Recent Research in Psychology

Edward E. Roskam (Ed.)

Mathematical Psychology in Progress

Springer-Verlag
Berlin Heidelberg New York
London Paris Tokyo Hong Kong

Editor

Edward E. Roskam
University of Nijmegen, Department of Psychology
P.O. Box 9104, 6500 HE Nijmegen, The Netherlands

ISBN 3-540-51686-7 Springer-Verlag Berlin Heidelberg New York
ISBN 0-387-51686-7 Springer-Verlag New York Berlin Heidelberg

Printed in Germany

Printing and binding: Druckhaus Beltz, Hemsbach/Bergstr.
2126/3140-543210 – Printed on acid-free paper

Preface

This volume is the third volume of papers originating from the European Mathematical Psychology Group. Earlier volumes were: E. Degreef & J. van Buggenhaut (Eds.), *Trends in Mathematical Psychology*, Amsterdam, North-Holland Publ. Cy., 1984, and E.E. Roskam & R. Suck (Eds.), *Progress in Mathematical Psychology*, Amsterdam: Elsevier Science Publ. As the title indicates, this volume presents work in progress, which was reported in one of the recent annual meetings of the European Mathematical Psychology Group. The Group finds it worthwhile to disseminate this work, using a review process which is somewhat less strict, and a publication lag which is shorter, than would be the case for standard international journals.

The editor is happy that the meetings of the European Mathematical Psychology Group are regularly attended by colleagues from overseas. Their contributions also appear in this volume, as was the case in earlier volumes.

Despite apparent heterogeneity, the reader will observe that European mathematical psychologists have a keen interest in basic issues of mathematical modeling and measurement theory, and that also substantive topics, such as decision making, perception, and performance are studied in the context of formal modeling. Also, and perhaps of more than casual importance for future developments, is the fact that theory, experiment, and data analysis go closely together. It should therefore not surprise that psychometric topics, and topics in scaling are represented in this volume, alongside with topics of a more 'purely' mathematical nature.

The present collection of papers is partitioned into three groups: first: Theory, Metatheory, and Measurement; secondly: Choice, Perception, Cognition, and Performance; and thirdly: Psychometrics and Theory of Data. For some papers, the allocation to one of these areas may appear arbitrary: this demonstrates how close these main streams are intertwined.

The editor wishes to express his gratitude to many friends and colleagues who assisted in the review process. The editor is especially indebted to Yvonne Schouten for her invaluable assistance in the editorial process, and to Geert-Jan van Engelen for his assistance in preparing the indices.

Edward E. Roskam

TABLE OF CONTENTS

Preface v

PART I - THEORY, METATHEORY, AND MEASUREMENT

P. Suppes 3
Current directions in mathematical learning theory

P. Wakker 29
Transforming probabilities without violating stochastic dominance

Edw. E. Roskam 49
Formal models and axiomatic measurement

A. Diederich and B. Orth 69
An axiomatic approach towards testing bilinear attitude models

R. Hübner 77
The representation of dynamic structures

R. Suck 85
Random variables and qualitative probability representations

D. Heyer and R. Niederée 99
Elements of a model-theoretic framework for probabilistic measurement

PART II - CHOICE, PERCEPTION, COGNITION, AND PERFORMANCE

G.J.P. Van Breukelen 115
Some modified inhibition models for response time series

R.W. Jansen and Edw.E.Roskam 133
Mental processing and distraction

C.E. Müller 157
A procedure for facilitating an expert's judgements on a set of rules

R. Mausfeld and R. Niederée 171
A generalized "discounting the background" model extending the traditional Grassmannian approach to colour vision

J.P. Barthélemy and E. Mullet 179
Choice basis, a model for multi-attribute preference: some more evidence

A.J. Smolenaars 197
An elementary formal categorization of a corpus of spelling errors

M. Müller 215
Rules for parallelprocessing networks with adaptive structure

PART III - PSYCHOMETRICS AND THEORY OF DATA

W.H. Batchelder and A. Kimball Romney ... 229
New results in test theory without an answer key

M.A. García-Pérez ... 249
Item sampling, guessing, partial information and decision-making in achievement testing

L. van Maanen, P.H. Been, and K. Sijtsma ... 267
The linear logistic test model and heterogeneity of cognitive strategies

B. Orth ... 289
Testable conditions for the existence of a qualitative J-scale in unfolding

B.Orth ... 299
Graph theoretical representations of proximities by monotonic network analysis (MONA)

R.A.W. Van Blokland-Vogelesang ... 309
Midpoint sequences, intransitive J scales, and scale values in unidimensional unfolding

P. Theuns ... 329
Predicting an optimal threshold in Boolean analysis of questionnaires

M.B. Gassner ... 345
An impossibility theorem for fair bidimensional representation: towards a biproportional solution

X. Hubaut ... 367
Thresholds and independence in proportional representation

Subject index ... 375

Author index ... 381

PART I

THEORY, METATHEORY AND MEASUREMENT

Current Directions in Mathematical Learning Theory

*Patrick Suppes**
Stanford University

The first part of this article surveys different current trends in mathematical learning theory. The main divisions of the subject covered are stimulus-response theory, language learning, formal learning theory, perceptrons, cellular automata, and neural networks. The second part is concerned with extending the ideas of stimulus-response theory to universal computation. This is done by using register machines rather than Turing machines. The main theorem is that any partial recursive function can be asymptotically learned by a register learning model. In the discussion of this result the emphasis is on the need for a carefully organized hierarchy of concepts in order to have a rate of learning that is realistic for either organisms or machines.

I have organized this lecture into two parts. In the first part I survey a number of different current trends in mathematical learning theory, with some attempt also to give some background of the developments leading up to them. In this part the main topics that I cover are stimulus-response theory, language learning, formal learning theory, and a group of related approaches I have entitled perceptrons, cellular automata, and neural networks. (The survey given here extends considerably the one given in Suppes, 1977a.)

In the second part I return to some of my own earlier work on stimulus-response theory of finite automata and give an extension to universal computation via register machines, rather than Turing machines. In this context I also discuss the feasibility of applying these theoretical ideas directly to actual learning situations.

General Survey

1. *Stimulus-response Theory*

For the period running from the late 1930s to the late 1960s, that is, roughly a period of 30 years, the dominant theoretical view of learning was some variant of stimulus-response theory. We could, of course, begin earlier with the work of Thorndike, but for the period to which I am referring we can start with the papers of Clark Hull, and especially his *Principles of Behavior* (1943). On the other hand, Hull's theory does not have a genuine mathematical feel about it. It is impossible to make nontrivial derivations leading to new quantitative predictions of behavior. This is so in spite of the valiant attempts to formalize Hullian theory (Hull et al., 1940). In my judgment the first serious paper that had an impact in the history of mathematical

---

***Institute for Mathematical Studies in the Social Sciences, Stanford University, Ventura Hall, Stanford, California 94305-4115, U.S.A.**

learning theory was William K. Estes' article "Toward a Statistical Theory of Learning" (1950). Estes presented in statistical learning theory a theory that has the kind of formulation that we expect of theories in physics. Nontrivial quantitative predictions can be made, and especially we can vary experimental conditions and derive new predictions. Another early and important publication was the 1955 book of Robert Bush and Frederick Mosteller, *Stochastic Models for Learning.* In the period roughly from 1955 to 1970, a large number of additional theoretical and empirical studies appeared and I will not attempt to survey them here. I do want to mention my own 1969 article, "Stimulus-Response Theory of Finite Automata," because in the second part I will return to the framework of this article and extend it to register machines, thereby establishing connection with some of the other directions characteristic of mathematical learning theory in the last several decades. The main theorem of the 1969 article is the following:

THEOREM 1. *Given any finite automaton, there is a stimulus-response model that under appropriate learning conditions asymptotically becomes isomorphic to the finite automaton.*

There are one or two features of stimulus-response theory as developed in the period I have described that have not been really satisfactorily replicated in the two decades since. It is important to recognize that progress has not been uniform in this respect. The most important of these features is the one mentioned above, the ability to make new predictions based upon change in experimental parameters. What is important about these predictions, moreover, is that the predictions of stochastic learning models derived from stimulus-response theory were detailed in character compared to the often qualitative or single predictions made from learning theories derived from the current fashion in cognitive psychology. To give some sense of this, I cannot resist showing some results on stimulus-response theory for a continuum of responses. Figure 1 shows a comparison between an observed response histogram conditioned upon a preceding reinforcement with a corresponding predicted density for a continuum of responses with noncontingent bimodal reinforcement distribution. Details can be found in Suppes, Rouanet, Levine, and Frankmann (1964). (For a recent application of these ideas to learning by robots, see Crangle and Suppes, 1989.) The derivation of this highly nonsymmetric curve is very much in the spirit of the kinds of derivations which one makes in physics and which work so well in stochastic learning models. The weakness of such models is that they work well in narrowly defined experimental settings, which I must say, by the way, is true of very many physical theories as well. The moral of the story is that in learning theory as in other subjects one cannot have one's cake and eat it too. If one wants precise mathematically derived predictions, then the experimental situations will probably be relatively narrowly circumscribed. On the other hand, if one wants to deal with a wide range of significant phenomena the predictions will not be nearly as satisfactory.

2. *Mathematical Models of Language Learning*

Although the theory of language learning in general form has a long history, we can date the mathematical theory in the modern period from an important paper of Gold (1967). He established the following important theorem.

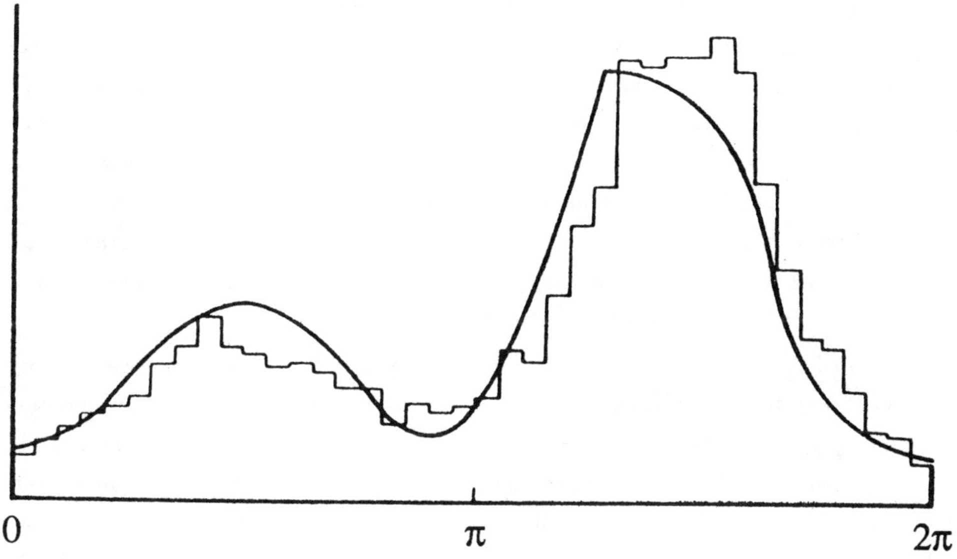

Figure 1: Observed response histogram conditional upon preceding reinforcement with corresponding predicted density.

THEOREM 2 (Gold). *Regular or context-free classes of grammars are not text-learnable.*

By *text-learnable* is meant that just by being presented instances of text the grammar as such cannot be learned, that is, asymptotically identified. Note that the sense of learnable in this theorem is a very weak sense. One has in mind that the grammar cannot be learned even with an infinite number of trials. On the other hand, on the assumption that one could ask an informant whether something were grammatical in the language being spoken and therefore according to the grammar which was to be learned, Gold proved the following theorem.

THEOREM 3 (Gold). *Regular or context-free classes of grammars are informant-learnable.*

It is important to note, of course, that Gold's framework is completely nonpsychological and is based really just on formal properties of regular and context-free grammars.

The most notable effort to develop a mathematical but psychological theory of language learning is to be found in the various publications of Kenneth Wexler and his associates. Perhaps the first article to be mentioned is Hamburger and Wexler (1973), in which they study the identifiability of a class of transformational grammars, and their 1975 article on a mathematical theory of learning transformational grammar. Here I shall refer especially to the large book of Wexler and Culicover (1980), entitled *Formal Principles of Language Acquisition.* The general idea of their theory is that when one is given surface data, for example, spoken sentences, then each surface sentence is paired with a base phrase marker and this structure is then passed to a learning mechanism. The intuitive idea is that every pair (b, s) in a certain range has a fixed probability greater than zero of appearing at time t, and that this probability of appearing at time t is bounded away from zero independent of the past history of the system. Exactly which pairs do show up, that is, what the theory permits as possible transformations, is a matter for linguistic analysis, to which we turn in a moment. The learning mechanism is a hypothesis formation procedure that is familiar from many other contexts. At any particular time t, the state of the learner is represented by a finite set of transformations, and on each "trial" the learner is presented with a pair (b, s). In response to the pairing, that is, the given phrase structure of grammars is used to decide if it is correct and thereby make no change, or if it is incorrect try another hypothesis. Such learning only from errors is a familiar mathematical model of learning. So the learning mechanism itself is simple, easy to describe, and very much in the tradition of earlier mathematical models of learning.

Notice that knowledge of the base structure is assumed in Wexler and Culicover's theory of learnability. Moreover, this base structure is the carrier of meaning. This assumption is certainly psychologically unrealistic but can be accepted in the context of their theory in order to permit concentration on the problem of learning a transformational grammar. But what is actually going on in a young child is undoubtedly very much more complicated than such a simple theory postulates. What is complicated, and I shall not attempt to describe in detail here, is the set of transformations derived from the theory of transformational grammars. Wexler and Culicover impose five important structural restrictions on transformations, which can be justified linguistically. The five basic restrictions that they impose on the class of transformational grammars can be described in the intuitive terms I used in my original review of the book (Suppes, 1983).

1. The *freezing principle* asserts that if a transformation changes the structure of a node so that that part of the base structure is no longer a base structure (i.e., able to be generated by the context-free grammar of the base), then no transformations may be applied to subparts of the structure of the node. (The intuitive picture here is of a grammatical tree structure, and the "structure" of a node refers to that part of the tree lying below the node.) For example, if we applied a passive transformation (I am not claiming such transformations are psychologically or linguistically sound) to *John who loved Mary loved Jane* to obtain *Jane was loved by John who loved Mary,* we could not then apply a transformation to the subordinate relative clause.

2. The *binary principle* restricts transformations to applying to constituents that cut across more than two embedded sentences in the base structure. Primarily because of this principle, Wexler and Culicover are able to prove that the learner need never encounter base sentences more complex than having two stages of embedding. Thus, base sentences of the complexity of the familiar nursery rhyme *This is the dog that worried the cat that killed the rat that ate the malt that lay in the house that Jack built* need not be encountered.

3. The *raising principle* asserts that if a node is raised, a transformation cannot be applied to a node beneath this node. For example, consider the sentence *John believes that the man who shot Bill loves Mary.* By raising we obtain *John believes the man who shot Bill to love Mary,* the noun phrase *the man who shot Bill* has been raised from subject of the complement clause to object of the main verb, and by the raising principle no transformation can be applied

to the relative clause of this noun phrase.

4. The *principle of no bottom context* is rather technical, and I shall not try to illustrate it here. What it does is rule out lower structures that overly determine whether a transformation at a higher level fits exactly and is thus applicable.

5. The *principle of the transparency of untransformable base structures* is also technical. It asserts that base structures that cannot be transformed must turn up in the surface structure and thus be transparent.

THEOREM 4 (Wexler and Culicover). *With restriction of input to sentences satisfying the binary principle stated above, a transformational grammar also satisfying the other four principles listed above may be asymptotically learned with probability one.*

I have already remarked in several places criticisms of the theory of the kind that are standard of mathematical theories of learning, namely, simplifications that all recognize are simplifications. There is another point of the Wexler and Culicover work that needs remarking of a different sort. They do not offer any evidence about the rate of learning. It could very well be that, on the assumption that sentences appear once a minute, it would still take several hundred years to learn a working grammar. In fact, the amount of time required could really be astronomical. It is an important aspect of theories of this kind to get, even if necessary by simulation, some idea of the rate of learning. Without doubt, the detailed features of the transformational grammar will have by far the largest impact on the rate of learning. Of course, by putting in hierarchical principles restricting in a given situation the transformations available, one can see how it would speed up very much the rate of learning and it may be by efforts of this kind a reasonable rate of learning could be achieved. What is probably needed in the tradition of this work at the present time is to get closer to some actual experiments–or actual data perhaps even better–of children's language learning, but the difficulties of testing quantitative theories in this fashion are also well known.

To some extent, this moving closer to the data is characteristic of the theory set forth in Pinker (1984). Also of interest is the fact that Pinker builds his theory around lexical functional grammars (Kaplan & Bresnan, 1982). Lexical functional grammars represent one of the new generalized phrase-structure grammars, which currently seem very promising from a linguistic standpoint and therefore represent a better target choice than the transformational grammars used by Wexler and Culicover. On the other hand, as Pinker explicitly states, he has not attempted to give a formal theory of language learning, so that consequently his main efforts fall outside the framework of this paper. His book is full of interesting remarks about problems of theorizing in this area and also about a great variety of psycholinguistic experimental and naturalistic data. But it would at the present time be extremely difficult to formalize his ideas as formulated in the book, and the standard questions we would want to ask of such a theory, as, for example, computations about rates of learning, etc., to show practical feasibility, are simply out of the question.

3. *Formal Learning Theory*

Based on the kind of idea characteristic of Gold's important early work (1967), a discipline known as formal learning theory has developed. The mathematical tools are essentially ideas of computability and recursion. There is no use of probabilistic notions and no appeal to actual empirical data. Thus, for example, the processes being modeled are not really actual learning processes, as exhibited in animals, persons, or even practical computer programs. The theorems mainly consist of possibility and impossibility theorems of the kind already exemplified in Theorems 2 and 3, due to Gold. The most recent summary of work in this field is the 1986 book *Systems That Learn* of Osherson, Stob, and Weinstein. Various combinations of these three authors have published a number papers as well. I will not try to summarize the variety of results that are proved but will state only one typical theorem that I think gives a sense of the kinds of results established. It is important to remember that this theorem is typical—it is not some conclusion of a large buildup.

THEOREM 5 (Osherson, Stob and Weinstein). *A learning strategy with limited memory restricts the set of languages that can be learned.*

Sketch of Proof. Let the memory for sentences of the strategy φ be only for the sentence currently being processed. Let $\mathfrak{L}$ be the set of languages consisting of

$$\begin{aligned} L &= \{(0,i) | i \in N\}, \\ L_j &= \{(0,i) | i \in N\} \cup \{(1,j)\}, \\ L'_j &= \{(0,i) | i \neq j, i \in N\} \cup \{(1,j)\}. \end{aligned}$$

When φ first sees $(1,j)$ for some j, φ cannot remember whether it previously saw $(0,j)$ or not, and so cannot distinguish between L_j and L'_j. This argument may easily be extended to a φ having any fixed finite memory.

Osherson, Stob, and Weinstein have a lot of informal remarks about human learners and language learning as well as about children's learning of first language, but it is obvious enough that their approach could not possibly supply anything like an empirically adequate theory of language learning. They establish within the framework of recursion theory a variety of positive and negative results but they do not move from general theorems of a recursive sort even to theorems about feasibility. Typically it has been important in the recent literature on complexity in computer science, for example, to distinguish a recursive result from special cases that are also feasible. The typical case is that a decision procedure that is exponential in terms of some essential parameter is recursive but not feasible. In order to be feasible it must be no more than polynomial in number of steps in the parameter. A typical example of this would be Tarski's well-known decision procedure for elementary algebra. It is known to be strongly exponential in the length of the algebraic formula whose validity is being decided. Feasible procedures can be given only for special subsets.

In spite of the general references to children, for example, and other aspects of human learning, there is no direct analysis of data of any kind and it would not seem appropriate with the self-imposed restrictions of the authors. Along with their absence of any detailed complexity results there are also no concrete or numerical results on the rate of learning of the various learning strategies they investigate. The results are either negative, for example, something cannot be learned, or the results are asymptotic. The concrete and positive study of learning must lie elsewhere, even though the kinds of results given can be useful in establishing the boundaries of substantive learning theories.

Also to be mentioned is the sophisticated independent work of Ehrenfeucht and Mycielski (1973a, 1973b, and 1977). The general framework is similar to that of Osherson, Stob, and Weinstein, but Ehrenfeucht and Mycielski introduce different conceptual ideas in order to characterize asymptotically learnable functions. Equally important in this connection is the independent work of Pentti Kanerva (1988), who goes further than Ehrenfeucht and Mycielski on the difficult problems of the organization of memory for formal learning theories or for related computing performance issues.

4. *Perceptrons*

I have grouped under this heading a great variety of work that I cannot attempt to survey in any depth but all of which needs at least some mention. The work on perceptrons goes through a line beginning with McCulloch and Pitts (1943), Rosenblatt (1959), and Minsky and Papert (1969). Minsky and Papert were quite successful in setting perceptron theory in a mathematical framework in which useful results could be proved. Their most important results were negative, showing that simple perceptrons of the kind mainly discussed in the prior literature were not capable of learning some quite simple geometrical concepts. I will not enter into the details of these negative results but define the concepts necessary to state the main positive result, the perceptron convergence theorem, particularly in the form given by Minsky and Papert.

The conceptual apparatus is of the following sort. There is a set D of perceptual displays and a subset G that we want the device to learn to select correctly, that is, to identify correctly membership or nonmembership in G. More particularly, on each trial the device responds *yes* to the presented display d if it classifies d as a member of G; otherwise it responds *no*. If the answer is correct, the device receives positive reinforcement (e_1), and, if the answer is incorrect, it receives negative reinforcement (e_2). Notice that the reinforcement is symmetric with respect to yes-no responses and depends only on the correctness or incorrectness of the response. This type of reinforcement is what I shall term standard nondeterminate reinforcement. Later on I shall discuss more complex and more informative reinforcement structures. The heart of the idea of the perceptron is that there is a set ϕ of elementary predicates. Each of these predicates is assigned a weight, and the perceptron combines in linear fashion the weighted 'answers' of the predicates to answer more complex questions. We can state the basic definition and the basic theorem without specifying more exactly the character of the elementary predicates because the results are relative to the set ϕ of predicates. For notational purposes, let A be a k-dimensional vector of real numbers that gives the weights assigned to each of the k-elementary predicates with a_i being the weight assigned to elementary predicate ϕ_i . The set ϕ can also most easily be represented as a k-dimensional vector of the k-elementary predicates. For each perceptual display d in D, $\phi_i(d)$ has the value 1 if d has the property expressed by ϕ_i and 0 otherwise. We can thus use standard inner product notation for vectors so that in place of $\sum a_i\phi_i(d)$ we can write $A \cdot \phi(d)$. It is understood that the response of the perceptron learning model is *yes* if this inner product is greater than 0 and *no* otherwise. To refer to a particular trial, the vector A_n of coefficients can also be referred to as the state of conditioning of the perceptron learning model at the beginning of trial n, and d_n is the object presented on trial n.

In the present context, finally the sample space X consists of all possible experiments, with each experiment, of course, being a sequence of trials. A trial in the present case is simply a triple (A, d, e), where A is the state of conditioning as described already, d is a perceptual display that is a member of D, and e is a reinforcement.

We thus have the following definition.

DEFINITION 1. *A structure* $\mathfrak{A} = (D, \phi, E, X)$ *is a perceptron learning model if and only if the following axioms are satisfied for every sequence of trials in* X.

(i) *If* e_1 *occurs on trial* n, *then* $A_{n+1} = A_n$.

(ii) *If* e_2 *occurs on trial* n *and* $A_n \cdot \phi(d_n) \leq 0$, *then* $A_{n+1} = A_n + \phi(d_n)$.

(iii) *If* e_2 *occurs on trial* n *and* $A_n \cdot \phi(d_n) > 0$, *then* $A_{n+1} = A_n - \phi(d_n)$.

Note that the main feature of the learning of perceptrons is that learning occurs only when an error is made, that is, when an e_2 reinforcement occurs. The vector expressing the state of conditioning changes in one of two directions, depending upon the type of error.

In terms of these concepts we can then state the standard theorem.

THEOREM 6 (Perceptron Convergence Theorem). *For any set* D *and any subset* G *of* D, *if there is a vector* A *such that* $A \cdot \phi(d) > 0$ *if and only if* $d \in G$, *then in any perceptron learning model there will only be a finite number of trials on which the conditioning vector changes.*

What is particularly important to note about this theorem is the ergodic property of convergence independent of the particular choice of weights A_1 at the beginning of the experiment. The finite number of changes also implies that the perceptron learning model will make only a finite number of mistakes. The hypothesis about G expressed in the theorem is equivalent to saying that G and its complement with respect to D are linearly separable.

The perceptron convergence theorem is asymptotic in character. The more important question of rate of learning is not settled by the theorem, although there exist some results in the literature that are of some interest. I say no more about perceptrons here because work on them in many ways converges into other work to be mentioned.

5. *Cellular Automata*

To illustrate ideas, here is a simple example of a one-dimensional cellular automaton. In the initial state, only the discrete position represented by the coordinate 0 has the value 1. All other integer coordinates, positive or negative, have the value 0. The automaton can in successive 'moves' or steps produce only the values 0 or 1 at any given location. The rule of change is given by a function that depends on the value of the given position and the values for the simple case to be considered here of the adjacent values on either side. Thus, using a_i' as the value at site i, after applying the function for change, we can represent the rule of change as follows:

(1) $$a_i' = \Phi(a_{i-1}, a_i, a_{i+1}).$$

Note that because of the restriction in the values at any site this function takes just eight arguments, the eight possibilities for strings of 0's and 1's. The automata being discussed here are at the very lowest rank on the number k of possible values: $k = 2$ is the number of possible values and $r = 1$ is the distance away. Updating may depend on adjacent values. The characterization here in terms of the infinite line can be replaced by a finite characterization, for example, in terms of a discrete set of points on a circle. The same kind of function as given in equation (1) applies.

Cellular automata have the following obvious characteristics:

Discrete in space

Discrete in time

Discrete state values

Homogeneous–in the sense all cells are identical

Synchronous updating

Deterministic rule of change corresponding to a deterministic differential equation of motion in the case of classical mechanics

Locality of change rule: the rule of change at a site depends only on a local neighborhood of the site

Temporal locality: the rule of change depends only on values for a fixed number of preceding steps–in the present example just one step.

The study of cellular automata by physicists has to a large extent been concerned with their usefulness as discrete idealizations of partial differential equations. Both computer simulation and mathematical analysis by use of cellular automata are simplifications of the difficult problems of the behavior of fluids and other complicated phenomena that in principle are governed by nonlinear differential equations.

The learning aspects of cellular automata have not been a real focus of study, but the closely related topic of self organization has been. The investigation of simple self-organizing phenomena goes back at least to the early work on chemical systems by Turing (1952). Even before that von Neumann began lecturing and talking about cellular automata. It seems that the idea of cellular automata originated in conversations between von Neumann and Stanislaus Ulam (von Neumann, 1966) as idealized mathematical models of biological systems capable of self-reproduction. Von Neumann's construction of a self-reproducing automaton was one of the early conceptual successes. Von Neumann's two-dimensional cellular automaton construction consisted of a universal Turing machine embedded in a cellular array using 29 states per cell with 5-cell neighborhoods. Moreover, his automaton can construct in the cellular array any configuration of machine which can be described on its input tape. For this reason von Neumann's cellular automaton is called a universal constructor. Also important is the fact that transcription takes place: von Neumann's automaton also makes a copy of the input tape and attaches it to the constructed automaton.

THEOREM 7 (von Neumann). *There exists a self-reproducing finite cellular automaton.*

As would be expected, there are a large number of subsequent results about self-reproduction. A good review is given in Langton (1984), which includes a description of Codd's substantial simplification of von Neumann's construction (Codd, 1968), as well as his simplification of Codd. The earlier articles on self-reproduction are well represented in the volume edited by Burks (1970). The abstract theory of self-reproduction is especially well set forth in Myhill (1964), reprinted in Burks' volume.

Although there has been almost no literature on cellular automata directly focused on learning, there has been considerable interest in adaptive automata as models of biological systems. For general theory, see Holland (1975); for a review of what is known about emergent properties of random cellular automata, see Kauffman (1984) and references therein. Especially suggestive is the work of Burks and Farmer (1984) on the modeling of DNA sequences as automata. A recent encyclopedic review of automata and computer models in biology is Baianu (1986).

Because of their great definitional simplicity, cellular automata provide a good framework for contrasting determinism and predictability. Clearly, the nonprobabilistic cellular automata are deterministic in character, but predictability of their behavior is another matter. Knowing the transition rule for a cellular automaton and given an initial configuration, can one predict in closed form the configuration after n steps? In general, this is certainly not the case. Of course, we can get predictability in another way by directly simulating the automaton but this is not what we ordinarily mean by predictability. There is in fact a concept that is useful to introduce at this point. This is the concept of being *computationally irreducible* (Wolfram, 1985). A system is computationally irreducible if a prediction about the system cannot be made by essentially shorter methods than simulating the system or running the system itself. Wolfram (1986) has shown that the following $k = 2, r = 1$ cellular automaton generates highly complex sequences that pass many tests for randomness, in spite of its totally elementary character. The automaton is defined by equivalent equations, one in terms of exclusive or and the other in terms of mod 2 arithmetic.

$$a'_i = a_{i-1} XOR (a_i OR a_{i+1})$$
$$a'_i = (a_{i-1} + a_i + a_{i+1} + a_i a_{i+1}) \ mod\ 2$$

Another good example of a physical process that is computationally irreducible is the addition of a column of numbers on the fastest computer available. For numbers randomly chosen but that do not have some special tricky features, there is no shorter way to compute their sum than simply to run the algorithm of addition itself. Because of our great interest in predictability we often forget how many processes are not predictable in the sense that they can be predicted in advance of their actual running or direct simulation of running. Of course, we can learn many things about the behavior of a system, including the asymptotic behavior of a learning system, without having it be computationally reducible. A tantalizing conjecture is that the network of neurons in a human brain constitute in their complete computational capability a computationally irreducible system. The implications of this conjecture for having theories of learning or performance as detailed as one might ask for are quite pessimistic.

6. *Neural Networks*

Just as cellular automata and perceptrons grow out of a common background, so do neural networks arise from the same background. Above all, neural networks are close to perceptrons in general conception. Neural networks differ from cellular automata in two essential respects. One is that updating is asynchronous, and, secondly, connections can be continually changed. (Cellular automata have been studied with these two changes in mind, but not extensively.)

Among the early work on neural networks we mention especially the voluminous research in various forms by Grossberg and his colleagues. Simply for reference I mention here Grossberg (1974, 1978, 1980, 1982). Grossberg's and his colleagues' research is concentrated on a psychophysiological theory of sensory processing and development. He gives an excellent overview of the theory in Grossberg (1978). As he puts it there, the theory is organized into four stages. The first stage is concerned with the question how fluctuating patterns of data are processed in cellular tissues so that problems of noise and dynamic range are solved. In particular, what are the mechanisms that keep the patterns of data from either being saturated or hopelessly confounded with noise? Stage two concentrates on the question how do persistently correlated presentations of two or more events yield an enduring reorganization of system dynamics. Grossberg's intention is to discuss problems at this stage, for example, classical conditioning, in a way that is fundamental in terms of schematic analysis of chemical and electrical properties of cellular structures. I emphasize the word schematic. It would be misleading to give a sense that he is dealing with the complete details of cellular dynamics.

The third stage concerns the question how sensory codes reorganize themselves or develop in response to environmental pressures. The theory at this stage particularly deals with the hierarchical organization of feature detectors, and in particular their interaction. Stage four deals with the fundamental question of how the information code can be held stable in an environment that is changing both internally and externally.

To give a sense of how Grossberg attacks these matters, a familiar and typical instance would be his analysis of adaptation and automatic gain control in on-center and off-surround networks which are hypothesized as schematic models of important aspects of the visual system. The models proposed are meant to account for psychologically known facts about perception of overlapping colored patches of light. Models are formulated in terms of population of cells which themselves have schematic properties in terms of activation decay. I hope it is clear that I am quite positive about the level of schematization that Grossberg is attempting. It is certainly out of range at the present time to try to use all the detailed information that is known about cell structure and, in particular, about the structure and function of neurons. How complicated the details are and how little we still know about function are well brought out in the chapter on the cerebral cortex by Crick and Asanuma in McClelland, Rumelhart, et al. (1986).

On the other hand, I will not try to review Grossberg's work in detail for another reason. He has concentrated on problems that are rather different from my focus here, namely, the computational power of learning models. There are certainly remarks in various publications that bear on this but he has mainly concentrated on specific network models of vision that account for visual illusions, on the development of feature detectors in the visual cortex, adaptive pattern classification, networks that account for psychological facts of olfaction, and especially the excellent recent monograph on the neural dynamics of ballistic eye movements (Grossberg & Kuperstein, 1986).

The surprising ability of neural networks to self-organize themselves to have emerging computational properties has recently been studied in simulations by Hopfield (1982) and Hopfield and Tank (1985). In the latter article it is shown how a neural network can be constructed to compute a surprisingly good solution of the traveling salesman problem, which is the hard combinatorial problem of finding the minimum-distance route a salesman should take in visiting n cities exactly once.

Within psychology the recent surge of interest in neural networks has been led by Rumelhardt, McClelland and the PDP Research Group (1986). Their massive and discursive two-volume treatise summarizes in one form or another most of the work done to date. What is especially interesting is the intellectual conflict that has already surfaced and is certain to continue between cognitive psychologists who are devoted to rule learning, and learning psychologists like Rumelhardt who do not believe that explicit rules, e.g., grammatical rules, play an important part in language learning or other cognitive domains. Chapter 18 of the work cited above–this chapter is by Rumelhardt and McClelland–provides a good example in its application of neural networks to learning the past tense of English verbs. Nothing like a complete sample of verbs is presented but enough is done to show what is a practical conceptual approach to developing a more extensive and detailed theory.

For an essentially negative critique of this work on verbs and related developments, see Pinker and Mehler (1988). The negative arguments by various cognitive psychologists in this volume are by no means conclusive, even though some excellent criticisms of neural networks, or connectionism as the theory is often called, are given. The important point from the standpoint of the present paper is that none of the criticisms by Pinker and others are precisely formulated from a mathematical standpoint. In other words, unlike other work cited here, no impossibility results are proved or even explicitly formulated.

There is a considerable development of formal theory in various other chapters of the work, with many of the ideas derived more from physics than psychology, even though some of the theorems state learnability results. An example is Chapter 6 by Smolensky on the foundations of harmony theory, a particular approach to information processing in dynamical systems, a topic close to some of the extensive work done by others on cellular automata. Smolensky contrasts his "subsymbolic" paradigm using concepts of activation, relaxation, and statistical correlation to the symbolic paradigm forcefully presented by Newell (1980), which emphasizes the central role of symbolic computation in cognitive science. This is the conflict mentioned above under another guise. The main characteristics of harmony theory, which is in its way a new descendant of older perceptron theories, are these: inference is through activation of schemata, stored knowledge atoms are dynamically assembled into context-sensitive schemata, schemata are coherent assemblies of knowledge atoms, harmony derives from making inferences that are consistent with the knowledge represented by the activated atoms, and the self-consistency of a possible state is assigned a quantitative value by a harmony function. What I have said here is only meant to be suggestive, and many of Solensky's remarks are of the same sort. However, and I emphasize this point, in the appendix to the chapter he gives a straightforward mathematical development of harmony theory. It is just not feasible to state here in technical detail the three theorems on competence, realizability, and learnability.

II. Learning Theory for Universal Computation

1. *Finite Automata Again*

The main purpose of this section is to straighten out confusions that have been the sources of criticisms of Theorem 1 (Suppes, 1969) on stimulus-response models of finite automata. I begin with a brief summary of this earlier work.

The central idea is quite simple–it is to show how by applying accepted principles of conditioning an organism may theoretically be taught by an appropriate reinforcement schedule to respond as a finite automaton. When an automaton is presented with one of a finite number of letters from an input alphabet, as a function of this letter of the alphabet and its current internal state, it moves to another one of its internal states. In order to show that an organism obeying general laws of stimulus conditioning and sampling can be conditioned to become an automaton, it is necessary first of all to interpret, within the usual run of psychological concepts, the notion of a letter of an alphabet and the notion of an internal state. In my own thinking about these matters, I was first misled by the perhaps natural attempt to identify the internal state of the automaton with the state of conditioning of the organism. This idea, however, turned out to be clearly wrong. In the first place, the various possible states of conditioning of the organism correspond to various possible automata that the organism can be conditioned to become. Roughly speaking, to each state of conditioning there corresponds a different automaton. Probably the next most natural idea is to look at a given conditioning state and use the conditioning of individual stimuli to represent the internal states of the automaton. In very restricted cases this correspondence works, but in general it does not. The correspondence that turns out to work is the following: the internal states of the automaton are identified with certain responses of the organism.

I now turn to the discussion of Theorem 1. The most technically detailed and in many ways the most interesting criticism of this representation theorem has been by Kieras (1976). The intuitive source of Kieras' confusion in his claim that the theorem as stated is too strong is easy to identify. Because I identified the *internal states* of a given automaton with the *responses* of the representing stimulus-response model, Kieras inferred I had unwittingly restricted my analysis to automata that have a one-one correspondence between *their* internal states and responses. On the basis of this confusion on his part he asserts that the representation theorem is not correct as it stands.

My purpose now is to lay out this dispute in an explicit and formal way in order to show unequivocally that Kieras is mistaken and the representation theorem is correct as originally stated.

From a mathematical standpoint Kieras' mistake rests on a misunderstanding of representation theorems. The isomorphism of a representation theorem is a formal one. In the case of Theorem 1 above, the isomorphism is between the internal states of the automaton and the responses of the representing stimulus-response model. The Rabin-Scott definition of automata used in the 1969 article does not have an explicit response mechanism, but that this is a trivial addition to their definition is shown by the *general* definition of a sequential machine with output given by Harrison (1965, p. 294), who is referenced by Kieras and who acknowledges he is mainly following the terminology of Rabin and Scott (see p. 292). An automaton or sequential machine with output is for Harrison just an automaton in the sense of Rabin and Scott with the additional condition that the set F of final states are those "giving a one output." As Harrison and others have remarked, a restriction of output to 1's and 0's is no restriction on the generality of the sequential machine.

The addition of this output apparatus to the formal definitions I gave in the original article is trivial. We just pick two responses r_0 and r_1 not used to represent internal states, but one of them, say r_0, represents 0 and the other 1. Whenever the machine is in an internal state that is not a final state but a response is required, it outputs r_0. When it is in a final state it outputs r_1 . To modify Definition 1 to take account of these output responses is easy. I note once again that the two output responses are in no way intended to correspond to internal states of the automata being represented. Other responses of the stimulus-response model represent the internal states. I emphasize, also, that this modification of adding output responses would not be correcting an error in Theorem 1 but would only be providing an additional closely related result.

2. *Register Machines*

Another misconception in the literature is that stimulus-response theory can only deal with machines that have the power of finite automata. The purpose of this section is to show that this is not the case by giving the construction of register machines, which are equivalent to Turing machines, corresponding to that for finite automata. The development here extends and modifies substantially that in Suppes (1977b). To give the results formal definiteness, we shall develop a learning theory for any partial recursive function. Such functions can be defined explicitly in a fairly direct way but we shall not do so here. I shall rely upon the fact that partial recursive functions are computable functions. We then use the basic theorem in the literature, whose technical framework we shall expand upon somewhat later, that any function is partially recursive if and only if it is computable by a register machine or, equivalently, by a Turing machine. The concept of a register machine used here was introduced by Shepherdson and Sturgis (1963). The reason for using register machines rather than Turing machines is that their formal structure is simpler. For example, the proof of equivalence between a function being a partial recursive function and being computable by a register machine is much simpler than the corresponding proof for Turing machines. First, let me recall how simple a classical register machine for a finite vocabulary is. All we have is a potentially infinite list or sequence of registers, but any given program uses only a finite number. Exactly three simple kinds of instructions are required for each register. The first is to place any element of the finite vocabulary at the top of the content of register n; the second is to delete the bottommost letter of the content of register n if the register is nonempty; because any computation takes place in a finite number of steps, the content of any register must always be finite in length. The third instruction is a jump instruction to another line of the program, if the content of register n is such that the bottommost or beginning letter is a_i; in other words, this is a conditional jump instruction. Thus, if we think of the contents of registers as being strings reading from left to right we can also describe the instructions as placing new symbols on the right, deleting old symbols on the left, and using a conditional jump instruction in the program when required.

It is straightforward to give a formal definition of programs for such an unlimited register machine, but I delay this for the moment. It is clear that a program is simply made up of lines of instructions of the sort just described. The potentially infinite memory of an unlimited register machine both in terms of the number of registers and the size of each register is a natural mathematical idealization. It is also possible to define a single-register machine with instructions of the kind just stated and to show that a single register is also adequate.

An important point about the revision of stimulus-response theory given here is that the internal language used for encoding stimulus displays is all that is dealt with. In other words, in the present formulation of the register-machine theory I shall not enter into the relation between the set of external stimuli and the encoding language, but deal only with the already encoded representation of the display. This level of abstraction seems appropriate for the present discussion but of course is not appropriate for a fully worked out theory. It is a proper division of labor, however, with the proper modularity. I am assuming that the sensory system passes to the central nervous system such encoded information, with the first level of encoding taking place well outside the central nervous system. Thus, in one sense the concept of stimulus becomes nonfunctional as such, but only because the encoding is already assumed. It is obvious enough that no serious assumptions about the actual perceptual character of stimuli is a part of classical S-R theory. Secondly, the concept of a program internally constructed replaces the direct language of responses being conditioned to stimuli. A natural question would be why not try to give a more neural network or hardware version of this construction. Given how little we know about the actual way in which information is transduced to the central nervous system and then used for encoding and programming, it seems premature, and in fact may well be premature for much longer than many of us hope, to try to move to any hardware details. Certainly what does seem to be the case is that there is internal programming. I am not suggesting that the abstract simple theory of a register machine catches the details of that internal programming–it is only a way of representing it–, and it is a matter for detailed additional theory to modify the abstract representation to make it more realistic.

On the other hand, without giving anything like a detailed neural analysis, the register-machine programs can be replaced by computationally equivalent stimulus-response connections, but without further specification such postulated S-R conditioning connections are no more concrete, i.e., closer to empirical realization, than the register-machine programs. It seems to me that it is therefore better to think of the programs as being realized by neural "hardware" we cannot presently specify. What is presented in the remainder of this section is formally adequate, but can surely be improved upon in many ways either to more closely imitate the learning of different organisms or to make machine learning more efficient. Moreover, given some feature coding of presented stimuli, there is every reason to think that to any software program there is a corresponding neural net, and vice versa, for solving a particular class of problems with essentially the same rate of learning. But this likely equivalence cannot be pursued further here.

To make matters more explicit and formal but without attempting a complete formalization, I introduce the following definitions. First, $\langle n \rangle$ is the content of register n before carrying out an instruction; $\langle n' \rangle$ is the content of register n after carrying out an instruction. Second, a *register machine* has (1) a denumerable sequence of registers numbered $1, 2, 3, \ldots$, each of which can store any finite sequence of symbols from the basic alphabet V, and (2) three basic kinds of instructions:

$(a)\ P_N^{(i)}(n):$ Place a_i on the right-hand end of $\langle n \rangle$.

$(b)\ D_N(n):$ Delete the leftmost letter of $\langle n \rangle$ if $\langle n \rangle \neq 0$.

$(c)\ J_N^{(i)}(n)[q]:$ Jump to line q if $\langle n \rangle$ begins with a_i

If the jump is to a nonexistent line, then the machine stops. The parameter N shown as a subscript in the instructions refers to the set of feature registers holding sensory data and not used as working computation registers. (This point is made more explicitly in the definition given below.)

A *line* of a program of a register machine is either an ordered couple consisting of a natural number $m \geq 1$ (the line number) and one of the instructions (a) or (b), or an ordered triple consisting of a natural number $m \geq 1$, one of the instructions (c), and a natural number $q \geq 1$. The intuitive interpretation of this definition is obvious and will not be given.

A *program* (of a register machine) is a finite sequence of k lines such that (1) the first number of the ith line is i, and (2) the numbers q that are third members of lines are such that $1 \leq q \leq k+1$. The parameter k is, of course, the number of lines of the program. I shall also refer to programs as *routines*. How a register machine *follows* a program or routine is intuitively obvious and will not be formally defined. *Subroutines* are defined like programs except (1) subroutines may have several exits, and (2) third members of triples may range over $q_1, \ldots, q_k$–these variables being assigned values in a given program.

I shall not give the formal definition of a partial recursive function defined over the alphabet V. It is any intuitively computable function. Given V, the finite vocabulary, then, as usual in such matters, $V*$ is the set of finite sequences of elements of V; in the present context, I shall call the elements of $V*$ feature codings. Let f be a function of n arguments from $V * x \cdots xV*$ (n times) to $V*$. The basic definition is that f is computable by a register machine if and only if for every register x_i, y and N with $y \neq x_i$ for $i = 1, \ldots, n$ and $x_i, \ldots, x_n, y \leq N$ there exists a routine $R_N(y = f(x_1, \ldots, x_n))$ such that if $\langle x_1 \rangle, \ldots, \langle x_n \rangle$ are the initial contents of registers $x_1, \ldots, x_n$ then

(1) if $f(\langle x_1 \rangle, \ldots, \langle x_n \rangle)$ is undefined the machine will not stop,

(2) if $f(\langle x_1 \rangle, \ldots, \langle x_n \rangle)$ is defined, the machine will stop with $\langle y \rangle$, the final content of register y, equal to $f(\langle x_1 \rangle, \ldots, \langle x_n \rangle)$, and with the final contents of all registers $1, 2, \ldots, N$, except y, the same as initially.

I turn now to the axioms for register learning models that in a very general way parallel those given for stimulus-response models with nondeterminate reinforcement in Suppes and Rottmayer (1974). I axiomatize only the model, and not the full probability space that serves as a formal framework for the learning trials. Extension to the latter, possibly via random variables and leaving the probability space implicit, is straightforward but tedious.

The axioms are based on the following structural concepts:

(i) the set R of registers,

(ii) the vocabulary V of the model,

(iii) the subset F of feature registers,

(iv) the subset C of computation registers,

(v) the subset Rp of response registers,

(vi) the working memory WM,

vii) the long-term memory LTM,

(viii) the responses r_0 and r_1 ,

(ix) the real parameters ρ and c.

It will perhaps be useful to say something briefly and informally about each of the primitive concepts. The feature registers in F just encode the features of the presented stimulus. This encoding and computation as well is done by using the vocabulary V. The computer registers in C are working registers available as needed for computation. The working memory WM stores programs being constructed. For simplicity here I shall assume there is only one such memory, but clearly this is too restrictive for general purposes. The long-term memory LTM is where programs that are found by repeated trials to be correct are stored.

One distinction is essential between the two memories and the registers. The memories store the program, so to the feature vocabulary $v_1, \ldots, v_n$ in V is added notation for the three types of instruction: P for placing or adding on the right, D for deleting on the left, and J for a jump instruction. V must also include notation for referring to registers used and to program lines. For the purpose I add the digit 1 (thus $2 = 11$, $3 = 111$, etc.), the most rudimentary counting notation.

The set Rp of response registers is also here for simplicity assumed to be a singleton set. This register corresponds in the general register machine characterized earlier to be the register that holds the value of the partial recursive function being computed. Here also I make an inessential simplifying assumption, namely, that learning will be restricted to concept learning, which is in principle no restriction on the set of computable functions. In the present case, given that the program is completed, if the register is cleared, the response is r_0, which means that the stimulus displayed–whose features are encoded in F–is an instance of the concept being learned, and if the register is not empty the response is r_1 , which means the stimulus presented is not an instance of the concept. Moreover, if the program at any step is halted before completion, the response is r_0 with guessing probability ρ, and r_1 with probability $1 - \rho$.

The two real parameters ρ and c enter in the axioms in quite different ways. As just indicated, ρ is the response guessing probability, and c is the constant probability of stopping construction of a program. These parameters, and others introduced implicitly in the axioms, are surely context dependent, and will naturally vary from task to task.

As formulated here, each line of a program is run as it is selected for the program construction and placed in working memory (WM). A program is transferred to long-term memory (LTM) only when it is completed and is successful in correctly identifying an instance of the concept being learned. The mechanism of completely erasing a constructed program that is in error is too severe, but is a simplifying assumption that holds for some animal learning, e.g., the all-or-none elimination of habituation in aplysia by sensitiving stimuli (Kandel, 1985).

The three types of register-machine instructions–adding on the right, deleting on the left, or conditional jump—mentioned earlier are modified in one respect. To jump to a nonexistent line and thereby halt the program, rather than jumping to $m + 1$ where m is the number of lines, the jump is to 0, which is a possible number for no line. The reason for this change should be apparent. As the program is probabilistically constructed line by line by the learning model, there is no way of knowing in advance how long the program will be. So it is convenient to have in advance a fixed "place" to jump to in order to halt the program.

DEFINITION 2. *A structure* $\mathfrak{R} = (R, V, F, C, Rp, WM, LTM, r_0, r_1, \rho, c)$ *is a* register learning model for concept formation *if and only if the following axioms are satisfied:*

Register Structure Axioms

R1. *The subsets* F, C, *and* Rp *of registers are nonempty and pairwise disjoint.*

R2. *Subsets* F *and* Rp, *and the set* V *are finite and nonempty.*

R3. *Each register in* R *can hold any word of* V_1^*, *i.e., any finite string of elements of* $V_1 = V - \{1, P, D, J\}$.

Stimulus Encoding Axiom

D1. *At the start of each trial, the stimulus presented is encoded as having features* $\langle f \rangle$ *in the registers* f of F.

Program Construction Axioms

P1. *If at the start of the trial, the* LTM *is nonempty, no program construction occurs.*

P2. *Given that* LTM *is empty:*

(i) *With probability* $c, 0 < c < 1$, *construction of the program in* WM *terminates after each line, independent of the trial number and any preceding subsequence of events;*

(ii) *Given that a line is to be added to the program, the probability of sampling an instruction of any type with any argument is positive, independent of the trial number and any preceding subsequence of events; in the case of the line number* n *to which a jump is to be made the probability is geometrically distributed.*

Program Execution Axioms

E1. *If* LTM *is nonempty, the contents are copied into* WM, *and then the program is executed.*

E2. *If* LTM *is empty, then a program is constructed probabilistically, line by line according to Construction Axioms P1 and P2, and is executed as each line is constructed.*

E3. *When a jump instruction is executed, there is a fixed positive probability the program is halted after one step, with this probability being independent of the trial number and any preceding subsequence of events.*

Response Axioms

Rp1. *If when the program is complete, register Rp is empty, the response is* r_0 .

Rp2. *If when the program is complete, register Rp is nonempty, the response is* r_1 .

Rp3. *If the program is halted by Axiom E3, response* r_0 *is made with guessing probability* ρ, *and response* r_1 *with probability* $1 - \rho$, *the probability* ρ *is independent of the trial number and any preceding subsequence of events.*

Program Erasure Axioms

Er1. *If positive reinforcement occurs at the end of a trial, the program in* WM *is copied in* LTM *if* LTM *is empty.*

Er2. *If negative reinforcement occurs at the end of a trial, the program in* WM *is erased and so is the program in* LTM *if it is nonempty.*

A few of the axioms require comments that were not made earlier in the informal discussion. The probabilistic program construction axiom P2 is similar to a stimulus sampling axiom which guarantees accessibility for conditioning of all relevant stimuli. Axiom P2 is obviously formulated in such a way as to bound sampling probabilities away from asymptotically approaching zero except in the case of the geometric distribution for sampling line numbers. The stopping probability required in program execution axiom E3 is required in order to prevent staying with programs that generate infinite loops. Finally, the informal concept of reinforcement used in the program erasure axioms has an obvious meaning and is easily formalized. Positive reinforcement here just means that the concept classification of a stimulus by the response r_0 or r_1 is correct, and negative reinforcement that it is incorrect. Obviously, more informative reinforcement methods can and are widely used in learning and without question facilitate the speed of learning. More is said on this point in the final remarks on hierarchical learning.

On the basis of the axioms stated above we may prove an asymptotic learning theorem corresponding in a general way to Theorem 1 for stimulus-response models.

THEOREM 8. *Let f be any partial function of n arguments over the finite alphabet V and having just two values in V. Then f is a partial recursive function if and only if f is asymptotically learnable with probability one by a register learning model $\mathfrak{R}$ of concept formation.*

Proof. Let $\wp$ be a program for $\mathfrak{R}$ that computes f. We know there must be such a program by virtue of the fact that a function f over a finite alphabet is partial recursive if and only if it is computable by a register machine. Furthermore, given a definition of f we have a constructive method for producing $\wp$. Our objective is to show that in the learning environment described by the axioms there is a positive probability of constructing $\wp$ on each trial.

Let $C \subseteq V^* \times \cdots \times V^*$ (n times) be the set of encoded stimulus instances of the f-computable concept C–without loss of generality in this context I identify the concept with its set of instances, and let $\neg C$ be the complement of C. We take as a presentation distribution of stimuli, where $(\langle f_1\rangle), \ldots, \langle f_n\rangle)$ is the encoding representation of a stimulus,

$$P((\langle f_1\rangle, \ldots, \langle f_n\rangle) \in C) = P((\langle f_1\rangle, \ldots, \langle f_n\rangle) \in \neg C) = \frac{1}{2}.$$

Moreover, we design the experiment to sample from C and $\neg C$ in the following geometric fashion. Let f_i be the coding in V^* of feature i of stimulus σ and let $|f_i|$ be the number of symbols in f_i. Then $\sum |f_i|$ is the total number of symbols used to encode σ. We use a geometric distribution for the total number of symbols, and a uniform distribution for selecting among those of the same total number of symbols. (In a completely formalized theory, these assumptions about probabilistic selection of presented stimuli would be part of the axioms, which I have restricted here just to the register learning model, and have not included axioms on stimulus presentation or reinforcement procedures in any detail.)

Suppose now that initially LTM is nonempty. If the program stored in LTM correctly computes f, we are done. If the program does not for some stimulus σ, then by the assumptions just stated there is a fixed positive probability that σ will be presented on every trial and hence with probability one asymptotically LTM will be cleared by virtue of Axiom Er2.

The probability of then constructing $\wp$ is positive on every trial. The detailed calculation is this. First, let $\wp$ have m lines. By Axiom P2(i), the probability of constructing a program of exactly m lines is equal to $c(1-c)^{m-1}$. If line i is not a jump instruction, then by Axiom P2(ii), the probability of line i being of the desired form is greater than some $\epsilon_1 > 0$. And if line i is a conditional jump instruction, where the jump is to line n_i , then also by Axiom P2(ii), the probability of line i being exactly line i of program $\wp$ is equal to $\epsilon_2^2(1-\epsilon_2)^{n_i-1}$ for some $\epsilon_2 > 0$.

So, independent of trial number, the finite product of these probabilities is positive on every trial. Explicitly, let $i_1, \ldots, i_{m_1}$ be the lines that are not jump instructions and let $j_1, \ldots, j_{m_2}$ be the lines that are, with $m = m_1 + m_2$. Then

(I) $$\text{Prob of } \wp > \epsilon_1^{m_1} \prod_{i=j_1}^{i=j_{m_2}} \epsilon_2^2 (1-\epsilon_2)^{n_i - 1} \cdot c(1-c)^{m-1} > 0.$$

From this inequality, we infer at once that asymptotically $\wp$ will be learned with probability one, which completes the proof, except to remark that to prove the constructed program characterizes a partial recursive function is straightforward.

Criticisms of the purely asymptotic character of this theorem are as appropriate as they were in criticisms of the perceptron convergence theorem (Theorem 6) or the language-learning theorem of Wexler and Culicover (Theorem 4). The next section addresses these problems.

3. *Role of Hierarchies and More Determinate Reinforcement*

For the theory of register-model concept learning, as formulated in Definition 2, we cannot improve on inequality (I). Treating it as an equality it is evident that for programs $\wp$ of any length learning will be very slow, much slower than we observe in most human learning and even much animal learning.

Within the framework of the present theory, the only practical hope for learning to occur in a reasonable time is to organize learning into a hierarchy of relatively small tasks to be mastered. It might be thought that this conclusion could be avoided by making the reinforcement more informative or determinate than what was assumed in Axioms Er1 and Er2 above. There is something correct and important about this view, and it can be supported by detailed computations on significant examples. On the other hand, there is also a question of interpretation. For the completely deterministic reinforcement used in the proof of Theorem 1, we could regard conditioning of each internal state of the finite automaton as a task–here task is defined by what gets reinforced, and in this view, the most fine-grained hierarchy is created by completely deterministic reinforcement.

It will be useful to end with application of the theory to a small, familiar task, to show that the theory can be brought down to earth and applied to data. Of course, in the present context I shall not try to be serious about actual parameter estimation. The task selected is that of 5-year-old children learning the concept of a triangle by recognizing triangles when presented with triangles, quadrilaterals and pentagons.

I make the following assumptions about the register model being used by the children. (It has the sort of simplifications necessary in such matters.)

(i) The language V_1 has a single element, α, which is used for counting.

(ii) There are two feature registers, #1 for number of segments and #2 for size, with α = small, $\alpha\alpha$ = medium and $\alpha\alpha\alpha$ = large.

(iii) The conditional jump is either to a previous line or to 0 (for a nonexistent line and stop).

(iv) To simplify formulation, computations are made directly on the feature registers rather than first copying their contents to a working register. (Characterizing copying from one register to another in terms of the three types of primitive instructions is straightforward.)

(v) *Rp* is the single response register.

(vi) Let a be the probability of selecting the delete instruction, b the probability for the jump instruction, and $1 - a - b$ the probability of the place or add instruction.

(vii) Let p be the probability of selecting feature register 1, and $1-p$ that of selecting feature register 2 for reference in a line of program.

A simple correct program is:

1. D(1)	Delete α from register 1.
2. D(1)	Delete α from register 1.
3. D(1)	Delete α from register 1.
4. Copy(1,Rp)	Copy the contents of register 1 in the response register Rp.

All programs, in the short form used here, must end in copying the contents of a feature or working register to the response register. A response is then made. So the probability of lines 1-3 is: $p^3a^3c(1-c)^2$, where c is the parameter for the distribution of number of lines introduced in Axiom P2(i).

It is important to recognize that many different programs will produce the correct response, and so the probability of a correct response is considerably greater than $p^3a^3c(1-c)^2$. The complexity of a full analysis even for the simple experimental situation considered is much greater if the task is recognition of quadrilaterals rather than triangles. Still, under reasonable assumptions, the probabilities of the correct programs that are near the minimum length should dominate the theoretical computation of a correct response.

The learning setup defined axiomatically here is in terms of its scope comparable to the definition of partial recursive functions or the definition of register machines for computing such functions—namely, the definitions apply to each function considered individually. But for extended learning of a hierarchy of concepts, the structure must be enriched to draw upon concepts that have been previously learned in order to reach a practical rate of learning. Here is a very simple example to illustrate the point. Consider a disjunctive concept made up of n disjoint cases. Only one register is required, the alphabet V_1 is the set $\{\alpha, \beta\}$, and there is no jump instruction, but only the four instructions for deleting letters on the left or adding them on the right. Let the program be at most 10 lines for each case. Then assuming a uniform distribution on sampling of instructions and of the number of lines (1 to 10), the probability of each program of at most 10 lines can be directly computed. More importantly in the present instance, we can easily compute the possible number of programs: 4 of length 1, 16 of length 2, and in general 4^n of length n, with $1 \leq n \leq 10$, for a total of $(4^{11}-4)/3$, which is approximately 4^{10}. If now at the second stage programs are put together using only original instructions and the n subroutines from individual cases, with programs of length at most $2n$ permitted, then there are $[(n+4)^{2n+1} - (n+4)]/(n+3)$ possible programs, which is approximately $(n+4)^{2n}$. On the other hand, if a single program is developed in one step with $10n$ lines, the number of possible programs is approximately 4^{10n}. Consider, for example, the case $n = 3$. Then

4^{30} is many orders of magnitude larger than $7^6 + 3.(4^{10})$. The details of this example are not important, and I have not attempted to fix them sufficiently to determine in each of the two approaches the number of possible programs that are correct. Ordinarily in both the hierarchical and nonhierarchical approach this number would be a very small percentage of the total. The gain from the hierarchical approach is evident enough.

More generally, clever ways of dynamically changing the probability of using a previously defined concept, i.e., its recognition program, are critical to actual machine learning, for example, and sound hypotheses about such methods seem essential to any sophisticated study of human or animal learning of an extended hierarchy of concepts. Of equal importance is the introduction of forms of information feedback richer than the simple sort postulated in Definition 2, but the mathematical study of alternatives seems still to be in its infancy—only the extreme cases are relatively well understood. Much human learning depends upon verbal instruction and correction, but an approximately adequate theory of this process of feedback is as yet out of reach from a fundamental standpoint. Various gross simplifying assumptions, as used, for example, in protocol analysis, seem uneliminable at the present time. This is one measure of how much remains to be done.

References

Baianu, I. C. (1986). Computer models and automata theory in biology and medicine. *Mathematical Modeling*, 7, 1513-1577.

Burks, A. W. (Ed.) (1984). *Essays on cellular automata.* Urbana, IL: University of Illinois Press.

Burks, C., and Farmer, D. (1984). Towards modelling DNA sequences as automata. In D. Farmer, T. Toffoli, and S. Wolfram (Eds.), *CellularAutomata* (Proceedings of an interdisciplinary Workshop, Los Alamos, New Mexico, March 7-11, 1983, pp. 157-167). Amsterdam: North-Holland.

Bush, R., and Mosteller, F. (1955). *Stochastic models for learning.* New York: Wiley.

Codd, E. F. (1968). *Cellular automata.* New York: Academic Press.

Crangle, C. and Suppes P. (1989). Instruction dialogues: Teaching new skills to a robot. In G. Rodrigues (Ed.), *Proceedings of the NASA Conference on Space Telerobotics* (January 31 - February 2, 1989, Pasadena, California). Jet Propulsion Laboratory, California Institute of Technology, Pasadena, California.

Crick, F., and Asanuma, C. (1986). Certain aspects of the anatomy and physiology of the cerebral cortex. In J. L. McClelland, D. E. Rumelhart, and the PDP Research Group (Eds.), *Parallel distributed processing. Explorations in the microstructures of cognition.* Vol. 2. *Psychological and biological models* (pp. 333-371). Cambridge, MA, and London: Massachusetts Institute of Technology Press.

Ehrenfeucht, A., and Mycielski, J. (1973a). Interpolation of functions over a measure space and conjectures about memory. *Journal of Approximation Theory, 9*, 218-236.

Ehrenfeucht, A., and Mycielski, J. (1973b). Organisation of memory. *Proceedings of the National Academy of Sciences U.S.A., 70*, 1478-1480.

Ehrenfeucht, A., and Mycielski, J. (1977). Learnable functions. In R. E. Butts and J. Hintikka (Eds.), *Foundational problems in the special sciences, Proceedings of the Fifth International Congress of Logic, Methodology and Philosophy of Science*, London, Ontario, Canada, (Vol. 2, pp. 251-256). Dordrecht, Holland: Reidel.

Estes, W. K. (1950). Toward a statistical theory of learning. *Psychological Review, 57,* 94-107.

Gold, E. M. (1967). Language identification in the limit. *Information and Control, 10*, 447-474.

Grossberg, S. (1974). Classical and instrumental learning by neural networks. In R. Rosen and F. Snell (Eds.), *Progress in theoretical biology* . New York: Academic Press.

Grossberg, S. (1978). A theory of visual coding, memory, and development. In E. L. J. Leeuwenberg and H. F. J. M. Buffart (Eds.), *Formal theories of visual perception* (pp. 7-26). New York: Wiley.

Grossberg, S. (1980). How does a brain build a cognitive code? *Psychological Review, 87,* 1-51.

Grossberg, S. (1982). Associative and competitive principles of learning and development: The temporal unfolding and stability of STM and LTM patterns. In S. Aman and M. A. Arbib (Eds.), *Competition and cooperation in neural nets. Lecture Notes in Biomathematics, 45*, 295-341.

Grossberg, S., and Kuperstein, M. (1986). *Neural dynamics of adaptive sensory-motor control. Advances in Psychology 30.* Amsterdam: North-Holland.

Hamburger, H., and Wexler, K. (1973). Identifiability of a class of transformational grammars. In K. J. J. Hintikka, J. M. E. Moravcsik, and P. Suppes (Eds.), *Approaches to natural language* (pp. 153-166). Dordrecht, Holland: D. Reidel.

Hamburger, H., and Wexler, K. (1975). A mathematical theory of learning transformational grammar. *Journal of Mathematical Psychology, 12,* 137-177.

Harrison, M.A. (1965). *Introduction to Switching and Automata Theory.* New York: McGraw-Hill.

Holland, J. H. (1975). *Adaptation in natural and artificial systems.* Ann Arbor, MI: University of Michigan Press.

Hopfield, J. J. (1982). Neural networks and physical systems with emergent collective computational abilities. *Proceedings of the National Academy of Sciences, 79,* 2554-2558.

Hopfield, J. J., and Tank, D. W. (1985). "Neural" computation of decisions in optimization problems. *Biological Cybernetics, 52,* 141-152.

Hull, C. L. (1943). *Principles of behavior.* New York: Appleton.

Hull, C. L., Hovland, C. I., Ross, R. T., Hall, M., Perkins, D. T., and Fitch, F. B. (1940). *Mathematico-deductive theory of rote learning.* New Haven, CT: Yale University Press.

Kandel, E. R. (1985). Cellular mechanisms of learning and the biological basis of individuality. In E. R. Kandel and J. H. Schwartz (Eds.), *Principles of neural science* (2nd ed.). Amsterdam: Elsevier.

Kanerva, P. (1988). *Space distributed memory.* Cambridge, MA: Massachusetts Institute of Technology Press.

Kaplan, R. M., and Bresnan, J. (1982). Lexical-functional grammar: a formal system for grammatical representation. In J. Bresnan (Ed.), *The mental representation of grammatical relations.* Cambridge, MA: Massachusetts Institute of Technology Press.

Kauffman, S. A. (1984). Emergent properties in random complex automata. In D. Farmer, T. Toffoli, and S. Wolfram (Eds.), *Cellular automata* (Proceedings of an Interdisciplinary Workshop, Los Alamos, New Mexico, March 7-11, 1983, pp. 145-156). Amsterdam: North-Holland.

Kieras, D. E. (1976). Finite automata and S-R models. *Journal of Mathematical Psychology, 6*, 127-147.

Langton, C. G. (1984). Self-reproduction in cellular automata. *Physica, 10D,* 135-144. Reprinted in D. Farmer, T. Toffoli, and S. Wolfram (Eds.), *Cellular automata* (Proceedings of an Interdisciplinary Workshop, Los Alamos, New Mexico, March 7-11, 1983, pp. 135-144). Amsterdam: North-Holland.

McCulloch, W. S., and Pitts, W. (1943). A logical calculus of the ideas immanent in nervous activity. *Bulletin of Mathematical Biophysics, 5*, 115-133.

Minsky, M., and Papert, S. (1969). *Perceptrons.* Cambridge, MA: Massachusetts Institute of Technology Press.

Myhill, J. (1970). The abstract theory of self-reproduction. In A. W. Burks (Ed.), *Essays on cellular automata* (pp. 206-218). Urbana, IL: University of Illinois Press.

Newell, A. (1980) Physical symbol systems. *Cognitive Science, 4,* 135-183.

Osherson, D. N., Stob, M., and Weinstein, S. (1986). *Systems that learn.* Cambridge, MA: Massachusetts Institute of Technology Press.

Pinker, S. (1984). *Language learnability and language development.* Cambridge, MA: Harvard University Press.

Pinker, S. and Mehler J. (Eds.) (1988). *Connections and Symbols.* Cambridge, MA: The MIT Press.

Rosenblatt, F. (1959). *Two theorems of statistical separability in the perceptron* (Proceedings of a symposium on the mechanization of thought processes). London: HM Stationery Office.

Rumelhardt, D. E., McClelland, J. L., and the PDP Research Group. (1986). *Parallel distributed processing: Explorations in the microstructures of cognition* (2 vols.). Cambridge, MA: Massachusetts Institute of Technology Press.

Shepherdson, J. C., and Sturgis, H. E. (1963). The computability of partial recursive functions. *Journal of the Association of Computing Machinery, 10,* 217-255.

Suppes, P. (1969). Stimulus-response theory of finite automata. *Journal of Mathematical Psychology, 6,* 327-355.

Suppes, P. (1977a). A survey of contemporary learning theories. In R. E. Butts and J. Hintikka (Eds.), *Foundational problems in the special sciences* (Part two of the Proceedings of the Fifth International Congress of Logic, Methodology and Philosophy of Science, London, Ontario, Canada, 1975, pp. 217-239). Dordrecht, Holland: D. Reidel.

Suppes, P. (1977b). Learning theory for probabilistic automata and register machines. In H. Spada and W. F. Kempf (Eds.), *Structural models of thinking and learning* (Proceedings of the 7th IPN-Symposium on Formalized Theories of Thinking and Learning and their Implications for Science Instruction, pp. 57-79). Bern: Hans Huber Publishers.

Suppes, P. (1983). Learning language in the limit, review of K. Wexler and P. W. Culicover, *Formal principles of language acquisition. Contemporary Psychology, 28,* 5-6.

Suppes, P., and Rottmayer, W. Automata. (1974). In E. C. Carterette and M. P. Friedman (Eds.), *Handbook of perception* (Vol. 1, pp. 335-362). New York: Academic Press.

Suppes, P., Rouanet, H., Levine, M., and Frankmann, R. W. (1964). Empirical comparison of models for a continuum of responses with noncontingent bimodal reinforcement. In R. C. Atkinson (Ed.), *Studies in mathematical psychology* (pp. 358-379). Stanford, CA: Stanford University Press.

Turing, A. M. (1952). The chemical basis of morphogenesis. *Philosophical Transactions of the Royal Society, London, Series B 237,* 37-72.

von Neumann, J. (1966). *Theory of self-reproducing automata,* edited by A. W. Burks. Urbana, IL: University of Illinois Press.

Wexler, K., and Culicover, P. W. (1980). *Formal principles of language acquisition.* Cambridge, MA, and London, England: Massachusetts Institute of Technology Press.

Wolfram, S. (1985). Undecidability and intractability in theoretical physics. *Physical Review Letters, 54,* 735-738.

Wolfram, S. (1986). Random sequence generation by cellular automata. *Advances in Applied Mathematics, 7,* 123-169.

TRANSFORMING PROBABILITIES WITHOUT VIOLATING STOCHASTIC DOMINANCE

*Peter Wakker**
University of Nijmegen
Nijmegen Institute for Cognition research and Information technology (NICI)

Abstract

The idea of expected utility, to transform payments into their utilities before calculating expectation, traces back at least to Bernoulli (1738). It is a very natural idea to transform, analogously, probabilities. This paper gives heuristic visual arguments to show that the, at first sight, natural way to do this, at second thought seems questionable. At second thought a sound and natural way is the way of anticipated utility, as indicated by Quiggin (1982).

SECTION 1. INTRODUCTION

In this paper we present a new argument, heuristic and visual, for a new approach to decision making under risk, the 'anticipated utility' approach. It has been initiated by Quiggin (1982) and Yaari (1987a) (and Schmeidler, 1982), and deals with the idea to transform probabilities. While being very old, this idea until recently did not lead to sound theories. As we shall argue this is because, loosely spoken, the old approaches to transformed probabilities 'transformed the wrong probabilities' when calculating expectation. This prevented the idea from becoming full-blown. Only recently, through the references mentioned above, it has become understood how to integrate with respect to transformed probabilities, i.e., how to calculate expectations with respect to transformed probabilities. This is best done by means of the 'Choquet-integral', introduced by Choquet (1953-4), or its analogues as used in this paper. The purpose of this paper is to give a visual presentation by means of which the reader may come to the intuition that the anticipated utility approach, rather than older approaches, is a natural analogue of expected utility. Hopefully this will interest the reader in getting to know more about anticipated utility to decision making under risk, and to consult the references given at the end. Finally a remark on terminology. Instead of 'anticipated

*The research has been made possible by a fellowship of the Royal Netherlands Academy of Arts and Sciences. Author's address: University of Nijmegen (NICI), Department of Mathematical Psychology, P.O. Box 9104, 6500 HE Nijmegen, The Netherlands

utility' one also finds in the literature terms such as 'rank-dependent expected utility', 'rank-ordered expected utility', 'expected utility with rank-dependent probabilities'. The latter term reflects best the idea of the new approach, but is not concise.

SECTION 2. LOTTERIES AND EXPECTATIONS

The simplest approach to decision making under risk consists of the maximization of 'expected value'. Let $(p_1; x_1, \ldots, p_n; x_n)$ be a **lottery** yielding $\$x_j$ with probability p_j, $j = 1, \ldots, n$. Then the **expected value** of the lottery is

$$\sum_{j=1}^{n} p_j x_j \; . \tag{1}$$

With the reader's indulgence we present, as a necessary preparation for the sequel, two elementary illustrations. In Figure 2.1a the shaded area indicates the expected value. The first column has height x_1 and breadth p_1, hence its area gives the first term $p_1 x_1$ of the summation of expected value; etc. **Let us emphasize that we assume in the sequel that the outcomes $x_1, \ldots, x_n$ have been ordered so that** $x_1 > x_2 > \cdots > x_n$.[1] Also we assume that all x_j's are positive; this is merely done for convenience. Figure 2.1b shows an alternative illustration of expected value. It has simply been obtained from Figure 2.1a by rotating to the left and flipping (as the reader may imitate with this paper). Obviously, the size of the shaded area is not affected by these operations. If one considers the shape in Figure 2.1b as the graph of a function, denoted by G, then the area in it is the integral of G. This function G in fact is the 'decumulative distribution function' of the lottery; the **decumulative distribution function**[2] assigns to any real number t the probability that the lottery will yield at least $\$t$, i.e.,

$$G : t \mapsto P(\text{lottery yields \$t or more}) \; .$$

Indeed, for every $t \in \Re_+$ the height of the graph is the sum of the probabilities of the x_j's to the right of t. Hence the expected value of the lottery can also be obtained as the integral of the decumulative distribution function, i.e.,

$$\sum_{j=1}^{n} p_j x_j = \int_{\Re_+} G(t)\, dt \; .$$

(By elementary means, such as integration by parts, the above integral can be reduced to the more common $\int_{\Re_+} t f(t)\, dt$, with f the usual density function, so f the derivative of $-G$.)

A challenge to the maximization of expected value was posed by the 'St. Petersburg paradox'. Suppose $p_j = 2^{-j}$ for all j, and $x_j = 2^j$ for all j. Then the expected value of the lottery $(p_1; x_1, \ldots, p_n; x_n, 2^{-n}; 0)$ is n. It turned out however that for large n

[1]For formula (3) the inequalities $x_1 \neq x_2 \neq \cdots \neq x_n$ will be essential. For section 4 the weak inequalities $x_1 \geq x_2 \geq \cdots \geq x_n$ will be essential.

[2]Probably better known than the decumulative distribution function is the usual '(cumulative) distribution function', assigning $P(\text{lottery yields \$}t\text{ or less})$ to every real number t. For the visual presentation of this paper the decumulative distribution serves best; we are following Yaari (1987a) in this. Yaari also uses such a visual presentation to consider anticipated utility as dual to expected utility.

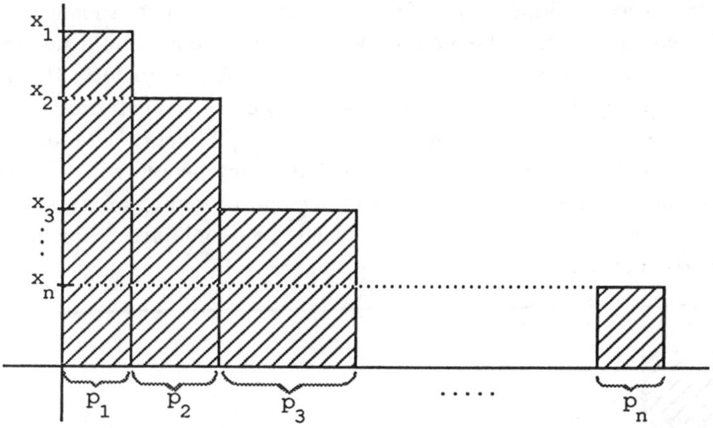

FIGURE 2.1a. *Expected value.* The area shaded by ▨ gives the expected value.

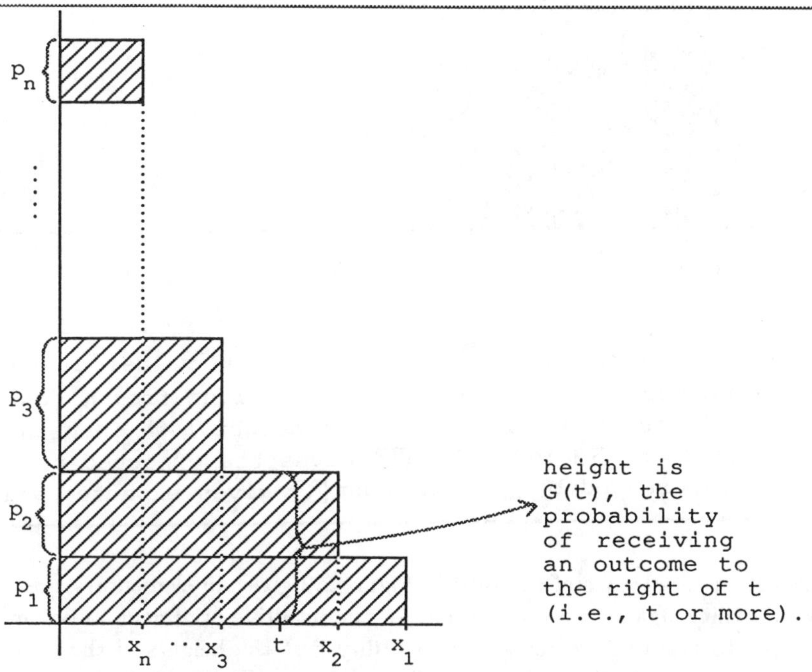

FIGURE 2.1b. *Alternative presentation of expected value.* Figure 2.1a has been rotated to the left, and flipped horizontally. Of course the area shaded by ▨ still gives the expected value. The figure gives the graph of the decumulative distribution function G; the area is its integral.

FIGURE 2.1. *Expected value represented as area.*

individuals were in no way willing to pay $\$n$ to participate in such a lottery. Usually not more than \$4 would be paid. Bernoulli's idea was that one should not calculate the expectation of the outcomes of money, but one should first transform the amounts of money by a 'utility function' U, and only then calculate expectation. As utility function Bernoulli proposed the logarithm. Indeed, $\sum_{j=1}^{n} 2^{-j} \log(2^j)$ tends to $\log(4)$ as n increases, so Bernoulli's approach indeed explains that people will not pay more than \$4 for participation in the lottery. (We prefer the presentation as above, with 'large' n, to the presentation with $n = \infty$. Intuitions of people are frequently misled by meaningless mathematical conventions concerning ∞.)

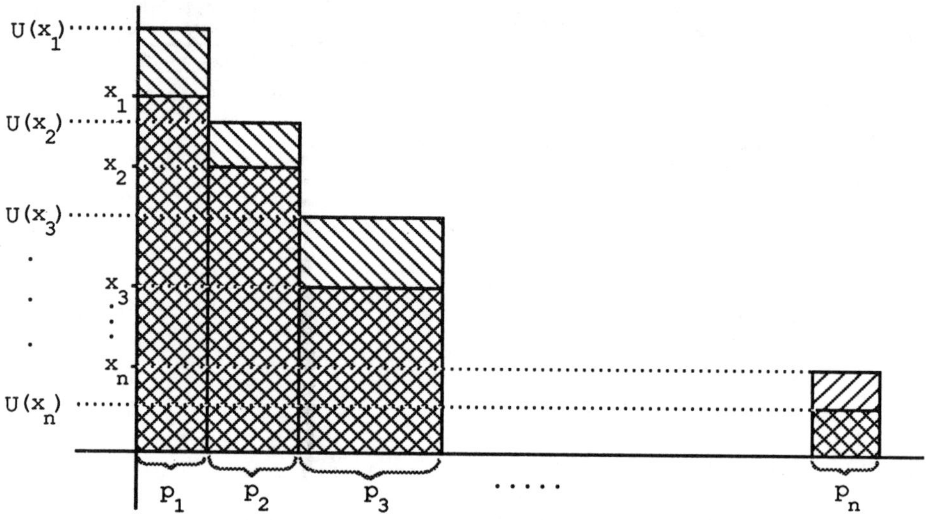

FIGURE 2.2. *Expected utility (and expected value)*. To calculate expected utility, for all j the height from x_j down to the x-axis is transformed into the height $U(x_j)$. Then the area shaded by ⧅, including ⊠, gives the expected utility. (The area, shaded by ⧄, including ⊠, gives expected value.)

With further indulgence of the reader, Figure 2.2 gives an elementary presentation of expected utility, again as a preparation for the intuitive argument to be developed. As compared to Figure 2.1a, for expected utility first the heights of the columns are transformed; the height x_1 is transformed into $U(x_1)$, the height x_2 (down to the x-axis!) is transformed into $U(x_2)$, etc. Finally, the **expected utility** of the lottery is the area shaded by \\\ in Figure 2.2 (including the xxx-area), i.e.,

$$\sum_{j=1}^{n} p_j U(x_j) \,. \tag{2}$$

The expected utility approach became full-blown when it received behavioural foundations by von Neumann & Morgenstern (1944) and Savage (1954). It stirred statistical literature, a topic we shall not pursue here. Expected utility was used to explain phenomena related to risk. For instance 'risk aversion' was explained through concavity of the utility function. If the utility function is concave then indeed a lottery is never preferred to its expected value. Also expected utility was used to model comparisons of attitudes of decision makers towards risk. A first decision maker is at least as risk averse as a second if the values $-U''/U'$ for the first decision maker are nowhere smaller than those for the second. Indeed, if then the first decision maker prefers a lottery with nonconstant outcomes (so with risk involved) to a certain amount of money, then the second decision maker will also prefer the risky lottery. This has been found independently by Pratt (1964) and Arrow (1965, 1971).

Still, people have not been fully satisfied by the above results of expected utility. When being informed about the explanation of risk aversion through concavity of the utility function for the first time, most people feel a moment's disappointment. One would think that the utility function rather reflects the decision maker's appreciation of money, than his attitude towards risk. (Be it that the appreciation of money concerns the dealing with risk, which is possibly different from -interval scale = cardinal-appreciations of money in other contexts.) And one would want to reflect attitudes towards risk by means of the way in which probabilities are incorporated, rather than the way in which money is incorporated. An idea is that maybe this can be achieved by transforming probabilities, just as well as Bernoulli transformed payments. Let us denote the transformation by φ. At first sight it may seem self-evident that a lottery is now to be valued by the following modification of (1) :

$$\sum_{j=1}^{n} \varphi(p_j)x_j \ . \tag{3}$$

It is then natural that φ should be nondecreasing, and that $\varphi(0) = 0$; further we may normalize $\varphi(1) = 1$. This idea was proposed for instance in Edwards (1955, p. 201, second column, lines 34–38, and formulas (3) and (4)); it was considered natural. We shall dispute that naturalness. A first-sight-heuristic argument to suggest that there may be a difference between the payments and the probabilities in (1) is that the payments are free variables, whereas the probabilities are restricted to sum to one. The aim of this paper is to give a more sophisticated heuristic to see the difference.

The new valuation of the lottery of Formula 3 is illustrated in Figure 2.3, by the area shaded by \\\ (including the ×××-area). Not the heights of the columns, but the breadths, have now been transformed.

The importance of (3) may appear from the central role given to it in 'prospect theory' of Kahneman & Tversky (1979). The idea already occurred in older papers, see for instance Preston & Baratta (1948). Further references are Edwards (1962), Coombs, Bezembinder & Goode (1967), Tversky (1967), and Wallsten (1971). More references are given in Edwards (1954), Luce & Suppes (1965), and Machina (1982, pp. 290–292). Sometimes the transformed probabilities $\varphi(p_j)$ in this approach are called subjective, and the probabilities p_j are called objective. Let us emphasize that the 'subjective probabilities', additive and summing to one, as occurring in Savage (1954), are 'quite different' (Edwards, 1962, p. 109) from the, nonadditive, not-summing-to-one, transformed probabilities. For this reason Edwards (1954) proposed to consider transformed probabilities not as probabilities, but as 'decision weights', a term also used in prospect theory.

We hope to convince the reader that the approach which deals with transformed probabilities as in (3), simply is not very suited.

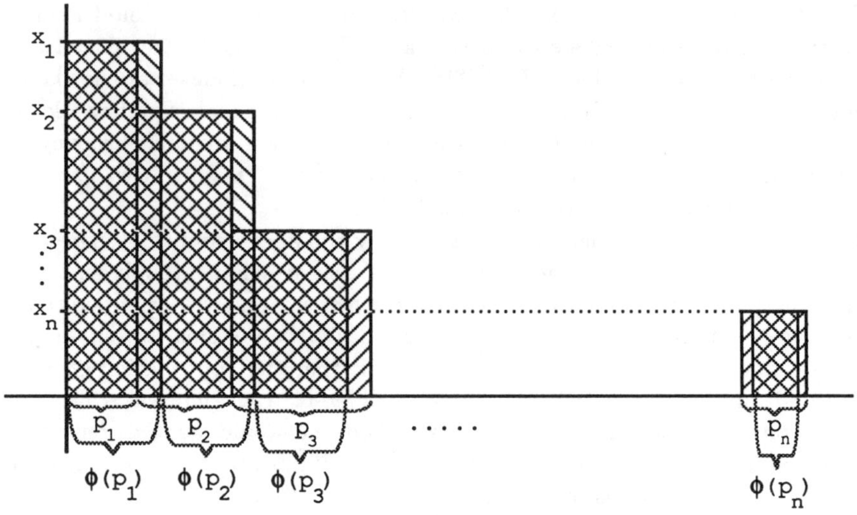

FIGURE 2.3. *Transforming probabilities in the 'old way'.* Breadths of single columns have been transformed. The lottery is now valued by the area, shaded by , including . (The area, shaded by , including , gives expected value.)

SECTION 3. THE PROBLEM WITH (3)

In this section we show what the problem is with (3). This has been pointed out for instance in Kahneman & Tversky (1979). Obviously, if the transformation φ is identity, then we deal with decision making as described by older approaches, and no new problems will occur. We shall show that problems occur as soon as φ is not identity. So say φ is not identity. Then, as we shall argue below, there must exist p_1 and p_2 so that :

$$\varphi(p_1 + p_2) \neq \varphi(p_1) + \varphi(p_2) \ . \tag{4}$$

It is well-known that a function which has equality in (4) for all p_1 and p_2 can only be nonlinear if it is 'very strange'. For instance it can then only be obtained through the 'choice axiom'[3] from mathematics, so that it will never be met in practice; its graph must be dense in $[0,1] \times \Re$, the function is nowhere continuous, is not Lebesgue measurable, and is nowhere monotone (see Aczél, 1966). The latter shows that our nonlinear and monotone φ must indeed for some p_1 and p_2 satisfy the inequality of (4). Suppose

$$\text{Case 1)}: \ \varphi(p_1 + p_2) > \varphi(p_1) + \varphi(p_2).$$

To show what may go wrong, we consider what happens if x_1 is decreased in Figure 2.3. That is illustrated in Figure 3.1. At first, not much interesting happens; see Figure 3.1a. The height of the first column has decreased somewhat, and with that

[3] See Maddy (1988) for its controversial history. It should not be confused with the choice axiom for probabilistic choice theory as in Luce (1959).

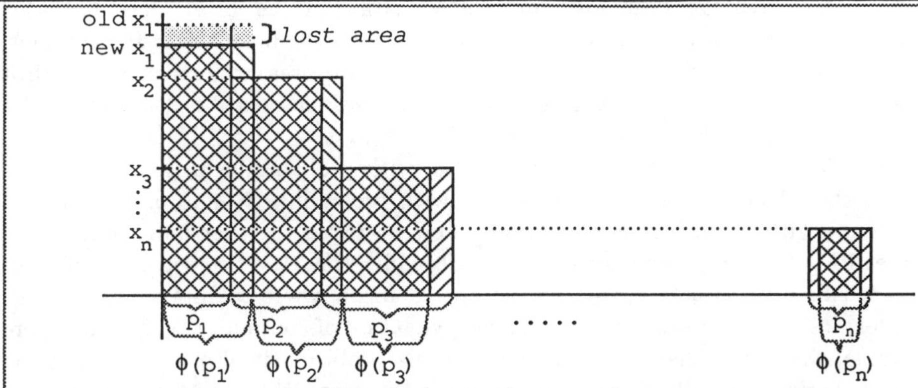

FIGURE 3.1a. *Moving* x_1 *of Figure 2.3 down somewhat.* Nothing interesting happens yet. Some area is lost, and the valuation of the lottery decreases somewhat. No breadths of columns are changed.

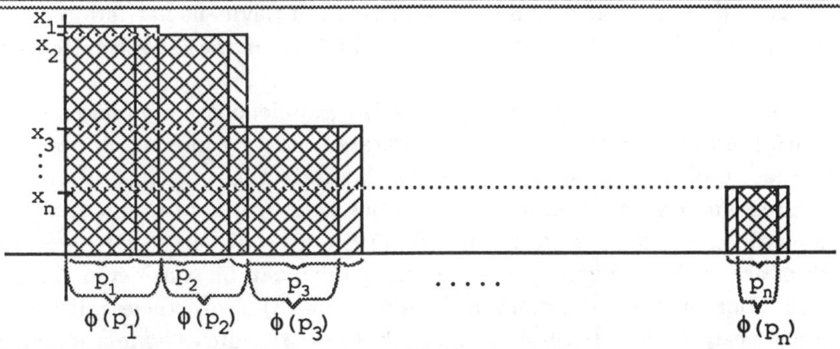

FIGURE 3.1b. *Moving* x_1 *further down.* It has gotten very close to x_2.

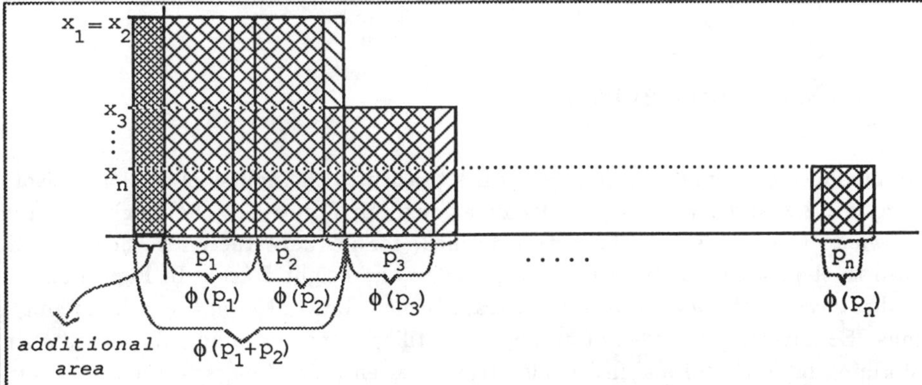

FIGURE 3.1c. x_1 *'hits'* x_2. An 'explosion' of new area to the left occurs. It has been shaded denser. We added it to the left for easy comparison. The two columns have been taken together into one broader column. Because of this, the area is larger than in Figure 3.1b. A decrease in payment has led to an increase in area and valuation.

FIGURE 3.1. *Formula (3) violates dominance.* Applying Formula (3) to different lotteries, differing w.r.t. payment x_1, reveals violation of stochastic dominance.

its area. Some area has been lost, and the valuation of the lottery has decreased somewhat. Note that the ordering of the outcomes, and the breadths of the columns, have remained unaffected. In Figure 3.1b, x_1 has been decreased further, and with it the area and the valuation of the lottery; x_1 here is very close to x_2. The problematic phenomenon occurs in Figure 3.1c, where x_1 'hits' x_2, i.e., $x_1 = x_2$. Then no longer x_1 and x_2 should be treated as different outcomes, with probabilities p_1 respectively p_2. Now they should be treated as one outcome, with probability $p_1 + p_2$ of occurrence.[4] The columns with heights x_1 and x_2 should now be taken together into one column, with breadth $\varphi(p_1 + p_2)$. As one sees, this is broader than the two separate columns with joined breadth $\varphi(p_1) + \varphi(p_2)$. So at the moment where x_1 hits x_2, at the left side an 'explosion' of area occurs. This gives a violation of continuity, which may seem undesirable. However, there is a far more serious problem: it also gives a violation of 'stochastic dominance'! To see this, compare the area, in Figure 3.1b, when x_1 is approaching x_2 so that still $x_1 > x_2$, but x_1 is very close to x_2, with the area in Figure 3.1c, when $x_1 = x_2$. Because of the 'explosion of area' on the left side, the area in Figure 3.1c is larger. That means that a decrease of payment has induced an increase in valuation! This is exactly what a violation of **(first-order) stochastic dominance** can be defined to be.

In Case 2, where $\varphi(p_1 + p_2) < \varphi(p_1) + \varphi(p_2)$, analogously a violation of stochastic dominance (and continuity) can be demonstrated, now by moving x_2 up to x_1 and by revealing an 'implosion' of area. We do not elaborate this.

The problem that transformed probabilities no longer sum to one has been known for a long time, see for instance Edwards (1954, p. 397/398). Because of this, the breadth of areas like in Figure 3.1 is variable, which can be considered the main cause for the violation of stochastic dominance of formula (3). Nevertheless, it is unknown to us who has been the first to observe explicitly that (3) induces a violation of stochastic dominance.

SECTION 4. ANTICIPATED UTILITY

To introduce anticipated utility, let us first return to the figures of section 2. Note that Figures 2.2 and 2.3 are not fully analogous. In Figure 2.2 the heights all the way down to the x-axis have been transformed, for instance the entire height from x_2 down to the x-axis has been transformed into the height $U(x_2)$. In Figure 2.3 no entire distances to the y-axis have been transformed, but only the breadths of single columns. So naturally the idea of anticipated utility comes to mind: Why not, when transforming breadths/probabilities, also transform entire distances to the y-axis, like it is done in expected utility? This is illustrated in Figure 4.1. First the outcomes are 'rank-ordered' so that $x_1 > x_2 > \cdots > x_n$ (in fact only $x_1 \geq x_2 \geq \cdots \geq x_n$ is essential). Then the procedure is as follows :

[4]The cruciality of this 'notational' detail in the application of Formula (3) is sometimes felt as unsatisfactory.

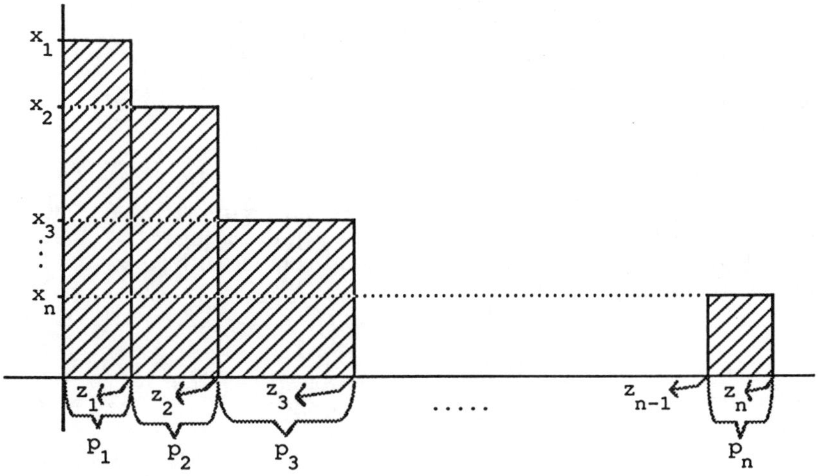

FIGURE 4.1a. *Endpoints of columns.* In the illustration of expected value we have now indicated the points $z_1, \ldots, z_n$, the endpoints of columns. These points will be shifted in Figure 4.1b.

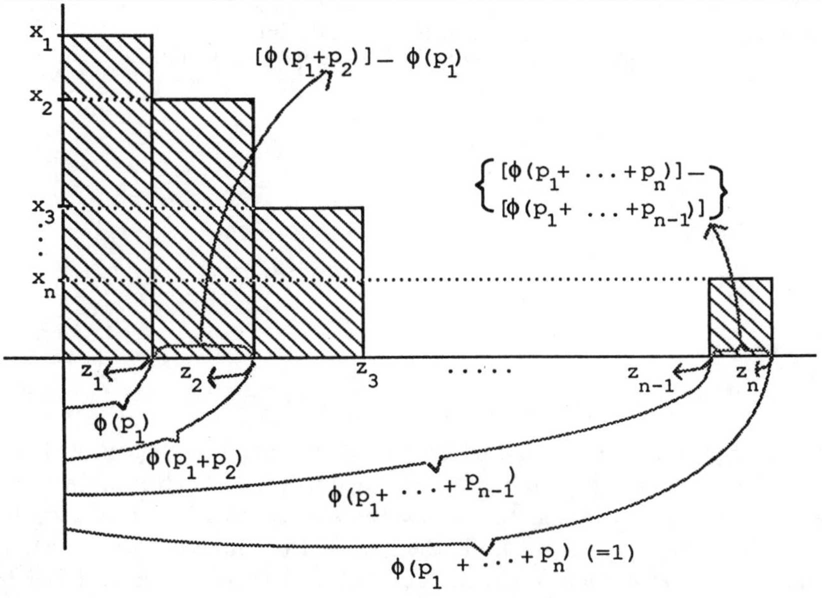

FIGURE 4.1b. *Anticipated utility.* Now entire distances from the points z_j to the y-axis have been transformed. And now z_n remains at a distance 1 from the y-axis.

FIGURE 4.1. *The anticipated utility approach to transformed probabilities.*

Replace p_1 *by* $\varphi(p_1)$.

So the distance p_1 from z_1 to the y-axis in Figure 4.1a is transformed, in Figure 4.1b, into $\varphi(p_1)$, as it was done in Figure 2.3. The breadth of the first column with height x_1 is now $\varphi(p_1)$.

Replace $p_1 + p_2$ *by* $\varphi(p_1 + p_2)$.

So the distance $p_1 + p_2$ from z_2 to the y-axis in Figure 4.1a is transformed, in Figure 4.1b, into $\varphi(p_1 + p_2)$, deviating from Figure 2.3. The breadth of the second column with height x_2 is now $\varphi(p_1 + p_2) - \varphi(p_1)$.

.

.

.

Replace $p_1 + p_2 + \cdots + p_{n-1}$ *by* $\varphi(p_1 + p_2 + \cdots + p_{n-1})$.

Replace $p_1 + p_2 + \cdots + p_n$ *by* $\varphi(p_1 + p_2 + \cdots + p_n)$.

The distance $p_1 + p_2 + \cdots + p_n$ $(= 1)$ from z_n to the y-axis in Figure 4.1a is 'transformed', in Figure 4.1b, into $\varphi(p_1 + p_2 + \cdots + p_n)$ $(= 1)$, deviating from Figure 2.3. The breadth of the n-th column with height x_n is now $\varphi(p_1 + p_2 + \cdots + p_n) - \varphi(p_1 + p_2 + \cdots + p_{n-1})$.

The lottery is now valued by :

$$[\varphi(p_1)]x_1 + [\varphi(p_1 + p_2) - \varphi(p_1)]x_2 + \cdots + [\varphi(p_1 + p_2 + \cdots + p_n) - \varphi(p_1 + p_2 + \cdots + p_{n-1})]x_n \,. \qquad (5)$$

□

This valuation can be reformulated exactly as the valuation by expected value was reformulated in Figure 2.1b. See Figure 4.2. Again, this is obtained from Figure 4.1b by rotating and flipping. Again the size of the shaded area is not affected by these operations. The shape in Figure 4.2 is the graph of the function $\varphi \circ \mathrm{G}$, with again G the decumulative distribution function: All heights $G(t)$ have been replaced by their φ-values $\varphi(\mathrm{G(t)})$. So the lottery is now valued by

$$\int_{\Re_+} \varphi \circ G(t)\, dt \;\; (= \; [\varphi(p_1)]x_1 + [\varphi(p_1 + p_2) - \varphi(p_1)]x_2 + \cdots + [\varphi(p_1 + p_2 + \cdots + p_n) - \varphi(p_1 + p_2 + \cdots + p_{n-1})]x_n) \,. \qquad (6)$$

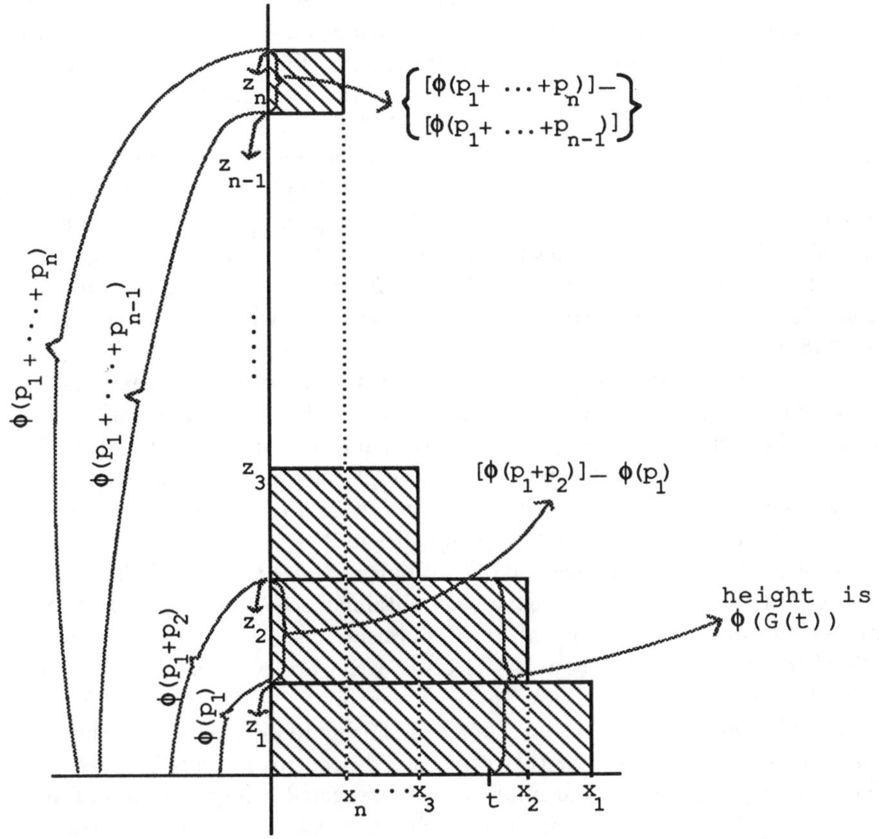

FIGURE 4.2. *An alternative presentation of anticipated utility.* Figure 4.1b has been rotated left, and flipped horizontally. The figure gives the graph of $\phi \circ G$.

SECTION 5. DISCUSSION AND EXAMPLE

The valuation by means of the integral in (6) is exactly the expected value of the lottery which has $\varphi \circ G$ as decumulative distribution function, instead of G.[5] So one may say that anticipated utility first transforms the decumulative distribution function, and then calculates expected value. Also $\varphi \circ G$ can be considered a 'capacity', and the valuation of the lottery the 'Choquet-integral' with respect to this capacity. (See for instance Wakker, 1989b, section VI.2 for definitions.) In Wakker (1989d) it is shown how anticipated utility for decision making under risk can be identified with 'Choquet-expected utility', the Choquet-integral approach for decision making under

[5] If φ is continuous of the right then indeed $\varphi \circ G$ is a decumulative distribution function of a σ-additive probability distribution.

uncertainty,[6] for the special case where objective probabilities are known.

To be taken serious, anticipated utility should be able to stand some questions. One of the first questions coming to mind (for instance when one sees the 'main message' in the concluding section 6) is a minor heuristic one: Why should one transform the probabilities of receipt of a fixed outcome or anything *better*, and not the probabilities of receipt of a fixed outcome or anything *worse*? The answer to this question is that it does not matter which of these two is taken. The two methods are 'data-equivalent', i.e., the set of decision strategies that can be modeled by the one method is identical to the set of the other. If one uses a transformation φ in the approach of this paper, then one should use the transformation $\psi : p \mapsto 1 - \varphi(1-p)$ for the other approach. In (6) one should then replace $\varphi \circ G$ by $\psi \circ$F, with F the usual (cumulative) distribution function. Relations between transformations such as φ and ψ above are central in Gilboa (1989).

Further anticipated utility and the integral in (6) can directly be extended to lotteries with infinite range, and can for instance deal with continuous distributions.

Of more importance is the question of the empirical implications of anticipated utility. We shall not elaborate these. An example of the most important empirical implication will be given in the sequel. Further we confine ourselves to the observation that anticipated utility is free from anomalies in its empirical implications, such as violations of stochastic dominance and of continuity.[7] Indeed sensible behavioural characterizations of anticipated utility have been obtained, see Quiggin (1982), Schmeidler (1982) and the simultaneous work of Yaari, published in 1987(a); and Gilboa (1987a). Also Wakker (1989a, 1989b Chapter VI) gives a characterization of anticipated utility in its version for decision making under uncertainty; here both transformation of payments and of probabilities are incorporated. For more information on the empirical implications of anticipated utility the reader should consult these references.

The most important empirical implication of expected utility is a kind of 'independence' condition, varying somewhat from context to context. Of course, since anticipated utility is more general than expected utility, its empirical implications will be less restrictive and less strong, so the most important empirical implication of anticipated utility consists of the weakening of (the several versions of) independence to 'comonotonic independence'. Schmeidler (1982) and Wakker (1989c) consider a version of comonotonic independence where probabilities are mixed, Yaari (1987a,b) considers a version of comonotonic independence where payments are mixed. All these versions apply only under the restrictive assumption that there is a kind of linearity w.r.t. the mixtures. We shall not elaborate these conditions, but instead present a version of comonotonic independence that is not restrictive: 'comonotonic coordinate independence'. It was introduced in Wakker (1989a, 1989b Chapter VI), as adaptation of Savage's 'sure-thing principle' (called 'coordinate independence' in Wakker's papers; see end of the following example). In Yaari (1987a,b) and Wakker (1989c, e) intuitive explanations are given in terms of hedging respectively optimism/pessimism. Also Gilboa (1987a) considers a variation of Savage's sure-thing principle, but his variation is more complicated.

---

[6]In decision making under uncertainty no 'objective' probabilities have to be known in advance; lack of information is modeled through a 'state space' as in Savage (1954).

[7]The latter is a somewhat more technical condition. Still it can add empirical content to other conditions. See Wakker (1988, Example 7.3).

EXAMPLE 1 [*The main empirical implication of the anticipated utility-approach ('comonotonic coordinate independence')*].

Suppose a die will be thrown. Either 1, or 2, ..., or 6 will come up, each with probability $\frac{1}{6}$. By $x = (x_1, \ldots, x_6)$ we denote the 'lottery' giving $\$x_1$ if 1 comes up, ..., $\$x_6$ if 6 comes up. Suppose a person prefers a bet $(x_1, \ldots, x_6)$ to a bet $(y =)\ (y_1, \ldots, y_6)$. Suppose further that $x_1 > x_2 > \cdots > x_6$ and that $y_1 > y_2 > \cdots > y_6$[8]. In anticipated utility the latter is central; to this the term 'comonotonic' refers. Suppose further that x and y have a common outcome, say $x_2 = y_2$. Then, if the person adopts anticipated utility to determine his preferences, **he will not change preference if the common outcome is changed into another common outcome**, say some $x'_2 = y'_2$, **as long as the change of outcome does not affect the rank-ordering of the outcomes.** I.e., if still $x_1 > x'_2 > \cdots > x_6$ and $y_1 > y'_2 > \cdots > y_6$, then still $(x_1, x'_2, x_3, x_4, x_5, x_6)$ is preferred to $(y_1, y'_2, y_3, y_4, y_5, y_6)$. Figure 5.1 illustrates how this can be derived.

The term comonotonic, abbreviating 'common monotonic', and introduced by Schmeidler, refers to the fact that the considered lotteries have the same rank-ordering of 'coordinates'. Indeed the involved outcomes can be considered coordinates, associated with fixed results of the throw of the die (such results are called 'states of nature' in decision making under uncertainty); the term 'coordinate' should distinguish this independence condition from the other ('mixture-')versions. 'Coordinate independence' is short for 'independence of equal coordinates'.

If the change of outcome does affect the ordering of outcomes, the preference may be changed. To see this, suppose the person is a ('super-pessimistic') maximin decision maker, i.e., values a lottery by its lowest outcome. This behavior, deviating from expected utility, can be described by anticipated utility, by taking $\varphi(p) = 0$ for all $p < 1$ (then in Figure 4.2 all area to the right of x_n vanishes). Then the above preference holds if $x_6 > y_6$. If x'_2 $(= y'_2)$ becomes smaller than y_6, so that indeed the rank-ordering of outcomes has been affected, then indeed the preference changes. Then $(x_1, x'_2, x_3, x_4, x_5, x_6)$ becomes equivalent to $(y_1, y'_2, y_3, y_4, y_5, y_6)$, each lottery having value $x'_2 = y'_2$. This phenomenon distinguishes anticipated utility from traditional expected utility. Under expected utility a change of a common outcome can never change the preference (this is the meaning of the 'sure-thing principle'/'coordinate independence'), irrespective of whether or not the rank-ordering of outcomes is affected. □

Let us take the opportunity to comment on (non-)differentiability of the valuation of lotteries in anticipated utility. The most influential recent deviation of expected utility, available in literature, is Machina (1982). He showed that results concerning ('higher-order') stochastic dominance, and comparisons of risk attitudes, considered before among the most important results of expected utility, could be obtained in a very general framework, not needing expected utility; only a 'Fréchet differentiability' assumption is used. This assumption by itself is technical, but in the presence of other assumptions may get empirical meaning, the status of which is not easy to determine. (Compare Wakker, 1988, Example 7.3.) It is the kind of assumption that is often made without further ado in applied literature. However, as shown by Chew, Karni & Safra (1987, Lemma 1), anticipated utility is *not* Fréchet differentiable. As Karni (1988) pointed out to the author, Figure 4.2 shows this in an easy way. Consider the shift of

[8] $\geq$ instead of $>$ would suffice

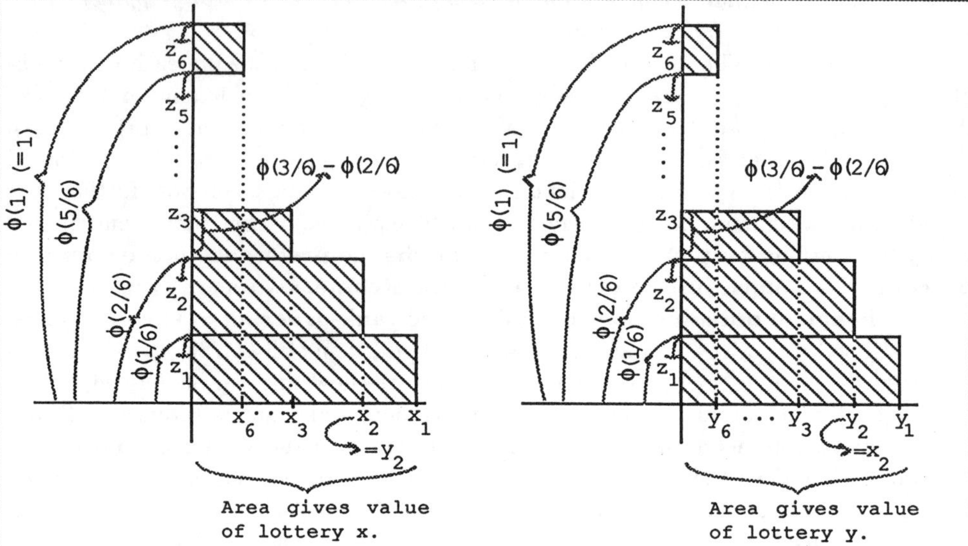

FIGURE 5.1a. *A preference with equal second coordinate.* x is preferred to y: the left area is somewhat larger than the right area.

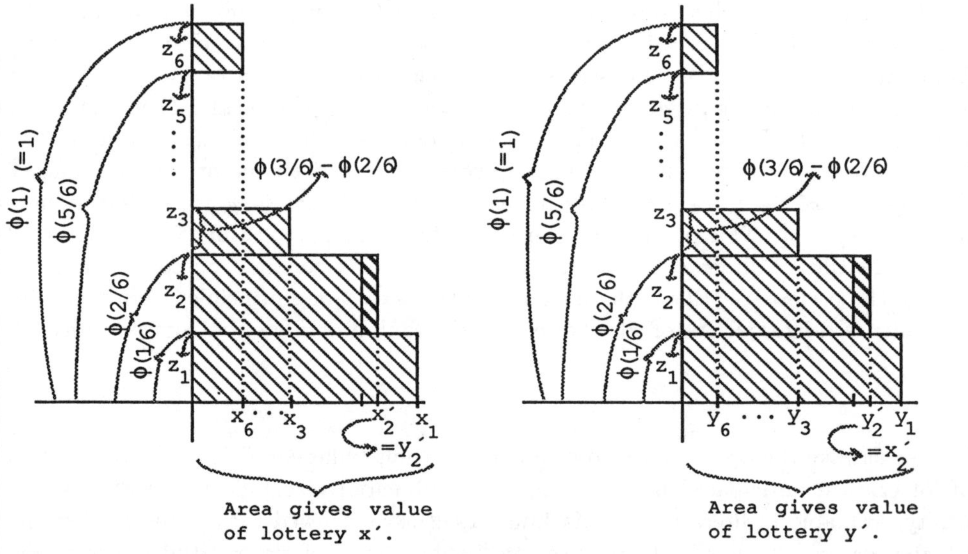

FIGURE 5.1b. *Adding same boldprinted area to left and right.* Still left area is somewhat larger than right area.

FIGURE 5.1. *Comonotonic coordinate independence.* The common outcome $x_2 = y_2$ from Figure 5.1a is replaced in Figure 5.1b by the common outcome $x_2' = y_2'$ in such a way that the rank-ordering of outcomes has not been affected. By this the areas of the left and right lottery have been increased by the same amount, indicated by ▧. Hence the ordering of the lotteries cannot have been affected, still the left lottery must be preferred to the right.

x_1 towards x_2. At first this induces a decrease in (Choquet-integral)-value at 'constant speed' $\varphi(p_1)$. However, at the moment that x_1 has 'hit' x_2 and continues becoming smaller than x_2, the constant speed suddenly changes into the speed $\varphi(p_1+p_2)-\varphi(p_2)$.[9] Loosely spoken, for Fréchet differentiability it is necessary that the speed of decrease is the same in all directions, as long as the shifts are infinitesimally small; a sudden change in speed as found above is not allowed. This means that the results of Machina's theory cannot be directly applied to anticipated utility. The above study of Figure 4.2 suggests that 'speed of decrease' is constant for infinitesimal shifts, as long as these shifts go in one direction; this is a loose-hand way to formulate 'Gateaux-differentiability'. Indeed, Chew, Karni & Safra (1987, Corollary 1) show that anticipated utility as presented in this paper[10] is Gateaux-differentiable. We think that the 'sudden change of speed' as observed above, and the implied non-Fréchet differentiability, is one of the most serious intuitive issues of anticipated utility.

SECTION 6. CONCLUSION

The new anticipated utility approach is, in a natural way, dual to expected utility. In the usual expected utility one takes Figure 2.1a, transforms the heights, then takes area. In the new anticipated utility approach one first flips and rotates Figure **2.1a** into Figure 2.1b, and only then transforms heights, and takes area. Let us phrase the **main message** of this paper:

> *If one transforms probabilities, then one should not transform the probabilities of receipt of a fixed outcome, but one should transform the probabilities of receipt of a fixed outcome or anything better.*

A final comment: The argumentation of this paper can be no more than heuristic, with arguments based on flippings of figures; this of course depends upon the particular way of illustration chosen in this paper, and the particular arrangement of columns in the Figures. Still we hope that this paper will help the reader getting interested, and encourage him/her to study the firm non-heuristic axiomatic justifications as provided in the references.

ACKNOWLEDGEMENT. Clarifying remarks have been added on the basis of suggestions of Th.G.G. Bezembinder.

REFERENCES

Aczél, J., (1966), '*Lectures on Functional Equations and Their Applications*'. Academic Press, New York.

[9]The latter is most easily seen by comparing it with the 'constant speed of decrease' $\varphi(p_2+p_1)-\varphi(p_1)$ when in Figure 4.2 in its present version (with $x_1 > x_2$) x_2 is shifted to the left. Also note that the inequality $\varphi(p_1) \neq \varphi(p_1+p_2)-\varphi(p_2)$ can always be established, according to Formula (4).

[10]In fact utility is assumed to be linear, so certainly differentiable, in this paper.

Allais, M. (1988), 'The General Theory of Random Choices in Relation to the Invariant Cardinal Utility Function and the Specific Probability Function'. *In* B. R. Munier (Ed.), *Risk, Decision and Rationality*, Reidel, Dordrecht.

Anger, B. (1977), 'Representations of Capacities', *Mathematische Annalen* 229, 245–258.

Arrow, K.J. (1965), '*Aspects of the Theory of Risk-Bearing*'. Academic Bookstore, Helsinki.

Arrow, K.J. (1971), '*Essays in the Theory of Risk-Bearing*'. North-Holland, Amsterdam.

Bernoulli, D. (1738), 'Specimen Theoria Novae de Mensura Sortis', *Commentarii Academiae Scientiarum Imperialis Petropolitanae* 5, 175–192. Translated into English by L. Sommer (1954), 'Exposition of a New Theory on the Measurement of Risk', *Econometrica* 12, 23–36; or in A.N. Page (Ed., 1968), '*Utility Theory: A Book of Readings*', Chapter 11, Wiley, New York.

Chateauneuf, A. (1988a), 'Uncertainty Aversion and Risk Aversion in Models with Nonadditive Probabilities'. *In* B. R. Munier (Ed.), *Risk, Decision and Rationality*, 615–629, Reidel, Dordrecht.

Chateauneuf, A. (1988b), 'Decomposable Measures, Distorted Probabilities and Concave Capacities', Working paper, Groupe de Mathématiques Economiques, Université de Paris I.

Chateauneuf, A. & J.-Y.Jaffray (1987), 'Some Characterizations of Lower Probabilities and Other Monotone Capacities', *Mathematical Social Sciences*, forthcoming.

Chew, S.H. (1985), 'An Axiomatization of the Rank-Dependent Quasilinear Mean Generalizing the Gini Mean and the Quasilinear Mean', Economics Working Paper # 156, Johns Hopkins University.

Chew, S.H., E. Karni, & Z. Safra (1987), 'Risk Aversion in the Theory of Expected Utility with Rank Dependent Probabilities', *Journal of Economic Theory* 42, 370–381.

Choquet, G. (1953-4), 'Theory of Capacities', *Annales de l'Institut Fourier* (Grenoble) 5, 131–295.

Coombs, C.A., Th.G.G. Bezembinder, & F.M. Goode (1967), 'Testing Expectation Theories without Measuring Utility or Subjective Probability', *Journal of Mathematical Psychology* 4, 72–103.

Dellacherie, C. (1970), 'Quelques Commentaires sur les Prolongements de Capacités', *Seminaire de Probabilités V Strasbourg*, (Lecture Notes in Mathematics 191), Springer Verlag, Berlin.

Denneberg, D. (1988), 'On Non-Expected-Utility Preferences', paper presented at 4th FUR conference, Budapest, 1988.

Dubois, D. & H. Prade (1988), 'Modelling Uncertainty and Inductive Inference: A Survey of Recent Non-Additive Probability Systems', *Acta Psychologica* 68, forthcoming.

Ebert, U. (1987), 'Measurement of Inequality: An Attempt at Unification and Generalization', *Social Choice and Welfare*, forthcoming.

Ebert, U. (1988), 'Rawls and Bentham Reconciled', *Theory and Decision* 24, 215–223.

Edwards, W. (1954), 'The Theory of Decision Making', *Psychological Bulletin* 51, 380–417.

Edwards, W. (1962), 'Subjective Probabilities Inferred from Decisions', *Psychological Review* 69, 109–135.

Fellner, W. (1961), 'Distortion of Subjective Probabilities as a Reaction to Uncertainty', *Quarterly Journal of Economics* 75, 670–690.

Fishburn, P.C. (1988), '*Nonlinear Preference and Utility Theory*'. Johns Hopkins University Press, Baltimore.

Gilboa, I. (1985), 'Subjective Distortions of Probabilities and Non-Additive Probabilities', Working paper 18–85, Foerder Institute for Economic Research, Tel-Aviv University, Ramat Aviv, Israel.

Gilboa, I. (1987a), 'Expected Utility with Purely Subjective Non- Additive Probabilities', *Journal of Mathematical Economics* 16, 65–88.

Gilboa, I. (1987b), 'Expectations and Variations in Multi-Period Decisions', *Econometrica*, forthcoming. Working paper 10–87, Foerder Institute for Economic Research, Tel-Aviv University, Ramat Aviv, Israel.

Gilboa, I. (1989), 'Duality in Non-Additive Expected Utility Theory'. *In* P.C.Fishburn & I.H.LaValle (Eds.), *Choice under Uncertainty*, Annals of Operations Research, J.C. Baltzer AG., Basel, forthcoming.

Hilton, R.W. (1988), 'Risk Attitude under Two Alternative Theories of Choice under Risk', *Journal of Economic Behaviour and Organization* 9, 119–136.

Huber, P.J. (1981), '*Robust Statistics*'. Wiley, New York.

Kahneman, D. & A. Tversky (1979), 'Prospect Theory: An Analysis of Decision under Risk', *Econometrica* 47, 263–291.

Karni, E. (1988), Personal communication.

Krantz, D.H., R.D. Luce, P. Suppes, & A. Tversky (1971), '*Foundations of Measurement, Vol. I. (Additive and Polynomial Representations)*'. Academic Press, New York.

Luce, R.D. & P. Suppes (1965), 'Preference, Utility, and Subjective Probability'. *In* R.D. Luce, R.R. Bush, & E. Galanter (Eds.), *Handbook of Mathematical Psychology*, III, Wiley, New York.

Machina, M.J. (1982), "Expected Utility' Analysis without the Independence Axiom', *Econometrica* 50, 277–323.

Machina, M.J. (1987), 'Choice under Uncertainty: Problems Solved and Unsolved', *Economic Perspectives* 1, 121–154.

Maddy, P. (1988), 'Believing the Axioms. I', *The Journal of Symbolic Logic* 53, 481–511.

Nakamura, Y. (1989), 'Subjective Expected Utility with Non-Additive Probabilities on Finite State Space', Discussion paper No. 400, April 1989, University of Tsukuba, Tsukuba, Ibaraki, Japan.

Pratt, J.W. (1964), 'Risk Aversion in the Small and in the Large', *Econometrica* 32, 122–136.

Preston, M.G. & P. Baratta (1948), 'An Experimental Study of the Auction Value of an Uncertain Outcome', *American Journal of Psychology* 61, 183–193.

Quiggin, J. (1982), 'A Theory of Anticipated Utility', *Journal of Economic Behaviour and Organization* 3, 323–343.

Röell, A. (1987), 'Risk Aversion in Quiggin and Yaari's Rank- Order Model of Choice under Uncertainty', (Supplement to the) *Economic Journal* 97, 143–160.

Savage, L.J. (1954), '*The Foundations of Statistics*'. Wiley, New York. (Second edition 1972, Dover, New York.)

Schlee, E. (1988), 'The Value of Information in Anticipated Utility Theory', University of Alabama, Department of Economics, October 1988.

Schmeidler, D. (1982), 'Subjective Probability without Additivity', Foerder Institut of Economic Research, Tel Aviv University, Tel Aviv, Israel. (Rewritten as Schmeidler, 1984.)

Schmeidler, D. (1984), 'Nonadditive Probabilities and Convex Games'. Caress working paper 84–21 (second part), University of Pennsylvania, Center for Analytic Research in Economics and the Social Sciences, Philadelphia, PA.

Schmeidler, D. (1986), 'Integral Representation without Additivity'. *Proceedings of the American Mathematical Society* 97, 255–261.

Segal, U. (1988), 'Anticipated Utility: A Measure Representation Approach', Working paper 8803, University of Toronto, Department of Economics and Institute for Policy Analysis, Toronto, Canada. Submitted to Annals of Operations Research. Rewritten version of Segal (1984), 'Nonlinear Decision Weights with the Independence Axiom', Working paper 353, University of California, Department of Economics, Los Angeles, USA.

Tversky, A. (1967), 'Additivity, Utility, and Subjective Probability', *Journal of Mathematical Psychology* 4, 175–201.

von Neumann, J. & O. Morgenstern (1944, 1947, 1953), '*Theory of Games and Economic Behavior*'. Princeton University Press, Princeton NJ.

Wakker, P.P. (1987), 'From Decision Making under Uncertainty to Game Theory'. *In* H.J.M. Peters & O.J. Vrieze (Eds.), *Surveys of Game Theory and Related Topics*, 163–180, CWI Tract 39, Centre for Mathematics and Computer Science, Amsterdam.

Wakker, P.P. (1988), 'The Algebraic Versus the Topological Approach to Additive Representations', *Journal of Mathematical Psychology* 32, 421–435.

Wakker, P.P. (1989a), 'Continuous Subjective Expected Utility with Nonadditive Probabilities', *Journal of Mathematical Economics* 18, 1–27.

Wakker, P.P. (1989b), '*Additive Representations of Preferences*, A New Foundation of Decision Analysis'. Kluwer Academic Publishers, Dordrecht.

Wakker, P.P. (1989c), 'A Behavioral Foundation for Fuzzy Measures', Internal report 89 MA 01, University of Nijmegen, NICI, Department of Mathematical Psychology, Nijmegen, The Netherlands. Submitted to *Fuzzy Sets and Systems.*

Wakker, P.P. (1989d), 'Stochastic Dominance Implies the Equality [Choquet-Expected Utility = Anticipated Utility]', Internal report 89 MA 02, University of Nijmegen, NICI, Department of Mathematical Psychology, Nijmegen, The Netherlands.

Wakker, P.P. (1989e), 'Characterizing Optimism and Pessimism Directly through Comonotonicity', Internal report 89 NICI 06, University of Nijmegen, NICI, Department of Mathematical Psychology, Nijmegen, The Netherlands.

Wallsten, T. (1971), 'Subjective Expected Utility Theory and Subjects' Probability Estimates: Use of Measurement-Free Techniques', *Journal of Experimental Psychology* 88, 31–40.

Wallsten, T.S. & B.H. Forsyth (1985), 'On the Usefulness, Representation, and Validation of Non-Additive Probability Judgements for Risk Assessment', Department of Psychology, University of North Carolina, Chapel Hill, NC, USA.

Yaari, M.E. (1987a), 'The Dual Theory of Choice under Risk', *Econometrica* 55, 95–115.

Yaari, M.E. (1987b), 'Univariate and Multivatiate Comparisons of Risk Aversion: a New Approach'. *In* W.P. Heller, R.M. Starr, & D.A. Starrett (Eds.), *Uncertainty, Information and Communication, Essays in honor of Kenneth J. Arrow*, Vol. III,

173–187, Cambridge University Press, Cambridge.
Yaari, M.E. (1988), 'A Controversial Proposal Concerning Inequality Measurement', *Journal of Economic Theory* 44, 381–397.
Yager, R.R. (1988), 'On Ordered Weighted Averaging Aggregation Operators in Multicriteria Decisionmaking', *IEEE Transactions on Systems, Man, and Cybernetics* 18, 183–190.

Formal Models and Axiomatic Measurement*)

*Edward E. Roskam***)
University of Nijmegen

Abstract
The paper addresses questions related to the interpretation of numerical representations of structures satisfying certain axiomatic properties. It is argued that a statement like 'situation *A* is two times as risky as situation *B*', is not meaningful as it depends on the particular representation chosen out of many ones which are axiomatically equivalent, even though each of them entails a ratio scale. Instead, it is meaningful that 'the risk of *A* is equivalent to the risk of (*B* and *B*)'. Furthermore, it is demonstrated that a different equivalent representation may imply a property which was not axiomized, but which is empirically meaningful and testable. Finally it is shown that a numerical representation which satisfies the axioms of an empirical structure, may not be meaningful as it may entail empirically contradictory implications, due to, e.g., violation of dimensional invariance.

On the axiomatic foundation of multidimensional scaling Tversky & Krantz (1970, p. 596) wrote: "The present approach is characterized by treating multidimensional scaling models as quantitative psychological theories rather than as methods for data reduction. It rests on the supposition that the axiomatic analysis of these models combined with the experimental investigation of their consequences will result in a deeper understanding of the metric and dimensional structures that underly similarity data". Beals, Krantz & Tversky (1968, p. 128) wrote: "If on the other hand, the necessary consequences of such models are rejected, on empirical or theoretical grounds, the 'blind' application of multidimensional scaling techniques is quite objectionable".

The axioms of measurement theory are abstractly algebraically formulated assumptions about the structure of empirical data, on the basis of which a certain numerical representation exists. The representation is actually of secondary importance. The theory about the empirical structure is the main thing, which is contained in the abstract algebraic axioms. The actual calculation of numbers is an 'encore' of the theory.

---

*) This is a modified and extended version of a paper earlier published in Dutch as: Formele modellen en axiomatische meetmethoden, of: wat betekent een kwantitatieve formulering?, In H.F.M. Crombag, L.J.Th. van der Kamp, & C.A.J. Vlek (Red.) (1987): *De Psychologie Voorbij, (Bundel aangeboden aan prof.dr.J.P.van der Geer bij zijn afscheid als hoogleraar methodenleer).* Lisse: Swets & Zeitlinger. I am grateful to R.Duncan Luce for pointing out a weakness in my exposition of Pollatsek & Tversky's Theory of Risk in an earlier version of this paper.

**) Nijmegen Institute of Cognition and Information, Department of Mathematical Psychology, University of Nijmegen, P.O. Box 9104, 6500 HE Nijmegen, The Netherlands, Bitnet-Earn U212753 @ HNYKUN11.

It is regrettable that the aim of measurement theory has been misunderstood by some (De Groot, 1977; De Groot & Medendorp, 1986). De Groot (1977, p. 229) wrote: "...is it interesting to see that Mario Bunge (1973, p. 121) in a chapter 'On confusing "measure" with "measurement" in the general methodology of behavioral science', states that the general 'theory of measurement' of psychologists is based on an illusion (which according to him originated in a translation error anno 1901), namely: 'the illusion (...) that a purely mathematical, hence *apriori* theory, could account for measurement - of anything and apart from both substantive theories and the praxis of measuring'. Concerning the error of translation: Hölder (1901) wrote *die Lehre vom Mass*, which was translated as *theory of measurement*, probably because the term *measure theory* (which may have been better) was already used as translation of *Masstheorie*, which has a fully different meaning. Bunge has, however, made a mistake himself in considering the term 'measurement' in 'theory of measurement' like he chose to define it, namely as *quantification*, and De Groot followed him in that error. Bunge distinguishes carefully between *quantitation* and *quantification*. By *quantitation* Bunge means (ib. p. 105-106) "the introduction of quantitative concepts": (it) is an armchair occupation scientists engage in when intent on building quantitative theories. It should therefore be kept distinct from *measuring* (italics mine, E.R.), which is an empirical operation - the more so since quantitation precedes measurement". Naturally I agree with these statements of Bunge. What Krantz *et al.* (1971) denoted as *measurement* is not in the first place quantification, but *quantitation*. Bunge (ib. p. 108) states: "Quantitation (...) consists in the introduction of some function mapping degrees of some property into *bona fide* numbers", and that is exactly where the *Foundations of Measurement* is about: the foundations of the 'introduction of quantitative concepts': the empirical conditions which must be satisfied, so that a numerical representation exists, and - in abstracto - the formal procedure to arrive at quantification. In so doing, measurement theory may be doing slightly more than Bunge intended when he meant 'quantitation': not only the introduction of quantitative concepts, but also their empirically testable justification and the constructive method to assign numbers.

In another respect too, it appears that Bunge is not right in his judgement. His proposition that apriori theory "could not account for measurement" ignores that measurement can also not do without apriori considerations, like the last example in this paper will demonstrate. Theory construction is always more than merely aposteriori inductive generalization or description of empirical structures.

Yet, it seems to me that many psychologists consider measurement theory and related matters more as an aspect of the technique of data analysis than as a metatheory for substantive theory-development. My opinion is that mathematical psychology is (at least a form of) *theoretical* psychology. A theoretical psychology which has a position in psychology which is comparable to the place of theoretical physics in physics, hardly exists. Mathematical psychology should be the natural partner of experimental psychology.

What should measurement theory, mathematical psychology, mathematical-theoretical psychology do? A starting point to discuss this can be found in the four problem themes which can be distinguished in the theory of measurement: (a) providing *representation* theorems, which show how empirical systems can be represented numerically, and because of which empirical conditions this is possible, (b) providing *uniqueness* theorems about these representations, (c) the problem of the *meaningfulness* of (quantitative) statements, (d) the *scaling* problem and data analysis. These four are closely related to each other. From the axioms - that is: from the content of the theory - the existence of a formal representation is proven, together with its uniqueness, and usually also its construction. The representation permits of deriving statements, e.g. in the form of quantitative relations: the effect of this is x times the effect of that. Which statements can, or can not, be made constitutes the *meaningfulness* problem, which - in brief - comes down to the question whether a relational statement which is valid in the formal representation, also is valid empirically, assuming that the theory is valid. This is basically the question what the theory says, and what it does not say. The answer is found in principle by investigating whether or not the statement is valid in all alternative representations (models) of the pertinent theory. The question of meaningfulness concerns, among others, the invariance of statements under permissible scale transformations. In that form it was already formulated by Stevens (1946, 1951). (See also Michel, 1986). It reaches, however, farther, and has a broader significance when also alternative representations of the same axiomatic system and metatheoretical considerations are taken into account. Analysis of formal models can show to which extent they are meaningful and useful as representation of the observed reality.

Mathematics as "science of making necessary conclusions" (Pierce, quoted in Davis & Hersh, 1981, p. 7), is for the empirical sciences the pre-eminent way to investigate consistence and tenability of theoretical statements and derivations.

In this paper, we will present some examples to show where such an analysis can lead us. We are explicitly concerned here with theoretical analysis, and hope to show that this is a means of critically examining the content and possible validity of a theory.

We discuss four cases which illustrate different aspects of the problem of 'meaningfulness'. In the first we discuss, in a fairly general way, which meaning can be attached to quantitative statements. In the second we discuss a case in which different quantitative representations of the same theory are possible, which, on closer inspection, differ in their empirical content. The third example concerns quantitative unfolding, which is shown to be less quantitative than its name suggests. In the fourth example, we discuss a model of risk perception which turns out not to be unequivocal. It is shown that a different model, satisfying the same theoretical assumptions, satisfies the requirement of unequivocality.

How much is two times as much?
Different scales or different operations?

The measurement of basic quantities in physics, like mass, is in general a rather unequivocal and transparent matter, despite the fact it is not simple to define the mass of sub-atomic particles. An object has a mass of 2 (gram) if it is balanced by two standard weights of 1 (gram). Measurement of mass (and the same holds for length, time, current, and various other quantities) is so transparent since it is performed with overt operations. No processes going on in a 'black box', of which we only see the outside, appear to be involved. For a psychological process 'in' a person, measurement seems less simple. Suppose that the effect of a training condition is equal to the effect of a different training condition which is administered two times in succession. It seems obvious that we call the effect of the one training condition two times as large as that of the other. The training effect itself needs not be measured. We only have to be able to compare the effects, and concatenate one training condition with itself. One might, however, object that the effect of a repeated condition is smaller than the effect of the first, and thus a training condition which has the same effect as a succession of two times a standard condition, is not 'two times' as effective, but less than two times (just like two times the same sweet does not give twice as much pleasure as once that sweet). But how can we find out? The consideration that we could measure the training effect per se would only displace the problem. To clarify the problem I choose an example that is comparable to the example of the weights in the balance, but I turn it into a psychological example by locating it, as it were, in a black box.

To measure, e.g. the magnitude of jars, different processes are conceivable. The next example is adapted from an example of Ellis, 1968, p. 80.

We site the measurement first outside the 'black box'. Take two (cylindrical) jars which are equally high, but with different diameter. Fill the smallest jar with sand and pour it over in the other. Repeat that and suppose that after, e.g., the fourth time, the larger jar is full. Thus we find that the larger jar is *four* times as large as the smaller jar. Now wrap a piece of paper around the small jar, such that it is exactly covered, and put that paper on the larger jar. Repeat that also until the larger jar is covered. We find now that the larger jar is fully covered with two wrappings of the smaller jar, and therefore, we find the larger jar *two* times as large as the smaller one.

Now take a lot of similar jars (all equally high, all exactly cylindrical), a supply of paper and a supply of sand, as well as a subject. Hand the subject pairs of jars, and ask him to choose a jar of which he finds - disregarding how he decides to determine this - that it is equivalent to the two given jars. However: let the subject do his task behind a screen (in a 'black box'), such that we can not see how he arrives at his response. Suppose that the responses perfectly satisfy the axioms of extensive measurement. The details of these axioms need not be discussed here. (See e.g. Roberts, 1979; see also equation [1], below, and footnote 6.)

The experimenter, ignorant of what goes on inside the black box, has little trouble in assigning numerical values to the jars, which represent how the subject judges these jars, according to the rule *f(C)=f(A)+f(B)* when the subject finds that *C* is equivalent to *(A with B)*, where *f(X)* is the number assigned to jar *X*. But how would the experimenter know what the subject did? Note that the question is analogous to the question how a subject after two times training condition *A*, reaches the same training effect as after once condition *B*.

The experimenter takes a different subject, chooses for both the same jar as unit, and finds that the numbers for the jars which he obtains for the second subject, are exactly the squares of those of the first subject.

With *E* as unit jar subject 1 says that[1)]

$E \oplus E =_o B$, making $f(B) = 2$, and $f(C) = 1.41$ [2)].

Subject 2 finds:

$E \oplus E =_o C$,
$C \oplus C =_o B$, making $f(B) = 4$, and $f(C) = 2$.

Our experimenter is very satisfied and concludes that the first subject used the paper (obviously judging circumference), and the second used the sand (judging volume). After some reflection, the experimenter realizes that with this conclusion he can choose a common measurement scale (the volume of the jars) but different operations: It is easily seen that he can assign the same numerical values to both subjects' perceptions of the jars, but assume that they performed the task differently.

The first subject satisfies the rule $f(C) = \sqrt{\{[f(A)]^2 + [f(B)]^2\}}$,

The second subjects satisfies the rule $f(C) = f(A) + f(B)$.

The preceding example may be too transparent. With respect to jars we 'know' already that only circumference and volume can be involved, and we know their numerical relation. However, one might as well define the magnitude of a jar by its radius, and represent the responses of the two subjects by:

---

1) With the symbol $=_o$ we denote an empirical equivalence. The symbol $\oplus$ means an empirical composition or concatenation: $A \oplus B$ is read as *A with B*.

2) The calculation of $f(C) = 1.41$ is a technical matter, which we can ignore here.

for the first subject: $g(C)=g(A)+g(B)$, and

for the second subject: $g(C)=\{\sqrt{[g(A)]}+\sqrt{[g(B)]}\}^2$, where

$g(\cdot)=[f(\cdot)]^2$.

Suppose that we present a subject with various *risky situations*, like 'a sailing tour on the North Sea', 'living next to an ammunition plant', 'living near a nuclear plant', and have him compare these, as well as combinations of such situations, as to 'risk'. Different subjects can give different responses which satisfy the axioms of an extensive measurement model. Let us assume that all subjects perceive the same *rank order* of risk. When we choose an additive representation for all, we get different scales; we can also choose the same scale for all, and assume that different persons judge differently about combinations of risky situations.

Stated in general terms: when data satisfy the axioms of an extensive measurement model, there exists a scale f such that[3]:

$$f(a) \geq f(b) \leftrightarrow a \geq_o b ,$$

$$f(c) = f(a) + f(b) \leftrightarrow c =_o a \oplus b . \qquad [1]$$

If t is a strictly monotone function (e.g. $t: x \rightarrow e^x$), which transforms the scale f into the scale $g=t \circ f$, then g also satisfies the axioms when we take the composition rule:

$$g(c) = t\{t^{-1}[g(a)] + t^{-1}[g(b)]\} \leftrightarrow c =_o a \oplus b . \qquad [2]$$

Some examples are (see Krantz *et al.*, 1971, p. 99 e.v.)[4][5]:

1. $t(x) = \text{signum}(x) \times |x|^{1/p},$ for $p > 0,$

$$t^{-1}(x) = \text{signum}(x) \times |x|^p,$$

$$g(a \oplus b) = \{[g(a)]^p + [g(b)]^p\}^{1/p} ;$$

2. $t(x) = \tanh(x) = \dfrac{\exp(x) - \exp(-x)}{\exp(x) + \exp(-x)},$ for $0 \leq x \leq 1,$

$$t^{-1}(x) = \tfrac{1}{2}\ln[(1+x)/(1-x)] ,$$

---

[3] We use the symbol $\geq_o$ to denote an empirical weak order relation. (connected and transitive; see Krantz *et al.*, 1971, p.14).

[4] Unless indicated otherwise, x^p means: $|x|^p$signum(x).

[5] Example 2 is known as the 'addition' of relativistic velocity, where velocity is proportional to distance divided by elapsed time, and g is scaled in such a way that $g(light)=1$, and $g(\cdot) \leq 1$. Schönemann, Dorcey & Kienapple (1985) use this subadditive concatenation also in the context of MDS.

$$g(a \oplus b) = \frac{g(a) + g(b)}{1 + g(a) \times g(b)} \ .$$

Imagine that *a, b, c, ...* represent situations, and that *f*, and *g*, resp., are scales which represent the (subjective) risk of those situations.

When we choose the value of *p* greater than 1 in example 1, the concatenation of risk is subadditive: $g(a \oplus b) < g(a) + g(b)$, that is: risk adapts (as *p* increases, the value of the concatenation approaches the value of the largest element). If the value of *p* is less than 1, then the concatenation of risk is superadditive: risk escalates. The value of *p* can be interpreted as an aspect of the perception of combinations of risk, where "risk, like beauty is in the eyes of the beholder" (Coombs & Huang, 1970). But when a subject says that living next to a nuclear plant is as risky as living between 10 chemical plants, would that not mean that a nuclear plant is ten times as risky as a chemical plant (at least according to the judgement of this subject)? That would only be a valid conclusion if living between ten chemical plants is experienced as 10 times as risky as living next to a single chemical plant (assuming, of course, that the risks are independent) which, however, is not self evident: At the market in my town, a herring costs *ƒ* 2.00, and six herrings cost *ƒ* 10.00. Is a tenner thus 6 times the value of two guilders? Only when 6 herrings are six times as 'valuable' as one herring (see Davis & Hersh, 1981, p. 71)).

In other words: when $A \oplus A$ is equivalent to *B*, that is insufficient reason to consider the value of *B* equal to two times the value of *A*. The numerical value of $A \oplus A$ may as well be more or less than 2. But precisely the latter can not be falsified, unless we already have an independent measurement of *A*. That other measurement should, however, in order to be not arbitrary, be based upon the algebraic structure of an empirical system, and so the problem is merely displaced. The question whether something 'really' is "two times as much", is almost a metaphysical problem, for which there exists no answer.

Yet, there is a way out of the dilemma whether we should choose a scale or should choose a certain numerical operation: If we find empirically that *B* is equivalent to $A \oplus A$, we can meaningfully say that *B* equals *2A* if and only if we specify explicitly by which empirical concatenation and observation we have found that *B* is equivalent to $A \oplus A$. For example: 'training condition A is two times as effective as training condition B' means then, literally, nothing but 'the effect of training condition A is equal to the effect of B followed by once again B'[6]. In other words: the number 'two' has a specific empirical referent. Numbers are thus considered as descriptive terms which are the domain of a suitable representational structure. There is a certain correspondence with the Aristotelian point of view that numbers are abstractions taken from reality (cf. Niederee, 1987). When we find different scales for different operations and observations (or for different subjects) we can interpret each of these as representations of different properties of the pertinent situation-person-systems,

[6] Assuming, of course, that the axioms of an extensive measurement model are satisfied, notably that *A* followed by *B* is equivalent to *B* followed by *A* (commutativity). See also the next section.

which are related by a certain function *t* (like circumference and area). But like it is meaningless to say that the area of a circle is two times as large as its circumference[7], it is also meaningless to say that persons *i*'s subjectively perceived risk of *A* is two times as large as that of person *j* (even when for both the same unit of measurement holds). Whatever way we look upon it, when someone finds that *A⊕A* is equivalent with *B*, we can not simply say that *B* is two times as much as *A*.

In this respect, there is a correspondence with *magnitude estimation*. When a subject finds that *B* is ten times *A*, can we then say that the subjective intensity of *B* is equal to 10 (taking *A* as the unit)? I believe that magnitude estimation is not measurement in the sense of a formal representation founded in a theoretical structure (but see also Eisler, 1982).

The problem is of course different when already independent measurements of *A* and *B* exist. When *A* and *B* are physical quantities (e.g. loudness intensities), *B* may appear less loud than *A⊕A* (binaurally presented), and when the *physical* intensity of *B* is equal to two times the physical intensity of *A*, we can meaningfully say that the psychophysical function is subadditive (concave). Similarly, with a theory of risk perception which describes risk as a function of the utilities of the outcomes, we also have a different case.

These examples demonstrate that meaningful statements are possible about the *relation* between measurement scales, but not about numerical quantities themselves. Krantz (1972) reached a similar conclusion. When at best statements about relations between scales are meaningful, and a certain scale never follows necessarily from the empirical structure, one should perhaps for pragmatic reasons adopt a certain scale as standard scale. (Just so as we choose an arbitrary unit for a scale). An example is the temperature scale (Ellis, 1968, 95-100).

Fischer's Axioms and Measurement Models for Change

A measurement model is always also a theory (or a system of substantive assumptions) about empirical phenomena. Via mathematical deduction, we prove the existence of a certain numerical model to represent the empirical structure which satisfies the assumptions. Different models may be possible - like was demonstrated above - and a comparison can show that a certain model offers possibilities for extensions which have empirical meaning (a related example in physics is negative mass or anti-matter).

Fischer (1987) has formulated a number of principles for the measurement of change. This concerns, e.g., the effect of a therapeutic treatment on the occurrence of a symptom, or the effect of an instruction on correct performance of a task. Let δ be a treatment effect, and

[7] The circumference of a circle with 1 cm radius is 2π cm = 6.28 cm; the area is π cm^2 = 3.14 cm^2; the numerical ratio of circumference to area is thus 2. Measuring the same circle in inches, the radius is 0.394 inch, the circumference 2.474 inch, and the area .487 inch^2. The numerical ratio of circumference to area is now 5.08.

ξ a person trait or property.The occurrence of a symptom or a correct performance is a function of ξ. According to Fischer, the change $\xi_1 \rightarrow \xi_3$ is written as a function of the changes $\xi_1 \rightarrow \xi_2$ and $\xi_2 \rightarrow \xi_3$, and the total effect is independent of the sequence of intermediate effects. Fischer's approach is based on the metatheoretical requirement of specific objectivity, namely that it is only meaningful to attribute an effect to a treatment if that effect does not depend on the subject under treatment. It is an empirical question whether or not specific objectivity in this sense exists. Statements about treatments per se are, however, meaningless when this requirement is not satisfied, or should be amended by a reference to certain properties of the person under treatment. Fischer's principles are:

$$\delta_1 = U(\xi_1,\xi_2), \quad \delta_2 = U(\xi_2,\xi_3), \quad \delta_3 = U(\xi_1,\xi_3),$$

$\delta_3 = H(\delta_1,\delta_2)$, independent of ξ_2,

$F(F(\xi_1,\delta_2),\delta_1) = F(F(\xi_1,\delta_1),\delta_2) = \xi_3$, (a kind of commutativity).

U is a function which defines δ as function of successive values of ξ, *H* is a function which defines a δ as function of other δ's (independent of the 'intermediate' positions), and *F* is a function which writes ξ as function of the first ξ and a commutative series of δ's. Different models satisfy these properties:

1. U: $\delta_1 = \xi_2 - \xi_1$, $\quad \delta_2 = \xi_3 - \xi_2$, $\quad \delta_3 = \xi_3 - \xi_1$,

   H: $\delta_3 = \delta_2 + \delta_1$,

   F: $\xi_1 + \delta_1 + \delta_2 = \xi_1 + \delta_2 + \delta_1 = \xi_1 + \delta_3 = \xi_3$, making:

   $\xi_2 = \xi_1 + \delta_1$ $\quad \xi_3 = \xi_2 + \delta_2$ $\quad$ etc., $\xi \in (-\infty,+\infty)$

2. U: $\delta_1 = \xi_2/\xi_1$, $\quad \delta_2 = \xi_3/\xi_2$, $\quad \delta_3 = \xi_3/\xi_1$,

   H: $\delta_3 = \delta_2 \times \delta_3$,

   F: $\xi_1 \times \delta_1 \times \delta_2 = \xi_1 \times \delta_2 \times \delta_1 = \xi_1 \times \delta_3 = \xi_3$, making:

   $\xi_2 = \xi_1 \times \delta_1$, $\quad \xi_3 = \xi_2 \times \delta_2$, $\quad$ etc., $\xi \in (0,\infty)$

3. U: $\delta_1 = \ln(\xi_2)/\ln(\xi_1)$, $\quad \delta_2 = \ln(\xi_3)/\ln(\xi_2)$, $\quad \delta_3 = \ln(\xi_3)/\ln(\xi_1)$,

   H: $\delta_3 = \delta_1 \times \delta_2$,

   F: $\xi_1^{(\delta_1 \times \delta_2)} = \xi_1^{(\delta_2 \times \delta_1)} = \xi_1^{\delta_3} = \xi_3$, making:

   $\xi_2 = \xi_1^{\delta_1}$, $\quad \xi_3 = \xi_2^{\delta_2}$, $\quad$ etc., $\xi \in (1,\infty)$

Model 2 follows from model 1 by the transformations $\xi \rightarrow \exp(\xi)$ and $\delta \rightarrow \exp(\delta)$. Model 3 follows by applying the transformation $\xi \rightarrow \exp(\xi)$ to model 2.

These three representations satisfy the same theory and statements about effects of treatments which are not valid in each of these representations are meaningless. Yet, the contents of these representations are different when we remove the fore mentioned restrictions on the range of ξ. One can therefore try and derive from its implications new statements which are empirically testable. When we remove the restrictions on the range of ξ, and in the third representation permit that ξ is in the open interval $(0,\infty)$, then this representation permits that the same δ has a positive (increasing) effect when $\xi > 1$, but a negative effect when $\xi < 1$. Empirically, that would mean that the same treatment has a favorable effect in some persons, but an adverse effect in others. Clearly, the direction of the effect is the same when the treatment is repeated. We see that this possibility is also present in the second representation, with $\xi \in (-\infty,+\infty)$, but not in the first representation.

It is not self evident that the restrictions on the range of ξ are necessary. Fischer's principles are satisfied even without these restrictions (except if $\xi \in (-\infty,+\infty)$ in model 2, which can not be represented in model 1 unless ξ and δ are allowed to be complex numbers).

This example demonstrates the heuristic value of exploring different representations. The theoretical assumptions by themselves as mentioned above, permit the construction of different representations, which each satisfy these assumptions. The extension of a certain representation appears to entail statements which are empirically testable, notably the possibility that the direction of an effect varies systematically with the person. When we extend the assumptions, a representation which would violate these extensions, must be rejected.

Quantitative Unfolding

According to Coombs' Unfolding theory, preference is a single peaked function on a cognitive continuum. The basic assumption of the theory is that there exists a unique ordering of alternatives such that in each triple, *A, B, C,* nobody ever prefers the middle one over the extremes. The theory in its basic form has nothing to say about the form of the preference function. However, if we assume that each subject's preference function is symmetric around the so-called ideal point, preference is a monotonely decreasing function of the distance between an alternative and the subject's ideal point. This permits of extracting information concerning the partial order of inter-alternative distances from a set of preference rank orders. Also the assumption of a symmetric preference function restricts the number of permissible preference rank orders to a number which is smaller than the number of permissible preference rank orders when the preference functions are not symmetric for every subject. The assumption of symmetric preference function and the ensuing possibility to extract more than ordinal information from these rank orders, is denoted as *quantitative* unfolding.

It is, however, easily seen that quantitative unfolding promises more than it really can give. Even if a set of data satisfies the restrictions of the quantitative unfolding model, there is nothing to prevent us from shrinking or stretching the scale monotonely, and thereby distorting the shape of the preference functions without affecting the preference rank order generated by these functions. In other words, although a set of preference rank orders may perfectly satisfy the restrictions of the quantitative unfolding model, we have no way of identifying the ordered metric structure of the scale, unless by the purely ad hoc assumption that the preference function is symmetric.

Pollatsek and Tversky's Theory of Risk

The next case shows that the choice of a certain model, although in agreement with empirical assumptions, may lead to contradictory conclusions, which disappear when we choose another model, equally corresponding to the empirical assumptions. What is paradoxical about this example is that the choice between them - contrary to Fischer's theory of change - apparently can not be based on empirical relations.

Imagine Peter and Paul, visiting the casino in Monte Carlo. They each have 600 french francs. Paul considers putting his money on black-odd, which he thinks is only twice as risky as putting his money on black. Peter, however, finds 'black-odd' three times as risky as just 'black'. Whether or not Paul or Peter are willing to play the gamble is another matter. Now Peter and Paul travel to Las Vegas, duely exchanging their french francs for dollars at the rate of six francs to the dollar. In Las Vegas, they consider the same wagers, but now Paul thinks that putting his 100 dollars on black-odd is four times as risky at putting it just on black, whereas Peter now finds 'black-odd' five times as risky as just 'black'. Suppose that we have a theory of risk perception, and that both Paul's and Peter's judgements are in accordance with that theory, both in Monte Carlo and in Las Vegas. Could that theory be correct?

Pollatsek and Tversky (1970) have proposed a theory of risk which says that the risk $R(g)$ of a situation, g, with unsure outcomes, is a linear function of the variance of the outcomes, $V(g)$, and of their expected value, $E(g)$. The theory is meant to be a theory about the perceived or subjective risk of a situation or option for action, which formally is considered as a probability distribution of utilities (advantages, disadvantages, gains, losses), that is: a probability distribution of possible effects or outcomes of g. The prototypical example is a lottery or a gamble.

Although experiments (e.g. Coombs and Bowen,1971; Coombs & Lehner, 1981a, 1981b, 1984) have shown that judgements of risk can not be written as an (additive) function of only (a monotone transformation of) variance and expectation[8)], the theory of Pollatsek & Tversky is interesting as an example showing that assumptions which in themselves are consistent and meaningful, do not automatically lead to a meaningful formula. Pollatsek & Tversky derived the following 'law' of perceived risk (but see also eq. [10] and the discussion at the end of this section):

[8)] Recently, Luce & Weber (1986) presented a theory of risk, by which the risk of a gamble is a weighted sum of the risks of its positive and its negative parts.

$$R(g) = tV(g) - (1-t)E(g) , \qquad (0 \leq t \leq 1) , \qquad [3]$$

where *t* is an individual parameter, which can be considered as a *V*(variance)-*E*(expectation) weighing parameter. They derived this law from the assumptions of an extensive measurement model for risk, the assumption that adding a positive value to all possible outcomes decreases risk, and the assumption that the risk order among gambles is not changed by convolution of a gamble with itself. The convolution of two gambles is a concatenation, which consists in playing both gambles independently.

We will demonstrate by some examples that formula [3] entails peculiar consequences, namely that

a *R, V, and E* can not be measured independent of each other,

b the parameter *t* depends on the unit of measurement of the utilities, and therefore can not be considered as a simple VE-weighing parameter, and

c certain risk-ratios are not invariant with a change of the unit of measurement of the utilities.

Consider the following pair of gambles:

g_1: (\$1.00, .50, -\$0.50) and g_2: (*ƒ* 2.56, .50, -*ƒ* 1.28) ,

i.e. g_1 is the option to win one dollar with a probability of one half, or else loose half a dollar. The definition of g_2 is the same, but now in guilders. When the value of the dollar is exactly *ƒ* 2.56, g_1 is equal to g_2, except for the choice of unit of measurement.

Now let *t* e.g. have the value .70. Consider the following gambles:

	gamble	E(g)	V(g)	t	R(g)
g_1:	(\$1.00, .5, -\$0.50)	+0.25	0.5625	.7	0.31875
g_2:	(*ƒ* 2.56, .5, -*ƒ* 1.28)	+0.64	3.6864	.7	2.3885
g_3:	(\$0.00, .5, -\$1.25)	-0.625	0.3906	.7	0.4609
g_4:	(*ƒ* 0.00, .5, -*ƒ* 3.20)	-1.6	2.56	.7	2.272

When the dollar is equal to *ƒ* 2.56, then g_1 is the same as g_2, and g_3 is the same as g_4. But with *t=.70* we get $R(g_1)<R(g_3)$ and $R(g_2)>R(g_4)$, meaning that the risk order of the two dollar gambles is opposite to the risk order of the same gambles expressed in guilders.

This obviously anomalous result can be eliminated by taking different values for *t*, one for dollars and one for guilders.

A simple calculation shows that $R(g_1)=R(g_3)$ when $t_\$=.83582$, and that $R(g_2)=R(g_4)$ when $t_f=.6654$. Now consider the next three gambles[9]:

	gamble	E(g)	V(g)	$t_\$$	R(g)
g_1:	(\$1.00, .5, -\$0.50)	+.250	.5625	.8358	.4291
g_3:	(\$0.00, .5, -\$1.25)	-.625	.3906	.8358	.4291
g_5:	(\$0.58, .5, -\$0.82)	-.119	.49	.8358	.4291

The same gambles transformed to guilders are[10]:

	gamble	E(g)	V(g)	t_f	R(g)
g_2:	(*f* 2.56, .5, -*f* 1.28)	+0.643	3.6864	.6654	2.2387
g_4:	(*f* 0.00, .5, -*f* 3.20)	-1.602	2.56	.6654	2.2387
g_6:	(*f* 1.48, .5, -*f* 2.10)	-0.305	3.2112	.6654	2.2387

One sees that the risk scale of the guilder-gambles is different from the scale of dollar-gambles, but that gambles which are equivalent on one scale, are also equivalent on the other scale.

The equivalence of g_1, g_3 *and* g_5, above, depends of course on the value of *t*. A different value, e.g. $t_\$=.70$, may make g_1 and g_3 not equivalent. The risk ratios of g_1 and g_3, and of g_2 and g_4 are still the same when t_f has the a value with which $t_\$=.70$ corresponds (see footnote 10):

g_1	with $t_\$ = .70$	$R = .3187$	the ratio
g_3	with $t_\$ = .70$	$R = .4609$	$R(g_3)/R(g_1) = 1.446$
g_2	with $t_f = .47684$	$R = 1.4230$	the ratio
g_4	with $t_f = .47684$	$R = 2.0577$	$R(g_4)/R(g_2) = 1.446$

9) Exactly calculated: $t_\$=.8358208955$, taking g_1 and g_3 as given, and constructing g_5 such that $E(g_5) = -f\ 0.1190909$.

10) The transformation of $t_\$$ to t_f is obtained as follows: we write *t* as $t=a/(a+b)$. When we set $a=t$, for simplicity, we have $b=1-t$. Changing from dollars to guilders: $a_f=a_\$/(2.56)^2$ and $b_f=b_\$/2.56$. So, when $t_\$=.7$ we obtain $t_f=.47684$, and when $t_\$=.8358$, we have $t_f=.6654$, maintaining the risk ratios. Exact calculations give: $t_f = 0.6653992395$ for $t_\$ = 0.8358208955$, and g_6 has $E(g) = -f\ 0.304872$.

Yet, the introduction of scale dependent t_f and $t_\$$ is not satisfactory. Although adapting t to the currency unit of the outcomes renders the risk ratio independent of the currency unit, this still prohibits comparison between subjects with different VE-weighing parameters, as the next example shows.

The value

$t_\$ = .70$ is for g_1 the dollar equivalent of $t_f = .4768$ for g_2, and
$t_\$ = .8566$ is for g_1 the dollar equivalent of $t_f = .70$ for g_2.

Inserting these values, which represent different, but currency-wise equivalent VE-weighing parameters, in formula [3], we get:

g_1 with $t_\$ = .7$	$R = .3187$	$R(g_1 \mid t=.7)$ / $R(g_1 \mid t=.857)$
g_1 with $t_\$ = .857$	$R \doteq .4460$	$= .7146$
g_2 with $t_f = .477$	$R = 1.4230$	$R(g_2 \mid t=.4768)$ / $R(g_2 \mid t=.7)$
g_2 with $t_f = .7$	$R = 2.3885$	$= .596$

This demonstrates that the ratio of the perceived risks of two subjects (each having his own VE-weighing parameter) changes when the gamble is expressed in a different currency unit.

The cause of these anomalies is that the VE-theory adds quantities of unequal dimensions. We will see that the assumptions which make out the content of the theory do not enforce formula [3].

It will be clear that the dimension of $E(g)$ is equal to the dimension of g, whether we deal with dollars, or with guilders. We use the symbol U (Util) to indicate the dimension of utilities. So, the dimension of $E(g)$ is U, and the dimension of $V(g)$ is U^2. When we want the dimensions in formula [3] to be invariant, then t should have the dimension U^{-2} and $(1-t)$ should have the dimension U^{-1}. This is evidently impossible, and [3] can not be dimensionally invariant. A way-out would be to replace t and $1-t$ by two different parameters, one with dimension U^{-2} and one with dimension U^{-1}, but that would spoil the elegant interpretation of t as VE-*weighing* parameter and leave the question about the dimension of R unsettled.

A solution exists if we replace the ordinary addition in [3] by a different composition rule, satisfying the same axiomatic properties by which an extensive measurement system for risk can be constructed. To show what we can do, we first summarize Pollatsek and Tversky's derivation of their risk law. This law follows from the additivity of risk and the application of the central limit theorem to the convolution of probability distributions with expected value equal to zero (cf. p. 124-129 in Krantz *et al.*, 1971). When the expected values of gambles are equal to zero, we have:

$$R(h \oplus k) = R(h) + R(k) = a\{V(h) + V(k)\} , \qquad [4]$$

where h and k are gambles, $\oplus$ is the convolution of outcomes distributions, V is the variance, and a is a scale unit parameter. According to [4], U^2 is the dimension of R. Adding the sure thing (s) to all outcomes of the gamble, gives:

$$R(h \oplus s) = R(h) + R(s) . \qquad [5]$$

Pollatsek and Tversky have shown that $R(s)$ must be equal to $-bU_S$, where b is another free scale unit parameter. U_S is the expected value, $E(g)$, of a gamble g, when $g = h \oplus s$, and h has its expected value equal to zero. So, $R(g) = aV(g) - bE(g)$. We get [3] when t is written as $a/(a+b)$, and a suitable unit is chosen for R.

In order to eliminate the unequal dimensions of V and E we return to [4], but take a different numerical operation instead of common addition, +. We write $+_p$, which is defined as:

$$x +_p y \equiv (x^p + y^p)^{1/p} \qquad (x, y \text{ real numbers}, p > 0) ,$$

$$\text{where } x^p \equiv |x|^p \text{signum}(x) . \qquad [6]$$

Also Krantz *et al.* (p. 99) point out this possibility of alternative representations for extensive measurement. Let us replace [4] by:

$$R(h \oplus k) = \{R^2(h) + R^2(k)\}^{\frac{1}{2}} = a\{S^2(h) + S^2(k)\}^{\frac{1}{2}}, \qquad [7]$$

where $S = V^{\frac{1}{2}}$, the standard deviation. The justification to replace V by S, is that S is a strictly monotone function of V, in accordance with [2]. When all outcomes of a gamble are increased by a fixed value, we get:

$$R(h \oplus s) = \{R^2(h) + R^2(s)\}^{\frac{1}{2}} = \{\alpha S^2(g) - \beta E^2(g)\}^{\frac{1}{2}}, \qquad [8]$$

where $g = h \oplus s$ (for clarity we use α and β inside the braces, instead of a and b, as we did before).

Next, we define $t = \alpha/(\alpha+\beta)$, and change the scale unit of R, to get:

$$R(g) = \{tV(g) - (1-t)E^2(g)\}^{\frac{1}{2}}, \qquad [9]$$

where t is now dimensionless, and R has dimension U. One must remember that $x^2 = x|x|$, and $x^{\frac{1}{2}} = |x|^{\frac{1}{2}}$ signum(x). So E^2 is negative when E is negative.

Since now R has dimension U, it is clear that we can not arbitrarily set $R(g_1) = 1$ independent of the unit of the outcomes. Given g_1 the value of R follows from the value of t.

For the sake of completeness, we show that the risk values of our examples are invariant when we change from dollars to guilders, and that we need not make a difference between $t_\$$ and t_f. For t=.7, we get:

$$g_1:\ R(g_1) = \{.7(.5625) - .3(.250)^2\}^{\frac{1}{2}} = .6124\ ,$$
$$g_2:\ R(g_2) = \{.7(3.6864) - .3(.640)^2\}^{\frac{1}{2}} = 1.5677\ ,$$
$$g_3:\ R(g_3) = \{.7(.3906) + .3(.625)^2\}^{\frac{1}{2}} = .625\ ,$$
$$g_4:\ R(g_4) = \{.7(2.56) + .3(1.60)^2\}^{\frac{1}{2}} = 1.6\ .$$

Accordingly, $R(g_2)/R(g_1)$ is equal to $R(g_4)/R(g_3)$ and equal to 2.56, i.e. the dollar/guilders ratio.

Discussion. Originally, Pollatsek & Tversky formulated the theory of risk as:

$$R(g) = \eta V(g) - \mu E(g)\ , \qquad (\eta,\ \mu \geq 0)\ , \qquad [10]$$

which may be considered the 'correct' statement of their theory. Changing the unit of measurement of R by dividing through $\eta+\mu$ leads to [3]. However, this division is not dimensionally acceptable. Taking [10] as it is, and letting H denote the dimension of R, the dimension of η is H/U^2, and the dimension of μ is H/U. It appears that [10] is dimensionally consistent, and that t defined as $\eta/(\eta+\mu)$ is dimensionally inconsistent. However, it may be considered questionable to assume that R has a dimension of its own, and that it is a function of V and E weighted by dimensional constants. This seems to imply that R is defined and measured independently of V and of E. Independent measurement of R is not available in the derivation of Pollatsek and Tversky; Although it might be assumed, their theory only states that risk is additive, and in particular that it is additive in V and in $-E$. This leaves the dimension of R undefined. Moreover, it raises the question of the interindividual comparison of risk perception, and of the intra-individual weighing of variance and expectation. By [10], no meaningful statement can be formulated expressing the relative impact of variance and expectation, since η and μ have different dimensions and are therefore incomparable. Any attempt to construct a function of these parameters, like t, must fail, as our numerical exercises have demonstrated.

The reason why [3] is incompatible with the requirement of dimensional invariance is obvious. This might be considered tolerable, if it would suffice to adapt t to the currency unit (in general: to the unit in which utilities are expressed). But this still leaves the risk ratios depending on the currency unit, and that should not be, because the risk scale is a ratio scale. Statements about risk ratios would then not be meaningful, unless one assumes that the currency unit has an intrinsic effect on risk perception. That seems absurd.

But can data decide between [9] and [10]? The answer appears to be: no. We can only test if comparative judgements on gambles and their concatenations (convolutions) satisfy the axioms of the model, and no model which is compatible with these axioms can be rejected if the axioms are empirically satisfied. The apriori, purely metatheoretical requirement that lawful relations should be dimensionally invariant and the desirability to interpret t as an individual parameter, exclude, however, both formula [3] and [10]. It should be noted that [8] and hence [9], although they do not follow necessarily from the Pollatsek & Tversky's axioms, are compatible with these axioms. Also, both α and β in [8] have dimension H^2/U^2, and so t is dimensionless.

Conclusion

In a recent paper, Michel (1986) distinguishes between *classical*, *operational*, and *representational* measurement theory. It is clear that we adopted the latter. According to the operational point of view, a measurement is also a definition of a construct. According to the classical point of view, measurement is the assessment of a quantity. In both, measurement appears to be independent of theory construction. The representational view on measurement takes (meta-)theoretical considerations as its basis. Both the operational definition of (theoretical) concepts, and the assessment of quantity are thereby subject to theoretical criteria, which are empirically testable.

In the area of representational measurement theory and of formal modelling, we have seen a shift from axiomization of formal representations toward the question of the 'meaningfulness' of statements (Falmagne & Narens, 1983; Luce, 1978; Luce & Narens, 1981; Narens, 1981a,b, 1985). What began as mathematical justification of measurement in the behavioral sciences, has evolved into critical analysis of the meaning of quantitative statements, and even of ordinal statements. Above axiomizing of measurement models proving representation theorems and uniqueness theorems, these recent developments provide us with a metatheory for the structure of formal models and their substantive content. Statements, seemingly derived from theoretical assumptions, which are not 'meaningful', that is, have no empirical meaning, or are not consistent and invariant, can not be considered as meaningful hypotheses, and the theory from which they follow is either itself not meaningful and therefore afortiori not testable and not valid, or requires additional assumptions to produce meaningful statements. The same holds for methods of data analysis which are based on models of which it is not established that they entail meaningful inferences about the structure of psychological phenomena. Whether we consider a model as a means of data analysis or data-reduction or as the representation of a theoretical structure, in either case a very critical reflection on what can be meaningfully extracted from them, is of vital importance.

References

Beals, R., Krantz, D.H., & Tversky, A. (1968). Foundations of multidimensional scaling. *Psychological Review, 75*, 127-142.

Bunge, M. (1973). On confusing 'measure' with 'measurement' in the methodology of the behavioral sciences. In M. Bunge (Ed.). *The Methodological Unity of Science.* 105-122. Dordrecht: Reidel.

Coombs, C.H., & Bowen, J. (1971). A test of VE theories of risk and the effect of the central limit theorem. *Acta Psychologica, 35*, 15-28.

Coombs, C.H., & Huang, L. (1970). Polynomial psychophysics of risk. *Journal of Mathematical Psychology, 7*, 317-338.

Coombs, C.H., & Lehner, P.E. (1981a). Evaluation of two alternative models for a theory of risk: I: Are the moments of distributions useful in assessing risk? *Journal of Experimental Psychology: Human Perception and Performance, 7*, 1110-1123.

Coombs, C.H., & Lehner, P.E. (1981b). The conjoint analysis of the bilinear model, illustrated with a Theory of Risk. In: I. Borg (Ed.), *Multidimensional Thata Representations, When and Why, 565-589.* Ann Arbor Mathesis Press.

Coombs, C.H. & Lehner, P.E. (1984), Conjoint design and analysis of the bilinear model: An application to judgments of risk. *Journal of Mathematical Psychology*, 11, 1-42.

Davis, Ph. J. & Hersh, R. (1981). *The Mathematical Experience.* Boston: Birkhäuser.

Eisler, H. (1982). On the nature of subjective scales. *Scandinavian Journal of Psychology, 23*, 161-171.

Ellis, B. (1966, 2nd ed. 1968). *Basic concepts of measurement.* Cambridge University Press.

Falmagne, J.C. & Narens, L. (1983). Scales and meaningfulness of quantitative laws. *Syndese, 55*, 287-325.

Fischer, G.H. (1987). Applying the principles of specific objectivity and of generalizability to the measurement of change. *Psychometrika, 52*, 565-588.

De Groot, A.D. (1977). Gevraagd: Forum-convergentie inzake begrips-, theorie- en besluitvorming. *Nederlands Tijdschrift voor de Psychologie, 32*, 219-241.

De Groot, A.D., & Medendorp, E.L. (1986). *Term, Begrip, Theorie. Inleiding tot signifische begripsanalyse.* Meppel: Boom.

Hölder, O. (1901). Die Axiome der Quantität und die Lehre vom Mass. *Ber. Verh. Kgl. Sächsis. Ges. Wiss. Leipzig, Math.-Phys. Classe, 53*, 1-64.

Krantz, D.H. (1972). A theory of magnitude estimation and cross-modality matching. *Journal of Mathematical Psychology, 9*, 168-199.

Krantz, D.H., Luce, R.D., Suppes, P., & Tversky, A. (1971). *Foundations of Measurement, Vol I, Additive and Polynomial Representations.* New York: Academic Press.

Krantz, D.H., & Tversky, A. (1975). Similarity of rectangles: an analysis of subjective dimensions. *Journal of Mathematical Psychology, 12*, 4-34.

Luce, R.D. (1978). Dimensionally invariant numerical laws correspond to meaningful qualitative relations. *Philosophy of Science, 45*, 1-16.

Luce, R.D. & Narens, L. (1981). Axiomatic measurement theory. In S. Grossberg (Ed.). *Mathematical Psychology and Psychophysiology: proceedings of the symposium SIAM-AMS, 13*, 213-235. Hillsdale: Erlbaum.

Luce, R.D., & Weber, E.U. (1986). An axiomatic theory of conjoint expected risk. *Journal of Mathematical Psychology, 30*, 188-205.

Michel, J. (1986) Measurement scales and statistics: a clash of paradigms. *Psychological Bulletin, 100*, 398-407.

Narens, L. (1981a). A general theory of ratio scalability with remarks about the measurement-theoretic concept of meaningfulness. *Theory and Decision, 13*, 1-70.

Narens, L. (1981b). On the scales of measurement. *Journal of Mathematical Psychology, 24*, 249-275.

Narens, L. (1985). *Abstract Measurement Theory.* Cambridge, Mass.: MIT.

Niederee, R. (1987). On the reference to real numbers in fundamental measurement. In E.E.

Roskam & R. Suck (Eds.). *Progress in Mathematical Psychology*, 3-25. Amsterdam: North-Holland Publ. Cy.
Pollatsek, A., & Tversky, A. (1970). A theory of risk. *Journal of Mathematical Psychology, 7*, 540-553.
Roberts, F.S. (1979). *Measurement theory.* Reading: Addison-Wesley.
Schönemann, P.H., Dorcey, T., & Kienapple, K., (1985). Subadditive concatenation in dissimilarity judgments. *Perception and Psychophysics, 8*, 1-17.
Stevens, S. S. (1946). On the theory of scales of measurement. *Science, 103*, 677-680.
Stevens, S.S. (1951). Mathematics, measurement, and psychophysics. In S.S. Stevens (Ed.). *Handbook of Experimental Psychology.* New York: Wiley.
Tversky, A., & Krantz, D.H. (1970). The dimensional representation and the metric structure of similarity data. *Journal of Mathematical Psychology, 7*, 572-596.

An axiomatic approach towards testing bilinear attitude models*)

*Adele Diederich & Bernhard Orth***)
Universität Hamburg

Abstract
Two basic properties of bilinear models are what may be called "intra-attributive multiplicativity" and "interattributive additivity". The axiomatic foundations of bilinear models can thus be studied largely in terms of multiplicatiive conjoint measurement with 2 components) and additive conjoint measurement (with $n > 3$ components). A suitable combination of axioms from both types of conjoint measurement yields necessary conditions for bilinear models. These axioms were tested empirically in a study on attitudes towards some fictitious jobs constructed in accordance with an appropriate factorial design.

Introduction

A prominent class of attitude measurement models are so called product-summation models:

$$A = f\left(\sum_{i=1}^{n} X_i P_i\right)$$

Attitude (A) towards an object is represented by means of a bilinear combination of numerical values that determine the rank order of the preferences of a given subject. Each numerical value is considered as a sum of products where summation refers to various attributes belonging to the object. That is why these models are often called "multiattribute attitude models". Each term of sum is a product of two factors, for example, evaluation (X_i) and subjective probability or belief strength (P_i). f Is a positive linear or at least monotonically increasing function.

The main goal of our work was to look for necessary conditions for this representation. This task is much easier than it appears, if it is realized that two similar structures have already been analysed in the literature. Each term of the sum has a two-factor multiplicative form which calls for using multiplicative conjoint measurement methods. (This property may be called intra-attributive multiplicativity.) On the other hand, ignoring the factorization

*) This work was supported by grant Or53/1 from Deutsche Forschungsgemeinschaft.
**) Psychologisches Institut I, Universität Hamburg, Von-Melle-Park 6, D-2000 Hamburg 13, F.R. Germany.

of the terms we clearly have an additive conjoint structural form (inter-attributive additivity). The open question, however, is how to combine both structures - the multiplicative and the additive one - in an appropriate way.

Kahneman and Tversky (1979, Appendix) were faced with just the same problem in developing an axiomatic analysis of prospect theory. Each prospect (or lottery) is represented as a bilinear combination of the subjective values of the outcomes and the probability. However, their representation problem is formally a special case of the one pursued here in that we consider more than two "outcomes", that means more than two attributes.

Testable axioms

The representation we are looking for is of the following form:

$$(x_1p_1, x_2p_2, \ldots, x_np_n) \succsim (y_1q_1, y_2q_2, \ldots, y_nq_n) \quad \text{iff}$$

$$\sum_{i=1}^{n} \phi_i(x_i)\,\psi(p_i) \geq \sum_{i=1}^{n} \phi_i(y_i)\,\psi(q_i)$$

where the ϕ's and ψ are real valued functions. ϕ_i denotes the subject's evaluation of the attribute i and ψ is a function that converts verbal belief statements like "very likely" into a numerical subjective probability. This bilinear representation calls for the axioms of multiplicative and additive conjoint measurement.

First consider the necessary axioms of *multiplicativity*. For each attribute the following axioms must be satisfied (for all $x_1, x_2, x_3 \in X$ and $p_1, p_2, p_3 \in P$, with X denoting the set of evaluations and P the set of belief strengths).

Weak order

Connectedness: Either $x_1p_1 \succsim x_2p_2$ or $x_2p_2 \succsim x_1p_1$

Transitivity: If $x_1p_1 \succsim x_2p_2$ and $x_2p_2 \succsim x_3p_3$ then $x_1p_1 \succsim x_3p_3$

Sign dependence

P is sign dependent from X iff X is partitioned into X^+, X^- and X° such that (for all $x_1^+ \in X^+$, $x_2^- \in X^-$, $x_3^\circ \in X^\circ$, $p_1, p_2 \in P$)
$p_1x_1^+ \succsim p_2x_1^+$ iff $p_2x_2^- \succsim p_1x_2^-$ and $p_1x_3^\circ \sim p_2x_3^\circ$

Double cancellation

If $x_1p_2 \gtrsim x_2p_3$ and $x_2p_1 \gtrsim x_3p_2$, then $x_1p_1 \gtrsim x_3p_3$

The axioms of solvability and Archimedeaness are not being testable and will not be considered here. (For details s. Roskies, 1965)
The necessary axioms for *additivity* are (for all $a_i, b_i, c_i \in A_i$, $A_i \subset X_i \times P$, $i \in N$, $N = \{1,2,...,n\}$, $n \gtrsim 3$):

Weak order

Connectedness: Either $a_1...a_n \gtrsim b_1...b_n$ or $b_1...b_n \gtrsim a_1...a_n$

Transitivity: If $a_1...a_n \gtrsim b_1...b_n$ and $b_1...b_n \gtrsim c_1...c_n$,
then $a_1...a_n \gtrsim c_1...c_n$

Joint independence

For every subset M, $M \subset N$, the ordering $\gtrsim_M$ induced by $\gtrsim$ on $X_{i \in M} A_i$ for fixed choices $a_i \in A_i$, $i \in N-M$ is unaffected by those choices. (For details s. Krantz et al., 1971). Notice that the elements of A_i are pairs $(X_i \times P)$.

To guarantee that the multiplicative and the additive operation can be combined in an appropriate way we need some kind of distributivity axiom. The following one is obviously necessary:

A relation $\gtrsim$ on $\overset{n}{\underset{i=1}{X}} A_i$, $A_i \subseteq X_i \times P$, $i \in N$, satisfies *distributivity* iff for all $x_i, y_i \in X_i$ and $p, q \in P$:

$$(x_1p,\ x_2p,\ ...,\ x_np) \sim (y_1p,\ y_2p,\ ...,\ y_np) \quad \text{iff}$$
$$(x_1q,\ x_2q,\ ...,\ x_nq) \sim (y_1q,\ y_2q,\ ...,\ y_nq).$$

While necessity of this condition is evident, combined with the other axioms it will not be sufficient for our representation, as observed by a reviewer. It should be pointed out that the model actually tested below is of the following form:

$$\sum_{i=1}^{n} f\,[\phi_i\,(x_i)\ \psi\,(p_i)]$$

with f any increasing function.

Experiment

Up to now we empirically tested all these necessary axioms except distributivity. We investigated attitude towards employments or jobs. Each job was characterized on three dimensions:

income:	- above average - average - below average
duration of employment:	- 5 years - 2 years - 1/2 years
kind of activity:	- rarely dull - sometimes dull - often dull

The possible values on each dimension were chosen such that a subject would evaluate them as either positive, indifferent or negative. For example: a person might evaluate positive an above average income. Moreover the subject was given the level of certainty that a given job did in fact has those values on the dimensions. Twenty students participated in the study. We first looked at *multiplicativity*. For each attribute there was a three by three design of evaluation and belief strength. Each subject had to give all possible (thirty six) pair comparison judgements for each dimension.

Transitivity

For testing transitivity we calculated Kendall's zeta. That is

$$\text{zeta} = 1 - d/d_{max}$$

where d_{max} is the maximum number of intransitive triads and d is the number of intransitive triads actually observed. The results are given in Table 1. 35% of the subjects completely satisfied transitivity for the first attribute, 25% for the second attribute and 15% for the third.

Table 1: Percentage of persons satisfying the axioms (completely or according to a specified criterion (in parentheses)).

Multiplicativity

	income	duration	activity	all
Transitivity	.35 (.70)	.25 (.55)	.15 (.55)	.05 (.30)
Sign dependence	.70 (.95)	.05 (.50)	.80 (1.00)	.05 (.45)
double cancellation	.60 (.70)	.70 (.75)	.20 (.40)	.10 (.30)
all axioms	.25 (.55)	-- (.15)	-- (.15)	-- (--)

Using a weaker criterion - namely accepting at most 10% intransitivities of all possible intransitive triads - (that are 3 violations of maximal 30 possible ones) we get the following percentages: 70% of the subject satisfied transitivity for the first attribute, 55% for the second and 55% for the third attribute.

Sign dependence

70% of the subjects completely satisfied sign dependence for the first attribute, 5% for the second and 80% for the third attribute. Accepting one violation of three possible ones we got 95% for the first, 50% for the second and 100% for the third attribute.

Double cancellation

20% for the third. Accepting 4 violations of 36 possible ones we got 70% for the first, 75% for the second and 40% for the third attribute.

To sum up, the level of transitivity was rather low. Sign dependence and double cancellation seem to depend strongly on the attribute that is analysed.

Additivity

In order to test the axioms for an additive conjoint representation we omitted the neutral value of each dimension. Thus each job was characterized on three dimensions, but each dimension had only two different possible values to take on, a positive and a negative one. Moreover, only two different belief strength levels were considered. This results in $4 \times 4 \times 4$ different job descriptions. First, our subjects had to sort them into 11 subgroups of four to seven elements which they considered roughly equivalent. For example, the first subgroup contained those jobs they liked most, and so on ... Second, a pair comparison procedure was performed with every subgroup. Thus, due to this procedure, transitivity over the subgroups was constructed a priori and could only be tested within each subgroup.

Transitivity

For each subject, we computed Kendall's Zeta in each subsgroup. The median of these Zeta-values for each subject was used as a criterion.

There were 73% of the subjects having a median Zeta-value above 0.9 and 89% with a median Zeta-value above 0.85.

Joint Independence

Joint independence was assessed as follows: for each fixed value of one attribute, the rank order was compared with the rank orders corresponding to the other value of the same attribute. Consistency among these orders was computed by Kendall's coefficient W. For each dimension, we got the results shown in Table 2.

Table 2: Percentage of persons satisfying the axioms (completely or according to a specified criterion (in parentheses)).

Additivity

Transitivity:	Zeta-Median 73% (89%)			
Joint independence:	18%	(53%)	income	(duration, activity)
	53%	(94%)	duration	(income, activity)
	29%	(41%)	activity	(income, duration)

Taking a W of 0.8 or above as an indication of indepence, the proportion of subjects satisfying independence were: 18% showed independence of the first attribute from the second and the third, 53% showed independence of the second attribute from the first and the second, and 29% showed independence of the third attribute from the first and the second. Weakening the criterion further down to 0.7 we got the following percentages: 53% for the first, 94% for the second, and 41% for the third attribute.

To sum up, while transitivity is far from perfect, joint independence is severely violated. Overall, our results may be summarized as follows:
First, the degree to which multiplicativity holds depends pretty much on the attribute; second, additivity does not seem to capture the way attitude is constructed from the attributes. Thus, even using rather weak criteria for assessing multiplicativity and additivity, our results do not favor the product summation model approach for modelling attitudes.

References

Kahneman, D. & Tversky, A. (1979). Prospect theory. An analysis of decision under risk. *Econometrica, 47,* 263-291.

Kendall, M. (1975). *Rank correlation methods.* (4th. Ed.) London: Charles Griffin.

Krantz, D.H., Luce, R.D., Suppes, P. & Tversky, A. (1971). *Foundations of measurement, Vol. I.* New York: Academic Press.

Roskies, R.A. (1965). A measurement axiomatization for an essentially multiplicative representation of two factors. *Journal of Mathematical Psychology, 2,* 226-276.

The Representation of Dynamic Structures

Ronald Hübner *
Universität Regensburg

Abstract

While axiomatic measurement has been widely used to define static attributes of some objects, there scarcely has been an axiomatic treatment of dynamic attributes, i.e. attributes that change over time. Normally, such attributes are treated by system theoretic methods. Unfortunately, the application of linear system theory is based on assumptions, which are difficult to fulfill for most psychological applications. However, despite these difficulties it is possible to apply linear system theory to psychology if it is combined with axiomatic measurement theory. For systems with scalar input and output quantities it is shown that after some modifications the theory of additive conjoint measurement is suitable for system identification.

Introduction

This work attempts to give an axiomatization of certain types of dynamic behavior. The attempt is motivated by the fact that a theory generally is considered to be in an advanced stage when it is expressed in an axiomatic form. The advantage of the axiomatic form is that the whole content of a theory is reduced to a few sentences, the axioms. If it can be shown that these axioms are true then, on ground of logical arguments, all deducible conclusions are true, too. For the development of axiomatic psychological theories, it is necessary to state the axioms in terms of easily interpretable, qualitative data. Since it usually turns out to be quite difficult to fulfill these conditions, there are only a few axiomatic psychological theories until now.

One exception, however, is modern measurement theory (cf. Krantz, Luce, Suppes & Tversky, 1971). The aim of modern measurement theory is the representation of empirical structures by numerical structures. A structure is defined as a set with some relations on it. A representation is given by a homomorphism from an empirical structure into a numerical structure. At first, only single attribute structures such as length were represented. Then it became possible to represent more complex attributes by conjoint structures.

One domain not yet treated by measurement theory is the representation of dynamic structures. The expression "dynamic structure" refers to a structure that defines attributes affected by other attributes in time. To clarify this, consider ordinary conjoint measurement. Here we have an attribute which is affected by two or more components. Usually it is assumed that all components affect the attribute simultaneously. But why should they not affect it successively ? We will see that it is possible to represent dynamic structures by conjoint structures and that such structures are representable by dynamic linear systems. Therefore, for these linear systems it is possible to give a qualitative axiomatization.

System Theory

In system theory, a system to be modeled is regarded as a black box (see Figure 1). Only the input and the output of the black box are directly observable. In the modern state

*Institut für Psychologie, D-8400 Regensburg, West-Germany

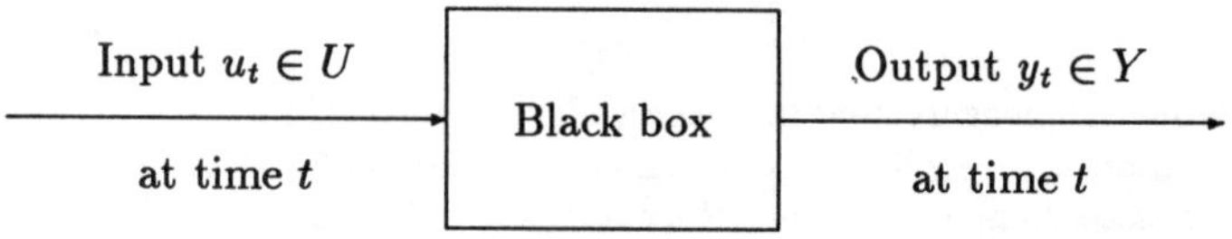

Figure 1: A system as a black box.

space approach, the intent is to replace the black box with a set of states in such a way that the knowledge of the current state and the input is sufficient to determine the next output. Let us state this approach more formally, thereby restricting our considerations to discrete-time systems. First, we will define a discrete linear system.

Definition 1 A structure $\Sigma = \langle X, \mathbf{F}, U, \mathbf{G}, Y, \mathbf{H}\rangle$ is a *discrete linear system* iff U, X, Y are *vector spaces* over a field and $\mathbf{F} : X \to X$, $\mathbf{G} : U \to X$ and $\mathbf{H} : X \to Y$ are linear mappings, such that

$$\begin{aligned} \mathbf{x}_{t+1} &= \mathbf{F}\mathbf{x}_t + \mathbf{G}\mathbf{u}_t \ \text{ and} \\ \mathbf{y}_t &= \mathbf{H}\mathbf{x}_t \ \text{ for all } \mathbf{x} \in X \text{ and } \mathbf{u} \in U. \end{aligned}$$

U is the *input set*, X the *state set* and Y the *output set.* Accordingly, $\mathbf{G}$ is the *input function*, $\mathbf{F}$ the *state transition function* and $\mathbf{H}$ the *output function.* $t \in \mathbf{Z}$ is a *time index.*

The set of all finite input sequences ω is: $U^* = \{\omega | u_0, u_1, \ldots, u_i \in U\}$. The *zero state response* δ_0 of Σ is given by the function[1]

$$\delta_0 : u_k, ..., u_1, u_0 \mapsto \sum_{l=0}^{k} \mathbf{H}\mathbf{F}^l\mathbf{G}u_l.$$

The starting-point of a system realization is an input-output function $f : U^* \to Y$, that gives for any input sequence ω the output y. The task is to identify the three linear operators $\mathbf{F}$, $\mathbf{G}$, and $\mathbf{H}$, such that $\delta_0 = f$. At first, U^* has to be made a vector space because only then f can be linear. To do this, we use the fact that $f(\omega)$ does not change if we prelode ω with any sequence of zeros. Then we can replace U^* by $U^\#$, where $U^\#$, if $\mathbf{N}$ denotes the natural numbers including zero, is defined by:

$$U^\# = \{\omega : \mathbf{N} \to U | \omega(l) \neq 0 \text{ only for a finite number of } l\}.$$

Every function ω corresponds to a left-infinite sequence $\ldots\omega(l)\ldots\omega(1)\omega(0)$. By appropriate definitions of the operations $U^\#$ becomes a vector space.

It can be shown that the following holds (cf. Padulo & Arbib, 1974):
Let $f : U^\# \to Y$ be a linear mapping. Then there exists a minimal system

$$\Sigma = \langle X, \mathbf{F}, U, \mathbf{G}, Y, \mathbf{H}\rangle,$$

[1]The indices of the input sequences are in reversed order for technical reasons.

such that

$$f(u_k, ..., u_1, u_0) = \sum_{l=0}^{k} \mathbf{H}\mathbf{F}^l\mathbf{G}u_l.$$

Σ is minimal in the sense that the state space X of Σ has a minimum number of dimensions. If there exist other minimal linear systems, then they are isomorphic. [2]

The theorem gives no method to realize a given function. But an iterative algorithm can be given that is applicable to most cases (cf. Padulo & Arbib, 1974). If there is any limitation known with respect to N the dimension of Σ, then $\langle\omega\rangle$ for all $\omega \in U^*$ is defined by:

$$\langle\omega\rangle = \begin{bmatrix} f(\omega) \\ f(\omega, 0) \\ \vdots \\ f(\omega, 0^{N-1}) \end{bmatrix},$$

where 0^N denotes a seqence of N zeros. If U has the basis $\mathbf{e}_1, \ldots, \mathbf{e}_m$ then a basis is selected for the space spanned by the array of vectors:

$$\mathcal{K}_N = [\langle\mathbf{e}_1\rangle, \ldots, \langle\mathbf{e}_m\rangle, \langle\mathbf{e}_1, 0\rangle, \ldots, \langle\mathbf{e}_m, 0\rangle, \ldots, \langle\mathbf{e}_1, 0^{N-1}\rangle, \ldots, \langle\mathbf{e}_m, 0^{N-1}\rangle]$$

Let this basis consist of the vectors $\langle\omega_1\rangle \ldots \langle\omega_{n'}\rangle$ with $n' \leq N$, and let $[\omega]$ be the column vector whose components are the coefficients of $\langle\omega\rangle$ with respect to this basis. Then Σ is defined by the matrices:

$$\begin{aligned} \mathbf{F}_N &= [[\omega_1, 0], \ldots, [\omega_{n'}, 0]] \\ \mathbf{G}_N &= [[\mathbf{e}_1], \ldots, [\mathbf{e}_m]] \\ \mathbf{H}_N &= [f(\omega_1), \ldots, f(\omega_{n'})]. \end{aligned}$$

For most practical applications the dimension of the system will not be known in advance. In this case we iteratively increase $\mathcal{K}$ until $\mathcal{K}_n$ and $\mathcal{K}_{n+1}$ have the same rank. Then we construct a basis for $\mathcal{K}_n$.

The realization algorithm has the disadvantage that the considered sets are restricted to vector spaces. Therefore, we have the difficult task to justify the assumption of vector spaces. This justification does not seem to be difficult for the realization of physical systems. Usually, an extensive measurement of the input and output quantities is possible. Therefore, we can measure them first and then work with the scale values. But in other areas such as psychology this is hardly possible. Although in psychophysics, for example, the input quantities can be measured directly it is problematic to measure the psychological output quantities. The psychological output quantity is neither directly observable nor is it easy to measure. Such a situation is described by what I call a "grey meta box" (see Figure 2).

The output of the system is not directly observable. But if we put any two input sequences ω_1, ω_2 into the grey meta box it tells us whether the output of the black box after processing the input sequence ω_1 is greater than or equal to the output after processing the sequence ω_2. The problem is to find a numerical representation of the system behavior and to realize it by a linear system.

[2]This result even holds if we take moduls over a unitary ring as input and output sets instead of vector spaces (cf. Padulo & Arbib, 1974). But we ignore this generalisation here.

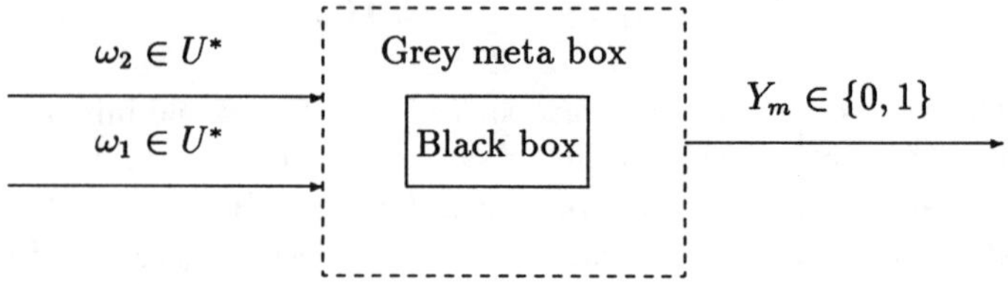

Figure 2: A system in a "grey meta box".

Additive Conjoint Structures

Some modifications of additive conjoint measurement will lead to a numerical representation of dynamic behavior. We can state some qualitative conditions which guarantee a numerical representation of some kind of dynamic structure, which will be defined soon. Further, these representations are realisable by linear systems.

We begin with an ordinary additive conjoint structure. Such a structure consists of a set $A_1 \times A_2$, a cartesian product. On this set we have a binary relation $\succsim$ (cf. Krantz et al., 1971). We define:

Definition 2 *A structure* $\langle A_1 \times A_2, \succsim \rangle$ is an additive conjoint structure iff there exist functions ϕ_i from A_i, $i = 1, 2$ in the real numbers such that for all $a, b \in A_1$ and $p, q \in A_2$

$$ap \succsim bq \text{ iff } \phi_1(a) + \phi_2(p) \geq \phi_1(b) + \phi_2(q).$$

For convenience, we give the definition directly in this way and do not specify the single axioms which guarantee such a representation. Here the elements consist of two components. But it is easy to generalize such structures to n-components. Then the set is a cartesian product over n sets $A_1 \times A_2 \times \cdots \times A_n$. Therefore, we define:

Definition 3 *A structure* $\langle A_1, \ldots, A_n, \succsim \rangle$,$n \geq 3$, is an n-component additive conjoint structure if there exist real valued functions ϕ_i on $A_i, i \in N$, such that for all $a_i, b_i \in A_i$

$$(a_1, \ldots, a_n) \succsim (b_1, \ldots, b_n) \text{ iff } \sum_{i=1}^{n} \phi_i(a_i) \geq \sum_{i=1}^{n} \phi_i(b_i).$$

Now, the question is how can we modify such structures to get close to the structures with which we are concerned in system theory ? The fact that the input sequences are of arbitrary length is very important. To get close to them we will generalize our structures to infinite components. Further, we have to specialize the structures to identical components.

Let us first specialize the n-component structures to identical components. Instead of the cartesian product over n different sets $A_1 \times A_2 \times \cdots \times A_n$ we have in this case a cartesian product over n identical sets A^n. For the conjoint structures with an infinite number of components we first must modify some well known conditions.

Definition 4 (Independence) A binary relation $\succsim$ on the infinite cartesian product $A_1 \times A_2 \times \ldots$ is *independent* iff for each $M \subset I$, $I = \{1, 2, \ldots\}$, the ordering $\succsim_M$ which is induced by $\succsim$ on $\times_{i \in M} A_i$ for fixed choices $a_i \in A_i, i \in I - M$ is not affected by those choices.

Definition 5 (Restricted solvability) A binary relation $\succsim$ on $A_1 \times A_2 \times \ldots$ satisfies *restricted solvability* iff for all $i \in I$, whenever

$$(b_1, \ldots, \bar{b}_i, \ldots) \succsim (a_1, \ldots, a_i, \ldots) \succsim (b_1, \ldots, \underline{b}_i, \ldots)$$

then there exists a $b_i \in A_i$, such that

$$(b_1, \ldots, b_i, \ldots) \sim (a_1, \ldots, a_i, \ldots).$$

Definition 6 (Standard sequence) Let $\succsim$ be an independent weak ordering on $A_1 \times A_2 \times \ldots$. For any set N of consecutive integers a set $\{a_i | a_i \in A_1, i \in N\}$ is a standard sequence (of component 1) iff there exists a set $A_j, j \in N$, $i \neq j$ and $p, q \in A_j$ such that not$(p \sim_j q)$ and for all $i, i+1 \in N$, $a_i p \sim_{1j} a_{i+1} q$. Parallel definitions hold for the other components.

Definition 7 Let $\succsim$ be a relation on $A_1 \times A_2 \times \ldots$. The component A_i is *essential* iff there exist $a, b \in A_i$ and $p \in A_j$, $i, j \in N, i \neq j$ such that not $ap \sim_{ij} bp$. Similar definitions hold for the other components.

Now, we take the infinite cartesian product over an identical set and define the following structure:

Definition 8 (I-component structure) Let A be a nonempty set and $\succsim$ a binary relation on A^I. The structure $\langle A^I, \succsim \rangle$ is an *I-component structure* iff for $\succsim$ the following five axioms hold:

1. Weak ordering (i.e. transitivity and connectedness).
2. Independence.
3. Restricted solvability.
4. Every strictly bounded standard sequence is finite.
5. At least three components are essential.

Now we have a structure in which we can include any set of input sequences. Unfortunately, it is not possible to give a global representation of such a structure, but it turns out that it is possible to represent certain subsets. One important subset for our purpose is the set of all sequences in which only the first $n \geq 3$ components are essential. Because of the independence condition such substructures are representable like n-component structures.

An interesting special representation is given if the standard sequence condition holds (cf. Krantz et al., 1971).

Definition 9 (Standard sequence condition) An I-component structure $\langle A^I, \succsim \rangle$ satisfies the *standard sequence condition* iff for all standard sequences a_i, b_i, c_i all distinct $j, k \in N$ and all $a_j, b_j, c_j, p_k, q_k \in A$, if $a_i = a_j$, $b_i = b_j$, $c_i = c_j$ and $a_j p_k \sim b_j q_k$ then $b_j p_k \sim c_j q_k$.

Now we can state the following representation theorem

Theorem 1 *Let $\langle A^I, \succsim \rangle$ be an I-component structure. If only the first $n \geq 3$ components are essential, then there exists an interval scale u on A and nonzero numbers $\lambda_1, \ldots, \lambda_n$ such that the representation*

$$\sum_{i=1}^{n} \lambda_i u(a_i)$$

is order preserving iff the standard sequence condition holds. The λ_i are unique up to multiplication with a positive constant.

Proof. The proof follows immediately from theorem 15 in chapter 6 of Krantz et al.(1971). □

If we introduce another property, called the *stationary property*, then an additional subset of the infinite sequences is representable. It was first stated by Koopmans(1960) for infinite structures and adapted for finite structures by Krantz et al.(1971).

Definition 10 (Stationarity) A binary relation $\succsim$ on A^I is *stationary* iff there exists a $x \in A$ such that

$$(x, a^{(1)}, a^{(2)}, \ldots) \succsim (x, b^{(1)}, b^{(2)}, \ldots) \text{iff } (a^{(1)}, a^{(2)}, \ldots) \succsim (b^{(1)}, b^{(2)}, \ldots)$$

for all $a^{(1)}, a^{(2)}, \ldots$ and $b^{(1)}, b^{(2)} \ldots \in A$.

This means if two sequences have identical first components then the ordering does not change if we remove these components. Let us now consider the subset of the infinite sequences which are bounded that is

Definition 11 A sequence (a_i) is *bounded* iff there exist $\underline{a}, \overline{a} \in A, \underline{a} \succsim_1 \overline{a}$, such that

$$\underline{a} \succsim_1 a_i \succsim_1 \overline{a} \text{ for all } i = 1, 2, \ldots$$

For such bounded sequences there is a representation which is given by the following theorem:

Theorem 2 (Koopmans, 1960) *Suppose $\langle A^I, \succsim \rangle$ is a stationary I-component structure. Then for the subset of all bounded sequences there exists an interval scale u on A and a unique number $0 < \lambda < 1$ such that the representation*

$$\Phi[(a_i)] = \sum_{i=1}^{\infty} \lambda^{i-1} u(a_i)$$

is order preserving.

Representation by Linear Systems

In this section we will show how dynamic behavior or attributes can be represented. The results are restricted to some special classes of linear systems with scalar input and scalar output. We take an I-component structure $\langle A^I, \succsim \rangle$ where A is an input set. The index i of the components of the sequences is now interpreted as a time index t such that

$$a_0, a_1, \ldots \Leftrightarrow a_t, a_{t-1}, \ldots.$$

If for such a structure the standard sequence condition holds then we call it a *dynamic structure.*

The correspondence of the input sequences of a system and the sequences of a dynamic structure then is

$$u_k, u_{k-1}, \ldots, u_0 \Leftrightarrow u(a_t), u(a_{t-1}), \ldots, u(a_{t-k}), 0, 0, \ldots.$$

If we have a structure where only the first n components are essential then it can be shown that the following theorem holds:

Theorem 3 *Suppose $\langle A^I, \succsim \rangle$ is a dynamic structure where only the first n components are essential. Then there exists an interval scale u and a linear system such that*

$$(a_t, a_{t-1}, \ldots) \succsim (b_t, b_{t-1} \ldots) \text{ iff } \sum_{i=0}^{n-1} \mathbf{HF}^i\mathbf{G}u(a_{t-i}) \geq \sum_{i=0}^{n-1} \mathbf{HF}^i\mathbf{G}u(b_{t-i}).$$

Proof. The result follows from theorem 1 and the realization algorithm mentioned above. □

Instead of pointing out the proof in detail let us consider an example. Suppose we have a dynamic structure where the first 3 components are essential. If we write u_i for $u(a_{t-i})$ then there exists a representation

$$\lambda_0 u_0 + \lambda_1 u_1 + \lambda_2 u_2.$$

With the realization algorithm (cf. Padulo & Arbib, 1974) the realization is given by:

$$\mathbf{x}_{t+1} = \begin{bmatrix} 0 & 0 & 0 \\ 1 & 0 & 0 \\ 0 & 1 & 0 \end{bmatrix} \mathbf{x}_k + \begin{bmatrix} 1 \\ 0 \\ 0 \end{bmatrix} u_k$$

$$y_k = \begin{bmatrix} \lambda_0 & \lambda_1 & \lambda_2 \end{bmatrix} \mathbf{x}_k.$$

Now we consider dynamic structures which satisfy the stationarity condition and state that the following theorem holds:

Theorem 4 *Suppose $\langle A^I, \succsim \rangle$ is a stationary dynamic structure. Then there exists an interval scale u and a linear system such that for the set of bounded sequences*

$$(a_t, a_{t-1}, \ldots) \succsim (b_t, b_{t-1}, \ldots) \text{ iff } \sum_{i=0}^{\infty} \mathbf{HF}^i\mathbf{G}u(a_{t-i}) \geq \sum_{i=0}^{\infty} \mathbf{HF}^i\mathbf{G}u(b_{t-i}).$$

Proof. We are given a stationary dynamic structure. If we abbreviate $\Phi[(a_t, a_{t-1}, \ldots)]$ by y_t we have the representation

$$y_t = \sum_{i=0}^{\infty} \lambda^i u(a_{t-i})$$

$0 < \lambda < 1$. If we introduce the *backshift-operator* B such that

$$\begin{aligned} Bu(a_t) &= u(a_{t-1}) \text{ and} \\ B^i u(a_t) &= u(a_{t-i}) \end{aligned}$$

then we can write the representation as

$$\begin{aligned} y_t &= (1 + \lambda B + (\lambda B)^2 + \cdots)u(a_t) \\ &= u(a_t) + \lambda B(1 + \lambda B + (\lambda B)^2 + \cdots)u(a_t) \\ &= u(a_t) + \lambda B y_t \\ &= u(a_t) + \lambda y_{t-1} \end{aligned}$$

And for this the realization algorithm mentioned above gives the linear system

$$\begin{aligned} x_{t+1} &= \lambda x_t + u(a_t) \\ y_t &= x_t. \end{aligned}$$

Concluding Remarks

We have shown that it is possible to give a representation of some kind of dynamic behavior by a linear system without specifying the input-output function. Only a qualitative binary relation on the input sequences with certain properties is required. Therefore, it is possible to simultaneously measure the input and output quantities and to identify the system. This enables us to handle systems with psychological input and output quantities. A successful application of this method to the modeling of loudness adaptation is given in Hübner(1988).

References

Hübner, R. (1988). Eine experimentelle Analyse eines meßtheoretisch fundierten dynamischen Modells zur Lautheitsadaptation. Unpublished dissertation: Regensburg.

Koopmans, T.C. (1960). Stationary ordinal utility and impatience. *Econometrica*, 28, 287-309.

Krantz, D.H.; Luce, R.D.; Suppes, P. & Tversky, A. (1971). *Foundations of measurement.* Vol I. New York, London: Academic Press.

Padulo, L. & Arbib, M.A. (1974). *System theory.* Philadelphia, London, Toronto: Saunders.

RANDOM VARIABLES AND QUALITATIVE PROBABILITY REPRESENTATIONS*)

Reinhard Suck
University of Osnabrück

Abstract
The widely practiced technique of conceiving of results of measurements as realisations of random variables is investigated in this paper. Theorems are presented in which the structure of a probability space is derived from well-known representation theorems of measurement theory. These theorems are related to the theory of qualitative probability representations. Furthermore representations are shown to be random variables, if the probability space on the measurement structure satisfies a natural condition. Moreover, it is shown how independent random variables which are required by most statistical applications can be constructed in this framework.

1. INTRODUCTION

Families of distributions, when used properly, are a powerful tool in the hand of the experienced research worker when it comes to drawing inferences from data. Theoretical statistics has provided science with many useful parametric families and a set of refined techniques enabling the scientist to decide which distribution taken from such a family fits the data best. The choice of the family, however, is in most cases left to assumptions and experience, or very general arguments such as limit theorems which render one supposition more plausible than another.

Whatever the reason may be for a distributional assumption, the empirical domain under scrutiny has already been mapped into the real numbers on the understanding that the numbers chosen reflect all (or much) of the information pertaining to the objects and the relations one is interested in and could get hold of.

This mapping procedure is usually dealt with in measurement theory. Especially in its recent developments e. g. Narens (1985), Luce & Narens (1983), Luce (1986), Luce & Narens (1985) great care is taken to separate those properties of the numerical scales which are extraneous to the empirical relational system and come in only by way of an arbitrary choice of the numerical domain, from those which are intrinsic i. e. which cannot be dispensed with and can be traced in the universe of discource by investigating its

*) University of Osnabrück, Postfach 44 69, D-4500 Osnabrück, F.R.G.

automorphisms or endomorphisms.

In this sence the distributional assumptions mentioned above seem to be extraneous. At least, there is no theorem of measurement theory which derives a family of distributions directly from the empirical system and its properties. Thus, a theory is called for which investigates the possibility of theorems of this kind. Let us call such a theory *"ab initio statistics"*. R. D. Luce sometimes asked the question whether it is possible to characterize the family of exponential distributions in terms of measurement theory. This is essentially the idea of ab initio statistics.

In this paper we want to investigate one possible line of research on this topic. At the outset we prove two theorems which are related to qualitative probability representations in the sense of Krantz, Luce, Suppes, & Tversky (1971, chap. 5) or Fishburn (1986).They differ, however, from the results obtained in this area, as we do not presuppose an algebra of events and a qualitative probability ordering of the events.

In our theorems the algebra is constructed from different primitives, and scales or numerical representations are used to define the probability measure.

In Theorem 3.1 we deal with a scalable weak order $(X,\lesssim)$ A probability space (X,A,P) is constructed where A contains the "intervals" of X, and P varies with the particular scale of $(X, \lesssim)$ chosen. Therefore P lacks strong uniqueness properties. One thing mandated by the structure $(X,\lesssim)$ is

$$\text{If } a < b \text{ then } P(\{x < a\}) \leq P(\{x < b\}) \text{ and} \qquad (1.1)$$
$$\text{if } P(\{x < a\}) \leq P(\{x < b\} \text{ then } a \leq b$$

which is satisfied. However, the relation of

$$P(\{a < x < b\}) \text{ and } P(\{c < x < d\}) \text{ for } a,b,c,d \in X \qquad (1.2)$$

is not determined by the initial system. This can be incorporated if we are willing to assume more structure on $(X, \lesssim)$. In Theorem 3.2 we investigate a relation W on the intervals on X defined by $\lesssim$. Subsequently we give an interpretation of the theorem in statistical terms which demonstrates that the assumptions made are far less restrictive than distributional assumptions.

In the next section we try to take one more step in pursuit of the program of ab initio statistics: We demonstrate that, drawing on the theorems of section 3, it is possible to construct random variables from scales. This turns out to be quite simple once the probabilistic prerequisites are thoroughly developed. However the random variables we arrive at are not independent. To guarantee independence we change the construction slightly, i. e. we apply Theorem 3.1 to the components of an additive conjoint measurement structure and define random variables on the product space. In this way pairs of independent random variables are generated.

The paper closes with a discussion of the possibility of extending the method and the results to justify distributional assumptions.

2. General properties of ordered sets and measure spaces

The prerequisites from ordered sets and measurement theory are introduced in this section. Futhermore the main concepts of measure spaces are summarized; in particular a method to construct a measure from a real valued set function is described.

2.1 Ordered sets and measurement theory.

A *weak order* $(X, \lesssim)$ consists of a nonempty set X and a binary relation $\lesssim$ on X satisfying connectedness (i. e. $x \lesssim y$ or $y \lesssim x$ for all $x, y \in X$) and transitivity. A weak order is *scalable* if and only if (iff) a function f exists mapping X into Re (the reals) such that $x \lesssim y$ iff $f(x) \leq f(y)$; f is a *scale* of $(X, \lesssim)$. A subset Y of a weakly ordered set X is *order dense* in X iff for each $x, x' \in X$ such that $x < x'$ there exists y in Y such that $x \lesssim y \lesssim x'$ $(X, \lesssim)$ is said to be of *order type* η iff

(1) $\lesssim$ is a total ordering (i. e. a weak order satisfying: $x \lesssim y$ and $y \lesssim x$ implies $x=y$).

(2) For each x, y in X, if $x < y$ then for some $z \in X$ $x < z < y$.

(3) X has no maximal and no minimal element.

(4) X is denumerable.

Obviously the rational numbers with the usual ordering are of order type η. More interestingly, however, this is the only example of this type, if we neglect isomorphisms, see Rosenstein (1982, chap. 2.2).

If $(X, \lesssim)$ is a weak order and x, x' in X are such that $x < x'$ and for all $y \in X$ either $y \lesssim x$ or $x' \lesssim y$, then xx' is a *gap* of X and x, x' are its endpoints.

If f is a scale then f(X) may have gaps; some of them are 'caused" by gaps in X and some are due to f, i. e. at the corresponding point in X there is no gap but nevertheless f has a jump at this point.

A scale f of $(X, \lesssim)$ is a *universal scale* iff all gaps af f(X) are 'caused' by gaps in X, i. e. the second type of gap of f(X) does not exist; for a precise definition see Droste (1987 a, b) where the existence of a universal scale is demonstrated.

Additive conjoint structures and positive difference structures, both standard notions from measurement theory, are used in the sequel. For a comprehensive discussion of the assumptions and the representation theorems see Krantz et al. (1971) or Roberts (1979). Here we will only give the definitions. (Note that sometimes (x,y) as an element of a Cartesian product is abbreviated by xy.) Let X_1, X_2 be nonempty sets. $(X_1, X_2, \lesssim)$ is an *additive conjoint* structure iff there exist functions $f_i: X_i \rightarrow Re$, i = 1,2 such that for all xy, uv $\in X_1 \times X_2$

$$xy \precsim uv \text{ iff } f_1(x) + f_2(y) \leq f_1(u) + f_2(v)$$

The pair (f_1,f_2) is an *additive representation* of $(X_1,X_2, \precsim)$. In an additive conjoint structure, weak orders $\precsim_i$ can be defined on X_i: for x,u $\in X_1$

$x \precsim_1 u$ iff $xy \precsim uy$ for some $y \in X_2$.
($\precsim_2$ is defined analogously on X_2).

$(A,A^*, \precsim)$ is a *positive difference* structure iff it satisfies:

(1) $(A^*, \precsim)$ is a weak order, $A^* \subset A \times A$
(2) If ab, bc $\in A^*$, then ac $\in A^*$
(3) If ab, bc $\in A^*$, then ab, bc < ac
(4) For ab, bc, a'b', b'c' $\in A^*$, if ab $\precsim$ a'b' and bc $\precsim$ b'c' then ac $\precsim$ a'c'
(5) Solvability: If ab, cd $\in A^*$ and ab < cd, then there exist c', d'$\in$ A such that cc', c'd, cd', and d'd $\in A^*$ and cc' $\approx$ ab $\approx$ d'd.
(6) Archimedean condition: If $a_1, a_2, \ldots$ are such that $a_{i+1}a \in A^*$ and $a_{i+1}a_i \approx a_2a_1$ (i. e. if it is a standard sequence) and if for some bc $\in A^*$, a_ia_1 < bc for all i (i. e. if it is strictly bounded), then it is finite.

The reader may wonder why we defined an additive conjoint structure in terms of representations, and a positive difference structure in terms of qualitative axioms. The reason is that in Theorem 3.2 we want to stress the qualitative aspect of the axioms with a numerical scale derived from a representation theorem, whereas in Theorem 4.2, an already existing numerical scale is shown to be interpretable as a random variable.

2.2 Measure spaces.

The basic concepts of measure theory are a σ-algebra *A* on a set X, an outer measure m on the subsets of X, and a (σ-additive) measure μ on the sets of *A*. The reader not acquainted with these notions is referred to Friedmann (1970, chapter 1.1 and 1.2) or Loève (1977, chapter I).

In the following we describe a method to constuct an outer measure m from a numerical function on a special set of subsets of X and subsequently to define a σ-algebra on X on which the restriction μ of m is a measure. For the proofs we refer to Friedmann (1970, chap. 1.3, 1.4) or Loève (1977, chap. I 1.4).

DEFINITION 2.1. Let K be a set of subsets of a nonempty set X. K is a *sequential covering class* of X if

(1) $\varnothing \in K$.

(2) For every subset A of X there is a sequence (I_n) in K such that

$$A \subset \bigcup_{n=1}^{\infty} I_n.$$

Any set of subsets containing the empty set and X is a sequential covering class.

Let δ be an extended (i. e. $\pm\infty$ is possible) real-valued, non-negative set function on a sequential covering class K such that $\delta(\varnothing) = 0$. Let

$$m(A) = \inf \{ \Sigma_n \delta(I_n);\ I_n \in K,\ \bigcup_{n=1}^{\infty} I_n \supset A \} \tag{2.1}$$

THEOREM 2.1. For any sequential covering class K *and for any extended real-valued, non-negative set function on* K *with* $\delta(\varnothing) = 0$ *the function m defined by (2.1) is an outer measure.*

THEOREM 2.2. Let m *be an outer measure on* X *and denote by* $\mathcal{A}$ *the set of all subsets* A *of* X *such that for all* $T \subset X$:

$$m(T) \geq m(T \cap A) + m(T - A). \tag{2.2}$$

Then $\mathcal{A}$ *is a* σ*-algebra and the restriction* μ *of* m *to* $\mathcal{A}$ *is a measure.*

It should be noted that the measurable sets constructed in this way strongly depend on the sequential covering class which is employed at the outset of this procedure. If we start with a trivial set K in Definition 2.1 then the resulting σ-algebra will not be very interesting, either.

In section 3 we shall use these theorems to construct measures and probabilities. The function δ will be derived from numerical representations of measurement structures; a sequential covering class which is empirically and mathematically interesting will be available if we define intervals on weakly ordered sets. In probability theory the measurable sets are called events.

The notation $\mu((a,b))$ will be abbreviated by $\mu(a,b)$ and the same applies to m and P.

3. Probability spaces on ordered sets

In this section we apply the construction described in Theorem 2.1 and 2.2 to scalable weakly ordered sets $(X, \precsim)$ to provide them with a probability structure.

The main idea is to take advantage from numerical representations of the relational system to define the function δ on a sequential covering class. In this way we can combine the measure-theoretic construction of a measure and the representational theory of relational systems in measurement theory.

We beginn by defining a sequential covering class which is available in every weakly ordered set.

DEFINITION 3.1. Let $(X, \lesssim)$ be a weak order

$(a,b) = \{x \in X;\ a < x < b\}$

$INT = \{(a,b);\ a,b \in X\} \cup \{X\}$

INT is the set of *intervals induced by* $\lesssim$ on X.

Obviously INT, containing X, is a sequential covering class. Thus, any extended real-valued non-negative function δ on X gives rise to a measure space $(X, \mathcal{A}, \mu)$. Since $(X, \lesssim)$ is scalable, any representation f can be used in various ways to define a function δ; for example:

$$\delta(I) = \begin{cases} f(b) - f(a) & \text{if } I = (a,b) \\ \sup\{f(b)-f(a);\ (a,b) \in NT\} & \text{if } I = X \\ 0 & \text{if } I = \emptyset \end{cases} \qquad (3.1)$$

The determination of the measurable sets $\mathcal{A}$ may pose a problem and even the proof of $INT \subset \mathcal{A}$ may be cumbersome. The difficulties lie in the discontinuous behaviour of the measure at the gaps of f(X). Both problems can be avoided, however. The first by extending X to a set containing an order dense subset of order type η which is always possible (see the proof of Theorem 2.3 of Narens (1985, pp 36 - 37). The second by using universal scales in the sense of Droste (1987a, b).

If f is a universal scale and X has an order dense subset of order type η then (3.1) can by shown to yield a measure μ_f closely resembling the Lebesgue-Stieltjes measure on the real line. In particular, we have

$$\mu_f(a,b) = f(b) - f(a).$$

It should be mentioned that this does not hold generally. If $X = \{a,b,c\}$, $a < b < c$, and $f(a) = 0$, $f(b) = 1$, and $f(c) = 2$. Then, since $(a,b) = \emptyset$ we have $\mu_f(a,b) = 0$ and $f(b) - f(a) = 1$.

In the following Theorems the universality of f and the 'no gaps' condition is not required. Whenever necessary we introduce the further assumption that the intervals be measurable. This is more general and can, depending on the structure under scrutiny, be verified without reference to the gaps of f(X).

If we transform f such that $||f||$ is bounded on X then $\mu_f(X)$ is finite and if $\mu_f(X) > 0$, a probability is defined on $(X, \lesssim)$ by $P_f(A) = \mu_f(A)/\mu_f(X)$.

DEFINITION 3.2. The probability space constructed from the sequential covering class INT and based on the function δ defined in (3.1) is called an *interval probability space* on X, and denoted by $(X, \mathcal{A}_f, P_f)$.

The considerations above are summarized in

THEOREM 3.1. Let $(X, \precsim)$ *be a scalable weak order, containing at least three mutually distinct indifference classes. For any bounded scale* f *there is an interval probability space on* X. *If for all* $a, b \in X$, $(a,b) \in A_f$ *and* $[a,b) \in A_f$, *then* $I(a) := \{x;\ x < a\} \in A_f$.

Proof. The proof of this theorem is contained in the description of the constructing process preceding it; $\mu_f(X) > 0$ follows from the assumption made on the three distinct indifference classes. The statement concerning I(a) needs a few new considerations. The case $I(a) = \emptyset$ is trivial. Suppose $I(a) \neq \emptyset$. Define $r = \inf \{f(x);\ x \in X\}$ and let (x_i) be a sequence in X, monotonically decreasing such that $f(x_i) \to r$ and $x_i \precsim a$.

Obviously $\bigcup_{i=1}^{\infty} [x_i,a) \subset I(a)$. For $x \in I(a)$ and for sufficiently large i we have $x_i \precsim x$. Thus $x \in [x_i,a)$, or $I(a) \subset \bigcup [x_i,x)$ This yields $I(a) = \bigcup [x_i,a)$. Since $[x_i,a) \in A_f$, $I(a) \in A_f$ follows.

As already mentioned in the introduction, the probability space (X,*A*,P) constructed from a mere weak order has no sensible interpretation that goes beyond the $\precsim$ relation. Eq. (1.1) is meaningful but is trivial, whereas the probabilities of (1.2) are comparable, but the comparison is meaningless as long as the representations f are not confined to a smaller set.

We address this question by introducing a new primitive, a binary relation W on INT. An empirical interpretation of this will be given at the end of this section.

THEOREM 3.2. Suppose X *is a non-empty set,* $\precsim$ *and* W *are binary relations on* X *and* $X \times X$, *respectively such that*

(1) $(X, \precsim)$ *is a weak order, with at least three mutually distinct indifference classes.*

(2) *Let* INT *be the set of intervals induced by* $\precsim$ *on* X *and* INT' *the set of pairs* $ab \in X \times X$ *such that* $(a,b) \in$ INT; *then* (X,INT',W) *is a positive difference structure.*

(3) *Every standard sequence of* (X,INT',W) *is finite.*

Then there is a σ*-algebra* *A* *and a measure* P *such that* (X,*A*,P) *is a probability space. Futhermore* INT $\subset$ *A and*

ab W cd *iff* $P(a,b) \le P(c,d)$. (3.2)

Remark: Compared with the definition of a positive difference structure given in section 2a, the assumption of two relations, $\precsim$ and W, seems superfluous. The reader should note, however, that the definition of the intervals depends on it. One can drop $\precsim$ altogether and postulate a 'probability ordering' W on a set INT' of abstract intervals. The proof given below applies with only minor changes. We chose the formulation given because the idea is to combine ordinal information about the objects (i. e. $\precsim$) and a qualitative probability i. e. 'is more probable than' for sets which are intervals in the $\precsim$-sense, to yield a probability space in which the intervals are events and the 'length' of an interval is measured by its probability.

Proof. By the representation theorem for positive difference structures (Krantz et al (1971) p. 147) there exists a positive function f: INT' $\rightarrow$ Re such that for all ab, cd$\in$ INT'

ab W cd iff $f(a,b) \leq f(c,d)$.

We define

$$\delta(I) = \begin{cases} f(a,b) & \text{if } I = (a,b) \\ \sup\{f(a,b); (a,b) \in \text{INT}\} & \text{if } I = X \\ 0 & \text{if } I = \emptyset \end{cases}$$

Because it is more convenient in later steps of the proof, we extend INT to INT_1 by adding the intervals [a,b), (a,b], and [a,b] to INT. δ is set to f(a,b) in all cases. Obviously INT_1 is a sequential covering class and by Theorems 2.1 and 2.2 a σ-algebra A and a measure μ is constructed. Next we prove $\mu(X) < \infty$. (Note that ab $\tilde{\tilde{W}}$ bc' is short for ab W bc' and bc' W ab)

Lemma 3.1. If ab W bc *then* c'b *exists such that* ab $\tilde{\tilde{W}}$ bc'.

Proof. By the solvability axiom x exists satisfying ab $\tilde{\tilde{W}}$ xc and again by solvability c' exists such that bc' $\tilde{\tilde{W}}$ xc, whence ab $\tilde{\tilde{W}}$ bc'. The proof of the second statement is similar.

To continue the proof of the theorem we pick two elements $x_0, x_1 \in X$, $x_0 < x_1$. If there is $y \in X$, $y \gtrsim x_1$, and x_0x_1 W x_1y, then by Lemma 3.1, $x_2 \in X$ exists, satisfying x_0x_1 $\tilde{\tilde{W}}$ x_1x_2. Accordingly x_{-1} can be found such that $x_{-1}x_0$ $\tilde{\tilde{W}}$ x_0x_1.

Next, we construct x_3 and x_{-2} in the same manner and so on. The procedure stops, when, after the construction of x_i, no y exists such that $x_{i-1}x_i$ W x_iy (and on the other end x_ix_{i+1} W yx_i). The ensuing sequence (x_i) is a standard sequence.

Condition (3) of the theorem guarantees that the process of constructing x_i finally comes to an end. Denoting u=max $\{x_i\}$ and v=min $\{x_i\}$ we observe

$f(x,y) \leq f(v,u) + 2f(x_0,x_1)$ for all $x, y \in X$.

The right side of this inequality is finite, since the standard sequence is finite. Thus we infer

$\sup\{f(x,y); x,y \in X\} < \infty$

But, on the other hand,

$0 < \mu(X) \leq \sup f(x,y)$.

By normalizing the probability P can be defined

$P(A) = \mu(A)/\mu(X)$.

Now, we have to prove that the intervals are measurable and that P is W-preserving.

Lemma 3.2. For all $I \in$ INT *follows* $I \in A$.

Proof. We must show that for all subsets T of X

$$m(T) \geq m(T \cap I) + m(T - I) \qquad (3.3)$$

Let $D = \{I_n; n=1,2,..\}$ be a system of intervals covering T and for (a small number) $\varepsilon > o$:

$$m(T) + \varepsilon \geq \Sigma_n \delta(I_n) \qquad (3.4)$$

Starting from D we construct systems B and C of intervals that cover $T \cap I$ and $T - I$ respectively. Thus, $m(T \cap I) \leq \Sigma_B \delta(J)$ and $m(T - I) \leq \Sigma_C \delta(J)$. Since $T \subset \bigcup_n I_n$, we have

$$T \cap I \subset \bigcup_n I_n \cap I = \bigcup_n (I_n \cap I)$$

and

$$T - I \subset \bigcup_n I_n - I = \bigcup_n (I_n - I)$$

However, $I_n \cap I \in INT_1$ and $I_n - I$ is in INT_1 or consists of the union of two intervals in INT_1. Thus, if we define $B = \{I_n \cap I; n=1,2,..\}$ and $C = \{I_n - I; n=1,2,..\}$, we get

$$T \cap I \subset \bigcup_{J \in B} J, \quad T - I \subset \bigcup_{J \in C} J$$

and

$$m(T \cap I) \leq \Sigma_B \delta(J), \quad m(T - I) \leq \Sigma_C \delta(J) \qquad (3.5)$$

But, if we denote the intervals which $I_n - I$ consists of, by I'_n and I''_n (one or both of them possibly empty), we have

$$I_n = (I_n \cap I) \cup I'_n \cup I''_n$$

and from the representation theorem for positive difference structures follows

$$\delta(I_n) = \delta(I_n \cap I) + \delta(I'_n) + \delta(I''_n).$$

Here we used the property $f(a,c)=f(a,b)+f(b,c)$ (Krantz et al. (1971) Theorem 4.1.). Thus

$$\Sigma_n \delta(I_n) = \Sigma_B \delta(J) + \Sigma_C \delta(J) \qquad (3.6)$$

Putting (3.4) and (3.6) together and observing (3.5) we arrive at (3.3) since ε is arbitrarily small. This finishes the proof of Lemma 3.2.

The proof of (3.2), i. e. that P is W-preserving is easily obtained from the definition of the outer measure m and the monotonicity with respect to W of f (and of δ) which is entailed in the representation theorem of positive difference structures. Theorem 3.2 is now fully established.

The assumption of Theorem 3.2 can be interpreted in the following way: ab W cd expresses the fact that observations in an experiment lying between c and d are more likely than between a and b. If, a, b, c, d are ordinal measures and are known as a result of an empirical investigation, W is also known. The empirical distribution function contains this information and the testable axioms of positive difference measurement are fulfilled. In fact, the empirical distribution function contains much more information; however, in a weak order this information is not meanigful and this is a good reason not to use it.

In this interpretation the conditions of Theorem 3.2 are very weak. More problems arise, however, if we take into account the problem of sampling. In this case, from Gliwenko's theorem we know that the empirical distribution functions are "close" to the distribution from which the sample is taken. This is true without any distributional assumptions.

4. Random variables

Once the probabilistic structure on the set X is established, real-valued functions on X can be regarded as random variables on $(X,\mathcal{A},P)$ provided the inverse images of the sets $(-\infty,r)$ are in $\mathcal{A}$ for all real numbers r. Theorem 4.1 describes one of the results concerning this subject in which the function is a representation of the weak order $(X, \precsim)$. This can come in handy when, in the program of ab initio statistics, the construction of random variables is called for. However, contrary to what one is likely to need, random variables constructed by this method are not independent.

In Theorem 4.2 we present a procedure which results in independent random variables.

THEOREM 4.1. Let $(X, \precsim)$ *be a weak order and* $(X,\mathcal{A},P)$ *a probability space such that* (a,b), $[a,b) \in \mathcal{A}$ *for all* $a, b \in X$. *If* α *is a real representation of* $(X, \precsim)$ *then* α *is a random variable on* X.

Proof. A function α is a random variable if $\alpha^{-1}(-\infty,r)$ is an event, i. e. an element of the σ-algebra. We prove two lemmas which investigate these sets.

Lemma 4.1. For all $a \in X$ $\alpha^{-1}(-\infty,\alpha(a)) = I(a)$.

Proof. $x \in I(a)$ implies $x < a$ and $\alpha(x) < \alpha(a)$. Thus $\alpha(x) \in \alpha(-\infty,\alpha(a))$ or equivalently $x \in \alpha^{-1}(-\infty,\alpha(a))$. Conversely $x \in \alpha^{-1}(-\infty,\alpha(a))$ implies $\alpha(x) < \alpha(a)$, whence $x < a$ or $x \in I(a)$.

Lemma 4.2. If $a_n \in X$ *such that* $\alpha(a_n) \geq r$ *and* $\alpha(a_n) \to r$, *then*

$$\alpha^{-1}(-\infty,r) = \bigcap_i \alpha^{-1}(-\infty,\alpha(a_i)).$$

Proof. The following conclusions hold true:

$$x \in \alpha^{-1}(-\infty,r) \text{ iff } \alpha(x) < r, \text{ iff } \alpha(x) < \alpha(a_n), \text{ iff } x \in \alpha^{-1}(-\infty,\alpha(a_n)).$$

Since this is correct for all n, the lemma follows.

To finish the proof of Theorem 4.1 we observe that, by Lemma 4.2, $\alpha^{-1}(-\infty,r)$ is a countable intersection of sets which are by Lemma 4.1 of the I(a)-type which was shown in Theorem 3.1 to be an event. If there is no sequence (a_n) satisfying the assumption of Lemma 4.2, we define $s = \inf\{\alpha(x); x \in X, \alpha(x) \geq r\}$.

We have $\alpha^{-1}(-\infty,r) = \alpha^{-1}(-\infty,s)$. Now either Lemma 4.2 can be applied to $\alpha^{-1}(-\infty,s)$ or $\alpha^{-1}(-\infty,s)$ is empty or the whole space X. In any of these cases it is an event and so is $\alpha^{-1}(-\infty,r)$.

THEOREM 4.2. Let $(X_1,X_2, \precsim)$ *be an additive conjoint structure. For* i=1,2 *let* (X_i,A_i,P_i) *be probabiliy spaces such that all intervals* (a,b) *and* [a,b) *defined by the induced orders* $\precsim_i$ *on* X_i *are events. Furthermore let* (f_1,f_2) *be an additive representation of* $(X_1,X_2, \precsim)$. *If for* $a \in X_1$, $b \in X_2$

$$\alpha_a(x,y) := f_1(a) + f_2(y)$$
$$\beta_b(x,y) := f_1(x) + f_2(b)$$

then α_a *and* β_b *are independent random variables on the product space* $(X_1{\times}X_2, A_1{\times}A_2, P_1{\times}P_2)$.

For the distributional questions of this section it would be more natural to drop the constants $f_1(a)$ and $f_2(b)$ in the definition of a and b respectively. This would lead to identical distributions. The definition given has the advantage of satisfying (1.1) for the weak orders induced by $\precsim$ on the components X_1 and X_2.

Proof. We have to prove that α_a and β_b are random variables on the product space. To this end it suffices to show that the inverse images of $(-\infty,r)$ for all $r \in Re$ are contained in the σ-algebra $A_1{\times}A_2$ (which is the σ-algebra generated by the "rectangles" $E_1{\times}E_2$ with $E_i \in A_i$.
If we define $\alpha(y) = \alpha_a(x,y) - f_1(a)$ and

$$\beta(x) = \beta_b(x,y) - f_2(b)$$

(notice that α does not depend on x and β not on y), we have functions defined on X_2 (X_1 respectively). They are random on (X_i,A_i,P_i) by Theorem 4.1. This implies

$$\alpha^{-1}(-\infty,r) \in A_2, \qquad \beta^{-1}(-\infty,r) \in A_1.$$

The randomness of α_a is proved by the following calculation.

$$\begin{aligned}\alpha_a^{-1}(-\infty,r) &= \{(x,y) \in X_1{\times}X_2;\ \alpha_a(x,y) < r\}\\ &= \{xy \in X_1{\times}X_2;\ f_1(a) + f_2(y) < r\}\\ &= \{xy;\ x \in X_1;\ f_2(y) < r - f_1(a)\}\\ &= X_1 \times \{y \in X_2;\ f_2(y) < r - f_1(a)\}\\ &= X_1 \times \alpha^{-1}(-\infty, r-f_1(a)) \qquad (4.1)\end{aligned}$$

Since this is a cylinder set it is contained in $A_1{\times}A_2$. The randomness of β_b is proved similarly.

To prove the independence of α_a and β_b we look at the joint distribution

$$\begin{aligned}P(\alpha_a < u, \beta_b < v)\\ &= P(\{xy;\ f_1(a) + f_2(y) < u,\ f_1(x) + f_2(b) < v\})\\ &= P(\{xy;\ f_2(y) < u-f_1(a),\ f_1(x) < v-f_2(b)\})\\ &= P(\{x{\in}X_1;\ f_1(x) < v-f_2(b)\} \times \{y{\in}X_2,\ f_2(y) < u-f_1(a)\})\\ &= P(\beta^{-1}(-\infty,v-f_2(b)){\times}\alpha^{-1}(-\infty,u-f_1(a)))\\ &= P_1(\beta^{-1}(-\infty,v-f_2(b))\ P_2\,\alpha^{-1}(-\infty,u-f_1(a)) \qquad (4.2)\end{aligned}$$

by the definition of a product measure.

Using (4.1) and $P_1(A) = P(A \times X_2)$, $P_2(B) = P(X_1 \times B)$ for all $A \in A_1$, $B \in A_2$ we can rewrite (4.2):

$$\begin{aligned} P(\alpha_a < u, \beta_b < v) &= P(\beta^{-1}(-\infty, v-f_2(b)) \times X_2)\ P(X_1 \times \alpha^{-1}(-\infty, u-f_1(a))) \\ &= P(\beta_b < v)\ P(\alpha_a < u) \end{aligned}$$

i. e., α_a and β_b are independent.

This completes the proof of Theorem 4.2. The rather complicated definition of the random variables α_a and β_b looks perhaps more plausible if one observes that α_a and $\alpha_{a'}$ for a, a' $\in X_1$ are not independent. The proof is left to the reader. Futhermore it is also fairly obvious that the theorem can be generalized by intro-ducing more than two components.

5. Discussion

It is of some interest to compare Theorem 3.2 with theorems on probability representations discussed in Krantz et al. (1971, chap. 5) for example Theorem 5.2. In this result the primitives are an algebra of events and a probability ordering on this algebra. In our theorem the primitives consists of a weak order and a probability ordering (W) on the intervals defined by the weak order. The algebra of events emerges from the construction. The conditions of both theorems are not easily comparable. However, from the proof of Theorem 5.2 of Krantz et al. (1971) and from the interrelation of concatenation structures and positive difference structures, we surmise that both are closely related.

If one wants to go one more step towards an axiomatization of distributions and families of distributions, two lines of research can be proposed from the results of this paper.

First, one can try to find axioms that should govern the relation between $\lesssim$ and W in Theorem 3.2. From the interpretation at the end of section 3 one can see that distribution functions can be "generated" by an adequate assigning of numerical values to the elements of X and correspondingly to the intervals in INT. Some procedures of psychological test theory and test construction seem to make use of this implicitly. However, at present we have no idea how this "adequate assigning" can be captured in qualitative conditions imposed on (X, $\lesssim$, W). It seems that the main problem of a theory of ab initio statistics is only reformulated by this remark.

Second, the potential of the construction of Theorem 4.2 is perhaps not fully exhausted. The following remark describes a possible course of research to derive results on distributions "ab initio". Each component together with the induced order allows for very many probability spaces. Theorem 3.1 shows that we can construct a probability measure from every monotonic representation g_i of $(X_i, \lesssim_i)$. Probably among the various possibilities there is one which results in a normal distribution of α_a and β_b. One can try to apply theorems which characterize the normal law, e. g. α_a, β_b are normally distributed if $\alpha_a+\beta_b$, $\alpha_a-\beta_b$ are independent. For reference, we mention the book of Mathai and Pederzoli (1977). Drawing on theorems of this kind leads to conditions on the function g_i; in the special case of the theorem mentioned, the required independence of $\alpha_a+\beta_b$, $\alpha_a-\beta_b$ leads to a complicated functional equation, the solution of which remains an open problem.

Finally we want to point out that a more general approach to the question raised in this paper is possible if one is willing to drop the constructive methods of measure theory (i. e. Theorems 2.1 and 2.2) employed in section 3. This leads to a parametrization of sets of random variables by sets of scales of measurement structures. The details and consequences of this theory are currently being investigated.

Acknowledgement

The author wishes to express his thanks to Duncan R. Luce and a reviewer for a number of helpful comments on an earlier draft of this paper.

References

Droste, M., (1987a). Ordinal scales in the theory of measurement. *Journal of Mathematical Psychology* 31, 60-82.

Droste, M., (1987b). Classification and transformation of ordinal scales in the theory of measurement. In E. Roskam & R. Suck (Eds.), *Progress in Mathematical Psychology*, Amsterdam: North Holland.

Fishburn, R. C., (1986). The axioms of subjective probability. *Statistical Science* 1, 335-358.

Friedmann, A., (1970). *Foundations of modern analyses.* New York: Holt, Rinehart and Winston, inc.

Krantz, D. H., Luce, R. D., Suppes, P., Tversky, A., (1971).*Foundations of measurement, Vol. 1*, New York: Academic Press.

Loève, M., (1977). *Probability theory I, II.* New York: Springer

Luce, R. D., (1986). Uniqueness and Homogeneity of Ordered Relational Stuctures. *Journal of Mathematical Psychology* 30, 391-415.

Luce, R. D., Narens, L., (1983). Symmetry, scale types, and generalizations of classical physical measurement. *Journal of Mathematical Psychology* 27, 44-85.

Luce, R. D., Narens, L., (1985). Classification of concatenation measurement structures according to scale type.*Journal of Mathematical Psychology* 29, 1-72.

Mathai, A. M., Pederzoli, G., (1977).*Characterizations of the normal probability law.* New Dehli: Wiley Eastern Ltd.

Narens, L., (1985). *Abstract measurement theory.* Cambridge, Mass.:MIT Press.

Roberts, F. S., (1979). *Measurement theory with applications todecisionmaking, utility, and the social science.* Reading,Mass.: Addison-Wesley.

Rosenstein, J. G., (1982). *Linear Orderings.* New York: Academic Press.

Elements of a Model-Theoretic Framework for Probabilistic Measurement

Dieter Heyer
University of Kiel[1]

Reinhard Niederée
University of Bonn[2]

Abstract
Standard model-theoretic concepts in the theory of fundamental measurement are extended so as to yield an abstract framework for probabilistic measurement based on the notion of a probabilistic structure. Conceiving probabilistic structures as 'P-mixtures' of deterministic structures allows to analyze certain probabilistic axioms satisfied by the former in terms of first-order axioms satisfied by the latter. Doing so introduces a new perspective into the theoretical discussion of probabilistic axioms as found in probabilistic measurement, and suggests a new scheme of classification. Some further prospects will be briefly discussed, in particular connections to probabilistic logic.

1. Introduction

In mathematical psychology two different, though loosely interrelated variants of measurement theory are dealt with: on the one hand, the representational approach of *fundamental measurement* in the tradition of Helmholtz, Campbell, and Suppes, on the other hand, *probabilistic* approaches as found in Fechnerian psychophysics, utility theory and probabilistic versions of extensive measurement. Both traditions are interested in formulating 'qualitative axioms' which are sufficient/necessary for certain 'numerical representations' to exist. While the former refers to 'deterministic' axioms such as the axioms of order or monotonicity (e.g. Krantz, Luce, Suppes and Tversky, 1971; Narens, 1985) the latter refers to 'probabilistic' axioms, such as $P_{a,b} + P_{b,c} + P_{c,a} \leq 2$ (e.g. Luce & Suppes, 1965; Falmagne, 1985; Colonius, 1984).

Traditional 'deterministic' measurement theory has benefited considerably from the introduction of the general and unifying model-theoretic framework based on the notion of homomorphic representation due to Scott & Suppes (1958). Thereby a link was established between measurement theory and first-order model theory, clarifying the concept of measurement itself and making a systematic treatment of axiomatizability and invariance issues possible.

To our knowledge, such a framework has not yet been discussed for probabilistic

1 Institut für Psychologie, Universität Kiel, Ohlshausenstr. 40-60, D-2300 Kiel 1, FRG.
2 Psychologisches Institut, Universität Bonn, Römerstr. 164, D-5300 Bonn 1, FRG.

measurement models, let alone a common concept formally bridging the probabilistic and the ordinary 'deterministic' case. In the sequel we will outline some fundamentals of such a unifying approach. Starting from the notions of probabilistic structure and probabilistic representation, questions will be pursued such as: In which ways can probabilistic structures and representations be conceived as derived from deterministic ones? And analogously, which probabilistic axioms can be conceived as probabilistic versions of certain first-order axioms? (What, for instance, should count as a 'probabilistic order'?) These questions will lead us to precise model theoretic notions which clear the way for a systematic distinction between probabilistic axioms which can be understood as 'structural assumptions' derivable from first order axioms and those which can not.

Some of the notions introduced in this connection will be 'canonical' extensions of their deterministic counterparts and allow tying probabilistic measurement in a precise way to disciplines such as probabilistic model theory. As the paper is introductory in character, we shall concentrate on comparatively elementary examples; logical notation will by and large be avoided. We hope to present more technical results in a later paper.

2. Some basic model-theoretic notions: Probabilistic structures and representations

Central to deterministic measurement theory is the concept of a relational structure $\mathfrak{A} = \langle A, R_1, \ldots, R_n \rangle$, R_i an n_i-placed relation on the domain A for $1 \leq i \leq n$. Subsequently such relations will be considered as two-valued functions, with $R_i(a_1, \ldots, a_{n_i})$ taking the value 1 or 0 depending on whether $(a_1, \ldots, a_{n_i})$ 'belongs' to R_i or not. Allowing R_i to be a mapping into the real interval $[0,1]$, whose elements are considered truth values denoting 'probabilities', leads to the notion of an *n_i-placed probabilistic relation.* Relational structures based on probabilistic relations will be called *probabilistic relational structures. Pair comparison systems* studied in psychophysics provide simple examples of such structures; they are of the form $\langle A, p \rangle$, where A denotes a set of stimuli and $p: A^2 \longrightarrow [0,1]$ is a mapping which assigns to each pair (a,b) of stimuli the probability $p(a,b)$ of b being judged to dominate a in a certain respect.

Another notion central to deterministic measurement theory is the concept of representation. A mapping $\varphi: \mathfrak{A} \longrightarrow \mathfrak{N}$, where $\mathfrak{N} = \langle N, S_1, \ldots, S_n \rangle$ is a numerical relational structure of the same type as $\mathfrak{A} = \langle A, R_1, \ldots, R_n \rangle$ (i.e. S_i is of the same arity, n_i, as R_i), is called a representation of $\mathfrak{A}$ in $\mathfrak{N}$ if and only if $R_i(a_1, \ldots, a_{n_i}) = S_i(\varphi(a_1), \ldots, \varphi(a_{n_i}))$ for all $a_1, \ldots, a_{n_i} \in A$, $1 \leq i \leq n$. Formulated this way, the definition readily carries over to the probabilistic case, yielding the notion of a *probabilistic representation* (expressed by $\varphi: \mathfrak{A} \longrightarrow \mathfrak{N}$). A one-one probabilistic representation which is onto, is called a *(probabilistic) isomorphism*.

The usual 'numerical representations' considered so far in probabilistic measurement theory can in fact be subsumed under this definition. While in the deterministic case N will typically be a subset of the reals, probabilistic representations will map $\mathfrak{A}$ into probabilistic numerical structures based either on a subset of the *reals* or on a set of real random variables or the like (in short *'random reals'* a term due to D. Scott). An example for the first case is Fechnerian scaling: given some pair comparison system $\mathfrak{A} = \langle A, p \rangle$, one is interested in a mapping $u: A \longrightarrow \mathbb{R}$ such that $p(a,b) = F(u(b) - u(a))$ for some strictly increasing function $F: \mathbb{R} \longrightarrow \mathbb{R}$. Translated into the above terminology this simply means that u is a probabilistic representation of $\mathfrak{A}$ in $\mathfrak{N} = \langle \mathbb{R}, G \rangle$ with $G(x,y) = F(y-x)$. More generally, constant utility models fall in this class. Random utility models, by contrast, correspond to probabilistic representations into a set of 'random reals'. Here one is interested in a mapping $X: A \longrightarrow \Theta$, where Θ is a set of random variables on some probability space, such that $p(a,b) = Pr(X_a \leq X_b)$. That is, X is a probabilistic representation in $\mathfrak{N} = \langle \Theta, \vartheta \rangle$, with $\vartheta(Y,Z) = Pr(Y \leq Z)$ for $Y, Z \in \Theta$. More complex examples for both cases are provided by probabilized versions of extensive measurement discussed in Falmagne (1980, 1985).

It is sometimes useful to regard probabilistic structures as being 'generated' from deterministic ones. For one thing, this will provide the tools needed for making precise the destinction between 'structural' and 'non-structural' probabilistic axioms. Furthermore, it is sometimes possible to construct probabilistic representations out of representations (in the traditional sense) of the corresponding deterministic structures. In this way, we believe, a deeper understanding in terms of general model-theoretic notions may be gained of the intuitions commenly underlying central concepts of probabilistic measurement theory.

Two interrelated methods for 'constructing' probabilistic structures out of deterministic ones will be outlined in the following section.

3. Understanding probabilistic structures in terms of deterministic ones: P-mixtures

Imagine we have an 'urn' of deterministic structures of the same type $\mathfrak{A}_\omega$, $\omega \in \Omega$, and a common underlying domain A. Consider the simple case where each structure contains a two-placed relation R^ω; a probabilistic two-placed relation R is then simply obtained by assigning to each pair of elements $(a,b) \in A^2$ the probability of 'drawing' a structure in which these elements stand in the corresponding deterministic relation.

In accordance with interpretations of related concepts sometimes found in the literature, one might conceive the deterministic structures $\mathfrak{A}_\omega$ as, say, 'possible worlds' or different deterministic 'states' of a given (possibly mental) system. Deterministic structures may then be thought of as playing the role of 'state descriptions', or, rather, descriptions of dispositions connected with each state. While an interpretation of that kind touches on subtle philosophical and conceptual problems, the corresponding abstract mathematical definition is simple and unproblematic.

Definition 1. Let $\mathfrak{F} = \langle \mathfrak{A}_\omega \mid \omega \in \Omega \rangle$ be a family of deterministic structures $\mathfrak{A}_\omega = \langle A, R_1^\omega, \dots, R_n^\omega \rangle$, R_i^ω n_i-ary relations and $\langle \Omega, \mathfrak{B}, P \rangle$ a probability space. Assume further that for all $a_1, \dots, a_{n_i} \in A$, $1 \le i \le n$, $\{\omega \mid R_i^\omega(a_1, \dots, a_{n_i}) = 1\} \in \mathfrak{B}$. Then a probabilistic structure $\mathfrak{F}/P = \langle A, R_1, \dots, R_n \rangle$ is defined by letting

$$R_i(a_1, \dots, a_{n_i}) = P\big(\{\omega \mid R_i^\omega(a_1, \dots, a_{n_i}) = 1\}\big).$$

It is called the *P-mixture of* $\mathfrak{F}$.

Remarks. (i) Most of the considerations made in this and the following section directly generalize to arbitrary set functions mapping some subset $\mathfrak{B}$ of the power set of Ω into $[0,1]$ (such as membership functions in fuzzy set theory). Only in sections 4 to 6 will properties of measures be invoked. It is sufficient to assume $\mathfrak{B}$ as a Boolean algebra and P as a finitely additive probability measure.

(ii) $R_i(a_1, \dots, a_{n_i})$ can be interpreted as a truth value assigned to an atomic formula $\mathbf{R}_i\mathbf{a}_1\dots\mathbf{a}_{n_i}$, where $\mathbf{R}_i$, $\mathbf{a}_1$, ..., $\mathbf{a}_{n_i}$ are symbols in a corresponding formal language.[3] Furthermore, since $\mathfrak{B}$ is assumed a Boolean algebra, the above construction allows analogously the assignment of probabilistic truth values to elementary quantifier-free formulas, i.e. Boolean combinations of atomic sentences of the above kind.

(iii) The concept of a P-mixture provides a general way of conceiving probabilistic structures. For any probabilistic structure $\mathfrak{A}$ can be written as a P-mixture for some $\mathfrak{F}$ and some P, though $\mathfrak{F}$ may be rather artificial (take, for instance, Ω as the set of all deterministic structures with the same domain and type as $\mathfrak{A}$, and $\mathfrak{A}_\omega = \omega$; suitable $\mathfrak{B}$ and P are then routine to define). Therefore only 'natural' special cases of P-mixtures are of interest, such as Σ-mixtures introduced in section 4 below.

Example. Let us, by way of illustration, discuss one of two standard ways of interpreting pair comparison experiments theoretically, and reconstruct it in terms of the

3 We refer to first-order predicate logic with identity. For simplicity logical notation will be used in an informal manner. Bold letters will be used to denote the relational symbols which belong to corresponding set-theoretical relations. We use the following notation: '$\forall x$' : 'for all x'; '$\exists x$' : 'there is an x such that...'; '$\wedge$' : 'and'; '$\vee$' : 'or' (non-exclusive); '$\neg$' : 'not'; '$\longrightarrow$' : 'if...then...' .

above concepts. Consider a well-known experimental paradigm in which subjects (or one subject at different times) are presented with pairs (a,b) of 'comparable stimuli' $a,b \in A$ (say, a set of achromatic lights of different intensity, commodity bundles,...), where 'being presented with a pair (a,b)' means that a and b are presented in different 'positions', subsequently labelled 0 and 1, respectively (corresponding to left/right, first/second,...). The subject may choose among two ways r_0, r_1, of responding (forced choice) according to the instruction that the response r_i $(i=0,1)$ is to be chosen when the stimulus presented in position i appears brighter, preferable,.... One is then interested in 'explaining' the observed response frequencies in terms of probabilities $p(a,b)$, where $p(a,b)$ denotes the probability of the subjects' response being r_1. (Note that this definition of $p(a,b)$ slightly deviates from the one customary in psychophysics.)

In the theoretical analysis it is usually assumed (if only tacitly) that each response is due to some all-over 'disposition' D_ω, $\omega \in \Omega$, corresponding to the subject's 'internal state' $\omega \in \Omega$, where $D_\omega\colon A^2 \longrightarrow \{0,1\}$ may be written as a function with $D_\omega(a,b)=i$ $(i=0,1)$. This is to be understood in the sense that the response is or would be r_i when or if a subject 'so disposed' is presented with the pair (a,b) of stimuli. It is assumed, then, that there is a family $\langle D_\omega \mid \omega \in \Omega \rangle$ of such dispositions endowed with a probability space $\langle \Omega, \mathfrak{B}, P \rangle$ (the probability of dispositions being 'realized'), such that

$$p(a,b) = P\big(\{\omega \mid D_\omega(a,b) = 1\}\big) .$$

The model to be discussed is based on the assumption that an 'internal ranking' $<_\omega$ of A is associated with each state $\omega \in \Omega$, along with some auxiliary disposition to react in the case of a pair (a,a) of equal stimuli being presented, denoted by $g(\omega) \in \{0,1\}$, such that

$$D_\omega(a,b) = \begin{cases} 1 \text{ if } a <_\omega b \text{ or } \big(a = b \text{ and } g(\omega)=1\big) \\ 0 \text{ if } b <_\omega a \text{ or } \big(a = b \text{ and } g(\omega)=0\big). \end{cases}$$

Clearly, then, $\mathfrak{A} := \langle A,p \rangle$ is the P-mixture of $\mathfrak{F} := \langle \mathfrak{A}_\omega \mid \omega \in \Omega \rangle$ where $\mathfrak{A}_\omega := \langle A, D_\omega \rangle$.

Furthermore, each $\mathfrak{A}_\omega$ satisfies certain structural assumptions, namely, transitivity, connectivity and antisymmetry (identifying D_ω with the corresponding subset of A^2), which to some extent determine the probabilistic properties of $\mathfrak{A}$ (see section 4). Note in passing that D_ω is a reflexive or irreflexive order depending on whether $g(\omega)=1$ or $g(\omega)=0$.

While in the construction described in Definition 1 relations were 'probabilized' over fixed objects, the second method of constructing probabilistic structures is guided by the idea of starting from fixed deterministic relations and 'probabilizing' the objects, as it were.

Definition 2. Let $\mathfrak{C} = \langle C, Q_1, \ldots, Q_n \rangle$ be a deterministic structure (called *background structure*) with Q_i an n_i-ary relation on C, $\langle \Omega, \mathfrak{B}, P \rangle$ as in Definition 1, and $\tilde{C} \subset {}^{\Omega}C$ $({}^{\Omega}C := \{ f: \Omega \longrightarrow C \})$. Assume that for all $X_1, \ldots, X_{n_i} \in \tilde{C}$, $1 \leq i \leq n$,

$$\left\{ \omega \in \Omega \mid Q_i\left(X_1(\omega), \ldots, X_{n_i}(\omega)\right) = 1 \right\} \in \mathfrak{B}. \tag{1}$$

Then $\tilde{\mathfrak{C}} := \langle \tilde{C}, \tilde{Q}_1, \ldots, \tilde{Q}_n \rangle$, where $\tilde{Q}_i(X_1, \ldots, X_{n_i}) := P\left(\{ \omega \mid Q_i(X_1(\omega), \ldots, X_{n_i}(\omega)) = 1 \}\right)$, is called the *probabilistic structure on* $\tilde{C}$ *induced from* $\mathfrak{C}$ *by P*.

Remark. In applications, $\tilde{C}$ will often be assumed to be a set of random variables, in the sense that $X \in \tilde{C}$ is measurable with respect to $\mathfrak{B}$ and some given Boolean algebra $\mathfrak{D}$ on C. Often the relations Q_i considered are $\otimes_{k=1}^{n_i} \mathfrak{D}$ -measurable (when understood as subsets of C^{n_i}), in which case (1) is trivially satisfied. If $\tilde{C}$ is the set of *all* measurable $X: \Omega \longrightarrow C$, the induced structure $\tilde{\mathfrak{C}}$ may be conceived as a probabilistic power of $\mathfrak{C}$ (generalizing the notion of an ultrapower in first-order model theory by substituting probability measures for two-valued measures, respectively ultrafilters; cf. Scott, 1969; Scott & Krauss, 1966; Narens, 1985).

Example. As an example consider the above-mentioned case (cf. section 2) of representing a pair comparison system $\langle A, p \rangle$ in a structure $\langle \Theta, \vartheta \rangle$ via a mapping $f: a \longmapsto X_a$, where Θ is a set of real random variables relative to an underlying probability space $\langle \Omega, \mathfrak{B}, P \rangle$ and $\vartheta(X, Y) = P(X \leq Y)$, $X, Y \in \Theta$. Choosing the background structure $\mathfrak{C}$ as $\langle \mathbb{R}, \leq \rangle$ and $\tilde{C} = \Theta$, $\langle \Theta, \vartheta \rangle$ turns out to be the probabilistic structure on $\tilde{C}$ induced from $\mathfrak{C}$ by P. Clearly the measurability condition is satisfied because of the preceding remark.

Probabilistic mixtures vs. induced probabilistic structures. In a canonical way, probabilistic structures induced from deterministic background structures (in short: *induced probabilistic structures*) can be written as P-mixtures:
Let $\mathfrak{C}_\omega = \langle \tilde{C}, \tilde{Q}_1^\omega, \ldots, \tilde{Q}_n^\omega \rangle$, $\mathfrak{F} = \langle \mathfrak{C}_\omega \mid \omega \in \Omega \rangle$, where

$$\tilde{Q}_i^\omega(X_1, \ldots, X_{n_i}) := Q_i(X_1(\omega), \ldots, X_{n_i}(\omega)),$$

$X_1, \ldots, X_{n_i} \in \tilde{C}$, $1 \leq i \leq n$. Then $\tilde{\mathfrak{C}} = \mathfrak{F}/P$.

Conversely, any P-mixture of $\mathfrak{F} = \langle \mathfrak{A}_\omega \mid \omega \in \Omega \rangle$ is isomorphic to some induced probabilistic structure as implied by the following proposition on the representation of P-mixtures in induced probabilistic structures.

Proposition 1. Let $\mathfrak{F} = \langle \mathfrak{A}_\omega \mid \omega \in \Omega \rangle$ be a family of deterministic relational structures of the same type with common domain A and $\langle \Omega, \mathfrak{B}, P \rangle$ a probability space such that the measurability condition of Definition 1 is satisfied. Assume there is a deterministic structure $\mathfrak{C}$ of the same type as $\mathfrak{A}_\omega$ and a family of representations $f_\omega : \mathfrak{A}_\omega \longrightarrow \mathfrak{C}$ $(\omega \in \Omega)$. Consider the set $\tilde{C}$ of all mappings X_a $(a \in A)$ defined by

$$X_a : \Omega \longrightarrow C \qquad (C = \text{domain of } \mathfrak{C})$$
$$\omega \longmapsto X_a(\omega) := f_\omega(a).$$

Then the mapping

$$f: A \longrightarrow \tilde{C}$$
$$a \longmapsto X_a$$

is a representation of $\mathfrak{F}/P$ in the probabilistic structure, $\tilde{\mathfrak{C}}$, induced on $\tilde{C}$ from $\mathfrak{C}$ by P.

The elementary proof is omitted.

Remark. By a simple, though 'artificial' construction, some $\mathfrak{C}$ can always be shown to exist which satisfies the above assumptions. Simply choose the 'disjoint union' of the $\mathfrak{A}_\omega$'s. The f_ω's can then be chosen as one-one representations, thereby yielding a one-one function f mapping A onto $\tilde{C}$, that is an isomorphism.

Of course, only those cases are of interest where $\mathfrak{C}$ can be chosen in a natural way. As an illustration, consider a pair comparison system $\mathfrak{A} = \langle A, p \rangle$. Theoretical reasoning might lead one to assume that there is a family $\mathfrak{F} = \langle \mathfrak{A}_\omega \mid \omega \in \Omega \rangle$ of orders $\mathfrak{A}_\omega = \langle A, \precsim_\omega \rangle$ (describing how the elements of A are deterministically ordered at 'state' ω) such that $\mathfrak{A} = \mathfrak{F}/P$ for some P; the $\mathfrak{A}_\omega$ are assumed to possess a countable dense subset. Under this assumption it is well-known (Krantz et al., 1971, p.40) that there is for each $\omega \in \Omega$ a representation f_ω of $\mathfrak{A}_\omega$ in $\langle \mathbb{R}, \leq \rangle$:

$$\mathfrak{A}_{\omega_0} \xrightarrow{f_{\omega_0}} \langle \mathbb{R}, \leq \rangle$$

$$\mathfrak{A}_{\omega_1} \xrightarrow{f_{\omega_1}} \langle \mathbb{R}, \leq \rangle$$

$$\vdots \qquad \vdots \qquad \vdots$$

$$\overline{\mathfrak{A} = \mathfrak{F}/P \xrightarrow{\;f\;} \langle \Theta, \vartheta \rangle = \mathfrak{F}/P}$$

By Proposition 1, then, $\langle f_\omega \mid \omega \in \Omega \rangle$ can be 'combined' to form a probabilistic representation f of $\mathfrak{F}/P$ in a probabilistic structure $\langle \Theta, \vartheta \rangle$ induced from the background structure $\langle \mathbb{R}, \leq \rangle$. Note that this situation relates to the example at Definition 2. That is, $a \mapsto X_a$ is a random-utility-like representation (though the X_a's need not be measurable).[4] This situation also allows a psychophysical interpretation in a 'Thurstonian' spirit (identify $\langle \mathbb{R}, \leq \rangle$ with a sensory continuum, and interpret A as a set of physical stimuli, $X_a(\omega)$ as the sensory output produced by the physical stimulus a at state ω, $\mathfrak{A}_\omega$ as the corresponding disposition to react in a pair comparison experiment, and $\langle A, p \rangle$ as the resulting pair comparison system).

This may suffice to illustrate that the notion of a P-mixture corresponds to ideas inherent in traditional probabilistic measurement. After having dealt with probabilistic/deterministic structures, let us now consider probabilistic/deterministic axioms. The concept of P-mixture will play a key role in the following discussion.

4. Deriving probabilistic axioms from deterministic ones: What is a probabilistic order?

In the example at Definition 1 we referred to a P-mixture of a family $\langle \mathfrak{A}_\omega | \omega \in \Omega \rangle$ of first-order structures. These structures shared certain structural properties such as transitivity, connectivity and antisymmetry, characterizing linear orders. On the other hand, we have probabilistic conditions like

$$p(a,b) + p(b,c) + p(c,a) \leq 2 \tag{2}$$

encountered in the literature dealing with representations of pair comparison systems $\langle A, p \rangle$. This section discusses within an appropriate model-theoretic framework how these two kinds of properties may be related to each other. By way of example, some simple probabilistic conditions found in the literature will be discussed. We shall focus on condition (2) (Gilbaud, 1953), which Falmagne(1980, p.284f) envisages as a "probabilistic version of the transitivity of a binary relation". This characterization relates condition (2) to the (first-order) structural condition of transitivity on more or less intuitive grounds. A model-theoretic approach, we think, is tailored to the objective of making such intuitions more precise. The following considerations are intended to convey some idea of how such a method could work. Let us start with a definition.

4 By way of comparison, a 'constant utility'-like representation of $\mathfrak{F}/P$ in a probabilistic structure with domain $\mathbb{R}$ may be achieved as follows: Choose a (bijectice) mapping $g: A \to \mathbb{R}$ and deterministic relations $\leq^*_\omega$ on $\mathbb{R}$ such that g represents $\mathfrak{A}_\omega$ in $\mathfrak{R}_\omega := \langle \mathbb{R}, \leq^*_\omega \rangle$ for all $\omega \in \Omega$. g is then a probabilistic representation of $\mathfrak{F}/P$ in $\langle \mathfrak{R}_\omega | \omega \in \Omega \rangle / P$.

Definition 3. Let Σ be a set of sentences of first-order predicate logic, $\mathfrak{K}$ the class of models of Σ (that is, the class of deterministic structures satisfying Σ). A probabilistic structure $\mathfrak{A}$ is called a Σ-*mixture* if there is a family $\mathfrak{F} = \langle \mathfrak{A}_\omega \mid \omega \in \Omega \rangle$ of structures in $\mathfrak{K}$ such that $\mathfrak{A} = \mathfrak{F}/P$ for some finitely additive probability measure P.

Remarks. (i) Note that for a given $\mathfrak{A}$ there can be two mutually inconsistent sets Σ, Σ' of first-order axioms, such that $\mathfrak{A}$ is a Σ-mixture *and* a Σ'-mixture. Consider, for example, a probabilistic structure $\mathfrak{A} = \langle \mathbb{R}, R \rangle$ where $R(a)=1$ for all $a \in \mathbb{R}$. Let $\Sigma = \{\forall z\, Rz\}$, $\Sigma' = \{\exists z\, \neg Rz\}$, then $\mathfrak{A}$ is both a Σ- and a Σ'-mixture. (To see that $\mathfrak{A}$ is a Σ'-mixture, choose $\Omega = \mathbb{R}$, a probability measure P such that $P(\{\omega\}) = 0$ for all $\omega \in \Omega$, and $\mathfrak{A}_\omega = \langle \mathbb{R}, R^\omega \rangle$ where $R^\omega(x) = 0$ if $x = \omega$ and $R^\omega(x) = 1$ otherwise.)

Thus each probabilistic structure $\mathfrak{A}$ determines a set of first-order theories, namely, its 'first-order spectrum' $S(\mathfrak{A}) = \{\Sigma \mid \mathfrak{A} \text{ is a } \Sigma\text{-mixture}\}$. However, in applications only certain sets Σ (and probability spaces $\langle \Omega, \mathfrak{B}, P \rangle$) will be of theoretical interest.

(ii) If $\mathfrak{A}$ is a Σ-mixture as described in Definition 3, then $P(\{\omega \mid \mathfrak{A}_\omega \in \mathfrak{K}\}) = 1$. The concept of a Σ-mixture can considerably be generalized, for instance, by allowing for arbitrary P-mixtures with $P(\{\omega \mid \mathfrak{A}_\omega \in \mathfrak{K}\}) \geq 1 - \varepsilon$ for some fixed $\varepsilon \in (0,1)$ (Σ-mixture with 'error' ε).

The concept of a Σ-mixture makes it possible to derive systems of probabilistic axioms from deterministic ones by looking for probabilistic conditions satisfied by all Σ-mixtures for fixed Σ. Let us consider the case of 'probabilistic order' which can be made precise as follows.

Definition 4. Consider the following first-order axioms

$\forall x \forall y \forall z\, ((x \sqsubset y \wedge y \sqsubset z) \longrightarrow x \sqsubset z)$	(in short φ_T; transitivity)
$\forall x \forall y\, ((x \sqsubset y \wedge y \sqsubset x) \longrightarrow x = y)$	(φ_A; antisymmetry)
$\forall x \forall y\, (x \sqsubset y \vee y \sqsubset x \vee x = y)$	(φ_C; connectivity)
$\forall x\, (x \sqsubset x)$	(φ_R; reflexivity)
$\forall x\, (\neg x \sqsubset x)$	(φ_I; irreflexivity)

(writing $x \sqsubset y$ in place of Rxy). A probabilistic structure $\mathfrak{A}$ is called a *probabilistic linear order*, if $\mathfrak{A}$ is a $\{\varphi_T, \varphi_A, \varphi_C\}$ - mixture; a $\{\varphi_T, \varphi_A, \varphi_C, \varphi_I\}$ - mixture is called a *probabilistic strict order*.

Remarks. (i) The axiom system $\{\varphi_T, \varphi_A, \varphi_C\}$ admits both reflexive, irreflexive and 'mixed' orders (compare the example at Definition 1).

(ii) Probabilistic weak orders, that is $\{\varphi_T, \varphi_C\}$-mixtures, are also of interest. This class includes those probabilistic structures, which can be probabilistically represented in a probabilistic structure induced from $\langle \mathbb{R}, \leq \rangle$.

(iii) There is another, well known, way of relating first-order axioms to probabilistic structures, which is quite different in nature. Each probabilistic structure, say, $\mathfrak{A} = \langle A, R \rangle$, R two-ary, induces a family of deterministic structures $\langle \mathfrak{A}_\rho | \rho \in]0,1] \rangle$, where $\mathfrak{A}_\rho = \langle A, R_\rho \rangle$ with $R_\rho(a,b) = 1 \leftrightarrow R(a,b) \geq \rho$, 0 otherwise. One may now for certain $\rho \in]0,1]$ require $\mathfrak{A}_\rho$ to satisfy specified first-order axioms, yielding probabilistic axioms like $R(a,b) \geq \rho \wedge R(b,c) \geq \rho \rightarrow R(a,c) \geq \rho$ (transitivity).

Proposition 2.

(i) Every $\{\varphi_T\}$-mixture $\mathfrak{A} = \langle A, p \rangle$ satisfies the following probabilistic condition

$$p(a,b) + p(b,c) \leq 1 + p(a,c). \tag{3}$$

(ii) Every $\{\varphi_A, \varphi_C\}$-mixture $\mathfrak{A} = \langle A, p \rangle$ satisfies

$$a \neq b \quad \Rightarrow \quad p(a,b) + p(b,a) = 1. \tag{4*}$$

(iii) By (i) and (ii), every probabilistic linear order $\mathfrak{A} = \langle A, p \rangle$ satisfies (3) and (4*), which in turn implies

$$\neq(a,b,c) \Rightarrow p(a,b) + p(b,c) + p(c,a) \leq 2 \tag{2*}$$

or somewhat stronger

$$\neq(a,b,c) \Rightarrow 1 \leq p(a,b) + p(b,c) + p(c,a) \leq 2 \tag{5*}$$

where $\neq(a,b,c)$ means $a \neq b \vee b \neq c \vee c \neq a$.

(iv) Every probabilistic strict order $\mathfrak{A} = \langle A, p \rangle$ satisfies $p(a,a) = 0$ and thus (2).

Proof. (i) Let $\mathfrak{F} = \langle \mathfrak{A}_\omega | \omega \in \Omega \rangle$ be a family with $\mathfrak{A}_\omega \models \varphi_T$ (short for: φ_T satiesfied by $\mathfrak{A}_\omega$), for all $\omega \in \Omega$, and $\langle \Omega, \mathfrak{B}, P \rangle$ be a probability space such that $\mathfrak{A} = \mathfrak{F}/P$. Since $\mathfrak{A}_\omega \models \varphi_T$ for all $\omega \in \Omega$, we have in particular $\{ \omega \mid a <_\omega b \;\&\; b <_\omega c \Rightarrow a <_\omega c \} = \Omega$ for every $a, b, c \in A$. Obviously this equation is equivalent to the relation $M_{(a,b)} \subset \Omega \setminus M_{(b,c)} \cup M_{(a,c)}$ ($M_{(a,b)} := \{ \omega \mid a <_\omega b \}$), which clearly implies (3).

(ii) Assume $\mathfrak{A}_\omega \models \varphi_A, \varphi_C$ for every $\omega \in \Omega$. Then for all $a, b \in A$ with $a \neq b$ it follows that $M_{(a,b)} \cup M_{(b,a)} = \Omega$ and $\Omega \setminus M_{(a,b)} \cup \Omega \setminus M_{(b,a)} = \Omega$, which immediatlely implies $M_{(b,a)} = \Omega \setminus M_{(a,b)}$, and consequently property (4*) follows.

(iii) and (iv) follow by easy computation. ▫

Remark. Due to Proposition 2, condition (3) could plausibly be called a "probabilistic version of the transitivity of a binary relation". For a full 'justification' one would like to have equivalence rather than only implication; dealing with the question whether the inverse of (i)/(ii) holds too goes beyond the scope of this introductory paper, however.

Condition (2), in contrast, does not imply that $\mathfrak{A}$ is a $\{\varphi_T\}$-mixture , nor is (2), or (2*) implied by $\mathfrak{A}$ being a $\{\varphi_T\}$-mixture. (Counterexamples: $A=\{1,2,3\}$, $p(x,y)=1$ if $(x,y)\in\{(1,2),(2,3)\}$, 0 otherwise; $\langle A,p\rangle$ satisfies (2), but, as easily seen, it is no $\{\varphi_T\}$-mixture. For the other direction define $p(a,b)=1$ for all $(a,b)\in A^2$; then $\langle A,p\rangle$ is a $\{\varphi_T\}$-mixture but does not satisfy (2*).) This suggests to modify the intuition cited above accordingly.

5. Towards a classification of probabilistic axioms: Structural vs. pooling assumptions

In Proposition 2 the probabilistic conditions (4*) and (5*) are referred to in place of their unrestricted variants (4) and (5) found in psychophysics and utility theory.[5]

In fact, (4) is equivalent to (4*) plus

$$p(a,a)=1/2, \tag{6}$$

and (5) is equivalent to (5*) plus

$$1/3\le p(a,a)\le 2/3. \tag{7}$$

The question now arises whether there is some Σ such that any Σ-mixture satisfies (4) or (5), respectively. In both cases the answer is in the negative as implied by the following proposition.

Proposition 3. Assume some Σ to be given such that there is a Σ-mixture $\langle A,p\rangle$ with $0<p(a,a)<1$ for some $a\in A$. Then for all $\rho\in[0,1]$ there is a Σ-mixture $\langle A,p'\rangle$ such that $p'(a,a)=\rho$.

Proof. Let $\langle\Omega,\mathfrak{B},P\rangle$ be a probability space, $\mathfrak{F}=\langle\mathfrak{A}_\omega\mid\omega\in\Omega\rangle$ a family of models of Σ, and $\mathfrak{F}/P=:\langle A,p\rangle$ such that $0<p(a,a)<1$ for some $a\in A$. Let $\mathfrak{A}_\omega=\langle A,Q^\omega\rangle$ and $M=\{\omega\in\Omega\mid Q^\omega(a,a)=1\}$ (which clearly is an element of $\mathfrak{B}$). Given some $\rho\in[0,1]$, a probability measure P' can then be defined by

$$P'(B)=\rho\cdot P(B\mid M)+(1-\rho)\cdot P(B\mid\Omega\setminus M).$$

The P'-mixture of $\mathfrak{F}$ $(=:\langle A,p'\rangle)$ then has the desired properties. ▫

---

5 '(4)'/'(5)' denotes condition (4*)/(5*) without restriction $\ne(a,b,c)$. As for (5) see e.g. Falmagne (1985, p.133).

Generalizing from our preceding considerations, the following programme may be proposed:

Given some probabilistic conditions $\mathfrak{P}_1,\ldots,\mathfrak{P}_n$ of the above kind, try to find a set of first-order axioms Σ such that for all $\mathfrak{A}$ (of a suitable type): $\mathfrak{A}$ is a Σ-mixture if and only if $\mathfrak{P}_1,\ldots,\mathfrak{P}_n$ are valid in $\mathfrak{A}$.

The 'if'-case could be illustrated by the following picture. The fact that a probabilistic structure satisfies the probabilistic conditions $\mathfrak{P}_1,\ldots,\mathfrak{P}_n$ can be 'explained' by assuming $\mathfrak{A}$ to be generated by 'probabilistically merging' a family of deterministic states $\mathfrak{A}_\omega$, each of which is described by Σ. In this case, therefore, Σ will be called a ***sufficient*** set of ***structural*** assumptions for the probabilistic condition $\mathfrak{P}_1,\ldots,\mathfrak{P}_n$ (recall in this connection the 'urn metaphor' at the beginning of section 3 and the example at Definition 1).

In some situations where there is no such 'explanation' (as with the probabilistic conditions (4) and (5)), it is still possible to account for $\mathfrak{P}_1,\ldots,\mathfrak{P}_n$ in terms of some set of structural assumptions by additionally making some *'pooling assumptions'* concerning aspects of how the different 'states' $\mathfrak{A}_\omega$ are distributed. The condition $p(a,a)=1/2$, which is implied by

$$P(\{\omega \mid \mathfrak{A}_\omega \models \varphi_R\}) = P(\{\omega \mid \mathfrak{A}_\omega \models \varphi_I\}) = 1/2,$$

may in the present context be conceived as such a pooling assumption; when added to the structural assumptions characterizing probabilistic linear orders, (4) and thus (2) follow. An analogous remark goes for (7) and (5).

This distinction shows that conditions such as (4) or (5), which at first sight look quite 'homogenous', split into two conditions of a different nature, when judged from a general model-theoretic perspective. This is of interest also from a psychological point of view, since this perspective may be related to intuitions underlying the corresponding psychological models, as outlined before.

6. Some further prospects

As indicated in Remark (ii) at Definition 1, probabilistic structures can be construed as valuations of atomic sentences of a corresponding formal language. In probabilistic model theory (which goes back to Carnap, e.g. 1950, and was further developed mathematically by Łos, 1962,Gaifman, 1964, Scott & Krauss, 1966, and others), probabilistic valuations defined on all of the sentences of a certain formal language are considered. In our opinion it would be interesting to relate both approaches to each other. One reason among others for doing so is the following observation: If Σ is a set of universal sentences then a probabilistic structure $\mathfrak{A}$ is a Σ-mixture if and only if the partial valuation determined by $\mathfrak{A}$ is extendable to a valuation μ of all sentences in such a way that $\mu(\varphi)=1$ for all $\varphi \in \Sigma$. In this connection, theorems regarding the extendability of measures on small fragments of Boolean algebras to the whole algebra (here: the Lindenbaum-Tarski algebra) play an important part. From a measure-theoretic theorem by Horn & Tarski (1948), for instance, it follows that for sets of universal sentences Σ the property of being a Σ-mixture is equivalent to satisfying a certain set of probabilistic conditions which have the form of inequalities between sums of elementary probabilities (such as the conditions discussed above).

Such a model-theoretic approach, which we intend to present in a separate paper, would allow further development of the concepts presented above, thereby making them more profitable for the analysis of probabilistic measurement models and the treatment of related axiomatizability issues.

A further consideration is that it seems to be possible to recast our approach in more 'fundamental' terms, either in formulating the notion of probabilistic structure more 'qualitatively' (using qualitative probability concepts), or in analyzing representations themselves in model-theoretic terms (analogously to the approach in Niederée, 1987).

However, the terms "qualitatively" and "fundamental" should not be understood in the sense of naive empiricism. Nor do we expect probabilistic and more generally Boolean-valued and related logics to yield a general practically feasible solution to the 'error problem', a position sometimes held in this connection (for criticism see Heyer & Mausfeld, 1987). The authors, on the contrary, believe that probabilistic measurement theory – perhaps, indeed, all current measurement theory – primarily serves theoretical purposes, viz. to make explicit the qualitative concepts and the intuitions associated with the term 'measurement' in general, and more specifically to clarify the structural content of the pictures underlying certain probabilistic geometrico-numerical models found in psychophysics and utility theory.

Thurstonian models are typical candidates for such an investigation, some possible elements of which the reader has probably already recognised in the course of the foregoing discussion. Doing full justice to the underlying ideas of such models, however, would require leaving the purely ordinal level of analysis in favour of incorporating further structural components (starting with probabilistic extensive measurement and the like). Eventually, we hope, a model-theoretical clarification of that kind will, among other things, result in a systematic classification of probabilistic conditions as discussed above (e.g. in terms of structural conditions vs. different types of pooling assumptions) and perhaps even make a measurement-theoretic characterization possible of families of distributions associated with random reals.

References.

Carnap, R.(1950). *Logical Foundations of Probability.* Chicago: Chicago Univ. Press.
Colonius, H.(1984). *Stochastische Theorien individuellen Wahlverhaltens.* Berlin: Springer.
Falmagne, J.C.(1980). A probabilistic theory of extensive measurement. *Philosophy of Science* , *47*, 227-296.
Falmagne, J.C.(1985). *Elements of Psychophysical Theory.* New York: Oxford University Press.
Gaifman, H.(1964). Concerning measures on first-order calculi. *Israel Journal of Mathematics, 2*, 1-18.
Guilbaud, G.(1953). Sur une difficulté de la théorie du risque. *Colloques Internationaux du Centre National de la Recherche Scientifique. (Econometric) 40*, 19-25.
Heyer, D. & Mausfeld, R.(1987). On errors, probabilistic measurement and Boolean valued logic. *Methodika, 1*, 113-138.
Horn, A. & Tarski, A.(1948). Measures in Boolean algebras. *Transactions of the American Mathematical Society, 64*, 467-497.
Krantz, D., Luce, R.D., Suppes, P. & Tversky, A.(1971). *Foundations of Measurement, Vol. I. Additive and Polynomial Representations.* New York: Academic Press.
Łos, J.(1962). Remarks on foundations of probability. *Proc. Intern. Congress of Mathematicians, Stockholm 1962*, 225-229.
Luce, R.D. & Suppes, P.(1965). Preference, utility, and subjective probability. In R.D. Luce, R.R. Bush & E. Galanter (Eds.), *Handbook of Mathematical Psychology.* Vol.3. New York: Wiley, 249-410.
Narens, L.(1985). *Abstract Measurement Theory.* Cambridge, Mass.: MIT Press.
Niederée, R.(1987). On the reference to real numbers in fundamental measurement: a model-theoretic approach. In: E. Roskam & R. Suck (Eds.), *Progress in Mathematical Psychology-1.* Amsterdam: North-Holland, 3-23.
Scott, D.(1969). Boolean models and nonstandard analysis. In: Luxemburg (Ed.), *Application of Model Theory to Algebra, Analysis, and Probability.* New York: Holt, Rinehart & Winston, 87-92.
Scott, D. & Krauss, P.(1966). Assigning probabilities to logical formulas. In: J. Hintikka & P. Suppes (Eds.), *Aspects of Inductive Logic.* Amsterdam: North-Holland, 219-264.
Scott, D. & Suppes, P. (1958). Foundational aspects of theories of measurement. *Journal of Symbolic Logic, 23*, 113-128.

PART II

CHOICE, PERCEPTION, COGNITION, AND PERFORMANCE

Some Modified Inhibition Models for Response Time series

Gerard J.P. Van Breukelen

University of Nijmegen *

Abstract

A modification of the Inhibition model of Van der Ven and Smit (Van Breukelen, Jansen, Roskam, Van der Ven & Smit, 1987), is derived which contains four parameters and conceptually lies between the three-parameter Poisson-Erlang model of Pieters and Van der Ven (1982) and the five-parameter Inhibition model, which both appeared to be partly valid in an earlier study. These models were derived to describe response time (RT) series on simple overlearned mental tasks, such as concentration tests, and assume that for a given subject, type of item and condition, the processing time is a constant whereas RT variability is due to the random occurrence of short distractions. The modified model, called the IMAX model, predicts an RT trend much like the exponential trend predicted by the Inhibition model, but in contrast with it, predicts a zero autocorrelation between successive RTs, and under stationarity reduces to the Poisson-Erlang model. Parameter estimators are derived and the model is shown to fit empirical data acceptably. Because some data indicate variability of the processing time, the IMAX and the original Inhibition model are next both derived by replacing the assumption of a constant processing time by the less restrictive assumption that the processing time is a stochast with finite mean and variance and stationary probability density. It is shown that then the IMAX model almost and the Inhibition model exactly predicts the same RT trend as the original Inhibition model with constant processing time. It is further shown that the autocorrelation predicted by the Inhibition model approaches zero as the processing time variance increases. As a result, the IMAX and Inhibition model may become empirically equivalent with respect to trend and autocorrelation, for increasing processing time variance.

1: Introduction: the Poisson-Erlang and the Inhibition model

The Inhibition model was originally devised by Van der Ven and Smit (see Van Breukelen et al., 1987, for its mathematical derivation) to describe response time (RT) series on simple, overlearned mental tasks, such as the dutch Bourdon-Wiersma test, or the german Brickenkamp and Pauli tests, which are generally considered to be concentration tests. The Inhibition model is a modification of the Poisson-Erlang model of Pieters and Van der Ven (1982).

----

* Author's full address: University of Nijmegen, The Nijmegen Institute for Cognition research and Information technology, Dept. of Mathematical Psychology, P.O. Box 9104, 6500 HE Nijmegen, the Netherlands.

Both models assume that RT variability on such tasks is due to the random occurrence of distractions, and that real processing time is constant for a given subject, speed level, test item and experimental condition. The latter is a restrictive assumption which may hold under certain experimental conditions, i.e. if successive items are equivalent and the solution strategy is homogeneous.

Empirical applications of these models suggested that they were globally valid, but with respect to some predictions incorrect. Among others, some data indicated that the assumption of processing time constancy might be too restrictive even for simple overlearned tasks (Van Breukelen et al., 1987). At the same time, a reinterpretation of the Inhibition process, yielding the so-called IMAX model, was suggested by R. Jansen (pers. comm.).

In line with these considerations, this paper discusses some modified Inhibition models. First, the IMAX model will be derived and a preliminary application to data from a concentration test will be given. Next, both for this IMAX model and the Inhibition model, the assumption of processing time constancy is dropped in order to obtain more realistic and flexible model versions, and to check which predictions then change and which remain unimpaired.

Before discussing these models we will restate the assumptions of the Poisson-Erlang (PE) model and the Inhibition (I) model. The PE-model is derived from the following assumptions:

1. Response time is the sum of processing time and distraction time.
2. The processing time is constant for a given subject, speed level, test item and experimental condition, and will be denoted by A.
3. The number of distractions per trial is Poisson distributed with parameter γ.
4. The duration of each distraction is exponentially distributed with parameter δ.

The Poisson distribution may be obtained by assuming that processing periods have an exponentially distributed duration with parameter λ, and by next restricting the total processing time to A. The number of distractions is then Poisson distributed with parameter $\gamma = \lambda A$. The parameters λ and δ are the so-called hazard rates[1] of shifting from processing to distraction and vice versa. The equations for mean and variance can be shown to be (Pieters, 1985):

$$E(T) = A + \gamma/\delta \tag{1}$$

$$\sigma^2(T) = 2\gamma/\delta^2 \tag{2}$$

---

[1] The hazard rate is defined as: $\lambda(t) = f(t)/(1-F(t))$, so: $\lambda(t)dt = P\{t<T<t+dt \mid T>t\}$, which is the probability that a shift will occur in the next time-interval dt, given that it has not occurred yet.

The Inhibition model differs from the PE-model with respect to the third assumption only: instead of assuming a constant hazard rate λ (= γ/A), the Inhibition model assumes that the hazard rate of shifting from work to distraction is equal to *MAX(0,I)*, where:

$$I = I_0 + \mu_1 T_p - \mu_2 T_d \qquad (3)$$

where I_0 is the hazard rate at (processing) time 0, T_p is the total amount of processing time so far, and T_d is the total amount of distraction time so far.

The rationale for this assumption is that processing results in an accumulation of inhibition (i.e. a tendency to stop working) which is reduced during distractions. So distractions may be looked upon as resting periods that serve to prevent excessive inhibition or "mental overload" (Bills, 1964; Pieters, 1985). The concept of "inhibition" should be understood as the tendency to stop processing, i.e. the 'inhibition' to continue work, which is represented by the hazard rate I in the model. No further connotation should be attached to this concept.

This difference with the PE-model has two empirical consequences: First, whereas the PE-model assumes that successive response times are independent, the Inhibition model predicts a negative autocorrelation. Secondly, whereas the PE-model assumes that for a given set of parameter values successive RTs are identically distributed, the Inhibition model predicts an exponentially increasing trend yielding stationarity in the long run, if the initial inhibition I_0 is lower than the stationary expectation of I, which is equal to $(\mu_1/\mu_2)\delta$.

The following equations can be shown to hold for the stationary mean, variance, and *m*-th lag autocorrelation[2], and for the trend across trials, i.e. the expectation of the *k*-th RT (Van Breukelen et al., 1987):

$$E(T) = \alpha \qquad (4)$$

$$\sigma^2(T) = 2(1-\theta)(\mu_1/\mu_2^2) \qquad (5)$$

$$\rho_m = -(1-\theta)(\theta^{m-1})/2 \qquad (6)$$

$$E(T_k) = \alpha + \beta\theta^{k-1} \qquad (7)$$

where: $\alpha = A(1+\mu_1/\mu_2)$, $\theta = \exp(-A\mu_2/\delta)$, $\beta = (1-\theta)(I_0-\delta\mu_1/\mu_2)/\mu_2$

----

[2] Only the first lag autocorrelation is derived in Van Breukelen et al. (1987), but the same procedure can be used to derive further lags. Using the method of induction, the autocorrelation function given here, can be shown to hold (Van Breukelen, 1989).

Application of the PE- and the Inhibition model to data from the dutch Bourdon-Wiersma concentration test (Van Breukelen et al., 1987) showed that:

1. In a continuous task condition, successive response times showed the exponentially increasing trend predicted by the Inhibition model (eq. 7).
2. No autocorrelation could be found in stationary (segments of) RT series, contrary to eq. (6), and the Poisson-Erlang model appeared to fit acceptably on those series.
3. If resting periods were inserted between trials, response times no longer showed a trend, but stayed at the initial level. This is in line with the Inhibition model, as resting periods presumably serve to reduce inhibition, thereby preventing distractions.

So RT trend was as predicted from the Inhibition model, but the stationary distribution appeared to be in line with the PE-model. Furthermore, some effects suggested processing time variability within RT series. Therefore, some new models were derived. The first model to be discussed below, the IMAX model, is intermediate between the Poisson-Erlang and the Inhibition model, conceptually as well as in its predictions. Next, for the IMAX model as well as the Inhibition model, a new version assuming a stochastic processing time *A*, is derived. Both new models are compared with their fixed-*A* counterparts with respect to predicted RT trend and autocorrelation.

2: The IMAX model with fixed processing time

2.1: Derivation of the IMAX model

The following reinterpretation of the concept of Inhibition was given by R. Jansen (pers. comm.): Inhibition represents the extent to which the testee can be distracted from processing the test item at hand by activation of irrelevant information, e.g. from earlier trials. Hence, the initial inhibition on the first trial is zero and inhibition is not broken down during short distractions, i.e $I_0 = 0$ and $\mu_2 = 0$. On the other hand, the inhibition is assumed to be bounded by an upper value I_{max}. So the model has four parameters. We will call this the IMAX model.

To understand the inhibition process as assumed by this model, we may imagine a table on which a box (a certain amount of load or inhibition) is placed on each trial. As soon as the table is filled, the addition of a new box on the table pushes another box from the other end of the table, and the total load on the table does not change anymore. The IMAX model may also be looked upon as a simple approximation of the Inhibition model.

These modifications of the Inhibition model have the following consequence: Until I_{max} is attained, the hazard rate of shifting from work to distraction is

$$\lambda(t) = \lambda(0) + \nu t,$$

where t refers to the processing time clock, and ν denotes the rate of inhibition increase during processing (i.e. μ_1 in the earlier I-model). So the hazard rate at the onset of the k-th trial is equal to $(k-1)\nu A$. Consequently, the number of distractions during the k-th trial is Poisson distributed (Cox & Miller, 1978, p.153-154; Van Breukelen, 1989) with parameter $m_k(A)$, where:

$$m_k(A) = \int_{(k-1)A}^{kA} \lambda(x)\,dx = (k-1/2)\nu A^2 \qquad (8)$$

As before, it is assumed that individual distractions have an exponentially distributed duration with parameter δ.

These distributions can be used to derive the expectation and variance of the k-th response time for all k. In these derivations we will assume that I_{max} is a multiple of νA, so that I_{max} is attained at the completion of a trial and not somewhere during a trial. Of course, the model may also be derived without this assumption, but at the expense of more cumbersome formulas without much gain. So this may be postponed until the model has been shown to hold reasonably well empirically.

We observe first that the total distraction time is a double stochast, as it depends on both the number of distractions and the duration of distractions. Therefore (Mood, Graybill & Boes, 1974, p.159),

$$E(T_k) = A + (E(N_k)/\delta)$$

$$\sigma^2(T_k) = \sigma^2\{E(T_k|N_k)\} + E\{\sigma^2(T_k|N_k)\} = \{E(N_k) + \sigma^2(N_k)\}/\delta^2$$

where N_k refers to the number of distractions during the k-th trial.

Using the fact that N is Poisson distributed, and hence that $\sigma^2(N) = E(N)$, the second equation can be rewritten as:

$$\sigma^2(T_k) = 2E(N_k)/(\delta^2)$$

Finally, inserting $E(N_k) = (k-1/2)\nu A^2$, we obtain:

$$E(T_k) = A + (k-0.5)\nu A^2/\delta \qquad (9)$$

$$\sigma^2(T_k) = (2k-1)\nu A^2/(\delta^2) \qquad (10)$$

These equations only hold as long as I_{max} is not attained, and imply a linearly increasing trend in both expectation and variance of the response times. If I_{max} is attained, the hazard rate of shifting from work to distraction becomes a constant and the model is equal to the PE-model with $\gamma = AI_{max}$. So:

$$E(T) = A(1 + I_{max}/\delta) \tag{11}$$

$$\sigma^2(T) = 2AI_{max}/\delta^2 \tag{12}$$

The trend in the RT expectation can be rewritten as:

$$E(T_k) = \alpha + \beta(k-0.5) \qquad \text{for all } k \leq \theta \tag{13}$$

$$E(T_k) = \alpha + \beta\theta \qquad \text{for all } k > \theta$$

where

$$\alpha = E(T_{stat}) - \beta\theta = A$$

$$\beta = dE(T_k)/dk = (\nu/\delta)A^2$$

$$\theta = I_{max}/(\nu A)$$

So, the model predicts a linearly increasing trend in RT mean (and variance) followed by stationarity from a certain (but unknown) trial on. This type of trend closely resembles the exponential trend predicted by the Inhibition model and may perhaps even be empirically indistinguishable from it (see figure 1). This may be even more likely because averaging across individual time series with different θ's, the IMAX model may even produce a negatively accelerated increasing trend, just like the original model. On the other hand, the model clearly predicts a zero autocorrelation: As inhibition is not broken down during distraction, the amount of distraction in trial *k-1* has no longer any consequence for the initial amount of inhibition and hence the occurrence of distraction on trial *k*.

The model may be evaluated empirically by testing its goodness of fit within experimental conditions (i.e. checking if the trend is as predicted, and if in the stationary part of each time series the autocorrelation is zero and the PE-model fits well), and by testing predictions about experimental effects on model parameters. For instance, the processing time *A* may be affected by item difficulty or by an instruction to work more precisely.

The distraction component may also be influenced, e.g. by the factor of 'massed' vs 'spaced' work. According to the original Inhibition model, we may expect that insertion of resting periods reduces distraction time, whether a resting period of 1 sec. is given after each trial or one of 10 sec. after each tenth trial. Underlying the IMAX model is the assumption that inhibition is not reduced during distractions and that it may be due to e.g. interference from earlier trials. We may then expect that only the second spaced version, i.e. longer but less frequent resting periods, will reduce distraction, through deactivation ('forgetting') of information from earlier trials.

In this paper, the model will only be tested with respect to the RT trend predicted and the goodness of fit under stationarity. Applications involving experimental effects are currently being studied by R. Jansen.

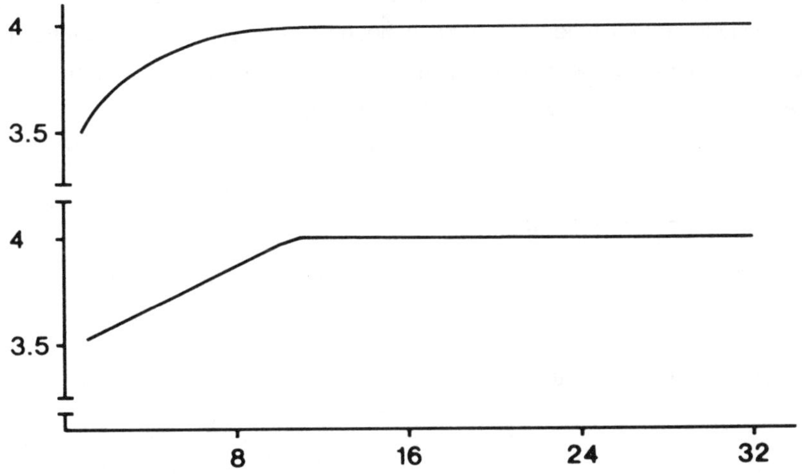

Figure 1: Trend in expected RT as predicted from the Inhibition model (eq. 7; α = 4.0, β = -0.5, θ = 0.7) and the IMAX model (eq. 13; α = 3.5, β = 0.05, θ = 10).

2.2: Parameter estimation and goodness of fit testing

The parameters of the IMAX model may be estimated in two stages: First, the parameters α, β and θ of equation (13) are estimated with a least squares procedure (see below). Next, all four model parameters may be calculated from the (estimates of the) trend parameters and the stationary RT variance, i.e. the variance of all RTs from trial number (θ+1) to the last trial[3], which is equal to $2AI_{max}/\delta^2$.

We will first explain the trend analysis procedure and give the results of some simulations. Next, the model will be applied to RT series obtained on a concentration test.

As shown by (13), the IMAX model predicts that:

$$E(T_k) = \alpha + \beta(k-0.5) \qquad \text{if } k \le \theta$$

$$E(T_k) = \alpha + \beta\theta \qquad \text{if } k > \theta$$

If we define a dummy variable X_k as $(k\text{-}0.5)$ for $k \le \theta$, and as θ for $k > \theta$, then for a given value of θ we obtain a normal linear regression equation, and parameters α and β may easily be estimated by the method of least squares. Next, we choose that value of θ from the alternatives 1,2,..., n, which yields the best fitting trend curve. We will call this the general least squares (gls) method.

A slightly different algorithm is more simple and has the advantage that it yields a strict equality of the stationary RT mean and $\alpha+\beta\theta$, although it may result in a goodness of fit inferior to that attained by the general least squares criterion: For each value of θ (= 1,2,..., n), α and β may be calculated without using least squares by:

$$\sum_{k=1}^{\theta} (T_k)/\theta = \alpha + \beta\theta/2$$

$$\sum_{k=\theta+1}^{n} (T_k)/(n-\theta) = \alpha + \beta\theta$$

thus using the mean RT of the non-stationary part (trials 1 to θ) in the first equation and the mean RT of the stationary part (trials θ+1 to n) in the second. Finally, we may choose θ according to the least squares criterion. Therefore we will call this the conditional least squares (cls) method as opposed to the general least squares (gls) method.

To give an impression of the quality of the gls and the cls methods, table 1 gives the results of three simulations. Each simulation consisted of 40 series of 32 response times. Parameter values were chosen in accordance with data from the first experiment reported in Van Breukelen et al. (1987).

The results suggest that the gls and cls method both yield fairly unbiased estimates for at

---

[3] The θ-th RT has expectation $\alpha + \beta(\theta\text{-}0.5)$ and must not be included in the calculation of the stationary variance. Consequently, this variance can only be estimated if θ is less than the number of trials minus one.

least α and β, and almost the same goodness of fit, as indicated by the proportion of variance explained by the trend function. Hence, the choice between these two methods is by and large arbitrary. We will use the cls method henceforth.

Table 1: Simulations with trend fitting procedures in the IMAX model. True values, mean (and standard deviation) of estimates, and fit as indicated by proportion of variance explained.

method	α	β	θ	fit
true	3.000	0.100	10.000	
gls	2.999	0.100	10.375	0.553
	(0.100)	(0.027)	(2.108)	
cls	2.998	0.100	10.375	0.552
	(0.108)	(0.027)	(2.108)	
true	3.000	0.200	5.000	
gls	2.981	0.222	6.125	0.394
	(0.181)	(0.117)	(5.115)	
cls	2.967	0.220	5.600	0.392
	(0.183)	(0.105)	(3.169)	
true	3.000	0.050	20.000	
gls	2.981	0.053	20.175	0.671
	(0.070)	(0.010)	(4.044)	
cls	2.981	0.052	20.200	0.670
	(0.070)	(0.010)	(3.976)	

The cls method was next applied to RT series obtained with the dutch Bourdon concentration test. In this test, subjects are given a number of equivalent blocks of patterns of 3, 4 and 5 dots, and are asked to distinguish between fours and non-fours as fast and precisely as possible. Response times are recorded per block rather than per response. Each RT series consisted of 32 RTs obtained under standard testing conditions, i.e. continuous working and an instruction to work fast without making errors. The sample consisted of 40 students who were each tested twice, and 36 children of about 10 years old who were each tested once.

The results of the trend analysis suggested that the IMAX model fitted as well as the Inhibition model. Both trend functions (eqs. 7 and 13) explained on the average about 20% of the RT variance and left hardly any trend in the expectation of residuals, while a clear heteroscedasticity (smaller residual variance in the non-stationary part) was observed in time series obtained under continuous work conditions, as predicted by both models. Furthermore, no clear autocorrelation could be detected in the stationary (segments of) series, which is at least as much in line with the IMAX model as with the Inhibition model.

As a measure of goodness of fit under stationarity, the average distance between the predicted and empirical distribution (a measure closely related to the Kolmogorov-Smirnov statistic which uses the maximum rather than the average distance) was calculated for all stationary (segments of) time series, i.e. series without significant ($p = .05$) trend. The IMAX model predicts a Poisson-Erlang distribution. As the probability density function of the Kolmogorov-Smirnov statistic is unknown when parameters have to be estimated from the data (Mood et al., 1974), simulations with the Poisson-Erlang model were done using parameter values derived from the data to estimate the average distance to be expected under the assumption of model validity. The average distance was .035 for the simulations as well as the students' data, and .050 for the childrens' data. Furthermore, most of the time series were positively skewed in their stationary part (trials $\theta+1$ to n), as predicted by the Poisson-Erlang model (Pieters, 1985).

So the model appears to fit the students' data (obtained in a laboratory with computerized testing) well and the childrens' data (obtained with a paper-and-pencil test) acceptably. Therefore, the IMAX model deserves further attention in future empirical studies of concentration tests and other simple mental tasks.

To give an impression of parameter values, table 2 shows average trend and model parameter values. Instead of δ, $1/\delta$ is given, which is the mean duration of distractions. The mean number of distractions is approximately equal to the product of the average A and the average I_{max}.

Table 2: Average values of the estimated parameters of the IMAX model, in two studies with the Bourdon cancellation test.

parameter	students	children
α	3.4	12.9
β	0.10	0.94
θ	15.0	10.3
σ	0.47	2.25
$1/\delta$	0.41	0.14
I_{max}	0.66	1.27
ν	0.024	0.017

In considering these data, it must be kept in mind that for reasons of experimental control (i.e. processing time constancy), each response time was obtained as the sum of 6 choice RTs in the students' experiment (i.e. a response had to be given to each stimulus), and 24 disjunctive RTs in the childrens' study (i.e. a response had to be given only to target stimuli). Furthermore, in the course of parameter estimation, 13 of the 80 students' time series and 7 of the 36 childrens' series had to be eliminated due to trend parameter estimates which prohibited proper model parameter estimation (i.e. $\beta < 0$ or θ near 0 or 32).

According to these estimates, the processing time per response (!) was near 0.55 sec. for both groups and distractions occurred on the average about once per three responses in the students' group and twice per three responses in the children's group.

3: The IMAX model with random processing time

Empirical tests of the PE- and Inhibition model suggested that in spite of thorough experimental control, the assumption of processing time constancy was too restrictive (Van Breukelen, 1989). Furthermore, the application of the IMAX model to the Bourdon series discussed in the previous section, with elimination of the few cases where $\beta < 0$ (indicating a decreasing trend), resulted in an average α above the average minimum RT. This is contrary to the model equation $\alpha = A$, while simulations suggest that α is estimated fairly unbiasedly and consistently by the conditional least squares method used (table 1). In addition, these simulations, which were done with parameter values comparable to those obtained from the students' series, yielded proportions of variance explained by trend, which were much higher than the 20% obtained from the Bourdon experiments (table 1). These findings are in line with a violation of the assumption of processing time constancy.

Therefore, we will now discuss a modification of the IMAX model in which this assumption is dropped. Instead, it is assumed that the processing time is a stochastic variable with finite mean and variance and that its (unknown) distribution is stationary across successive trials of a given RT series. For the case of simple, overlearned tasks, this assumption appears reasonable, as the major source of nonstationarity of the processing time will be practice effects. For the distraction component the same assumptions are made as in the preceding section.

The stationary RT expectation and variance may be derived by using the formulas for the expectation and variance of a double stochast (Mood et al., 1974, p.159) and eqs. 11 and 12, to obtain:

$$E(T) = E\{E(T|A)\} = \mu(1 + I_{max}/\delta) \tag{14}$$

$$\sigma^2(T) = \sigma^2\{E(T|A)\} + E\{\sigma^2(T|A)\}$$

$$= \{1 + I_{max}/\delta\}^2\sigma^2 + \{2I_{max}/\delta^2\}\mu \tag{15}$$

where μ and σ^2 denote the mean and variance of A respectively. This is a special case of the PE-model with stochastic processing time, assuming that $\gamma = A/I_{max}$.

To derive the RT trend, we will start with the expectation of the number of distractions on the k-th trial for the case that stationarity is not attained, i.e. $I_k < I_{max}$. For a given value of the k-th processing time, A_k, and a given inhibition level at the onset of the k-th trial, I_{k-1}, N_k is again Poisson distributed with mean and variance $m_k(A)$. However, both A_k and I_{k-1} (the latter depending on the sum of the preceding $(k-1)$ processing times) now are stochastic. So N_k is a doubly stochastic variable, and:

$$E(N_k) = E(E(N_k \mid \{A\}_k)$$

where $\{A\}_k$ denotes the vector $(A_1, ..., A_k)$.

Using the fact that given $\{A\}_k$, N_k is Poisson distributed with parameter $\nu(A_1 + ... + A_{k-1} + 0.5A_k)A_k$, and using the assumption that successive A's are independently and identically distributed, we obtain:

$$E(N_k) = (k-1)\nu E^2(A) + \nu E(A^2)/2$$

which is easily rewritten as:

$$E(N_k) = (k-1/2)\nu\mu^2 + \nu\sigma^2/2$$

So $E(N_k)$ is a linear function of the trial number k. Using $E(D_k) = E(N_k)/\delta$, with D_k denoting the total distraction time on the k-th trial, the expectation of the k-th RT is seen to be equal to

$$E(T_k) = E(A_k) + E(D_k) = \mu + (\nu/\delta)\{\sigma^2/2 + (k-1/2)\mu^2\} \qquad \text{or:}$$

$$E(T_k) = \alpha + \beta(\omega+k-1/2) \approx \alpha + \beta k \qquad (16)$$

$$\text{where } \alpha = \mu, \quad \omega = (\sigma^2/2\mu^2), \quad \beta = (\nu/\delta)(\mu^2)$$

and generally $\omega \leq 0.5$ to prevent negative processing time values. Now, define θ as $I_{max}/(\nu\mu)$, which is the trial number at the end of which stationarity is attained if all processing times are equal to their expectation. Then the stationary expectation given by (14) equals $\alpha + \beta\theta$, and it will be clear that (16) can only hold if:

- $k \leq \theta$ (as the nonstationary expectation can never exceed the stationary expectation), and:
- $I_k < I_{max}$.

Apart from ω, the RT trend thus seems the same as in the fixed-A model: a linear trend up to trial θ and stationarity afterwards.

However, whereas in the fixed-A model, the probability of stationarity, i.e. $I = I_{max}$, suddenly changes from 0 to 1 between trials θ and $(\theta+1)$, the present model implies that this probability is always greater than zero and smaller than one, and that it gradually increases for increasing trial number in the present model, as it is equal to the probability that the sum of all preceding processing times exceeds $\mu\theta$. This yields the following properties for the trend in $E(I_k)$ and consequently also in $E(T_k)$:

- $E(I_k) < I_{max}$ as $P(I_k = I_{max}) < 1.0$ for all k.
- a monotonely increasing trend in $E(I_k)$.
- a negatively accelerated trend, as the probability of a ceiling effect, $P(I_k = I_{max})$, increases with the trial number.

So the expected RT is a negatively accelerated increasing function of the trial number k with an asymptotic (stationary) value. This resembles the RT trend predicted by the Inhibition model (eq. 7), and may be empirically indistinguishable from it, depending on the distribution of the processing time A. The same effect can be obtained within the fixed-A model (eq. 13) if parameter θ (the trial at the end of which stationary is attained) varies across subjects, and RT series are averaged across subjects.

Without making assumptions about the distribution of A, the trend function can not be fully specified, and the model can not be tested parametrically. However, the usefulness of the present result mainly lies in the demonstration that if the processing time becomes stochastic, the RT trend predicted by the IMAX model approaches the RT trend predicted by the Inhibition model. Considering the fact that a negatively accelerated trend (eq. 7) may be more plausible than a linear trend which suddenly changes into stationarity (eq. 13), this result may be helpful in evaluations of the IMAX vs the Inhibition model.

4: The original Inhibition model with random processing time

We may finally derive the Inhibition model of Van der Ven and Smit with random processing time, in order to see whether this modification can, just like the IMAX model with random processing time, account for the presence of exponential trend and the absence of autocorrelation in empirical studies (Van Breukelen et al., 1987; Van Breukelen, 1989). Such a derivation seems worthwhile since the Inhibition model is intuitively more appealing than the IMAX model: analogously to the dissipation of fatigue during sleep, it assumes that inhibition dissipates during distraction. In this way, the model naturally yields stationarity in the long run, whereas the IMAX model has to assume an I_{max} to prevent RTs from continuing to increase.

We may easily derive the stationary RT mean, variance and first lag autocorrelation for this model. If the mean and variance of the processing time are denoted as μ and σ^2 respectively, then insertion of equations (4) and (5) in the formulas for the expectation and variance for double stochasts (Mood et al., 1974, p.159), yields:

$$E(T) \quad = \quad E(A) + E\{E(D|A)\} \quad = \quad \mu(1 + \mu_1/\mu_2) \tag{17}$$

$$\sigma^2(T) \quad = \quad \sigma^2\{E(T|A)\} + E\{\sigma^2(T|A)\} \quad = \quad \kappa\sigma^2 + \omega(1-\theta) \tag{18}$$

$$\text{where: } \kappa = (1 + \mu_1/\mu_2)^2, \quad \omega = (2\mu_1/\mu_2{}^2), \quad \theta = E\{\exp(-A\mu_2/\delta)\}$$

Finally, the first lag autocorrelation, ρ, may be derived as follows:

$$\sigma^2(T_{k+1}+T_k) = 2\sigma^2(T)\{1 + \rho\}$$

$$\sigma^2(T_{k+1}+T_k) = \kappa\sigma^2(A_{k+1}+A_k) + \omega\{1-E(\exp\{-(A_{k+1}+A_k)\mu_2/\delta\})\}$$

$$= 2\kappa\sigma^2 + \omega(1-\theta^2)$$

as A_{k+1} and A_k are assumed to be independently and identically distributed. Equating these two expressions and rearranging terms yields:

$$\rho \quad = \quad -(1-\theta) \ / \ 2(1+\{\kappa\sigma^2/\omega(1-\theta)\}) \tag{19}$$

As a special case, for constant *A*, ρ reduces to $-(1-\theta)/2$ and lies between 0.0 and 0.5 (eq. 6). As the variance of *A* increases, the autocorrelation becomes smaller and may finally vanish. Furthermore, $(\kappa\sigma^2)/\omega(1-\theta)$ is greater than the ratio of processing time variance to distraction time variance[4], as $\kappa > 1$.

Using the Jensen inequality (Mood et al., 1974, p.72), it is seen that $E\{\exp(-A\mu_2/\delta)\} > \exp\{-E(A)\mu_2/\delta\}$. Hence, θ in the random-*A* model is higher than θ in the fixed-*A* model for a given $E(A)$.

Using the same procedure as for the fixed-*A* Inhibition model, the following recursive formula may be shown to hold for the entire autocorrelation function:

$$\rho_m \quad = \quad \theta\rho_{m-1} \quad = \quad (\theta^{m-1})\,\rho_1 \tag{20}$$

which is eq. (6), but with a smaller ρ_1 and a somewhat higher θ.

----

[4] Application to the Bourdon experiment of Van Breukelen et al. (1987) yields the following result: if we assume that the insertion of resting periods between trials (i.e. spaced work) does not affect the processing time variance, but reduces distraction to almost zero, then comparison of the stationary RT variances obtained under massed (continuous) and spaced working conditions, suggests that about 44% of the massed RT variance was due to processing time variance. Inserting this in eq. (19), results in a reduction of the first lag autocorrelation with about 50%, in line with autocorrelation data from this experiment.

Finally, we may derive the RT trend function for the random-*A* model. First, observe that the following equations hold for the fixed-*A* model (Van Breukelen et al., 1987, p.191):

$$E(T_k) = A(1 + \mu_1/\mu_2) + E(I_{k-1}-I_k)/\mu_2$$

$$E(I_t) = c + (I_0-c)\exp(-bt)$$

where I_k = I at the end of trial k, I_t = I after processing time t, $c = \delta\mu_1/\mu_2$ and $b = \mu_2/\delta$

Using the fact that for random *A*, $E(I_k) = E\{E(I_k|\{A\}_k)\}$, with $\{A\}_k$ denoting the vector $(A_1,...,A_k)$, it can be shown that the trend function of the fixed-*A* model (eq. 7) also holds for the random-*A* model, when we assume that successive *A*'s are independently and identically distributed:

$$E(T_k) = \alpha + \beta\theta^{k-1} \qquad (21)$$

where: $\alpha = (1+\mu_1/\mu_2)E(A)$, $\theta = E\{\exp(-A\mu_2/\delta)\}$,
and $\beta = (1-\theta)\{I_0-(\delta\mu_1/\mu_2)\}/\mu_2$

The interpretation of the trend parameters is almost the same as in the fixed-*A* model.

As in the latter model, parameters may be estimated using the trend parameters, the minimum RT and the RT variance (Van Breukelen et al., 1987). But as the random-*A* model has six instead of five parameters (unless a one-parameter distribution is assumed for *A*), there are not enough equations to estimate the model parameters, unless the third moment, which is unstable, is used. However, we may test the model by trend analysis, autocorrelation analysis, and predictions about experimental effects on the trend parameters and the stationary RT variance.

More importantly however, the present derivation shows that processing time variability within RT series may mask the negative autocorrelation between successive response times, while leaving the RT trend unimpaired. Thus, the simultaneous presence of increasing trend and absence of a clear negative autocorrelation does not contradict the Inhibition model, at least if the assumption of processing time constancy is dropped.

In addition, it may be observed that a negative autocorrelation may be further attenuated by either of the following effects:

1. A non-significant trend in distraction time. As eqs. (7) and (23) show, strict stationarity is never attained, so a small trend may still persist after e.g. eight trials, although trend analysis reveals no significant trend after exclusion of the first eight trials.
2. A non-significant trend in the processing time.

5: Distraction models: a survey

We now have five models of response times on simple overlearned mental tasks. They reveal a trend toward more flexible models at the expense of additional parameters. Table 3 gives a summary of all models.

Table 3: A survey of distraction models and their parameters (+ indicates the generalized model with random processing time).

model	processing parameters	distraction parameters
PE	A	δ, γ
IMAX	A	δ, ν, I_{max}
INH	A	$\delta, \mu_1, \mu_2, I_0$
IMAX +	μ, σ	as IMAX
INH +	μ, σ	as INH

The oldest model is the Gamma-model (not treated here) which contains three parameters and only differs from the Poisson-Erlang model in its assumption that the number of distractions per response is a constant. The Poisson-Erlang model still contains three parameters, but replaces the assumption of a fixed number of distractions by a Poisson distribution. The PE-model appears to fit better than the Gamma-model (Pieters, 1985). However, both models assume that for a given set of parameter values response times are independently and identically distributed, whereas time series are generally non-stationary (Van Breukelen et al., 1987; Van Breukelen, 1989).

The Inhibition model of Van der Ven and Smit replaced the Poisson distribution for the number of distractions by an inhomogeneous Poisson proces. This model accomodates for exponentially increasing trend and predicts a negative autocorrelation in stationary time series at the expense of two more parameters. Recent experiments confirmed the prediction of an exponentially increasing trend, but no clear autocorrelation was found (Van Breukelen, 1989).

In this paper we first derived a four-parameter model, the IMAX model, which predicts a trend much like that predicted by the Inhibition model, but zero autocorrelation, and which under stationarity reduces to the Poisson-Erlang model. Thus, with respect to the number of parameters as well as the empirical implications this model is intermediate between the Poisson-Erlang and the Inhibition model.

All these models share the assumption of a constant processing time and an exponential distribution of the duration of distractions. The first assumption seemed too restrictive in the light of some experimental findings. Therefore, it was replaced by the assumption of a random processing time with stationary distribution and finite mean and variance. Both the Inhibition model and the IMAX model were generalized, assuming a random processing time, thus introducing an additional model parameter (except when a one-parameter distribution is assumed for *A*). Although the model parameters can not be estimated, at least not without making specific assumptions about the distribution of *A*, the models can be globally tested by trend analysis and experimental effects.

More importantly however, the models with random processing time show that empirical data from concentration tests do not necessarily contradict either the Inhibition model or the IMAX model, i.e. RT series may show a (negatively accelerated) increasing trend, without a clear negative autocorrelation in the stationary part. Furthermore, the IMAX and Inhibition model may be empirically indistinguishable as far as trend and autocorrelation analysis are concerned. They may perhaps be compared with respect to predictions about experimental effects, e.g. "massed vs spaced" work as suggested before.

Recapitulating, we see that two of the three assumptions of the oldest model, the Gamma model, have been relaxed gradually in successive models. First, the number of distractions was no longer constant (the PE-model), nor necessarily stationary (the Inhibition model). Now we have some models in which the processing time is no longer constant either.

A logical further development might be a model which drops the assumption that the processing time is stationary, e.g. a model which can accomodate for learning effects. For instance, in the fixed-*A* Inhibition model the RT trend equation can easily be derived if $A_k = (m+1-k)A$ or $(m/2^{k-1})A$, with m such that A_k is a multiple of *A*. These assumptions imply that the first RT has expectation equal to the sum of the first m trials as defined by eq. (7), i.e. $m\alpha + \beta(1-\theta^m)/(1-\theta)$. Analogous expectations may be derived for further RTs. Using the empirically plausible restriction that $\alpha > |\beta/(1-\theta)|$, with the latter term reflecting the difference between mean RT and stationary mean RT (α), it is then easily seen that a monotonely(!) decreasing RT trend is obtained, due to a masking of the increasing Inhibition trend by the decreasing trend in the processing time.

To maintain clear distinctive predictions, it is wiser to keep to simple overlearned tasks. As already recognized by Kraepelin and Oehrn at the end of the 19-th century, the measurement of distraction (or as they called it, "fatigue") should not be confounded by practice effects (Eysenck & Frith, 1977, p.20,32).

However, the value of a model with trend in the processing time lies in the demonstration that the finding of some RT series with (monotonely) decreasing trend do not necessarily falsify the Inhibition theory, just like the derivation of models with random processing time showed that a failure to find autocorrelation does not invalidate the Inhibition theory.

Concludingly, this paper shows that the failure to confirm all predictions derived from a given model (e.g. the Inhibition model) does not necessarily imply the rejection of this model altogether. Rather, it may suggest a modification of either the model or the task conditions under which the model may hold. Examples of the first alternative are the replacement of the Inhibition model by the IMAX model, and the skipping of the constancy assumption. The other alternative implies the use of tasks that are even more simple than the Bourdon task, and perhaps the administration of even more practice trials. To enable tests of the generalizability of the Inhibition theory to typical mental tasks, the first alternative may be preferred. Experimental factors, such as massed (continuous) vs spaced (interrupted) work may be used to estimate the relative contribution of processing and distraction time to the RT mean and variance, and to evaluate hypotheses concerning the exact nature and function of distraction without complete specification of the RT distribution.

Acknowledgements

- This research was supported by grant no. 560-267-003 from the PSYCHON foundation of the Netherlands Organization for Scientific Research (N.W.O.).
- Thanks are due to Prof. Dr. D. Vorberg for some very useful comments on an earlier draft of this paper.

References

Bills, A.G. (1964). A study of blocking and other response variables in psychotic, brain-damaged and personality-disturbed patients. ***Behaviour Research and Therapy, 2,*** 99-106.

Cox, D.R. & Miller, H.D. (1978). ***The theory of stochastic processes.*** London: Chapman and Hall (reprint of 1965 issue by Methuen & Co.).

Eysenck, H.J. & Frith, C.D. (1977). ***Reminiscence, motivation and personality: a case study in experimental psychology.*** New York: Plenum Press.

Mood, A.M., Graybill, F.A. & Boes, D.C. (1974). ***Introduction to the theory of statistics.*** Auckland/London: McGraw-Hill (3rd ed).

Pieters, J.P.M. & Van der Ven, A.H.G.S. (1982) Precision, speed and distraction in time-limit tests. ***Applied Psychological Measurement, 6,*** 93-109.

Pieters, J.P.M. (1985). Reaction time analysis of simple mental tasks: a general approach. ***Acta Psychologica, 59, 227-269.***

Van Breukelen, G.J.P., Jansen, R.W.T.L., Roskam, E.E.Ch.I., Van der Ven, A.G.G.S., & Smit, J.C. (1987). Concentration, speed and precision in simple mental tasks. In: E. Roskam & R. Suck (eds.) ***Progress in Mathematical Psychology, vol. 1.*** Amsterdam: Elsevier (North-Holland), pp. 175-193.

Van Breukelen, G.J.P. (1989). Concentration, speed and precision in mental tests. Doctoral dissertation, University of Nijmegen, the Netherlands.

Mental Processing and Distraction

Ronald W. Jansen and Edward E. Roskam)*
University of Nijmegen

Abstract

The domain of interest of this paper is limited to the continuous performance on simple two-choice reaction time (RT) tasks. It is generally found that the RTs, the RT variance and the error rate increase over trials. There is no simple explanation for these findings in terms of a speed-accuracy trade-off, nor in terms of some additive factor processing model. Evidently some time gets 'lost'. To tackle this problem the RT was split into two components: processing time and distraction time, which is time spent on other mental activities than those to solve the task. This is the basic assumption of the inhibition theory. This theory is introduced in some length along with its formalisation into some mathematical models and along with the presentation of some empirical evidence. The inhibition theory contains a mechanism that predicts an increase in RTs with time on task. In the experiments of this study a single task condition (the monotonous condition) was contrasted with an alternating task condition (the mixed condition). Whereas most other theories would predict more decrement in RT performance in the more demanding mixed condition, the inhibition theory predicts a larger increase of RTs in the monotonous condition. The results supported the inhibition theory. In the mixed condition the subjects lost less speed over the series of trials, made fewer errors, had lower RT variance and were on the average as fast as in the monotonous condition.

A decrement in reaction time (RT) performance in a condition with a continuous administration of well-practiced trials (a so-called massed condition) is consistently found across a number of different tasks and within different populations of subjects. In our own experiments (Breukelen & Jansen, 1987a; Jansen & Breukelen, 1987; Ven, Smit & Jansen, in press) the increasing RT curves in the massed condition were found using a dot counting task (the Bourdon task), a digit-addition task, and a letter-matching task with adults as well as with children, and even with paper and pencil tests administered in the school situation. Bertelson and Joffe (1963) and Sanders and Hoogenboom (1970) reported also the same kind of effects in massed series of their experiments. In a broader sense this impairment in performance is found in tracking tasks (Eysenck & Frith, 1977) and in vigilance tasks (Mackworth, 1969; Parasuraman, 1985). We hold the position that the same mechanism is responsible for the decrement in performance in each of the cases mentioned. Up till now no

*) Nijmegen Institute of Cognition and Information, Department of Mathematical Psychology, University of Nijmegen, P.O. Box 9104, 6500 HE Nijmegen, The Netherlands, Bitnet-Earn U212775 @ HNYKUN11.

satisfying answer was given to the question concerning the structure of this mechanism.

The aim of this study is to give an adequate explanation for the problem just described. Our approach is as follows. First, a mathematical model will be presented that can describe and predict the observed RT series. Secondly, a theory is proposed that explains the RT increase in the massed condition, as well as some other effects. Finally, several experiments are reported in which hypotheses of this theory are tested. The specific predictions are derived by means of the mathematical model. As a start, however, it is important to give a precise description of the problem dealt with.

The Problem: Decrement in continuous performance

In the present study RT is the dependent variable. A computerized administration of two choice RT tasks was used in all of the experiments to be discussed. A considerable amount of trials was given in a continuous manner in each task condition. On each trial a RT was recorded. Another important detail of the experimental paradigm was the instruction to work as fast as possible, but without making errors. In all of the series of trials subjects were urged not to commit any errors. Additional feedback was given in the practice series. Therefore, performance of the subject should depend solely on his speed.

An example of this kind of experiments is an experiment of Breukelen and Jansen (1987a). The Bourdon task (see for the original version Bourdon, 1895) served as the simple mental task. In this task dot patterns are shown containing either three, four or five dots. Subjects had to respond YES on a stimulus with four dots, and otherwise they had to respond NO. After considerable practice subjects got a condition with a continuous series of trials (the massed condition) and a condition with regular rest periods between blocks of trials (the spaced condition). The results of this experiment were as follows. In the massed condition the RTs tend to increase over trials. It can be added that both the $RT_{Variance}$ and the error rate increase during the session. No such increase is found in the spaced condition. Further, the RT_{Mean}, $RT_{Variance}$ and the number of errors are lower in the spaced condition than in the massed condition. In figure 1 the average RTs (averaged over 40 subjects) per block of six trials are given for the two conditions mentioned. Moreover, the fitted RT curves according to the INHIBITION model are depicted for the massed and the spaced condition.

No obvious explanation can be given for this increasing RT curve. For example, taking into account that besides the RTs also the error rate increased, it becomes evident that a speed-accuracy trade-off can not explain the observed RT series in the massed condition. Further, an appropriate additive factor processing model can hardly be constructed in an attempt to cover this problem, since the two conditions were absolutely equivalent with respect to the stimulus and response administration. As a last example, one could mention fatigue as an explanatory factor (skipping for the moment the objection that a label by itself is not an explanation). However, fatigue would *not* be expected to be present at the start of the time series, and furthermore, once fatigue is present, one would expect an accelerating

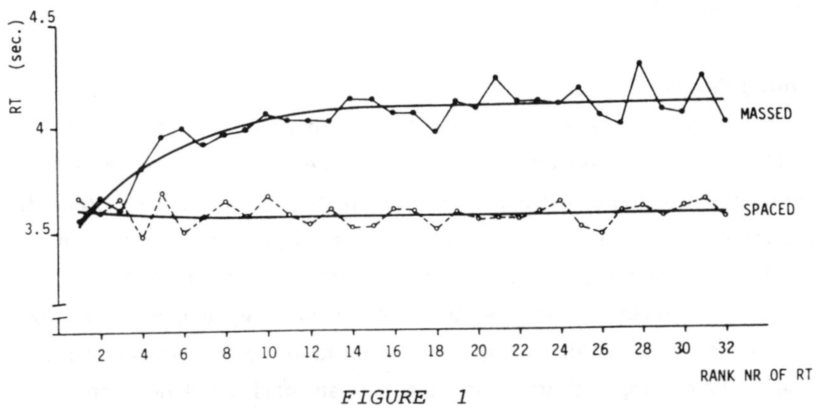

FIGURE 1

The massed versus spaced condition (Bourdon task, (Rearranged from Breukelen et al., 1987b)

time series. The observed RT series is decelerating from the start.

THE THEORY AND MATHEMATICAL RT MODELS

The developments of the RT models at our department started with the basic assumption that RT is the sum of alternating periods of *processing* and *distraction*. In other words, it is assumed that the RT per trial can be decomposed into processing time (PT) and distraction time (DT). DT was defined as time consumed by all mental activities which do not contribute to task performance. All RT models assume also that PT per trial is constant for a given subject, task and condition. The model parameter for this constant is denoted by the capital *A*. This assumption of a constant PT per trial implies that the experimental paradigm should control for the equivalence of trials. Further, all models assume that the duration of each simple distraction period is negatively exponentially distributed with parameter δ.

We consider a number of RT models, differing on the assumption regarding the number of the distraction periods. Breukelen, Jansen, Roskam, Ven & Smit (1987b) gave a complete review of the RT models developed sofar. The INHIBITION model of Ven and Smit (Ven et al., in press) is theoretically the most important model. A brief description will be given below. This model will not be pursued here, since there are some practical difficulties in its parameter estimation and since it predicts an autocorrelation which is very hard to find, even if it is in fact present (see for more information on this subject Breukelen & Jansen, 1987a). Instead of this model the IMAX model will be used. The IMAX model predicts about the same RT curve as the INHIBITION model, but predicts no autocorrelation. The parameters of the IMAX model are easier to estimate and they can be more easily interpreted. For more details of the comparison of the IMAX model and the INHIBITION model see Breukelen (1989a, this volume; 1989b).

The Inhibition theory

The following theory is proposed for the continuous processing of a repetitive task. At the beginning of the task almost no distractions are present. The task relevant processors become gradually inhibited during continuous task performance. As we assume that at any time some mental activity is executed, task *ir*relevant processing will gradually consume more time. These periods are called distractions. In other words, in the recovery periods of the task relevant processors some other mental activities take place, and these activities are called distractions. The main point of this theory is that a mechanism is constructed that is responsible for the eliciting of distractions. This mechanism is called inhibition.

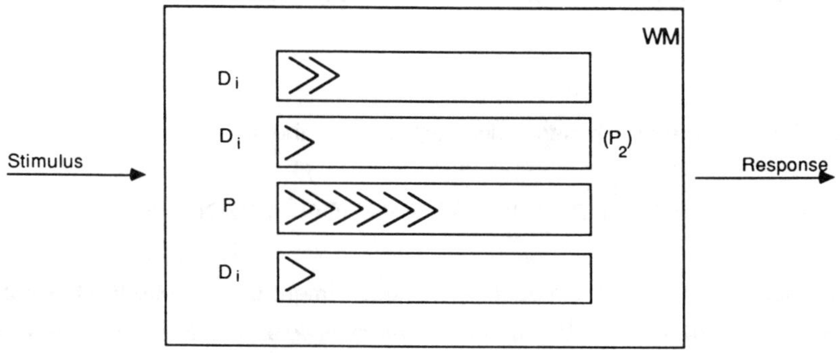

FIGURE 2

A cognitive model of the inhibition theory. The symbol > denotes the activation level of a processor.

In figure 2 an illustration is presented of a cognitive model for the inhibition theory. The task relevant processors are depicted as box P. Constantly activating these processors inhibits them. Putting this another way, the task relevant processors get blocked, and, subsequently, they need a recovery period. Within these recovery periods other mental processes are activated, as indicated by the boxes D_i in figure 2. All these processors are thought to be functionally equivalent to the central processor within the Working Memory (WM) concept of Baddeley (1986).

Evidence for the inhibition theory. The massed versus spaced experiment gives a nice illustration of how the inhibition mechanism works. In contrast to the prediction for the massed condition this theory predicts a stationary time series for the spaced condition. The rest periods between the blocks of trials give the task processors the opportunity to recover. This recovering property of the theory is formalized in the INHIBITION model, where the hazard rate[1)] of shifting from processing to distraction decreases with the distraction time. The rest pauses induced in the spaced condition are functionally equivalent to long distractions. The predictions that the $RT_{Variance}$ is lower under the spaced condition, and also that DT and, therefore, the RT_{Mean} are lower under spaced than under massed, all follow from the assumption that the hazard rate decreases during the rest pauses, i.e. that the task processors recover during these periods of forced rest. As was reported in the introduction, the results found in the experiment of Breukelen and Jansen (1987a), but also in some other experiments (Jansen & Breukelen, 1987), support these predictions and, therefore, corroborate the inhibition theory.

The INHIBITION model

The model assumes that the number of distraction periods depends on the hazard rate of shifting from processing to distraction. This hazard rate increases with the accumulated processing time and decreases with the accumulated distraction time, where accumulation is taken over an entire series of trials. In other words, the expectation of the number of distractions becomes larger with the accumulation of the processing time, but decreases with the time consumed by the distractions. In mathematical terms we get:[2)]

The number of distractions is approximately inhomogeneously Poisson distributed with parameter γ,

$$\text{where } \gamma = h(t) \times A$$

$$\text{with } h(t) = \max[0, I(t)]$$

$$\text{and } I(t) = \mu_1 T(P) - \mu_2 T(D) + I_0$$

where $T(P)$: *the accumulated processing time*
$T(D)$: *the accumulated distraction time*
I_0 : *the initial inhibition value* [1]

The INHIBITION model predicts a negative exponentially increasing RT curve, if $I_0 < 0$. Further, a negative autocorrelation is predicted in the stationary part of the RT curve.

The IMAX model

For the present purpose the INHIBITION model is replaced by a more convenient model. The simplification of the INHIBITION model is such that the hazard rate of shifting from processing to distraction increases linearly with the processing time, until a maximum of the

1) The hazard rate is defined as: ft/(1 - F(t)), so $\lambda t dt = P\{ t < T < t + dt \mid T > t \}$

2) The present parametrisation comes from Roskam and it is more completely described in Breukelen et al. (1987b). A different parametrisation was used by Ven et al. (in press).

hazard rate is reached. This maximum is called I_{MAX}.

The specific assumption of the IMAX model is:

The number of distraction periods is inhomogeneously Poisson distributed with parameter γ,

where $\gamma = h(t) \times A$

$$\text{with} \quad h(t) = \nu \times (\text{accumulated PT}) \quad \text{if } h(t) < I_{MAX}$$
$$h(t) = I_{MAX} \quad \text{else} \qquad [2]$$

It should be stressed that performing a single trial is considered as a continuous stream of alternating processing and distraction periods. Each trial (or a number of trials) is finished after a fixed amount of processing. The assumption of a constant processing time can easily be violated by systematic factors, affecting the processing time, such as repetition effects. Therefore blocks of trials, balanced with respect to such factors, were taken as the unit of analysis. A distraction is thought to be the processing of task irrelevant information. In fact, distractions are all other mental activities than those necessary for the performance of the task at hand. The predicted RT curve of the IMAX model is shown in figure 3. Both PT and DT are depicted.

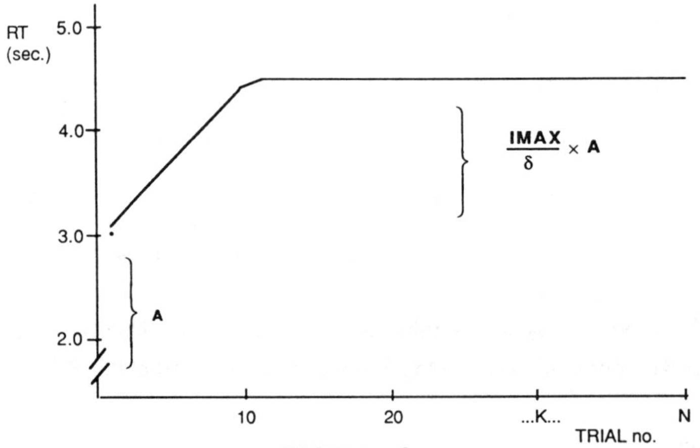

FIGURE 3

The predicted IMAX model RT curve, with $A=3.0$, $\delta=7.5$, $I_{MAX}=3.75$, *and* $\nu=0.125$

Estimation of the model parameters from the data. [3] The expectation of RT on trial *k* is depicted in figure 3. In formulas we get:

$$\begin{aligned}
&\text{for } h(t) < I_{MAX}\\
&E(RT_k) = A + (1/\delta)(k-\tfrac{1}{2})\nu A^2\\
&VAR(RT_k) = (2k-1)(1/\delta^2)\nu A^2\\
&\text{for } h(t) \geq I_{MAX}\\
&E(RT_k) = A + A(1/\delta)I_{MAX}\\
&VAR(RT_k) = 2I_{MAX}(1/\delta^2)A
\end{aligned} \qquad [3]$$

The model parameters are A, δ, I_{MAX} and ν. These parameters can be estimated by the following procedure. First, the parameters α,β and θ of the following trend function are estimated with a least squares procedure:

$$\begin{aligned}
&E(RT_k) = \alpha + \beta(k-\tfrac{1}{2}), && \text{for all } k \leq \theta\\
&E(RT_k) = \alpha + \beta\theta && \text{else}
\end{aligned} \qquad [4]$$

For reasons of convenience we assume that I_{MAX} is reached at the end of trial θ. Next all model parameters can be calculated from the trend parameters and the stationary variance of RT, σ^2, i.e. the variance of all RTs from trial number $(\theta+1)$ to the last, by means of the following equations:

$$\begin{aligned}
A &= \alpha\\
\delta &= \frac{2\beta\theta}{\sigma^2}\\
I_{MAX} &= \frac{\delta\beta\theta}{A}\\
\nu &= \frac{I_{max}}{\theta A}
\end{aligned} \qquad [5]$$

As shown in figure 3 the model predicts a linearly increasing trend in the expectation of RT, but also in $RT_{Variance}$, until stationarity is reached from a certain (unknown) trial on. This type of trend closely resembles the exponential trend predicted by the INHIBITION model (cf.Breukelen, 1989a, this volume).

A major disadvantage of the IMAX model is that the hazard rate of shifting from processing to distraction does not decrease with the distraction time. This means that we have to assume that this hazard rate decreases during the resting periods of the spaced condition. Once this additional assumption is made, the same predictions are derived from the IMAX model as from the INHIBITION model.

---

[3] All formulas were derived by Breukelen (see Breukelen, 1989b)

It should be stressed that the inhibition theory is at stake, and not the RT models. Further, it should be stressed that the INHIBITION model is the most important model, but that with respect to the prediction of PT and DT in the massed condition the IMAX model and the INHIBITION model are empirically almost equivalent. In the following experiments the inhibition theory is tested once more, and the IMAX model is used to derive specific predictions.

MONOTONOUS VERSUS MIXED TASKS

Monotony and boredom are two terms frequently encountered in the literature on ergonomics. They are relevant to situations in which people have to execute the same kind of operations for hours and hours, but also to tasks of a repetitive nature in the laboratory (see for a review Davies, Shackleton & Parasuraman, 1983). In such monotonous and boring situations an impairment in performance is always observed. Davies et al. (1983) pointed out that no common definition of monotony and boredom exists.

Welford (1965) expressed that boredom should be associated with 'underload'. Typically boring situations seem to be those in which attention is required, but little information is conveyed. The association of boredom with underload serves to distinguish boredom from fatigue. The latter is regarded by Welford as resulting from chronic overloading of the sensory, central, or response mechanism involved in task performance.

Baschera and Grandjean (1979) drew the same distinction between monotony and fatigue, associating monotony with underload and fatigue with overload. According to these authors the states of monotony and fatigue have in common that both produce impairment of performance and feelings of fatigue and sleepiness. A difference is that monotony is quickly reversible, while fatigue requires an adequate recovery period. They conclude from their experiments that repetitive tasks with a low degree of difficulty produce a state of monotony due to the lack of stimulation, whereas a repetitive task with a high degree of difficulty produces a state of fatigue due to a high mental load.

In the present study we are dealing only with well-practiced simple mental tasks. Such repetitive tasks are therefore called monotonous tasks in line with the remarks of Welford and Baschera and Grandjean. These authors put forward the concept of underload to explain the impairment of performance on such monotonous tasks. From that point of view task performance would improve if the monotonous task would be made more stimulating.

Whereas Welford (1965) and Baschera and Grandjean (1979) only describe and label the situation of monotony, the inhibition theory poses the mechanism that explains why performance on a monotonous task decreases, and what conditions lead to better performance. For example, one could call alternation of tasks more stimulating, and one could predict that stimulation leads to better performance. However, this labeling of a stimulating situation again does not explain why performance will improve. In case of the alternation of tasks the inhibition theory will explicitly give the reasons for the improvement of RT performance.

In this section a hypothesis of the inhibition theory will be tested which deals with the monotonous task condition versus the alternating tasks condition. This latter condition will be called mixed task condition. The inhibition hypothesis will be contrasted with a plausible alternative. In the experiments to be discussed monotonous tasks and mixed tasks were administered in a massed version. Monotonous means within this context that the subject is given only trials with stimuli of one kind of task, e.g. the Bourdon task. In the mixed task condition stimuli of two or three different tasks are alternated in a random order, e.g. alternating Bourdon trials with trials of a letter-matching task. It is important to notice that stimuli were presented self-paced with a negligible response stimulus interval in both task conditions. In this way subjects were forced to work continuously. Details of this experiment will be presented in a later section.

The inhibition hypothesis. It states that the processors of the task relevant information will become inhibited because of the repetition of the required action. These processors need a recovery period. Assuming that information is processed at any time, it follows that while the task relevant processors are 'blocked', only task irrelevant information can be processed.

This line of reasoning leads us to the notion that another task can be executed within the period of time that the first task processor is inhibited. In figure 2 the processors of the second task are indicated by P2 between parentheses. The processors of the first task can recover in the time consumed by the processors of the second task. The assumption is made that the two tasks have none or only a few processors in common. Therefore, this inhibition hypothesis predicts that the distraction time will be lower in the alternating task condition, since the two (or more) tasks work as each others distractions. The second task is irrelevant for the first task, but not irrelevant for the overall task performance.

An alternative hypothesis: loss of attentional capacity. To show that the above mentioned hypothesis is not at all trivial, an alternative hypothesis is presented. In some experiments on vigilance tasks Parasuraman (1985) found that performance got worse especially in those conditions that had a high event rate. From these and other results he concluded that loss of attentional capacity is the factor responsible for the decrement in performance in vigilance tasks. In case of the monotonous versus mixed tasks this hypothesis would state that the increase in RT would be largest in the condition with the largest demand for attentional capacity. Since in the mixed condition two task instructions have to be kept active in working memory, the prediction of this hypothesis would be that the decrement in performance would be larger in the mixed task condition.

Experiment 1

Method

Subjects. Five male and seven female students volunteered as subjects for about two hours per person. They received each about 8 US dollars for their participation.

Apparatus. An Olivetti M28 Personal Computer was used along with a so-called APLEX interface card and a panel with three buttons, which was especially designed and manufactured for this kind of experiments. The screen was placed about 40 cm in front of the subject. The stimuli (letters, digits, or dot patterns) were white against a black background. The hue was determined by the subject during the practice session and held constant afterwards.

Design. Seven conditions were administered in a full within subjects design. These conditions consist of three monotonous conditions, three mixed conditions of two alternating tasks (mixed-two conditions), and one mixed condition of three alternating tasks (the mixed-three condition). To keep the task for the subject workable, they received six of the seven conditions, i.e. three monotonous conditions, two out of the three mixed-two conditions, and the mixed-three condition. The presentation order of these conditions was: first the monotonous tasks, then the mixed-two conditions, and finally the mixed-three condition. Across subjects the sequence of the conditions was balanced as much as possible.

Procedure. The following tasks were used: 1) a letter-matching task, 2) the Bourdon task, and 3) a digit-addition task. This letter-matching task was introduced by Posner (1978). In this task stimuli are presented containing two characters. Both upper- and lowercase characters belong to the set of stimuli. In the Name match version of this task the subject is asked if both characters stand for the same Lexical symbol. In the Physical match version the subject has to respond to the question if the characters are identical with respect to their Physical appearance. For example, the combination 'A a' elicits a YES response under the Name match condition, but a NO response under the Physical match condition. The Name match version of the Posner task is used in all three experiments to be reported. The Physical match is only administered in experiment 3.

In the digit-addition task subjects are asked if the addition shown is correct or not. This task is a modification of the Pauli test (see Arnold, 1961). Hence, this task will be called the Pauli task.

Per condition two practice series of 120 trials were administered followed by the experimental series of 240 trials. The stimulus sequences were balanced per block of six trials, especially with respect to YES/NO stimuli. RT was recorded per trial, but the analyses were performed on RT per block. A short coffee break was given after the first three conditions. Instructions were presented on the screen, just before every new condition.

Results

Figure 4 shows the fitted RT curve of the average time series of the monotonous conditions and of the mixed conditions. Although this figure may be too global to state definite conclusions, the two curves are in line with the inhibition hypothesis, since the RT curves are less increasing in the mixed condition.

The results, presented in the following sections, are treated in three respects. Firstly the average curves of the mixed conditions are split by task. Secondly the individual time series

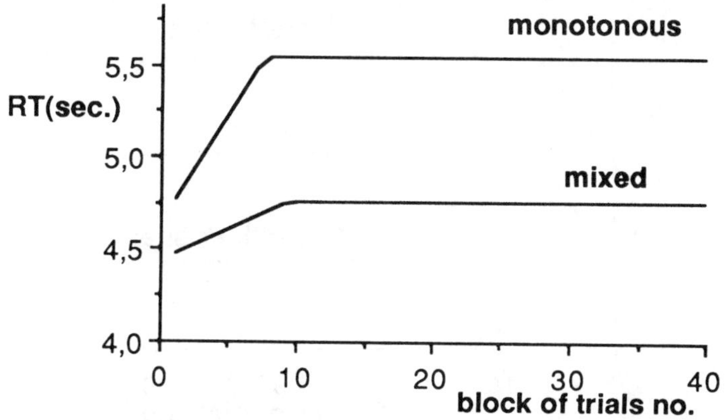

FIGURE 4

The fitted RT curves of the Monotonous and the Mixed task conditions.

will be examined. And finally, analyses of variances will be presented with the task variables (RT_{Mean}, $RT_{Minimum}$, error rate, etc.) as the dependent variables.

As described earlier, every condition contains 240 trials. In the mixed-2 conditions every 12 successive trials consisted of six trials of each task. Therefore, it was possible to decompose the time series of the mixed conditions into two reconstructed time series, one of each task. Taking again six trials for one RT, we got 20 RTs for each task in the time series. Since half of the trials (all belonging to the other task) are cut out of the original trial series, these 20 RTs should be plotted against the original horizontal axis of the total 40 blocks of trials. For example, figure 5 shows the reconstructed time series of the Bourdon trials out of the Bourdon-Posner condition and the reconstructed time series of the Bourdon trials from the Bourdon-Pauli condition. The monotonous condition of the Bourdon task is also depicted in figure 5. To give a fair comparison of the monotonous versus the mixed conditions this figure has two interpretations of the horizontal axis. The 40 blocks of trials of the monotonous condition cover the same range of trials as the 20 blocks of trials of the reconstructed Bourdon trials out of the mixed conditions.

So, in figure 5 the Bourdon RT curves of the monotonous condition and of the reconstructed mixed conditions are shown. The RT curves of the monotonous condition is much more increasing than the reconstructed RT curves of the mixed conditions. The same pattern of trend curves was found for the Pauli tasks and for the Posner tasks, in the monotonous, and mixed conditions, respectively.

We also fitted the IMAX model to each individual time series. If all monotonous conditions on the one hand and all mixed conditions on the other hand are taken together, table 1 shows that more curves increase in the monotonous conditions than in the mixed conditions.

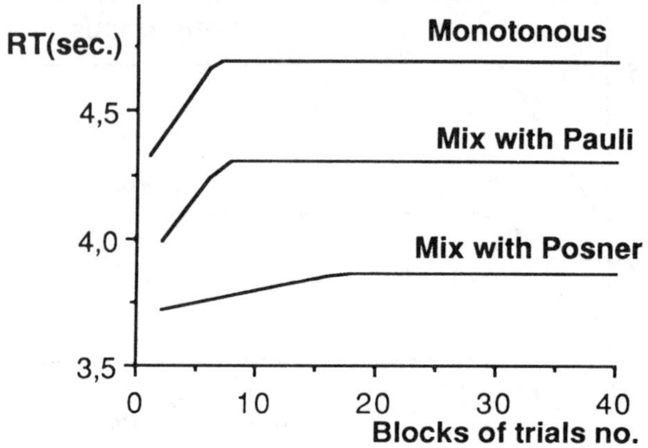

FIGURE 5

The fitted Bourdon`RT curves in both the monotonous and the mixed conditions.

Table 1 also yields the results of the experiments 2 and 3 (discussed below) with respect to the number of increasing and decreasing individual time series. In all three experiments the monotonous conditions have more increasing RT curves than the mixed conditions. The specific results of experiments 2 and 3 will be commented in a later stage.

The ANOVAs. The parameters of the IMAX model only have acceptable values in case the time series increases. For instance, $I_{MAX}A/\delta$ (the expression for DT in the stationary part of the time series) will have a negative value if the time series decreases. In order to have acceptable values for DT and PT in case of decreasing RTs, some robust approximations of PT and DT are proposed. A robust (though slightly biased) estimator of PT is the $RT_{Minimum}$ (see Breukelen, 1989b). DT can, then, be expressed as (RT_{Mean}-$RT_{Minimum}$). Therefore, DT/PT can be estimated by (RT_{Mean}-$RT_{Minimum}$)/($RT_{Minimum}$), i.e. the distraction time per unit processing time. Since $RT_{Minimum}$ and DT/PT can be calculated for every time series these task variables will be taken into account in the following ANOVAs, and not the IMAX model parameters.

The ANOVA results are very clear-cut. The mixed conditions have significantly lower values than the monotonous conditions (see table 2) on all task variables except for the error rate. To illustrate the amount of processing time and distraction time in the monotonous and the mixed conditions table 2 also gives the average values of all task variables in the monotonous and the mixed conditions.

It should be emphasized that DT/PT is a measure for the distraction time per unit of processing time. This means that the analyses on this measure are fairly independent of the analyses on PT, i.e. $RT_{Minimum}$. In fact, the correlation between $RT_{Minimum}$ and DT/PT was on the average near zero. The correlations between RT_{Mean}, $RT_{Minimum}$ and $RT_{Variance}$ are

TABLE 1

Number of increasing and decreasing individual time series for all three experiments

EXPERIMENT	CONDITION	INCREASING	DECREASING
1			
	Monotonous	30 (7)	6 (1)
	Mixed	25 (4)	11 (1)
2			
	Monotonous	27 (7)	9 (2)
	Mixed	4 (1)	20 (5)
3			
	Monotonous	34 (12)	14 (2)
	Mixed	26 (2)	22 (5)

NOTE. Between brackets the number of significant curves, $F(2,df_2)$=MS(IMAX-model)/MS(MEAN-model), $\alpha=.05$

usually quite substantial, ranging between 0.6 and 0.8.

Discussion

The results of Experiment 1 support the inhibition hypothesis. On the average the RT curves of the monotonous task increase more than those of the mixed conditions. The same accounts for the individual time series. The ANOVA on DT/PT shows that the proportion of distraction time is far greater in the monotonous condition than in the mixed conditions. All these results are in conflict with the loss of attentional capacity hypothesis and are in line with the inhibition hypothesis. Distraction time becomes less when two tasks are alternated.

The fact that the $RT_{Minimum}$ is significantly lower in the mixed conditions than in the monotonous conditions indicates a sequence effect. Subjects learn to do the task more efficient. However, reasoning in this way implies that the difference in distraction time found between monotonous and mixed conditions could be even larger, since a learning effect is masked in the monotonous conditions. Absence of that learning effect could lead to more detectable distraction time, because the estimated processing time would most probably be lower, and therefore the ratio DT/PT would be larger. The problem of a decreasing processing time has been handled elsewhere (Breukelen, Wollenberg & Ven, 1987c). For the moment, it should be recorded that the sequence effect in the presentation order may discredit the effects found in the ANOVA, but the conclusion that distraction time is larger in

TABLE 2

Means and F-values per task variable in experiment 1

VARIABLES	MEANS		F	Sign. of F
	MONO.	MIXED	(df=1,50)	
RT_{Mean}	5.5	4.7	15.63	$p < .001$
$RT_{Minimum}$	4.07	3.58	14.05	$p < .001$
$RT_{Variance}$	1.12	0.71	6.80	$p < .05$
Error Rate	5.33	5.49	0.11	$p > .05$
DT/PT	0.34	0.31	5.50	$p < .05$

DT/PT = $(RT_{Mean}-RT_{Minimum})/RT_{Minimum}$

MONO. = Average across Bourdon, Posner, and Pauli (3 times N=12)

MIXED = Average across all MIXED2 (3 × (N=8)), and MIXED3 (N=12)

monotonous conditions than in mixed conditions could be even more true.

Experiment 2

In Experiment 1 the sequence of the monotonous and mixed conditions was not balanced across subjects. Therefore, a sequence effect might have caused the differences found on the task variables between these two conditions. A replication of the first experiment was done in which the presentation order of all the conditions was balanced across subjects.

Method

This experiment was divided into two parts. The first part contains a comparison between the monotonous conditions of the Posner task and the Bourdon task, and the mixed condition of these two tasks. In the second part, a similar comparison was made using the Posner task and the Pauli task. Twelve subjects who did not participate in Experiment 1, volunteered in Experiment 2 receiving a financial reward. The apparatus was exactly the same in this experiment as in Experiment 1.

Procedure. Firstly, all practice series were administered in a counterbalanced design within subjects. Two practice series in every condition had to be performed. After these practice series a short break was given. Thereupon the three conditions (Bourdon, Posner, and their mix) were administered in a completely balanced design across subjects. A second break was given followed by the Pauli condition and the mix of the Pauli task and the Posner task. All details of this experiment were the same as in Experiment 1.

Results

With respect to the average RT curves the results of Experiment 1 and Experiment 2 are about the same. Again the RT curves of the monotonous conditions are increasing and those of the mixed conditions are even decreasing. This decreasing effect in the mixed task conditions is very well visible in table 1. This table shows that a vast majority of the curves of the mixed conditions are decreasing, whereas most of the curves of the monotonous conditions are increasing (see table 1).

The ANOVAs, however, are quite different from those of the first experiment. In the first part, in which the Posner task and the Bourdon task were compared with their mix, the $RT_{Minimum}$ was much lower in the monotonous conditions than in the mixed condition, $F(1,22)=17.7$, $p<0.001$. A similar effect was found on the RT_{Mean}, $F(1,22)=6.6$, $p<0.05$. No other significant difference was found. Notwithstanding this fact, DT/PT is lower in the mixed condition, $F(1,22)=3.37$, $p=0.08$, as was predicted by the inhibition hypothesis. Part of the difference in the $RT_{Minimum}$ can be caused by the smaller error rate in the mixed condition.

In part two of this experiment, i.e. the comparison of the Posner and the Pauli task with their mix, there was no difference in RT_{Mean} or $RT_{Minimum}$ between mixed and monotonous conditions, and only the $RT_{Variance}$ appears to differ significantly. The mixed condition had the lower value. This condition was the last one in the presentation order.

Discussion

Summarizing the results of Experiments 1 and 2 we get to the following conclusions. In Experiment 1 more individual time series are increasing in the monotonous condition than in the mixed condition. The same holds for Experiment 2. Only in Experiment 2 time a vast majority of the RT curves in the mixed condition is decreasing.

In Experiment 1, RT_{Mean}, $RT_{Minimum}$ and $RT_{Variance}$ were much lower in the mixed conditions than in the monotonous conditions. On the other hand, $RT_{Minimum}$ and RT_{Mean} are much higher in the mixed conditions than in the monotonous conditions in Experiment 2. Both experiments yield the same results with respect to DT/PT. This ratio is lower in the mixed condition as predicted by the inhibition theory.

Possible interpretations of these results are: (1) the effects found on RT_{Mean} and $RT_{Minimum}$ in Experiment 1 might be due mainly to a sequence effect, which is commonly labelled as learning, and (2) the design of Experiment 1 might have been very well chosen with regard to the requirement that a task should be overlearned. The mixed tasks of Experiment 2, however, clearly do not fulfill this requirement of overlearnedness, as the majority of the RT curves is decreasing in that condition. The design of Experiment 2, therefore, might have more confounding factors than that of Experiment 1. The mixed conditions of Experiment 1 have a learning advantage over the monotonous conditions, whereas the mixed conditions of Experiment 2 violate the assumption of overlearnedness of the task. In Experiment 1, however, the conclusions regarding the inhibition hypothesis hold a fortiori, whereas the conclusions in Experiment 2 are disputable.

Considering the shapes of the RT curves of the two conditions the conclusions of both experiments are in favor of the inhibition hypothesis stating that distractions occur because the processor of the task relevant information is inhibited. This hypothesis assumes that more than one processor operates in the human information processing system. During the period that the processor (of one task) is inhibited (the non-work period of that processor), the other processor can do its job in an alternating task condition. If, however, both tasks use mostly the same processors, then again the distraction time should be as large as in the monotonous task condition. Experiment 3 attempts to test that hypothesis.

Experiment 3

The hypothesis tested in this experiment states that the distraction time of two alternating tasks which require the use of mostly the same processors will be larger than the distraction time of two tasks using different processors. This hypothesis follows directly from the inhibition hypothesis stated earlier. Schematically figure 2 could be modified a bit for this purpose. In figure 6 the overlap between the processors of the two mixed tasks is illustrated.

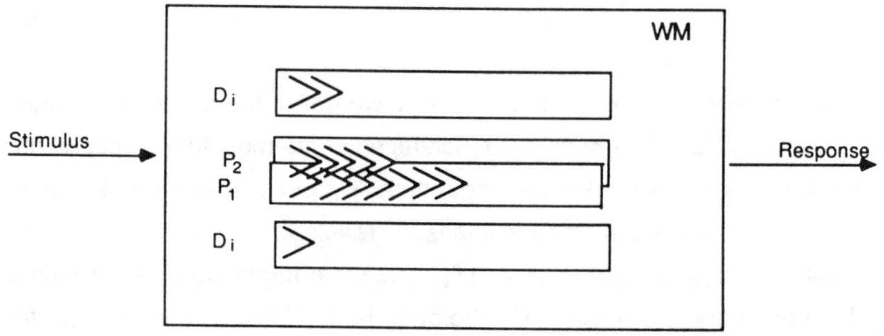

FIGURE 6

The cognitive model for the mixed task condition.

This experiment was worked out in the following way. Two versions of the letter-matching task of Posner, i.e. the Name match and the Physical match, were both used in this experiment. Further, the Bourdon task and a Lexical decision task were used. The idea was that the Bourdon task, a dot counting task, uses at least partly the same (figural) processors as the Physical letter-match, and that the Lexical decision task uses at least in part the same (verbal) processors as the Name match of the Posner task. Further, we assumed that the Bourdon task and the Name match task had less processors in common than the Lexical decision task and the Name match task. In the same way we assumed that the Physical match task had more processors in common with the Bourdon task than with the Lexical decision task.

The following predictions were formulated: 1) the condition of alternating the Bourdon task with the Physical match task will show more distraction time than the condition of alternating the Lexical decision task with the Physical match task, and 2) the condition of alternating the Bourdon task with the Name match task will show less distraction time than the condition of alternating the Lexical decision task with the Name match task.

Method

Subjects. Subjects were seven male and nine female student volunteers. They were paid about 8 US dollars for their session that took less than two hours.

Task and Procedure. The Bourdon task and the Posner Name match task were already mentioned. The Lexical decision task consisted of the presentation of a word with the question if this was a correct Dutch word. The word length and the familiarity of the word were controlled. The non-words were formed by changing one or two characters while keeping the word phonologically Dutch. The Posner Physical match had only a different instruction in comparison to the Posner Name match. This time subjects were asked only to match the characters on their shape. This means that the combination 'A a' has to be answered as different.

Subjects were partitioned into two groups of eight. The first group received the Posner Name match. The second group got the Posner Physical match. Both groups got furthermore the Bourdon task and the Lexical decision task. Within each group all possible mixed-two conditions were administered. The design of this experiment is depicted in table 3.

Table 3 shows that the monotonous conditions were administered first, followed by the mixed conditions. These mixed conditions were counterbalanced within and across subjects. For that purpose the subjects received the relevant mixed conditions two times. The Bourdon-Lexical decision combination is the non-relevant mixed condition, since the hypothesis makes no statement with respect to this combination. This Bourdon-Lexical decision condition was given as a filling condition in the administration order of the conditions without making the subjects suspicious with regard to purpose of the experiment.

Results

Preview. First, the overall average RT curves of the monotonous conditions and the mixed conditions are again in line with the inhibition hypothesis. This means that on the average the RT curves of the monotonous conditions are more increasing than the RT

TABLE 3

The design of experiment 3

GROUPS		CONDITIONS
1	BOURDON	1
	POSNER NAME	2
	LEXICAL DECISION	3
	LEX-DEC + NAME (1)	4
	BOURDON + NAME (1)	5
	BOURDON + LEX-DEC	6
	BOURDON + NAME (2)	7
	LEX-DEC + NAME (2)	8
2	BOURDON	1
	POSNER PHYSICAL	2
	LEXICAL DECISION	3
	BOURDON + PHYSICAL (1)	4
	LEX-DEC + PHYSICAL (1)	5
	BOURDON + LEX-DEC	6
	LEX-DEC + PHYSICAL (2)	7
	BOURDON + PHYSICAL (2)	8

NOTE. Condition 1 through 3, and 4 through 8 were balanced across subjects (per group)

curves of the mixed conditions. This difference in the shape of the time series is again illustrated by the number of increasing and decreasing individual time series. Table 1 shows that the monotonous conditions also have the larger number of increasing RT curves in experiment 3.

Monotonous versus Mixed. This section contains information concerning the comparison of the monotonous versus the mixed conditions for the total group of subjects. The next section deals with the ANOVAs per group, in which only the relevant mixed conditions are involved.

Table 4 shows the results of the ANOVAs comparing monotonous with mixed. Completely in line with the inhibition hypothesis, the mixed conditions have significantly lower values on DT/PT, on the $RT_{Variance}$, and on the RT_{Mean}, and no differences are found on the $RT_{Minimum}$ or the error rate. These ANOVA results are even more clear-cut than those of the first two experiments, since in this case the processing time (estimated by the $RT_{Minimum}$)

TABLE 4

Means and F-values of task variables in experiment 3 (first presentation of mixed, see design)

VARIABLES	MEANS		F	Sign. of F
	MONO.	MIXED	(df=1,70)	
RT_{Mean}	3.54	3.38	14.91	$p < .001$
$RT_{Minimum}$	2.78	2.76	0.19	$p > .05$
$RT_{Variance}$	0.23	0.15	16.02	$p < .001$
Error Rate	5.31	5.41	0.03	$p > .05$
DT/PT	0.28	0.22	14.18	$p < .001$

MONO. = Average across Bourdon, Posner, and Lexical-Decision (N=16, per task)

MIXED = Average across all three MIXED2 task combinations (N=16)

appears equal for both conditions. The differences found on DT/PT, the $RT_{Variance}$, and on the RT_{Mean} constitute clear evidence for the inhibition theory.

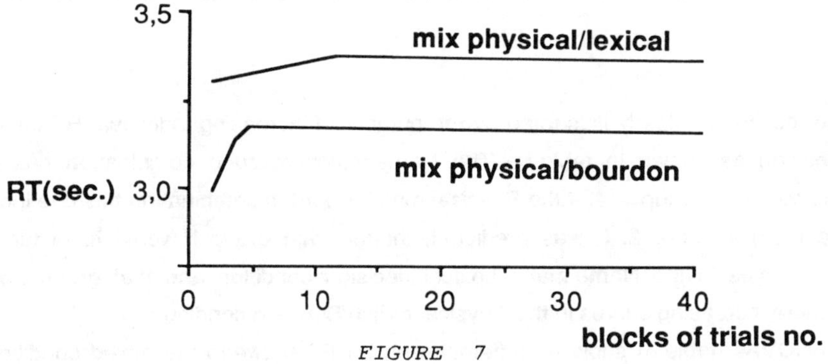

FIGURE 7

The RT curves of the Bourdon/Physical match condition and the Lexical-decision/Physical match condition

Same tasks mixed versus different tasks mixed. Figure 7 shows the curves of the Physical match/Bourdon condition versus the Physical match/Lexical decision condition for group 2. The differences in the slopes of the fitted RT curves supported only very slightly the predictions. The first combination of which it was assumed that the overlap of processors would be larger, indeed had the more increasing averaged RT curve.

In the other group (group 1), however, the results were contradictory to the predictions. The Name match/Bourdon combination had a more increasing curve than the Name match/ Lexical decision combination (see figure 8). It was assumed that the Name match and the Lexical decision task would have more processors in common, and therefore would show a larger inhibition effect, i.e. a more increasing curve.

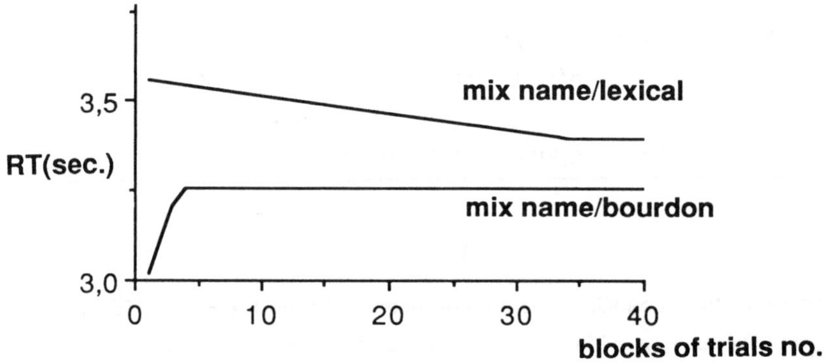

FIGURE 8

The RT curves of the Bourdon/Name match condition and the Lexical-decision/Name match condition

These results are clearly illustrated by the number of increasing individual RT curves in each condition as shown in table 5. The Name match/Bourdon combination has more increasing curves in group 1, and the Physical match/Bourdon combination has one increasing curve more in group 2. It was predicted, though, that group 1 would have far more increasing curves in the Name match/Lexical decision condition and that group 2 would have far more increasing curves in the Physical match/Bourdon condition.

The ANOVAs (table 6) show no difference on DT/PT between the mixed conditions in either group. Table 6 also shows no difference of the mean values of DT/PT between the mixed conditions per group. The conditions differ only markedly on the RT_{Mean}, but this difference can be ascribed to the higher difficulty of the Lexical decision task.

TABLE 5

Number of increasing and decreasing individual time series per condition per group

GROUP	CONDITION	INCREASING	DECREASING
1	NAME/BOURDON (N=8, 2 sessions)	8 (2)	8 (0)
	NAME/LEX-DEC (N=8, 2 sessions)	5 (0)	11 (4)
2	PHYSIC/BOURDON (N=8, 2 sessions)	9 (0)	7 (0)
	PHYSIC/LEX-DEC (N=8, 2 sessions)	10 (0)	6 (2)

NOTE. Between parentheses the number of significantly increasing, or decreasing curves (α=.05) are recorded

Discussion

Assuming that the Physical match task acts upon the same processors as the Bourdon task, and that on the other hand the Name match task uses the same processors as the Lexical decision task, the inhibition theory predicts that for each group separately the mixed conditions with the more similar tasks would yield more increasing RT curves, i.e. more DT, than the mixed conditions with the less similar tasks. The results did not support the predictions. The reasons for these negative findings can be either that the theory does not hold, or that the chosen tasks do not use the same processors.

The discussion needs some refinement on this point. Besides the overlap of processors there are at least two other factors that influence the inhibition mechanism, (1) the time needed by the processors to recover, and (2) the processing time of the alternative task. To start with the last factor, it is evident that the processor of the task with the shorter processing time has more time to recover than the processor of the other task. If, however, the response time of the shorter task, is long enough, the processor of the task with the larger processing time also has enough time to recover sufficiently. (In this reasoning we assumed that the processors of the two tasks do not overlap.)

These notions should be given more consideration in future research on mixed tasks with overlapping processors. Regarding Experiment 3 the first conclusion to be drawn is that the tasks did not have that much processors in common, as we supposed they would have.

TABLE 6

Means and F-values of the mixed conditions per group

VARIABLES	MEANS BOU/POS	MEANS POS/LEX	F (1,21)	Sign. of F
GROUP 1 (Name match)				
RT_{Mean}	3.25	3.46	12.23	$p < .001$
$RT_{Minimum}$	2.69	2.79	4.20	$p > .05$
$RT_{Variance}$	0.13	0.16	1.75	$p > .05$
Error Rate	4.9	5.8	0.92	$p > .05$
DT/PT	0.21	0.24	2.19	$p > .05$
GROUP 2 (Physical match)				
RT_{Mean}	3.14	3.35	17.58	$p < .001$
$RT_{Minimum}$	2.61	2.72	3.97	$p > .05$
$RT_{Variance}$	0.11	0.18	8.42	$p < .01$
Error Rate	4.9	4.7	0.50	$p > .05$
DT/PT	0.20	0.23	2.63	$p > .05$

NOTE. Both sessions are considered in these analyses.

Further, the Lexical decision task had the highest PT (3.8 seconds over a block of six trials), but this PT was not that much larger than the PTs of the other tasks (3.5 seconds for the Name match, 3.2 seconds for the Physical match, and 3.5 seconds for the Bourdon). No convincing evidence was found that the Lexical decision trials cut out of the mixed conditions show a more increasing RT curve than the RT curves of the trials of the other tasks.

Given the earlier results the inhibition theory is not abandoned at this moment. Instead the conclusion is drawn that apparently the human information processing system may be organized in a different way from what we assumed and that the tasks used in experiment 3 each have their own specific processors. A replication of this last experiment should be conducted with tasks, of which it is much more likely that they use the same processors. For example, the Physical match task can be administered either with alphabetic characters or mathematical symbols. Mixing these two tasks would render a task that could be seen as a monotonous task. Therefore, about as many increasing RT curves should be found in this mixed condition as in the two corresponding monotonous task conditions.

CONCLUDING REMARKS

The aim of this study was to give an adequate explanation for the consistently found decrement in continuous RT performance. The inhibition theory explains why RT performance gets worse. The main feature of this theory is the inhibition mechanism, which says that a continuous activated processor gets inhibited ('blocked') and consequently needs a recovery period. In some former studies the massed versus spaced experiments already demonstrated the explanatory value of the inhibition theory (see Breukelen et al., 1987b). The present study added empirical support, since the predicted monotonous versus mixed condition effect was found. The cognitive model depicted in figure 2 and figure 6 might be a helpful illustration in the development of theories in this field of attention and performance. For example, the inhibition mechanism seems a good candidate for explaining the decrement of RT performance in vigilance tasks, despite the work of Parasuraman (1985).

The distinction between underload and overload to characterize a specific task situation as given by Welford (1965) and others is of minor importance to the inhibition theory. The inhibition mechanism is thought to be present in every task situation, but it can be of less influence in some task situations, e.g. in tasks with a large processing time variability. For the domain of monotonous tasks the inhibition mechanism is responsible for the decrement in performance according to the theory presented in this study.

A challenging direction in extending the inhibition theory is the mathematical modeling of the mixed task performance. The activation of the non-overlapping processors of the second task is releaving the first task, whereas the activation of the overlapping processors inhibits by definition the processors of the first task. Pulling the line a bit further along this way of thinking the mixed task condition may prove a fruitful instrument in determining how much two tasks have in common i.e. how many processors the two tasks share. Theorizing, modeling, and experimenting are three parts of the same approach to get more insight in this area of cognitive performance.

References

Arnold, W. (1961). *Der Pauli-Test.* [The Pauli-Test.] München: Johan Ambrosius Barth.

Baddeley, A.D. (1986). *Working Memory.* Oxford: Oxford University Press.

Baschera, P., & Grandjean, E. (1979). Effects of Repetitive Tasks with Different Degrees of Difficulty on Critical Flicker Frequency (CFF) and Subjective State. *Ergonomics, 22, 4,* 377-385.

Bertelson,P., & Joffe, R. (1963). Blockings in prolonged serial responding. *Ergonomics, 6,* 109-116.

Bourdon, B. (1895). Observations comparatives sur reconnaissance, la discrimination et l'association. *Revue Philosophique, 40,* 153-185.

Breukelen, G.J.P. van (1989a, this volume). Some modified inhibition models for response time series.

Breukelen, G.J.P. van (1989b). *Concentration, Speed and Precision in mental tests: a psychonometric approach.* Unpublished Doctoral Thesis. University of Nijmegen.

Breukelen, G.J.P. van, & Jansen, R.W.T.L. (1987a). *The role of concentration in simple mental tasks: an experimental test of some models.* Internal Report 87-MA-08, University of Nijmegen, the Netherlands.

Breukelen, G.J.P. van, Jansen, R.W.T.L., Roskam, E.E.Ch.I., Smit,J.C., & Ven, A.H.G.S. van der (1987b). Concentration, speed and precision in simple mental tasks. In: Roskam, E.E.Ch.I. & Suck, R. (eds.) *Progress in Mathematical Psychology, vol.1.* Amsterdam: North-Holland Publ. Co.

Breukelen, G.J.P. van, Wollenberg, A.L. van den, & Ven, A.H. van der (1987c). *Decomposing Response Times with the Poisson-Erlang model: a comment.* Internal Report 87-MA-02, University of Nijmegen, the Netherlands.

Davies, D.R., Shackleton, V.J., & Parasuraman, R. (1983). Monotony and Boredom. In: G.R.J. Hockey (Ed.) *Stress and Fatigue in Human Performance.* Chichester: John Wiley & Sons Ltd.

Eysenck, H.J., & Frith, C.D. (1977). *Reminiscence, motivation and personality: a case study in experimental psychology.* New York: Plenum Press.

Jansen, R.W.T.L. & Breukelen, G.J.P. van (1987). *Distraction and Inhibition in continuous CRT performance.* Internal Report 87-MA-01, University of Nijmegen, the Netherlands.

Mackworth, J. (1969). *Vigilance and habituation: A neuropsychological approach.* Harmondsworth (U.K.): Penguin.

Parasuraman, R. (1985). Sustained Attention: A Multifactorial Approach. In: Posner, M. & Marin, J. (Eds.) *Attention and Performance XI.* Hillsdale, N.J.: Lawrence Erlbaum Associates.

Posner, M.I. (1978). *Chronometric Explorations of Mind.* Hillsdale, N.J.: Lawrence Erlbaum Associates.

Sanders, A.F. & Hoogenboom, W. (1970). On the effects of continuous active work on performance. *Acta Psychologica, 33,* 414-431.

Ven, A.H.G.S. van der, Smit, J.C. & Jansen, R.W.T.L. (in press). Inhibition in prolonged work tasks. *Applied Psychological Measurement.*

Welford, A.T. (1965) Fatigue and Monotony. In: Edholm, O.G. & Bacharach, A.L. (Eds.) *The Physiology of Human Survival.* London: Academic Press.

A Procedure for Facilitating an Expert's Judgements on a Set of Rules.

Cornelia E. Müller *

Technische Universität Braunschweig

Abstract

A knowledge structure that is known to be a formal basis for a system assessing students' knowledge is constructed from an expert's judgements. Such judgements refer to a body of questions from a specified field, and represent the information concerning which of these questions may be asked, and which can be considered redundant, depending on the answers given by a student during the assessment procedure. The expert's judgements therefore select rules of the form: "if a student has answered all questions of this subset of questions incorrectly, then do not ask this specific question."

The selection of the appropriate rules by an expert causes the following problems: firstly, the number of possible judgements grows exponentially with the size of the set of questions under consideration; secondly, contradictory judgements may eventuate, and, thirdly, the number of questions in the conditional part of the rules may be too large to permit a reliable judgement.

This paper therefore suggests a procedure for restricting the expert's judgements to those that do not logically follow from previous judgements. Contradictory judgements are avoided, and the number of questions in the conditional part of the rules to be judged is minimized within specific equivalence classes. This procedure is appropriate for use within an interactive system for supporting an expert when selecting rules.

1. Introduction

Expert systems frequently use knowledge represented by a set of rules (Buchanan and Shortliffe, 1984). This paper introduces an interactive procedure for supporting an expert in judging which set of rules is an appropriate representation of the knowledge in question.

By way of illustration, we will refer to the example of a procedure that supports an expert in judging which set of rules represents the meta-knowledge in the system of Doignon and Falmagne (1985), by which students' knowledge is to be assessed. Whereas such a system, on the one hand, might embody a large number of possible questions, on the other hand, it might also pose only a few but highly pertinent of these to the student. Those questions that a specific student is not asked during the assessment

* Technische Universität Braunschweig. Institut für Psychologie, Postfach 3329. 3300 Braunschweig, F.R.G. (West-Germany). E-MAIL: I3160501 at DBSTU1.EARN

procedure are successively determined on the basis of the student's answers to the previous questions.

The information concerning which of the possible questions are not asked may be derived from an expert's judgements (in the example, the expert is the teacher) each of which is a selection or rejection of a rule of the form: "if a student has answered all questions of this subset of questions incorrectly, then do not ask this specific question."

EXAMPLE 1.1. We consider a subcollection of four simplified questions from a system for the assessment of students' knowledge on binary relations: *

(*a*) Is the binary relation $S \times S$ on the set S an equivalence relation?

(*b*) Is the binary relation $S \times S$ on the set S a weak order?

(*c*) Is the binary relation $\emptyset$ on the set S an asymmetric relation?

(*d*) Is the binary relation $\emptyset$ on the set S a strict weak order?

An expert's judgements on these questions may be as follows:

(1) If a student answers question (*a*) incorrectly, then do not ask question (*b*).

(2) If a student answers the questions (*b*) and (*c*) incorrectly then do not ask question (*d*).

The diagram below illustrates these two judgements.

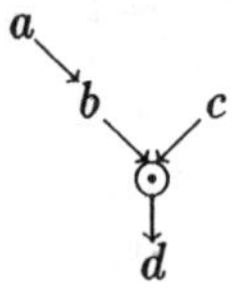

Asking an expert to select the appropriate rules from a large body of possible rules is difficult whenever the number of these questions is large. Firstly, the number of possible judgements grows exponentially with the size of the set of questions under consideration; secondly, contradictory judgements may eventuate, and, thirdly, the number of questions in the conditional part of a rule may be too large to permit a reliable judgement.

This paper suggests a procedure for restricting the expert's judgements to those that do not follow logically from previous judgements. Contradictory judgements are avoided, and the number of questions in the conditional part of the rules to be judged is minimized within equivalence classes, the nature of which is explained below. This procedure is appropriate for use within an interactive system for supporting an expert when evaluating rules.

The result of applying such a procedure to support an expert is a specific collection of accepted rules. These collections are shown to be in one-to-one correspondence with

* The system for assessing knowledge on binary relations developed at Braunschweig University currently comprises 217 questions.

knowledge structures suggested by Doignon and Falmagne (1985). Information concerning the parametrisation of such a knowledge structure is available (Doignon and Falmagne, 1988), and its relationship to irredundant assessment algorithms is investigated (Degreef, Doignon, Ducamp and Falmagne, 1986). Moreover, various probabilistic strategies for assessing a student's knowledge are developed within this framework (Falmagne and Doignon, 1988a; Falmagne and Doignon, 1988b; Falmagne, 1987).

2. Deriving a Failure Space from a Set of Rules.

A naïve procedure for asking an expert for judgements on a set of questions is introduced first, and will be refined later. Suppose a fixed and finite set V of questions is available, with $p_1, \ldots, p_k, q \in V$, and the expert selects a subset of rules from the set of all possible rules, each rule selected having the form:

$$\text{if } p_1 \text{ and } \cdots \text{ and } p_k \text{ are answered incorrectly, then assume } q \text{ to be unknown.} \qquad (2.1)$$

We can regard the set of questions as being a set of Boolean variables. Incorrect and correct answers to the questions are represented by a truth assignment $t: V \to \{T, F\}$. The value $t(p) = T$ is assigned to a question $p \in V$ if this question is answered *incorrectly*, and the value $t(p) = F$ otherwise. In this manner, the rule selected as above can be represented as a Boolean expression,

$$p_1 \wedge \cdots \wedge p_k \to q. \qquad (2.2)$$

In the following, we will describe a set of Boolean expressions of the form (2.2) compactly. Let $2^V \setminus \emptyset$ denote the powerset of the finite set V without the empty set. We define a relation R on $2^V \setminus \emptyset$ to V so that, for $P = \{p_1, \ldots, p_k\} \subseteq V$, and $q \in V$,

$$(P, q) \in R \quad \text{if and only if} \quad p_1 \wedge \cdots \wedge p_k \to q.$$

The relation $R \subseteq (2^V \setminus \emptyset) \times V$ is called *implication relation*. For a member $(P, q) \in R$ we will call the set P the *premise*.

The implication relation R constitutes a restriction on the set of all truth functions $t: V \to \{T, F\}$ for which the conjunction of the Boolean expressions characterized by R has the truth value T. We define a truth function t to be *admissible* for R if and only if, for $\{p_1, \ldots, p_k\} = P \subseteq V$, and $q \in V$,

$$t(p_1 \wedge \cdots \wedge p_k \to q) = T \text{ for all } (P, q) \in R.$$

A set of admissible truth functions is represented as a family of sets identifying a set $X \in 2^V$ with the truth function t_X where

$$t_X(p) = \begin{cases} T, & \text{if } p \in X; \\ F, & \text{otherwise.} \end{cases}$$

Note that a truth function t_X is admissible if and only if for every $(P, q) \in R$, if $P \subseteq X$, then $q \in X$.

DEFINITION 2.1. A subset X of V is called a *failure state* if and only if t_X is an admissible truth assignment for R. The family of all failure states is called the *failure space* $\mathcal{F}_R$ derived from the implication relation R.

The following proposition will establish the relationship between failure spaces derived from an implication relation and structures for the assessment of knowledge introduced by Doignon and Falmagne (1985).

PROPOSITION 2.2. *The failure space $\mathcal{F}_R$ derived from an implication relation $R \subseteq (2^V \setminus \emptyset) \times V$ is closed under intersection. The empty set and the set V are elements of $\mathcal{F}_R$.*

Proof. Suppose $(P, q) \in R$, and let $\mathcal{F}_{(P,q)} = \{X \subseteq V \mid P \not\subseteq X\} \cup \{X \subseteq V \mid q \in X\}$. With the definition of a failure space,

$$\mathcal{F}_R = \bigcap\{\mathcal{F}_{(P,q)} \mid (P, q) \in R\}.$$

We prove that $\mathcal{F}_{(P,q)}$ is closed under intersection. Suppose $\mathcal{S} \subseteq \mathcal{F}_{(P,q)}$. If $P \not\subseteq X$ for some $X \in \mathcal{S}$, then $P \not\subseteq \bigcap\mathcal{S}$, and $\bigcap\mathcal{S} \in \mathcal{F}_{(P,q)}$. Hence, suppose $P \subseteq X$ for all $X \in \mathcal{S}$. From the definition of $\mathcal{F}_{(P,q)}$, we have $q \in X$ whenever $P \subseteq X$; i.e., $q \in \bigcap\mathcal{S}$, and hence $\bigcap\mathcal{S} \in \mathcal{F}_{(P,q)}$. Since all families $\mathcal{F}_{(P,q)}$ are closed under intersection, the family $\mathcal{F}_R$ is also closed under intersection. Since $P \neq \emptyset$, $\emptyset \in \mathcal{F}_{(P,q)}$, and since $q \in V$, one obtains $V \in \mathcal{F}_{(P,q)}$ for all $(P, q) \in R$. ◊

REMARK. Note that in general a failure space is not closed under union. Families of subsets of an arbitrary set U which are closed under intersection and contain the empty set and U itself are known as *convexity structures* or *convexity spaces* (Kay and Womble, 1971).

For the example of assessing students' knowledge, the failure states and failure spaces $\mathcal{F}_R$ can be illustrated as follows: suppose a student has answered a subset I of the set V of questions incorrectly. Then we can assign to this student the smallest failure state F of the failure space $\mathcal{F}_R$ containing the set I of incorrectly answered questions. The members of the student's failure state F which are not in the set I are those which are *implied* by the Boolean expressions of the form (2.2) represented by the implication relation R. In this manner, the failure state of a student can be regarded as the set of questions the student is *incapable* of solving. The set complement $V \setminus F$ of a failure state F can be considered as the set of questions a student is *capable* of solving, that is, as a knowledge state in the sense of Doignon and Falmagne (1985).

Doignon and Falmagne define a *knowledge space* on a set U as a family of subsets of the set U that is closed under union and contains the empty set and the set U. By proposition 2.2, the family of the complements of the elements of a failure space $\mathcal{F}_R$ is a knowledge space on the set V, and will be refered to as the knowledge space derived from the implication relation R. Doignon and Falmagne derive knowledge spaces from specially defined AND/OR graphs called *surmise systems.*

From an implication relation representing a set of rules selected by an expert, we have derived a knowledge space, a structure of the sort already known to be an appropriate basis for the application of algorithms to assess students' knowledge. A one-to-one correspondence between knowledge or failure spaces and implication relations which contain all the members which follow from other members of the relation will be proven in the next section.

3. The Correspondence between Sets of Rules and Failure Spaces.

The refined procedure for questioning an expert for his judgements on a set of rules will be based on the relationship between failure spaces and implication relations. To clarify this relationship we need the following well known definition (see, for example, Ore, 1962).

DEFINITION 3.1. Let $(P, \leq)$ and $(Q, \leq)$ be two partial orders, and let (g, h) be a pair of mappings,

$$g: P \rightarrow Q, \qquad h: Q \rightarrow P.$$

The pair (g, h) is called a *Galois connection* between P and Q if the following four conditions hold, for all $p, p' \in P$ and $q, q' \in Q$:
(i) If $p \leq p'$, then $g(p) \geq g(p')$,
(ii) If $q \leq q'$, then $h(q) \geq h(q')$,
(iii) $p \leq (h \circ g)(p)$,
(iv) $q \leq (g \circ h)(q)$.
The elements $(h \circ g)(p) \in P$ and the elements $(g \circ h)(q) \in Q$ are called the *Galois closures* of p and q, respectively. The combined correspondences $(h \circ g)$ and $(g \circ h)$ are called *Galois closure operators.*

REMARK. The Galois closure operators $(h \circ g)$ and $(g \circ h)$ are closure operators of P into P and of Q into Q, respectively. The Galois closures in P and Q are therefore also called the *closed* members of P and Q, respectively. A Galois connection (g, h) induces an order reversing one-to-one correspondence between the closed members of P and the closed members of Q (see, for example, Ore, 1962). Note that $g(h \circ g)(p) = g(p)$ and $h(g \circ h)(q) = h(q)$, for a Galois connection (g, h).

With the following proposition, a Galois connection between families of subsets of a finite set and sets of implication relations will eventually be established. This proposition is related to the following results. Let us consider the special case of an implication relation $\dot{R}$ on $2^V \setminus \emptyset$ to V, which is defined as

$$P\dot{R}q \quad \text{if and only if} \quad |P| = 1.$$

In that manner we can identify a relation $\dot{R}$ with a binary relation on V. Birkhoff (1937) has proven that there is a one-to-one correspondence between the quasi-orders on a set U and knowledge spaces on U which are closed under intersection. Monjardet (1979) has shown that Birkhoff's result can be considered to be a consequence of the fact that a Galois connection can be established between the binary relations on a set U and the families of subsets of the set U. The idea of generalizing the results of Birkhoff (1937) and Monjardet (1979) and of applying the generalized result to the assessment of knowledge is due to Doignon and Falmagne (1985). Doignon and Falmagne establish a Galois connection between representations of AND/OR graphs called *surmise systems* and families of subsets of a set U. As closed families of subsets they obtain the knowledge spaces on U. Koppen and Doignon (1988) extend Monjardets work by constructing a Galois connection between the families of subsets of a set U and the binary relations on a set 2^U. The resulting Galois closures are the knowledge spaces and quasi-ordered relations on 2^U which the authors call *entail* relations. The one-to-one correspondence between knowledge spaces and entail relations has also been proven by Burigana (1988). The following proposition 3.2 can also be considered a generalization of Birkhoff's and Monjardet's work. *

PROPOSITION 3.2. *Let $\tilde{\mathcal{F}}$ be the set of all families of subsets of a finite set V, and let $\tilde{R}$ be the set of all implication relations on $2^V \setminus \emptyset$ to V, both ordered by the inclusion relation. Define a mapping $r: \tilde{\mathcal{F}} \to \tilde{R}$ by requiring that*

$$(P,q) \in r(\mathcal{F}) \text{ if and only if } q \in \bigcap\{X \in \mathcal{F} \mid P \subseteq X\}).$$

Similarly, define a mapping $f: \tilde{R} \to \tilde{\mathcal{F}}$ by setting

$$X \in f(R) \text{ if and only if for every } (P,q) \in R, \text{ if } P \subseteq X, \text{ then } q \in X.$$

Then the pair (r, f) is a Galois connection.

The Galois closure $(f \circ r)(\mathcal{F})$ is the smallest failure space containing $\mathcal{F}$. The Galois closure $(r \circ f)(R)$ is the largest implication relation with the same set of admissible truth assignments as R.

Proof. (i) To prove $\mathcal{F} \subseteq \mathcal{F}'$ implies $r(\mathcal{F}) \supseteq r(\mathcal{F}')$, suppose $\mathcal{F} \subseteq \mathcal{F}'$, and let $P \subseteq V$. Since $\mathcal{F} \subseteq \mathcal{F}'$, it follows that $\bigcap\{X \in \mathcal{F} \mid P \subseteq X\} \supseteq \bigcap\{X \in \mathcal{F}' \mid P \subseteq X\}$. Hence, for all $q \in \bigcap\{X \in \mathcal{F}' \mid P \subseteq X\}$, we obtain that $(P,q) \in r(\mathcal{F})$ whenever $(P,q) \in r(\mathcal{F}')$ by definition of the map r.

---

* **The results of Burigana, of Koppen and Doignon, and the proposition 3.2 below were obtained independently.**

(ii) To prove $R \subseteq R'$ implies $f(R) \supseteq f(R')$, suppose $R \subseteq R'$. Using the definition of the map f, $f(R) = 2^V \setminus \{X \subseteq V \mid (P,q) \in R \text{ and } P \subseteq X \text{ and } q \notin X\}$, whereas $f(R') = f(R) \setminus \{X \subseteq V \mid (P,q) \in (R' \setminus R) \text{ and } P \subseteq X \text{ and } q \notin X\}$. Hence, $f(R) \supseteq f(R')$.

(iii) To prove $\mathcal{F} \subseteq (f \circ r)(\mathcal{F})$, suppose $Y \in \mathcal{F}$. If $P \subseteq Y$, then $\bigcap\{X \in \mathcal{F} \mid P \subseteq X\} \subseteq Y$. Hence, if $q \in \bigcap\{X \in \mathcal{F} \mid P \subseteq X\}$ and $P \subseteq Y$, then $q \in Y$. By the definition of the map r, it follows that $q \in Y$ whenever $(P,q) \in r(\mathcal{F})$ and $P \subseteq Y$. By the definition of the map f, we have $Y \in (f \circ r)(\mathcal{F})$.

(iv) To prove $R \subseteq (r \circ f)(R)$, suppose $(P,q) \in R$. Using the definition of the map f, we have $q \in X$ for all $X \in f(R)$ with $P \subseteq X$, and hence $q \in \bigcap\{X \in f(R) \mid P \subseteq X\}$. By definition of the map r, $(P,q) \in (r \circ f)(R)$.

The specification of the Galois closures follows immediately from definition 2.1, from proposition 2.2, and from the fact that the Galois connection (r,f) induces a one-to-one corresponence between the Galois closures. ◇

COROLLARY. *The Galois connection (r,f) induces a one-to-one correspondence between the closed implication relations R on $2^V \setminus \emptyset$ to V and the failure spaces derived from the implication relations R, respectively.*

REMARK. Let T be the implication relation on $2^V \setminus \emptyset$ to V defined as

$$(P,q) \in T \text{ if and only if } q \in P.$$

The members of the implication relation T represent the Boolean expressions of the form (2.2) which are tautologies. The relation T is the smallest closed implication relation on $2^V \setminus \emptyset$ to V. The relation T is associated with the largest closed failure space 2^V by the mappings f and r,

$$f(T) = 2^V \text{ and } r(2^V) = T.$$

The largest closed implication relation $(2^V \setminus \emptyset) \times V$ is associated with the smallest failure space $\{\emptyset, V\}$,

$$r(\{\emptyset, V\}) = (2^V \setminus \emptyset) \times V \text{ and } f((2^V \setminus \emptyset) \times V) = \{\emptyset, V\}.$$

In the next section the Galois correspondence between implication relations and failure spaces will be used to avoid contradictory judgements, and judgements which follow from previous judgements in a procedure for questioning an expert.

DEFINITION 3.3. The members of the closed implication relation $(r \circ f)(R)$ are called the *consequences of* R. Two ordered pairs (P,q) and (Q,q) are called *equivalent with respect to* R, if, for all implication relations $R' \supseteq R$, and all $q \in V$,

$$(P,q) \in (r \circ f)(R') \quad \text{if and only if} \quad (Q,q) \in (r \circ f)(R').$$

The following proposition shows that the equivalence of two ordered pairs with respect to an implication relation R can be tested on the basis of R or on the basis of the failure space $f(R)$.

PROPOSITION 3.4. *Two members $(P,q),(Q,q) \in (2^V \setminus \emptyset) \times V$ are equivalent with respect to R if and only if*

$$\bigcap\{X \in f(R) \mid P \subseteq X\} = \bigcap\{X \in f(R) \mid Q \subseteq X\}.$$

Proof. (i) Suppose (P,q) and (Q,q) are equivalent with respect to R. Let $Y = \bigcap\{X \in f(R) \mid P \subseteq X\}$. Obviously $(P,q) \in (r \circ f)(R)$ if and only if $(Q,q) \in (r \circ f)(R)$. Since $(Q,s) \in (r \circ f)(R)$, for all $s \in Q$ by definition of the maps r and f in proposition 3.2, $(P,s) \in (r \circ f)(R)$ for all $s \in Q$. Also using the definition of the map f, since $f(R) = f(r \circ f)(R)$, and since $Y \in f(R)$ by proposition 2.2, it follows that $Q \subseteq Y$. Since $Z = \bigcap\{X \in f(R) \mid Q \subseteq X\}$ is the smallest set in $f(R)$ containing Q, it follows that $Z \subseteq Y$. The proof that $Y \subseteq Z$ is similar.

(ii) Suppose $Y = \bigcap\{X \in f(R) \mid P \subseteq X\} = \bigcap\{X \in f(R) \mid Q \subseteq X\}$. We prove $(P,q) \in (r \circ f)(R')$ implies $(Q,q) \in (r \circ f)(R')$, for all $R' \supseteq R$, and $R' \subseteq (2^V \setminus \emptyset) \times V$; hence, suppose $(P,q) \in (r \circ f)(R')$. By proposition 2.2, $Y' = \bigcap\{X \in f(R') \mid Y \subseteq X\} \in f(R')$. Since $(P,q) \in (r \circ f)(R')$, and $P \subseteq Y'$, it follows that $q \in Y'$, by definition of the map f. Since $R \subseteq R'$, one obtains $f(R) \supseteq f(R')$, using the axiom (ii) of the definition 3.1. Hence, there is no set in $f(R')$ containing Q and not containing Y, i.e., Y' is the smallest set in $f(R')$ containing Q. Since $q \in Y' = \bigcap\{X \in f(R') \mid Q \subseteq X\}$, we have $(Q,q) \in (r \circ f)(R')$ by definition of the map r. The proof that, if $(Q,q) \in (r \circ f)(R')$, then $(P,q) \in (r \circ f)(R')$ is similar.

EXAMPLE 3.5. Let $V = \{a,b,c,d\}$ be a set of questions, and suppose the rules 1 and 2 of the example 1.1 have been selected; i.e., $R = \{(\{a\},b),(\{b,c\},d)\}$. We obtain the failure space associated to R,

$$f(R) = \{\emptyset,\{b\},\{c\},\{d\},\{a,b\},\{b,d\},\{c,d\},\{a,b,d\},\{b,c,d\},\{a,b,c,d\}\}.$$

The consequences of R are the set,

$$(r \circ f)(R) = \{(\{a\},b),(\{b,c\},d),(\{a,c\},b),(\{a,c\},d),(\{a,d\},b),$$
$$(\{a,b,c\},d),(\{a,c,d\},b)\} \cup T,$$

where T is the implication relation representing Boolean expressions of the form (2.2) which are tautologies. Members of the relation T are, for example, $(\{a\},a)$ and $(\{a,b\},b)$. Some classes of ordered pairs that are equivalent with respect to R are, for example:

$$\{(\{a\},d),(\{a,b\},d)\} \text{ and } \{(\{a,c\},d),(\{a,b,c\},d),(\{a,c,d\},d),(\{a,b,c,d\},d)\}.$$

4. The Procedure for Supporting an Expert.

The Galois correspondence between failure spaces and implication relations representing sets of rules of the form (2.1) is used to build the interactive expert questioning procedure, as announced in the first two sections. This procedure will help an expert to omit judgements of rules that are consequences of rules judged previously thereby avoiding contradictory judgements, and to minimize the premise of the rules to be judged within equivalence classes determined by the definition 3.3.

It will be shown that the major calculations required by the procedure can be based on failure spaces instead of on sets of rules. In this fashion, the maximal number of iterations used by the interactive questioning program can be reduced, and the failure or knowledge space for the assessment of a student's knowledge can be considered an outcome of the questioning procedure.

We suggest a stepwise procedure presenting at each step l with $l > 0$, exactly one rule of the form (2.1) to the expert. The expert judges, i.e., accepts or rejects this rule. A new rule presented for judgement at step $l + 1$ must fulfill the restrictions [a], [b], and [c] given by the definition 4.1 below. The procedure terminates, at step m, say, whenever no new rule fulfills the restrictions.

DEFINITION 4.1. Let $\emptyset = J_0 \subseteq J_1 \subseteq \cdots \subseteq J_l \subseteq \cdots \subseteq J_m$ be a sequence of implication relations on $2^V \setminus \emptyset$ to V, such that $|J_{l+1} \setminus J_l| = 1$, and $m \leq (|2^V| - 1)|V|$. For $l > 0$, the member $(P,q) \in J_l \setminus J_{l-1}$ is called the *rule judged at the step l*. Let $\emptyset = R_0 \subseteq R_1 \subseteq \cdots \subseteq R_i \subseteq \cdots \subseteq R_n$ be a sequence of implication relations on $2^V \setminus \emptyset$ to V such that $R_i \subseteq J_m$, for all i. The largest relation R_i contained in the relation J_l is denoted by R_l. If $(P,q) \in R_l \setminus R_{l-1}$, then (P,q) is called the *rule accepted at the step l*. Let r and f be the functions defined in the proposition 3.2, so that $(r \circ f)(R_l)$ is the set of the consequences of the members of R_l.

If $(P,q) \in J_l \setminus (J_{l-1} \cup R_l)$, then (P,q) is called the *rule rejected at the step l*. The set $J_l \setminus R_l$ of rules rejected at the steps $j \leq l$ is denoted by $\bar{R}_l$. The members of the set

$$\bar{R}_l^* = \{(O,s) \in (2^V \setminus \emptyset) \times V \mid \bar{R}_l \cap (r \circ f)(R_l \cup \{(O,s)\}) \neq \emptyset\}$$

are called the *negative consequences* of $\bar{R}_l$ *with respect to* R_l or, briefly, the *negative consequences* of $\bar{R}_l$. The sets R_l and $\bar{R}_l$ are called *contradictory* if and only if

$$\bar{R}_l^* \cap (r \circ f)(R_l) \neq \emptyset.$$

The implication relations J_l are called *consistent,* if and only if for all $0 \leq l \leq m$, one has whenever $(P,q) \in J_{l+1} \setminus J_l$, then the conditions [a] and [b] below are fulfilled.

[a] $(P,q) \notin (r \circ f)(R_l)$.

[b] There is no $(Q,q') \in \bar{R}_l$ such that $(Q,q') \in (r \circ f)(R_l \cup \{(P,q)\})$.

Consistent relations J_l are called *minimally* consistent if and only if for all $0 \leq l \leq m$, the condition [c] below holds whenever $(P,q) \in J_{l+1} \setminus J_l$.

[c] $|P| \leq |Q|$ for every (Q,q) that is equivalent to (P,q) with respect to R_l.

By the proposition 3.2, the consequences $(r \circ f)(R_l)$ of the rules R_l accepted up to step l have been shown to be those members of $(2^V \setminus \emptyset) \times V$ the acceptance of which logically follows from the acceptance of the members of R_l. The negative consequences $\bar{R}_l^*$ of the rules $\bar{R}_l$ rejected up to step l are defined to be those members of $(2^V \setminus \emptyset) \times V$ the rejection of which logically follows from the rejection of the members of $\bar{R}_l$ and from the acceptance of the members of R_l. Hence we have defined a set R_l of accepted rules and a set $\bar{R}_l$ of rejected rules to be contradictory, if there is a member $(P,q) \in (2^V \setminus \emptyset) \times V$ the rejection as well as the acceptance of which follows from $\bar{R}_l$ and R_l.

PROPOSITION 4.2. *If the implication relations J_l, with $0 \leq l \leq m$, are consistent, then the conditions (i), (ii), (iii), and (iv) below are fulfilled:*

(i) No rule accepted at a step l is a consequence of a set of rules accepted at steps $0 \leq j < l$.

(ii) No rule rejected at a step l is a consequence of a set of rules accepted at steps $0 \leq j < l$.

(iii) No rule rejected at a step l is a consequence of a set of rules accepted at steps $m \geq j > l$.

(iv) The set of rules accepted at the steps $j < l$ and the set of rules rejected at the steps $j \leq l$ are not contradictory for all steps $0 \leq l \leq m$.

If the implication relations J_l are minimally consistent, then the condition (v) below is fulfilled.

(v) At most one member of an equivalence class with respect to a set R_l of accepted rules is judged at steps $j > l$. The size of the premise of this member is minimal within its equivalence class.

Proof. The conditions (i) and (ii) follow immediately from condition [a] of definition 4.1. The condition (iii) of follows immediately from condition [b] of definition 4.1. The condition (v) follows from condition [c] and from definition 3.3, together with conditions [a] and [b] of definition 4.1.

We prove condition (iv) by induction. Since $J_0 = \emptyset$, we obtain by definiton 4.1 of the implication relations $\bar{R}_l$ and $\bar{R}_l^*$ that $\bar{R}_0^* \cap (r \circ f)(R_0) = \emptyset$. We prove whenever $\bar{R}_l^* \cap (r \circ f)(R_l) = \emptyset$, then $\bar{R}_{l+1}^* \cap (r \circ f)(R_{l+1}) = \emptyset$. Hence, suppose $\bar{R}_l^* \cap (r \circ f)(R_l) = \emptyset$.

Firstly, suppose $(P,q) \in \bar{R}_{l+1} \setminus \bar{R}_l$. Further, suppose $(O,s) \in \bar{R}_{l+1}^*$ in order to prove that $(O,s) \notin (r \circ f)(R_{l+1})$. By definition 4.1, we have $R_l = R_{l+1}$ and $\bar{R}_{l+1} = \bar{R}_l \cup \{(P,q)\}$. If $(P,q) \notin (r \circ f)(R_l \cup \{(O,s)\})$, then $(O,s) \in \bar{R}_l^*$ by definition 4.1 of the set $\bar{R}_l^*$, and $(O,s) \notin (r \circ f)(R_l) = (r \circ f)(R_{l+1})$. Hence, suppose that $(P,q) \in$

$(r \circ f)(R_l \cup \{(O,s)\})$. Since $(P,q) \notin (r \circ f)(R_l)$ by condition [a] of definition 4.1, we have $(r \circ f)(R_l) \neq (r \circ f)(R_l \cup \{(O,s)\})$. Using proposition 3.2 and definition 3.1 we obtain that $(O,s) \notin (r \circ f)(R_l) = (r \circ f)(R_{l+1})$.

Secondly, suppose $(P,q) \in R_{l+1} \setminus R_l$. Further, suppose that $(O,s) \in (r \circ f)(R_{l+1})$ in order to prove that $(O,s) \notin \bar{R}^*_{l+1}$. From definition 4.1 it follows that $\bar{R}_l = \bar{R}_{l+1}$ and $R_{l+1} = R_l \cup \{(P,q)\}$. Hence, we obtain that $\bar{R}_{l+1} \cap (r \circ f)(R_{l+1}) = \emptyset$ from condition [b] of definition 4.1. Since $(O,s) \in (r \circ f)(R_{l+1})$, we have $(r \circ f)(R_{l+1}) = (r \circ f)(R_{l+1} \cup \{(O,s)\})$. Thus, $(O,s) \notin \bar{R}^*_{l+1}$ by definition 4.1 of the negative consequences of $\bar{R}_{l+1}$ at step $l+1$. ◇

EXAMPLE 4.3. Let $V = \{a,b,c,d\}$ be the set of questions introduced in example 1.1, and let the rules presented for judgement be selected so that the sets J_l of judged rules are minimally consistent for $0 \leq l \leq m$.

Suppose the rule $(\{a,c\},d)$ is presented for judgement, and accepted at step $l=1$, i.e., $R_1 = J_1 = \{(\{a,c\},d)\}$. Since the rule $(\{a,b,c\},d)$ is a member of $(r \circ f)(R_1)$, and hence a consequence of the rule in R_1, it will not be presented for judgement at later steps $l > 1$ by axiom [a] of definition 4.1.

Suppose the rule $(\{c,d\},b)$ is presented at step $l=2$ and rejected, i.e. $(\{c,d\},b) \in J_2 \setminus R_2$. By axiom [b] of definition 4.1, neither the rule $(\{c\},b)$, nor the rule $(\{d\},b)$ will be presented at later steps $l > 2$, since their acceptance would contradict the rejection of the rule $(\{c,d\},b)$.

At step $l=3$, the rule $(\{a,c,d\},b)$ cannot be presented for judgement by axiom [c] of definition 4.1, since the rules $(\{a,c,d\},b)$ and $(\{a,c\},b)$ are equivalent with respect to $R_2 \subseteq J_2$. The rule $(\{a,c,d\},b)$ will also not be presented at later steps $l > 3$ using definition 3.3 and the axioms [a] and [b] of the definition 4.1.

The procedure terminates at the step m where no new rule fulfills the restrictions [a], [b], and [c] of the definition 4.1.

By applying an interactive procedure presenting only those rules to an expert for judgement which fulfill the conditions [a] and [b] of definition 4.1 we can omit all judgements which might be redundant in the sense that a rule would be judged which is already a consequence of rules accepted at previous steps or a negative consequence of rules rejected at previous steps. Judgements that are redundant in the sense that a rule might be accepted which is a consequence of rules accepted at later steps of the questioning procedure cannot be avoided using only the conditions [a] and [b]. An interactive questioning procedure restricted by the conditions [a] and [b] is so that the sets of accepted rules and the sets of rejected rules are not contradictory at all steps.

By applying also the condition [c] of the definition 4.1 at each step of the questioning procedure the size of the premise of a rule judged at a given step is minimized within its class.

A procedure selecting the rules presented to an expert for judgement may be restricted by additional conditions which further reduce the number of rules to be judged. The conditions [a] and [b] of definition 4.1 are chosen so that they do not yet predetermine the sequence in which the rules are selected for judgement. Ordering the rules to be judged prior to presentation could influence the efficiency of the procedure. Whenever the set V of questions is large, an additional means of limiting the size of the premise of the rules to be judged to some upper bound will be necessary. For example, were a rule to fill a terminal screen, it would be unlikely that the expert could make a reliable judgement.

For a fixed set V, the maximal number of members of an implication relation is larger than the maximal number of failure states. Minimally consistent sets of judged rules should therefore be determined on the basis of the corresponding failure space. The following proposition states how the axioms [a], [b], and [c] of definition 4.1 can be tested for the failure spaces $f(R_l)$.

PROPOSITION 4.4. *If R_l is an implication relation on $2^V \backslash \emptyset$ to V, then the following conditions are fulfilled:*

(i) $(P,q) \in (r \circ f)(R_l)$ *if and only if* $q \in \bigcap\{X \in f(R_l) \mid P \subseteq X\}$.

(ii) (P,q) *and* (Q,q) *are equivalent with respect to* R_l *if and only if* $\bigcap\{X \in f(R_l) \mid P \subseteq X\} = \bigcap\{X \in f(R_l) \mid Q \subseteq X\}$.

(iii) Let $(Q,q') \notin (r \circ f)(R_l)$ *and let* $S = R_l \cup \{(P,q)\}$. *Then* $(Q,q') \in (r \circ f)(S)$ *if and only if the condition [d] below is fulfilled.*

[d] $P \subseteq \bigcap\{X \in f(R_l) \mid Q \subseteq X\}$ *and* $q' \in \bigcap\{X \in f(R_l) | Q \cup \{q\} \subseteq X\}$.

Proof. (i) follows immediately from the definition of the Galois connection (r,f) in proposition 3.2. (ii) is proven using proposition 3.4.

We prove (iii). Suppose $(Q,q') \in (r \circ f)(S)$. Let $Z = \bigcap\{X \in f(S) \mid Q \subseteq X\}$. Since $Z \in f(S)$ using proposition 2.2, and since $f(r \circ f)(S) = f(S)$, we obtain $q' \in Z$ by definition of f. Let $Y = \bigcap\{X \in f(R_l) \mid Q \subseteq X\}$. By proposition 2.2, $Y \in f(R_l)$. By condition (ii) of definition 3.1, we obtain $f(R_l) \supseteq f(S)$, and hence $Y \subseteq Z$. If $q' \in Y$, then $(Q,q') \notin (r \circ f)(R_l)$ contradicts the definition of the map r; hence, suppose $q' \notin Y$. Since $(Q,q') \in (r \circ f)(S)$, we have $Y \notin f(S)$ by the definition of f. Since $f(S) = f(R_l) \setminus \{X \in f(R_l) \mid P \subseteq X \text{ and } q \notin X\}$, and $Y \in f(R_l)$, and $Y \notin f(S)$, we have $P \subseteq Y$. Since if $P \subseteq Y$, it follows that $P \subseteq Z$, and by definition of f, we also have $q \in Z$. Hence, $Z = \bigcap\{X \in f(R_l) \mid Q \cup \{q\} \subseteq X\} \ni q'$.

Suppose $P \subseteq \bigcap\{X \in f(R_l) \mid Q \subseteq X\} = Y$, and $q' \in \bigcap\{X \in f(R_l) \mid Q \cup \{q\} \subseteq X\} = Z$. If $Y = Z$, then $(Q,q') \in (r \circ f)(S)$ by the definition of the map r. Hence, suppose $Y \neq Z$. Since $f(S) = f(R_l) \setminus \{X \in f(R_l) \mid P \subseteq X \text{ and } q \notin X\}$ by the definition of the map f, it follows that $Y \notin f(S)$, and that $Z \in f(S)$ with $Z = \bigcap\{X \in f(S) \mid Q \subseteq X\}$. Since $q' \in Z$, $(Q, q') \in (r \circ f)(S)$ using the definition of the map r. ◇

The condition (iii) of the proposition 4.4 can be used to calculate, at each step l of the questioning procedure, the consequences of the set R_l of accepted rules and the negative consequences of the set $\bar{R}_l$ of rejected rules which have not yet been determined at previous steps. For example, if the rule (P, q) is accepted at step l, then we obtain the members of the set $(r \circ f)(R_{l+1})$ by adding to the set $(r \circ f)(R_l)$ those rules $(Q, q') \notin (r \circ f)(R_l)$, for which the condition [d] of the proposition 4.4 is fulfilled at step l. In this manner we obtain a procedure for constructing the set of consequences of the rules accepted up to each step l which is non-iterative at a given step. Koppen and Doignon (1988) have suggested an iterative procedure for the same purpose, which requires repeated iterations through intermediate implication relations $I_1, \ldots, I_n$ at each step l, with $(r \circ f)(R_l) \subseteq I_1 \subseteq \cdots \subseteq I_n \subseteq (r \circ f)(R_{l+1})$. The rules (P, q) for which the condition [b] of the definition 4.1 is not fulfilled at a step l can also be determined using the condition (iii) of the proposition 4.4.

Once the interactive procedure of judging a consistent selection of rules is terminated, we obtain the failure space $f(R_m)$ associated with the largest set R_m of accepted rules by the proposition 3.2. Algorithms for assessing students' knowledge (Doignon and Falmagne, 1985; Falmagne and Doignon, 1985), can be applied to the failure space or to the corresponding knowledge space. Some of these assessment algorithms do, however, require restrictions, which do not hold for all knowledge or failure spaces derived from a set of rules (Falmagne and Doignon 1988b; Falmagne, 1987).

An important open problem in connection with developing a procedure facilitating an expert's judgements on a set of rules is the problem of defining and assessing the reliabilty and validity of the resulting judgements.

Acknowledgements

This work was supported by a Feodor–Lynen Fellowship of the Alexander von Humboldt–Stiftung and by the NSF Grant No. IST 84–18860 to New York University (PI J.-C. Falmagne). The author would like to thank Jean-Claude Falmagne for suggesting the subject.

References

Birkhoff, G. (1937). Rings of sets. *Duke Mathematical Journal*, **3**, 443–454.

Birkhoff, G. (1979). *Lattice Theory*. Providence: American Mathematical Society.

Buchanan, B. G. & Shortliffe, E. H. (1984). *Rule-Based Expert systems*. Reading: Addison-Wesley.

Burigana, L. (1988). Organization by rules in finite sequences. University of Padua.

Manuscript.

Degreef, E., Doignon, J.-P., Ducamp, A. & Falmagne, J.-C. (1986). Languages for the assessment of knowledge. *Journal of Mathematical Psychology*, **30**, 234–256.

Doignon, J.-P. & Falmagne, J.-C. (1985). Spaces for the assessment of knowledge. *International Journal of Man-Machine Studies*, **23**, 175–196.

Doignon, J.-P. & Falmagne, J.-C. (1988). Parametrisation of knowledge structures. *Discrete Applied Mathematics*, **21**, 87–100.

Falmagne, J.-C. (1987). A latent trait theory via a stochastic learning theory for a knowledge space. Technical Report MSCP 87–2, Department of Psychology, New York University.

Falmagne, J.-C. & Doignon, J.-P. (1988a). A class of stochastic procedures for the assessment of knowledge. *British Journal of Statistical and Mathematical Psychology*, **41**, 1–23.

Falmagne, J.-C. & Doignon, J.-P. (1988b). A Marcovian procedure for assessing the state of a system. *Journal of Mathematical Psychology*, **32**, 232–258.

Kay, D. C. & Womble, E. W. (1971). Axiomatic convexity theory and relationships between the Carathéodory, Helly, and Radon numbers. *Pacific Journal of Mathematics*, **38**, 2, 471–485.

Koppen, M. & Doignon, J.-P. (1988). How to build a knowledge space by querying an expert. New York University. Manuscript.

Monjardet, B. (1979). Tresses, fuseaux, préordres et topologies. *Mathematiques et Sciences Humaines*, **30**, 11–22.

Ore, O. (1962). *Theory of Graphs*, Providence: American Mathematical Society Colloquium publications Vol. XXXVIII.

A Generalized "Discounting the Background" Model Extending the Traditional Grassmannian Approach to Colour Vision*)

*Rainer Mausfeld and Reinhard Niederée***)
University of Bonn

Abstract
The paper gives a short account of a new model for asymmetric colour matching. It generalizes affine models previously proposed in the literature, starting from Walraven's (1976) "discounting the background" principle. The characteristic feature of the model proposed is that it allows different v.Kries-type multiplicative transformations for increments and decrements. Due to the qualitative laws implied, the model is particularly attractive from a measurement-theoretic 'Grassmannian' perspective. Some empirical and theoretical aspects of the model are briefly discussed.

1. Introduction

One of the most elegant applications of measurement theory is the measurement-theoretic reconstruction of the Newton-Young-Helmholtz theory of metamerism provided by Krantz (1975a). Here 'metamerism' is understood in terms of the '2°-paradigm' of colour vision: Two lights A,B (jointly presented to the dark-adapted eye in a bipartite field of a size of approximately 2° visual angle in a dark surround) are called metameric, formally: $A \equiv B$, if they are perceptually indistinguishable, i.e., if they yield the same colour appearance. This experimental paradigm arose in connection with both neurophysiological considerations (three-receptor hypothesis) and phenomenological observations related to foveal colour vision. As before Grassmann (1853) and Schrödinger (1920), Krantz (1975a) gave a mathematical analysis of the purely psychophysical aspects (i.e. the interaction of physics and phenomenology) of this situation, which turns out to be governed by particularly simple qualitative laws. Krantz' rigorous measurement-theoretic approach starts from an elementary physical 'structure of lights', which here will be denoted by $\langle D, \oplus, * \rangle$, D standing for the set of 'lights' (commonly identified with spectral energy distributions, i.e. non-negative measure functions over the visual spectrum),

*) This work has been supported by DFG grant MA 1025/2-1.
**) Psychological Institute, University of Bonn, Römerstr. 164, D-5300 Bonn 1, FRG, Bitnet-Earn UPS128 at DBNRHRZ1.

$\oplus$ for the operation of additive colour mixture in the sense of superimposing lights (addition of measures), and $t * A$ ($t \in Re^{>0}$) denoting intensity changes of light by factor t (i.e., the corresponding operation on measures, respectively). This structure is made into a psychophysical structure by adding the psychological relation $\equiv$ of metamerism. Krantz then proves a representation theorem to the effect that if certain qualitative laws are fulfilled by this structure, then there is a linear mapping $\phi : D \rightarrow Re^3$ that maps D onto a convex (three-dimensional) cone of Re^3 and satisfies the condition: $\phi(A) = \phi(B)$ if and only if $A \equiv B$. Cast in measurement theoretic terms this means that there is a homomorphic representation ϕ of the (qualitative) structure $<D, \oplus, *, \equiv>$ into the numerical structure $<Re^3, +, \cdot, =>$. A mapping ϕ of that kind will be called a *Grassmannian representation*. The corresponding qualitative laws include Grassmann's well-known *linearity laws* :

(i) $A \equiv B$ if and only if $A \oplus C \equiv B \oplus C$
(ii) if $A \equiv B$ then $t*A \equiv t*B$ (for all $t > 0$).

Clearly, ϕ is only determined up to non-singular linear transformations; that is, there is a family of representations including the familiar CIE tristimulus codes and the commonly postulated linear photoreceptor output functions. In this way, Krantz' analysis provides us with an abstract understanding of Uttal's concept of a 'neural code' as applied to primary colour codes, and lays bare in the clearest possible way the structural assumptions underlying CIE colour space, conceived as an 'appearance space'.

In separating psychophysical considerations neatly from neurophysiological ones, and in algebraically and qualitatively accounting for the geometrico-numerical concepts associated with the notion of colour space, such an abstract 'Grassmannian' framework is a particularly valuable contribution to the psychophysics of colour both from a theoretical and an experimental perspective. It therefore appears attractive to keep as much as possible of the measurement-theoretic Grassmannian spirit while extending it so as to comprise other fundamental psychophysical relations, too. This enterprise was pioneered by Krantz (1968, 1975b, see also 1974) by incorporating unique colours and (from still a more abstract point of view) cross-context matching into a measurement-theoretic framework.

A special case of cross-context matching is asymmetric colour matching (cf. Wyszecki & Stiles, 1982), which will here be understood in the sense of 'testspot A, when presented in surround S, appears equal to B in surround T' ('spatial adaptation'), symbolically $<A,S> \equiv <B,T>$, $(A,B,S,T \in D)$. When tying theory to experiment, one would, of course, have to make this notion more precise; for the present theoretical purposes the above coarse description suffices, however.

This extended notion of metamerism, which in a way generalizes the previous one (which in turn corresponds to dark surrounds $S,T = 0$, i.e. constant zero distributions), is related to phenomena traditionally subsumed under the headings of "colour induction", "colour contrast", or, more recently, "discounting the background". This situation, furthermore, does not only comprise 'luminous' colours, as the '2°-situation' underlying CIE space, but also 'dark' colours like brown, grey, maroon etc. associated with the perceived colour of surfaces. This is of special interest in developing a more comprehensive concept of colour space.

In this paper, a 'Grassmannian' type of model for asymmetric colour matching will be proposed which is a variant of affine models of colour coding as previously discussed in the literature (e.g. Burnham, Evans & Newhall 1957; Krantz, 1968; Jameson & Hurvich, 1972). It differs, however, in introducing an increment/decrement distinction and breaking the affine structure by assuming different multiplicative (v. Kries) coefficients for increments and decrements.

2. An Octant-Wise Linear Model of Incremental Colour Coding

Formally, the model to be discussed may be conceived as a generalization of Walraven's (1976) "*discounting the background*" principle to the effect that if a testspot $S \oplus \Delta$ is presented in surround S ($S, \Delta \in D$), the visual system essentially behaves as if only the increment Δ were processed and subjected to an S-dependent multiplicative 'gain control'. This means that the 'background' S on which the increment is presented is 'discounted', as it were. Cast in terms of metamerism, this hypothesis amounts to the following quantitative model.

The model is assumed to hold for some appropriately specified Grassmannian representation ϕ of $\langle D, \oplus, * \rangle$ with non-negative component functions ϕ^i, $i=1,2,3$, and for appropriately chosen S-dependent factors $\rho^i_S > 0$, $S \in D$, $i=1,2,3$. Consider now a testspot Δ which is incrementally presented *on* a background S, i.e. a stimulus $\langle A,S \rangle$ where $A = S \oplus \Delta$, and a corresponding stimulus $\langle B,T \rangle$, where $B = T \oplus \Delta'$ ($\Delta, \Delta', S, T \in D$).
The basic assumption of the model is that

$$\langle A,S \rangle \equiv \langle B,T \rangle$$

if and only if the values

$$\rho^i_S(\phi^i(A) - \phi^i(S)) = \rho^i_S \phi^i(\Delta) =: \Phi^i(A,S)$$

and

$$\rho^i_T(\phi^i(B) - \phi^i(T)) = \rho^i_T \phi^i(\Delta') =: \Phi^i(B,T)$$

coincide for $i=1,2,3$. That is, $\langle A,S \rangle$ and $\langle B,T \rangle$ are metameric if they yield the same value in terms of the 'incremental' code (Φ^1, Φ^2, Φ^3).

Clearly, from a psychophysical point of view, only the existence of such a representation ϕ can be postulated, i.e. neither ϕ nor the multiplicative coefficients are absolutely fixed by the above assumption. However, only certain non-negative Grassmannian representations ϕ will satisfy the condition "there are S-dependent factors ...": in fact, if the model is satisfied for some ϕ, and the corresponding factors differ sufficiently, then ϕ is uniquely determined up to permutations of components and componentwise multiplication by positive reals. (From a neurophysiological point of view, it would then be natural to extend the hypothesis so as to assume ϕ^1, ϕ^2, ϕ^3 to be conceivable as photoreceptor output functions. For an analogous argument in the framework of classical v.Kries theory see Wyszecki & Stiles, 1982, p.431ff.).

As it stands, this model only applies to *increments* $<S \oplus \Delta, S>$, but not to arbitrary stimuli $<A,S>$ such as *decrements*, where $S = A \oplus \Delta$, i.e. the surround exceeds the testspot.

We propose to consider the following general model which is assumed to hold for appropriately chosen factors $\rho_S^{i\pm}$ (with $\rho_S^{i+} = \rho_S^i$):

$$<A,S> \equiv <B,T> \text{ if and only if } \Phi^i(A,S) = \Phi^i(B,T) \text{ for } i=1,2,3$$

where

$$\Phi^i(A,S) = \begin{cases} \rho_S^{i+} (\phi^i(A) - \phi^i(S)) & \text{if } \phi^i(A) \geq \phi^i(S) \\ \rho_S^{i-} (\phi^i(A) - \phi^i(S)) & \text{if } \phi^i(A) < \phi^i(S) \end{cases}$$

and $\Phi^i(B,T)$ is defined accordingly.

This *octant model* may be illustrated by the following abstract receptor model (Fig.1). We stress the illustrative character since we do not want to leave the realm of psychophysics here by making premature and over-simplified neurophysiological commitments.

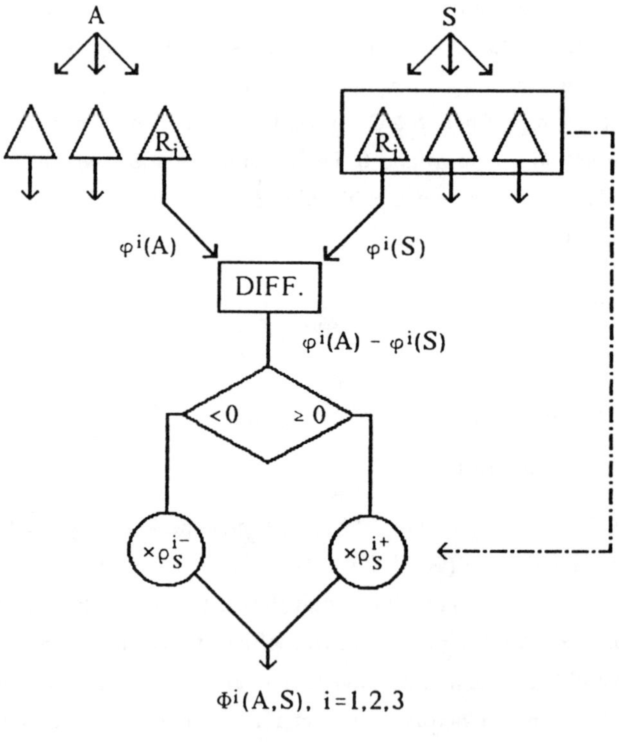

Fig.1 Illustration of the octant model
(R_i, i=1,2,3, denoting primary receptors)

Contrary to ϕ, which is assumed to be non-negative, $\Phi(A,S)$ can take on values in all octants of Re^3 and different factors $\rho_S^{1\pm}$, $\rho_S^{2\pm}$, $\rho_S^{3\pm}$ apply, dependent on the octant of Re^3 to which the incremental triple

$$(\phi^1(A) - \phi^1(S), \phi^2(A) - \phi^2(S), \phi^3(A) - \phi^3(S))$$

belongs. Increments pertain to the positive (more precisely, the non-negative) octant $(Re^{\geq 0})^3$, whereas decrements pertain to the 'negative' one, i.e. $(Re^{\leq 0})^3$. As a consequence, an increment $<A,S>$ with $\phi^i(A) > \phi^i(S)$ for some i will never match a decrement, so that increments and decrements constitute different 'worlds' of colour appearances, as it were. Observe that there are stimuli whose codes belong neither to the positive octant nor to the negative one; this means that the model does not simply fall into two different models for increments and decrements. It rather provides a coherent (continuous and piecewise affine) overall model.

3. Discussion

As already noted before, the octant model explicates Walraven's (1976) "discounting the background" principle for increments, and generalizes it to general stimuli $<A,S>$. A more subtle reading of the model ("discounting the level") allows to also accommodate the findings of "partial discounting" by Shevell (1978) and Larimer (1981). These studies applied a *colour cancellation* method to increments, whereas the present model is based on the more fundamental relation of *metamerism*. Since experiments based on an absolute judgmental method using equilibrium colours, as the ones just mentioned, can only yield indirect support for models on metamerism, further empirical support by asymmetric colour matching experiments seems desirable.

For the achromatic domain a discounting principle was already put forward by Whittle and Challands (1969), who used a form of binocular brightness matching and noted in passing that, as a rule, increments would not match decrements, regardless of their absolute intensities - as implied by the octant model (see above).

A point to be commented on in passing is that from the octant model it follows that $<A,A> \equiv <B,B>$ for any pair A,B of spectral energy distributions, the corresponding Φ-values being (0,0,0). This is a boundary case of the principle 'increment matches increment, decrement matches decrement' and a consequence of any kind of 'relational' approach to colour based on 'differences', 'ratios' or the like. It seems, at least at first sight, to strive against a direct empirical interpretation. At this point, the experimental realization of the stimuli $<A,S>$ becomes crucial: When S extends over the entire visual field except for the testspot, the case $A \equiv S$ corresponds to Ganzfeld conditions, where colour fades, whence $<A,A>$ and $<B,B>$ might formally be treated as metameric. (If S stands for an annulus in an otherwise dark surrounding field, the case $A \equiv S$ and 'its vicinity' require separate treatment, involving different 'mechanisms' such as, say, 'filling in'.)

Besides the implication that octants are closed under metamerism, the octant model has other attractive qualitative consequences, which can be stated in a precise formal manner, such as the *octant-wise validity of incremental* (i.w.s) *variants of Grassmann's linearity laws*. These allow to subject the octant model to a rigorous measurement-theoretic analysis.

Furthermore, owing to the 'v. Kries' coefficients $\rho_S^{i\pm}$, the octant model is consistent with 'ratio principles' as stated by Hess and Pretori (1894) and Wallach (1948) (for brightness) and, in a way, in Land (e.g. 1986) (where in the present context 'ratio principle' may be understood in the sense of $(A,S) \equiv (t{*}A, t{*}S)$ or the stronger assumption that colour appearance is essentially determined by the ratios $\phi^i(A)/\phi^i(S)$, $\phi^i(S) \neq 0$).

In achromatic experiments, Jacobson and Gilchrist (1988) showed a ratio principle to hold for a large range of decrements, but *not* for increments. While such an increment/decrement distinction is incompatible with the assumption that always $\rho_S^{i+} = \rho_S^{i-}$, i.e., with an affine model, it is indeed consistent with an octant model. There are, in fact, several other reasons for decoupling the multiplicative coefficients ρ_S^{i+}, ρ_S^{i-}, which, for sake of brevity, will be omitted here.

A more comprehensive discussion of the conceptual, theoretical and empirical background of this model and related principles, along with a qualitative description of the resulting 'appearance space' is given in Mausfeld and Niederée (1989a), where it is taken as a possible starting-point for a relational theory of colour perception. Measurement-theoretic aspects of the octant model are dealt with in Mausfeld and Niederée (1989b).

References

Burnham, R.W., Evans, R.W., & Newhall, S.M. (1957). Prediction of Color Appearance with Different Adaptation Illuminations. *Journal of the Optical Society of America, 47*, 35-42.

Grassmann, H. (1853). Zur Theorie der Farbmischung. *Poggendorff's Annalen der Physik, 89*, 69-84.

Hess, C., & Pretori, H. (1894). Messende Untersuchungen über die Gesetzmäßigkeit des simultanen Helligkeitskontrastes. *Gräfes Archiv für Ophtalmologie, 40*, 1-24.

Jacobson, A., & Gilchrist, A. (1988). Hess and Pretori Revisited: Resolution of Some Old Contradictions. *Perception & Psychophysics, 43, 7-14.*

Jameson, D., & Hurvich, L.M. (1972). Color Adaptation: Sensitivity, Contrast, After-Images. In D. Jameson & L.M. Hurvich (Eds.), *Handbook of Sensory Physiology, 568- 881.* Heidelberg: Springer.

Krantz, D.H. (1968). A Theory of Context Effects Based on Cross-Context Matching. *Journal of Mathematical Psychology, 5*, 1-48.

Krantz, D.H. (1974). Measurement Theory and Qualitative Laws in Psychophysics. In D.H. Krantz, R.C. Atkinson, R.D. Luce, & P. Suppes (Eds.), *Contempory Developments in Mathematical Psychology. Vol.II. Measurement, Psychophysics, and Neural Information Processing, 160-199.* San Francisco: Freeman.

Krantz, D.H. (1975a). Color Measurement and Color Theory: I. Representation Theorem for Grassmann Structures. *Journal of Mathematical Psychology, 12*, 283-303.

Krantz, D.H. (1975b). Color Measurement and Color Theory. II: Opponent-Colors Theory. *Journal of Mathematical Psychology, 12*, 283-303.

Land, E.H. (1986). Recent Advances in Retinex Theory. *Vision Research, 26*, 7-21.

Larimer, J. (1981). Red/Green Opponent Colors Equilibria Measured on Chromatic Adapting Fields: Evidence for Gain Changes and Restoring Forces. *Vision Research, 21*, 501-512.

Mausfeld, R. & Niederée, R. (1989a). Inquiries Into Relational Colour Theory I. A Relational Colour Space Based Upon a Principle of Incremental Colour Coding. *Bonner Methoden Berichte, 6, 21*. Bonn: Psychologisches Institut (To be submitted for publication).

Mausfeld, R. & Niederée, R. (1989b). An Incremental Octant-wise Linear Model for Asymmetric Matching Based on an Extended Grassmann Structure: A Measurement Theoretic Analysis. *Bonner Methoden Berichte, 6, 22*. Bonn: Psychologisches Institut. (To be submitted for publication).

Schrödinger, E. (1920). Grundlinien einer Theorie der Farbenmetrik im Tagessehen. *Annalen der Physik, 63*, 397-426, 427-456, 481-520.

Shevell, S.K. (1978). The Dual Role of Chromatic Backgrounds in Color Perception. *Vision Research, 18*, 1649-1661.

Wallach, H. (1948). Brightness Constancy and the Nature of Achromatic Colors. *Journal of Experimental Psychology, 38*, 310-324.

Walraven, J. (1976). Discounting the Background - The Missing Link in the Explanation of Chromatic Induction. *Vision Research, 16*, 289-295.

Whittle, P. & Challands, P. D. C. (1969). The Effect of Background Luminance on the Brightness of Flashes. *Vision Research, 9*, 1095-1110.

Wyszecki, G., & Stiles, W.S. (1982). *Color Science. Concepts and Methods, Quantitative Data and Formulae*. (2nd Edition). New York:Wiley.

Choice Basis, a Model for Multi-attribute Preference: some more Evidence.

J.P. Barthélemy *)

Ecole Nationale Supèrieure des Telecommunications, Paris.

E. Mullet

U.A. CNRS 656 et Université de Lille III.

Abstract

Several models for riskless choice involving the concept of bounded rationality, have been presented and tested under various conditions. In the special case of a binary choice between alternatives characterized on several attributes, present models include essentially the maximin and maximax rules, the dominance rule, the conjunctive and disjunctive rules, the majority and the weighted set of differences rules, the choice by greatest attractiveness rule, the lexicographic, the minimum difference lexicographic and the lexicographic semi-order rules, the addition of utility differences and the sequential accumulation of differences rules. To account for expert's information processing in a binary choice task, Barthélemy and Mullet (1986) proposed and tested a slightly more complex and flexible model, inspired by the work of Montgomery (1983). This model, called the moving basis heuristics, coordinates four types of rules: 1°) lexicographic rules, 2°) threshold rules, 3°) conjunctive rules, 4°) disjunctives rules. It builds on the principle that the dominance rule is used as a major one and that all the other rules are justused to obtain dominance structure as quickly as possible. Three basic principles are in fact involved in the model: (i) a parsimony principle, (ii) a reliability principle, (iii) a decidability principle. Empirical data supporting the model have been presented and discussed previously (Barthélemy and Mullet, 1986). In this paper we discuss the model in relation to other models and we present the results of three other experiments. The first two replicate the basic experiments; in the third one, experts' verbal justifications are analyzed.

1. Models of riskless choice

According to Simon (e.g. 1979), a human decision maker is able to show rationality, but restricted within the limits of the representation of the decision situation facing the decision maker (see also Klein, 1983; Payne, 1982). Several

---

ENST, département Informatique, 46 rue Barrault, 75634 Paris cedex 13, France.

models for choice, involving this concept of bounded rationality, have been presented and tested under various conditions (Montgomery and Svenson, 1976; Svenson, 1983). In the special case of a binary choice between alternatives characterized on several attributes, these rules or models include the following:

The *maximin* and the *maximax* rules (Dahlstrand and Montgomery, 1984).

The *dominance* rule (Lee, 1971).

The *conjunctive* and the *disjunctive* rules (Coombs, 1964; Dawes, 1963).

The *majority* rule (May, 1954; Russo and Dosher, 1976), and the *weighted set of differences* rule (Huber, 1979).

The *choice by greatest attractiveness* rule (Montgomery and Svenson, 1976).

The *lexicographic* rule (Fishburn, 1974); the *minimum difference lexicographic* rule (Montgomery and Svenson, 1976); the *lexicographic semi order* rule (Tversky, 1969).

The *addition of utility differences* rule (Tversky, 1969) and the *sequential accumulation of differences* rule (Aschenbrenner et al., 1984).

Most of these rules are well known. According to the *maximin* rule, the chosen alternative has the highest lower attribute value. The *maximax* rule implies that the chosen alternative has the highest of the highest evaluation. According to the *dominance* rule, an alternative is chosen over the other if it is better on at least one attribute and not worse on all other attributes. The *conjunctive* rule states that the attribute values for the chosen alternative must exceed a standard specific for each attribute and that, at least on one attribute, the other alternative falls below this threshold. The *disjunctive* rule states that the evaluation on at least one attribute, for the chosen alternative, must exceed a threshold specific to that attribute and that all aspects of the other alternative fall below a critical value specific to each attribute. The *majority rule* goes back to Condorcet (1785) in the context of social choice and the *weighted sets of differences* rule goes back to Benjamin Franklin (1772, cf. Debord, 1987) in the context of individual choice. The first rule states that, if alternative s_1 is better than alternative s_2 for a majority of attributes, then s_1 is chosen. According to the second rule the decision maker divides the set of attributes into two subsets. The subset A_1 (resp. A_2) contains all the attributes that speak for s_1 (resp. for s_2). These two sets are weighted and s_1 is chosen whenever A_1 has more weight than A_2. The *choice by greatest attractiveness difference* rule states that the decision maker first determines the attribute associated with the greatest attractiveness difference. Then the most attractive alternative on this attribute is chosen.

In the various *lexicographic* rules the attributes are assumed to be ranked in terms of importance. The (pure) *lexicographic* rule states that the chosen alternative has the highest evaluation on the most important attribute. In case of a tie on this attribute, the decision is based on the second most important attribute and so on. The *lexicographic semiorder* rule works like the lexicographic rule with the additional assumption that for the first attribute there is a difference threshold. If the difference between the evaluations of the two alternatives exceeds this threshold, then the alternative with the highest evaluation is chosen. If not, the second attribute is used, and so on, as in the lexicographic rule (i.e. without difference thresholds). As a generalization, one obtains the *minimum difference lexicographic* rule which states that each attribute is associated with a difference threshold and that the differences on attributes are lexicographically compared to these thresholds.

In all utility models a utility function u_i is applied to each attribute X_i. In the *addition of utility differences* rule, a difference function μ_i is applied to each attribute X_i and s_1 is chosen over s_2 whenever $\Sigma\mu_i(u_i(s_1)-u_i(s_2))>0$. The *sequential accumulation of differences* rule combines the lexicographic rule and the addition of utility difference rule. Attributes are ranked in terms of importance and a global threshold ∂ is given. A counter accumulates the differences $\mu_i(u_i(s_1)-u_i(s_2))$ and $\mu_i(u_i(s_2)-u_i(s_1))$ on the attributes taken in lexicographic order, until one of these two sums of differences exceeds the threshold. Hence, only the first k attributes are considered and the alternative s_1 such that $\Sigma_{i\leq k}\mu_i(u_i(s_1)-u_i(s_2))>\partial$ is chosen.

2. The moving basis heuristics

To account for experts' choices in a binary choice task, Barthélemy and Mullet (1986) proposed and tested a slightly more complex model, inspired by Montgomery (1983). This model, called the *moving basis heuristics*, coordinates four types of rules 1°) lexicographic rules, 2°) threshold rules, 3°) conjunctive rules, 4°) disjunctive rules. The general architecture of the model is described in Figure 1: Box 1 represents the subprocess of selection of one or more attributes at a given time (Montgomery's pre-editing phase). Box 3 shows the subprocess of comparing the relative superiority of one alternative over the other with one or several threshold values (dominance testing phase). If at least one difference is lower than the corresponding threshold, another set of attributes can be taken into account (Box 7, dominance structuring phase). After several loops, the expert may decide or provide a non-choice (Box 6).

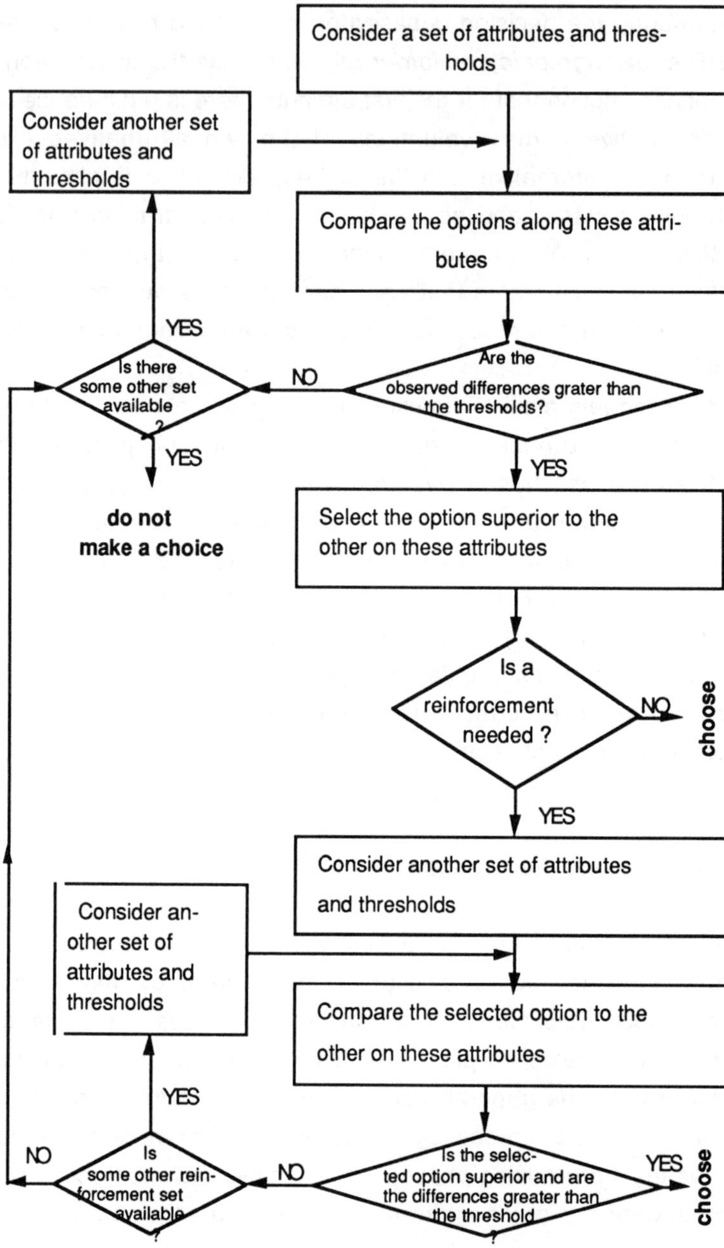

FIGURE 1. The moving basis heuristics

This model is a decision heuristic in the sense of Groner et al. (1983) and Hubert (1986). It builds on the principle that a "restricted" dominance rule is used as a major one and that all the other rules are just used to obtain a dominance structure as quickly as possible (Montgomery, 1983). Three basic principles are involved in the model.

1. A parsimony principle. Due to his/her inability to process the whole data set, the expert extracts some subsets whose size is small enough to be compatible both with human short-range storage abilities (there is no intermediate storage in a long term memory) and with human computational abilities (see Aschenbrenner, 1978;Johnson and Payne, 1985; Lindman and Lyons, 1978, ...).

2. A reliability/warrantability principle. This principle works, in some sense, as the opposite of the preceding one (de Hoog and Van der Wittenboer, 1986). Concerned by reliability (socially as well as personally), the expert extracts from the data set a subset large enough and composed in such a way as to appear meaningful (comparisons on several attributes, conjunctive rules). A decision is made if and only if the gap between two alternatives is large enough (threshold rules; see Adelbratt and Montgomery, 1980; Huber, 1983; McAllister et al., 1979; Montgomery, 1983; Raynard and Crozier, 1983, ...).

3. A decidability principle. Concerned with the necessity to achieve choice in almost all cases, the expert extracts subsets of data in a manner flexible enough to achieve, almost all the time, a decision, on relatively short notice. Minimal conflict corresponds to such a decision (see Huber, 1986; Klayman, 1982, p. 39; Montgomery, 1983; Svenson, 1979, p. 106-107, ...).

Applying such a heuristic is generally consistent with a low probability of error and a small cost for errors that may happen (Stillwell et al., 1981). A reason for this weakness of errors may be that the attributes are correlated (Vicariant Process, Einhorn et al., 1979, p. 466). Moreover it is worth noticing that although the information process is assumed to follow a flow chart, such a representation should not be considered literally. The sequence of events surely is not strictly determined at each time. Rather it corresponds to stochastic tendencies. As in the model of Aschenbrenner, Albert and Schmalhofer (1984), the sequence of selecting attributes may be varying (see also Montgomery, 1983).

Figure 2 represents an example of application of the heuristics. {L}, {L,F}, {F,M} are the sets of attributes one expert considered successively; in other words they are the successive points of view the expert uses. The ∂s are the results of the comparisons between alternatives on L, or LF, or FM. The numbers 3, 1, 4 are the corresponding threshold values. Clearly, in this example, the model presupposes a process that includes both interdimensional and intradimensional judgments.

This seems compatible with many previous observations (e.g. Bettman and Jacoby, 1976; Raynard and Crozier, 1983).

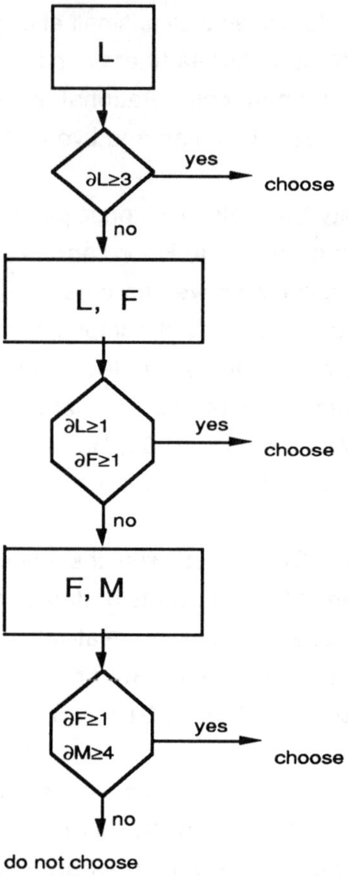

FIGURE 2. A realization of the heuristics

The whole process can be summarized as a single formula, which we call a *choice polynomial*:

$$L^3 + LF + FM^4$$

It reads: Each time there is a difference of at least three levels in L, favoring one alternative, then this alternative is chosen. If not, each time there is a difference of at least one level on L (exponent omitted in this case) *and* a difference of at least one level in F, favouring one alternative, then this alternative is chosen. If not, each time there is a difference of at least one level on F and a difference of at least four levels in M, favouring one alternative, then this alternative is chosen. In all other cases there is a non-choice.

In this formula, each 'monom' represents what is generally conceived as a *production rule* and the whole formula may be viewed as a *production system* (Huber, 1986). This is also what Kleinmuntz (1986) calls a "formal mathematical model of decision making at the process level".

3. Relationships to other models

In cases where all the monoms (sets of attributes with thresholds) of a polynomial are reduced to a single attribute (no conjunction), the model reduces to a minimum difference lexicographic rule (e.g., $L^3+F^4+M^5$). If there is only one threshold (on the first attribute), or no threshold at all, the model reduces to a lexicographic semi order rule (e.g., L^3+F+M), or a lexicographic rule (e.g., L+F+M). In cases where only one monom occurs (no disjunction, i.e. no loop in the process), the model reduces to a conjunctive one (e.g., LF^3). In cases where this set of attributes includes all the attributes, the model reduces to a strict dominance rule (LFM). In cases where the sets of attributes include each combination of a majority of attributes without threshold, the model reduces to the majority rule (LF+LM+FM).

More generally, the model is a collection of criterion dependent processing rules in the sense of Schmalhofer and Saffrich (1984) and Schmalhofer and Gertzen (1986). The more difficult the decision is, because of the similarities between alternatives, the more processed attributes are required to make a choice. The model can also express compensatory effects (as in the addition of utility difference rule, or as in the sequential accumulation of utility differences rule) in the following way: $L^3 + L^2F^2 + LF^4 + F^6$. In this polynomial, a decrease of the difference along the attribute L is compensated by an increase of the difference along F. According to Billings and Marcus (1983), it is an important property for a model to allow for the expression of compensatory, as well as non-compensatory effects (see also Montgomery, 1983). But the model is mainly a *satisficing model.* As soon as one particular set of attributes allows for a choice, the choice is made, despite the fact that another set of attributes may induce an opposite choice. In other words, the additive law in the polynomials cannot be used in a commutative way; the model is truly lexicographic. Finally, the model can account for intransitivities and non choices (Corbin, 1980), by assuming threshold rules and by allowing the consideration of non-overlapping sets of attributes, if any (Flament, 1960 a and b; Tversky, 1969; Huber, 1979).

From a quite different point of view, it is also possible to translate the moving basis to an *anchoring and adjustment* (Slovic, 1967; Lopes, 1982; Svenson, 1985) version as follows: Place two objects, a and b, on each side of a choice scale (Figure 3)

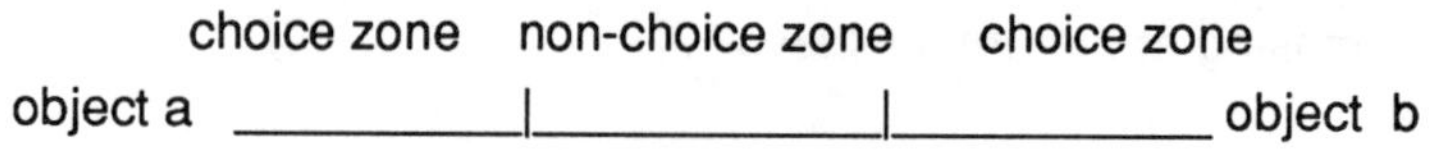

FIGURE 3

Suppose that an expert usually considers the attributes M, L, F (rule 1). Suppose he/she considers first (rule 1) attribute F (anchor) which favours b. We can represent the effect of F on the scale as in Figure 4:

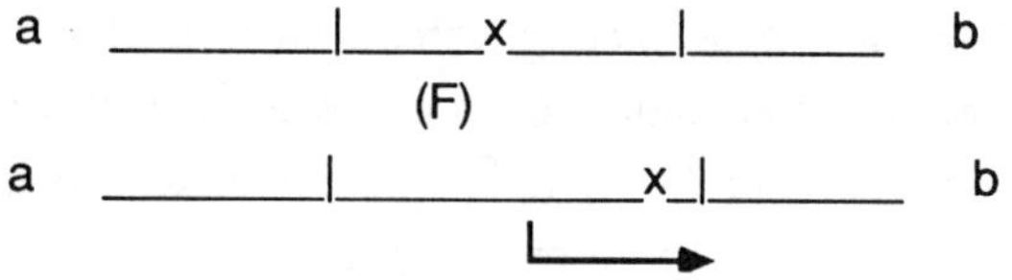

FIGURE 4

In the present case, the position of the cross, which expresses an internal state of the expert, is still in the non-choice zone. So, the expert needs to consider another attribute: M (rule 3). Suppose M also favors b. We can represent the additional effect of M on the scale of Figure 5. Now the cross lies outside of the non-choice zone and a choice can be produced (first case).

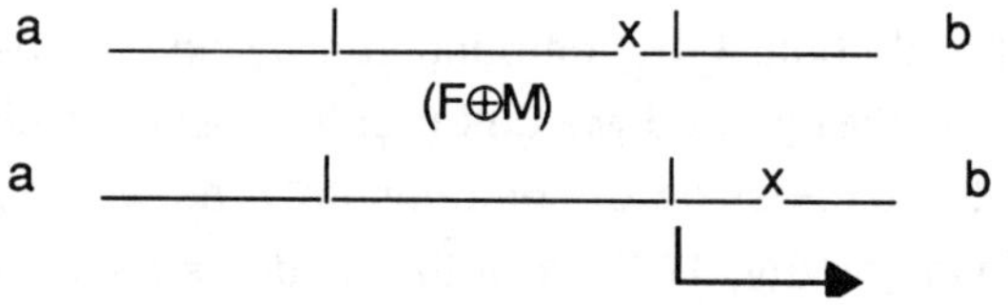

FIGURE 5

Suppose, on the contrary (second case), that M does not favor b or a. If this is the case one needs to process more information (L). Suppose now that after the processing of F, M and L, the internal state of the expert implies that no choice is possible. In this case, we can imagine that the expert turns his/her attention to another set of attributes (rule 4). The reasons of this swich are partly internal - the expert does not easily process more than three pieces of information, but they are also partly external - a major difference in V seems attractive ... Suppose that the expert processes that difference first, and that it favors a, as expressed in Figure 6.

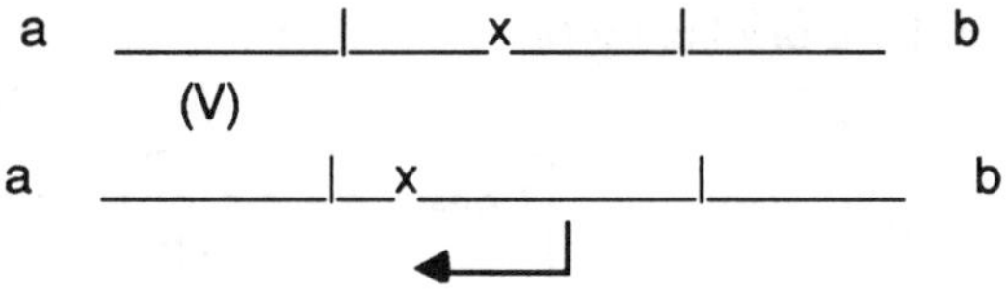

FIGURE 6

Suppose also that in the next step, he/she processes the difference on N, which also favors *a* in such a way that this time a choice can be made. With this choice the process can stop.

On the whole, the expert tried two bases: an {F,L,M} basis and a {V,N} basis. In the second case, the first, whose anchor was F, did not allow for a satisfactory choice. The second, whose anchor was V, allowed for a satisfactory choice. This anchoring and adjustment point of view may be generalized as follows:

Consider for instance the polynomial:

$$L^3 + LF + FM^4$$

and "factorize" it as:

$$L(L^2+F) + FM^4$$

This new expression suggests the following decision rule:

1°) [Anchor] Each time a one level difference is observed on L, the corresponding option is *selected*, but a reinforcement is needed.

2°) [Adjustment] Each time a difference of at least two more levels on L is observed, favouring the selected option, this option is chosen.

3°) [Alternative adjustment] When the request of 2°) is not satisfied, each time a difference of at least one level on F is observed, favouring the selected option, this option is chosen.

4°) [Alternative anchor] When the request of 3°) is not satisfied, the selected option is left and a difference of at least one level on F and at least four levels on M produces the choice.

The general architecture of this anchoring and adjustment model is given on figure 7 and its realization for the rules induced by $L^3+LF+FM^4$ is depicted in figure 8 (a). It is worth noticing that the way this polynomial is computed is not influenced by the assumption that the first (figure 1) or the second (figure 7) flow chart holds. Hence these cognitive processes are both compatible with the polynomial. Moreover for a given polynomial and within the anchor/adjustment model the same polynomial admits many factorizations. For instance, $L^3+LF+FM^4$ may be written as: $L^3+F(L+M^4)$: L and F are anchors, L does not need any adjustment and F need to be reinforced either by L or else by M.

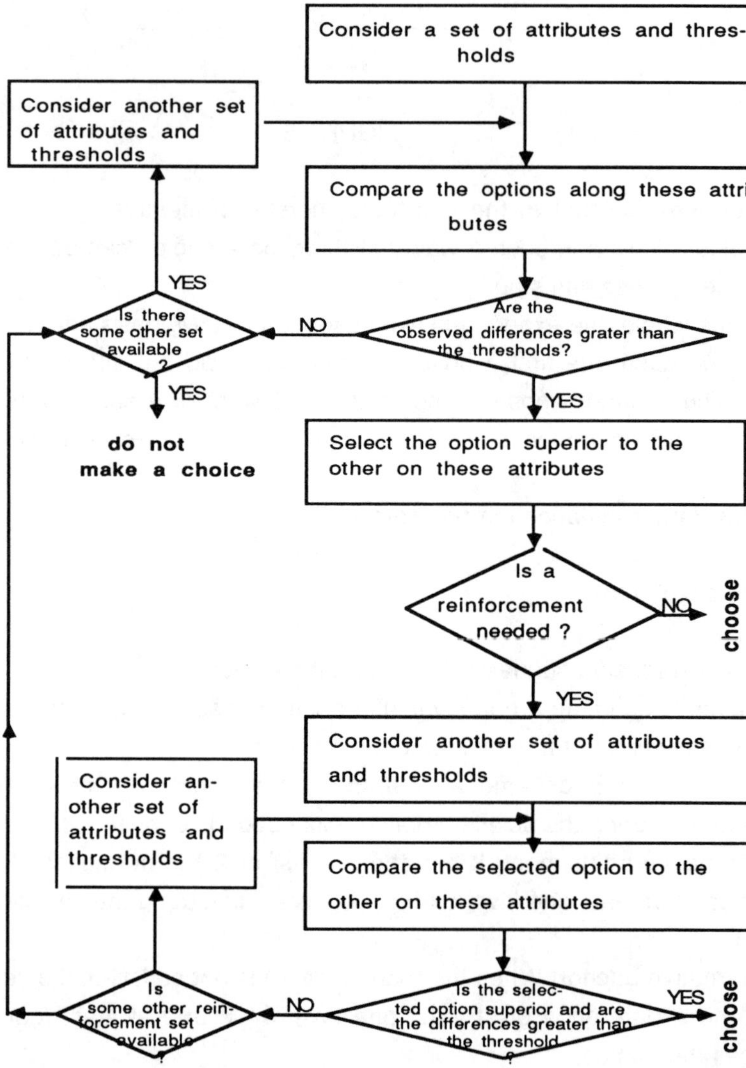

FIGURE 7

In addition, it seems reasonable to consider

$$L(L^2+F) + F(L+M^4)$$

as another factorization of $L^3+LF+FM^4$ (since LF+LF induces the same choices as LF !). This factorization leads to another realization of the process of Figure 7. This realization is depicted on Figure 8 (b).

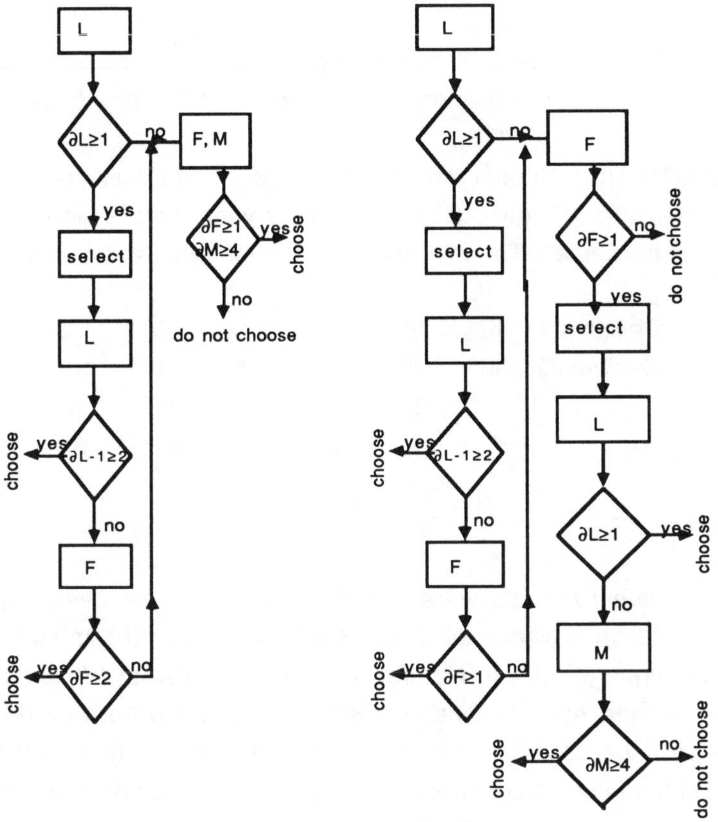

(a) (b)

FIGURE 8

4. Some more empirical evidence

Empirical data supporting the model as described in Section 2 have been presented and discussed previously (Barthélemy and Mullet, 1986). Here we will present the results of three other experiments. The first two are replications of the basic experiment; in the third one, however an analysis of verbal justifications given by the experts was performed.

4.1 Experiment 1

4.1.1 *Method*

4.1.1.1 SUBJECTS: The area of school guidance was used as the choice situation. The expert population consisted of 24 volunteer unpaid psychologists.

4.1.1.2 STIMULI: Stimuli consisted of 2x7 academic records (a to g) of (approximatively) 15 year-old students, three years before high school graduation ('classe de troisième'). The records were designed as two latin squares:

Design n°1	F	M	N	S	V	L	A
Design n°2	M	F	T	A	N	S	L
a	1	2	3	4	5	6	7
b	7	1	2	3	4	5	6
.	....						

These academic records were built from 12 attributes, seven of these varying across the records. These included: Grades in French (F), in Mathematics (M), in Foreign Languages (L), in Natural Sciences (S); Verbal (V) and non Verbal (N) Test scores and Age (A). The values held constant were: Sex (female), parents' profession (blue collars), type of school (high school), type of the Baccalaureat desired in the future (Economics), and health (good). Eighty-four additional records were compiled by extrapolation from real records to give a more realistic flavour to the set as a whole.

4.1.1.3 CHOICE TASK. Records a_1 to g_1 in design 1 were combined to make 21 pairs of records. Records a_2 to g_2 were combined in a similar fashion. The 84 additional records were randomly partitioned into 42 pairs. Thus the total number of comparisons was: 84 = 21+21+42. The presentation order for the pairs of experimental records (designs 1 and 2) was randomized. Each counseling psychologist was asked to compare each pair so as to be able to state which of the students was more likely to succeed in the desired Baccalauréat program. The experts indicate either a preference (a<b or b<a), or else a non-choice (a=b). They worked in their usual setting and at their own place.

4.1.2 *Results*

The number of choices made varies considerably across counselors (from 8 to 21, with 16,1 as average). No significant relationship was found for the number of choices expressed per counselor in Design 1 vs. Design 2.

4.1.2.1 IS REFERENCE TO PREFERENTIAL WEIGHING OF CERTAIN ATTRIBUTES NECESSARY TO EXPLAIN CHOICES ? This hypothesis was tested by computing the number of times the chosen record had the highest grade in French, Math., Sciences etc. Detailed examples are given in Mullet (1984). Significant effects were found for all but two counselors. In the majority of cases grades in F and/or M and/or L appeared as the most highly selected dimensions related to the choice.

4.1.2.2 IS REFERENCE TO THRESHOLDS NECESSARY TO EXPLAIN THE CHOICE PROCEDURE ? A systematic analysis of intransitivities involving non-choices (a=b, b=c and a<c) was performed. Following well known principles in perception theory, we claim that the hypothesis of a threshold seems possible when such intransitivities are observed. However without a well established mathematical model, we have to be careful in our conclusions (for instance, if the preference relation is transitive and numerically representable in one dimension, such a threshold would correspond to a semi-order. In our case the strict preference is not necessarily transitive...). Such intransitivities were found for 20 counselors. Thus, threshold rules probably are applied by these counselors.

4.1.2.3. IS REFERENCE TO CONJUNCTIVE PROCESSING OF MULTIPLE ATTRIBUTES NECESSARY TO EXPLAIN THE CHOICE BEHAVIOR ? This hypothesis was tested by the analysis of a minimal choice basis. The principle behind this analysis is to examine each choice made in each pair and to retain only those attributes required as a minimal choice basis given the entire set of choices. Two separate analyses were performed. In the first one, the attributes favouring the chosen alternative in each pair were selected (potential bases). In the second analysis, a minimal basis was extracted from each potential basis. Such a minimal basis appears as a monom like FM^4. It means that F and M are extracted from the potential basis and are minimal in the sense that a decrease of thresholds (1 and 4) on F or on M will inverse the preference or produce a non-choice in another pair. So a conjunctive process of multiple attributes must be inferred each time a minimal basis has at least two attributes. Globally, the 24 counselors made a total of 386 choices out of 504 possible (77%). In 256 cases (67%) a minimal basis with more than one attribute was observed. The hypothesis of the existence of information processing without joint evaluation of several attribute values has to be rejected.

4.1.2.4 IS REFERENCE TO A DISJUNCTIVE PROCESS INVOLVING ATTRIBUTES OR SETS OF ATTRIBUTES NECESSARY TO EXPLAIN CHOICE BEHAVIOR ? A change in information processing strategies reflects a procedure opposite to a systematic comparison of one or a set of attributes maintained for use throughout the entire choice procedure. In order to test the hypothesis of the presence of changes in strategies, intransitivities of strict preferences ($a<b$, $b<c$ and $c \leq a$) were scrutinized. The presence of intransitivities of this type can be explained by changes in the attributes or set of attributes under consideration from one comparison to the next (Tversky, 1969; Montgomery, 1977). Such high intransitivities were found for 17 counselors out of the 24 (or approximatively 2/3). Consequently, the attributes' processing is neither uniform nor stereotypic. Depending on the moment the comparison is made, the counselor forms a judgment according to one specific attribute, or another, or several others, until reaching a choice or a non-choice.

4.2 Experiment 2

Experiment 2 is an extension of Experiment 1 in which only counselors who gave emitted non choices (and only they) were asked to reexamine the corresponding pairs of records. This time, however, they were asked to make a forced choice. The aim of this procedure was to test the robustness of the preceding results relative to the intransitivities of the type: $a<b$, $b<c$ and $a=c$. As counselors are busy experts, it would not have been reasonable to ask them several times to compare the same pair of records. Experiment 2 took place one week after Experiment 1 for each counselor (one declined to participate). Intransitivities were again present in 14 out of the 23 counselors.

4.3 Experiment 3

Experiment 3 was designed to compare verbalizations of the experts about their own process with the inferences about the process based on the choices. The main question was to find out whether expressed choice basis was consistent with the choice basis inferred from observed choices. Would the expert mention conjunctions of attributes and changes into the choice basis? Another question concerned the generality of experts' choice behavior. Would the experts, facing real records, continue to mention variable conjunctions of attributes ?

4.3.1 *Method*

The experimental design was essentially the same as the one described in 4.1 . But at the end of the task, the expert was required to indicate what attributes had been used to make the choice. The experts were five counselors. They were separately asked to participate to the experiment.

4.3.2 *Results*

The same analysis of the choice data was made as in the previous experiments, but was completed by an analysis of experts' verbalization. These analyses were performed both on the 42 pairs of experimental records and on the 42 additional real records.

4.3.2.1 IS REFERENCE TO CONJUNCTIVE PROCESS OF MULTIPLE ATTRIBUTES NECESSARY TO EXPLAIN CHOICE BEHAVIOR? The results of the analysis of 4.1.2.3 and of experts' verbalization are shown in table 1.

The reader can see that all these results are similar in percentage. Moreover, in 63% of cases the declared basis contains the computed basis; in 20% of cases the two bases are similar, but without inclusion. In only 17% of cases we did observe relevant differences (in particular, the computed bases were greater than the expressed bases). Once again we must invoke conjunctive processes of several attributes.

TABLE 1

		Number of attributes			
		1	2	3	>3
Choice set1:	computed	12%	27%	10%	41%
	declared	5%	17%	23%	55%
Choice set 2:	computed	20%	16%	20%	44%
	declared	11%	22%	35%	32%
Additionnal records (declared)		12%	16%	21%	51%

4.3.2.2 IS REFERENCE TO A DISJUNCTIVE PROCESS OF ATTRIBUTES, OR SET OF ATTRIBUTES NECESSARY TO EXPLAIN CHOICE BEHAVIOR ? The number of strong intransitivities observed in choice sets 1 and 2 for each counselor was: 7, 0, 8, 15 and 17, respectively. Hence four counselors used a disjunctive strategy. In these records, changes in the basis from one comparison to another were spontaneously expressed by these experts. Some *examples* are shown below:

TABLE 2

counselor n°1		2	3	4	5
ab		F,L,M	F,V	=	F,M,V,N
af	A,F,M,S	A,F,L,M,S	A,F,L,S,V,N	M,S,V,N	A
bc		F,L,M	F,L,M,S,V,N	F,L,M	M
be	M,N	F,L,M,S	A,F,L,V,N	M,N	L,M,V,N
bg	A,V	=	A,F,L,V	L,M,S,V,N	A
cd	=	F,L,M	L,S,N	F,M,N	L,S,V
cg	A,F,N	F,L,M,S	A,F,V,N	A,F,M	A,F
dg	L,M,S,V	F,L,M	A,F,L,S,V,N	A,F,M,N	L,V

The reader may note that non overlaps are relatively common for the same counselor (excepted for the 'transitive' counselor 2).

These results are confirmed by the expressed bases for the additionnal records: frequent changes and non-overlap (except once more, for counselor n°2).

4.4 Discussion

Results from the three reported experiments provide evidence for the model depicted in Figure 1. Analyses of observed choices and analyses of verbal justifications lead to convergent conclusions: the coordination of conjunctive and disjunctive rules, the use of thresholds and the use of lexicographic rules. Changes of the choice basis, that can lead to strong intransitivities or preference reversions, are not to be considered as random errors. Rather they reflect experts' strategies, regardly whether they are computed according to the model (e.g. L^3+LF+FM^4) or are spontaneously expressed (even when the expert is faced with *real data*).

References

Adolbratt T. & Montgomery H. (1980), Attractiveness of decision rules, *Acta Psychologica*, 45, 177-185.

Aschenbrenner K.M. Albert D. & Schmalhofer F. 1984), Stochastic choice heuristics, *Acta Psychologica*, 56, 153-166.

Aschenbrenner K.M. & Kasubek (1978), Challenging the Cushing Syndrome: Multiattribute evaluation of cortisone drugs, *O.B.H.P*, 22, 216-234.

Barthélemy J.P. & Mullet (1986), Choice basis: A model for multiattribute preferences, *British Journal of Mathematical and Statistical Psychology*, 39, 106-124.

Bettman J.R. & Jacoby J. (1976), Patterns in consumer information acquisition, in B.B. Anderson (ed.) *Advances in Consumer Research, vol. 4,* Chicago: Association for Consumer Research.

Caritat M.J.A., marquis de Condorcet (1785), Essai de l'application de l'analyse à la probabilité des décisions rendues à la pluralité des voix, Paris (reprint, Chelsea publ. 6, New York, 1974).

Coombs C.H. (1963), *A Theory of Data*, New York, Wiley.

Corbin (1980), Decision that might not to get, in T. Wallenstein (ed.) Cognition processes in choice and behavior, Hillsdale: Erlbaum.

Dahlstrand V. & Montgomery H. (1984), *I*nformation search and evaluation processes in decision-making: A computer based process tracing study, *Acta Psychologica* 56, 113-123.

Dawes R.M. (1964), Social Selection based on multidimensional criteria, *Journal of Abnormal and Social Psychology* 68, 104-109.

Debord B. (1987), *Axiomatisation des procédures d'agrégation de préférences*, Thesis, Grenoble.

Einhorn M.J., Kleinmuntz D.N. & Kleinmuntz B. (1979), Linear regression and process tracing models of judgment, *Psychological Review* 86, 465-485.

Fishburn P.C. (1974), Lexicographic orders, utilities and decision rules: A survey, *Management Science* 20, 1442-1471.

Flament C. (1958), Analyse pluridimensionnelles des structures hierarchiques intransitives, *Bulletin du C.E.R.P.* 7, 171-179.

Flament C. (1960a), Comportement de choix et échelle de mesure I: Etude théorique, *Bulletin du C.E.R.P.* 9, 165-175.

Flament C. (1960b), Comportement de choix et échelle de mesure II: Etude expérimentale, *Bulletin du C.E.R.P.* 9, 177-186.

Groner R., Groner M., & Bischof W. (1983), The role of heuristics in models of decision, in R.W. SCHOLZ (ed.) *Decision Making under Uncertainty,* Amsterdam: North-Holland.

Hoog R. de & van der Wittenberg (1986), Decision justification, information structure and the choice of decision rules, in R.W. Bremmer, M. Jungermann, P. Lourens & G. Sevon (eds.) *New Direction in Research on Decision Making,* Amsterdam: North-Holland.

Huber O. (1979), Non transitive multidimensional preferences: Theoretical analysis of a model, *Theory and Decision* 10, 147-165.

Huber O. (1983), The information presented and actually processed in a decision task, in P.C. Humphrey, O. Svenson & A. Vari (eds.): *Analyzing and Aiding Decision Process*, Amsterdam: North-Holland.

Huber O. (1986), Decision making as a problem solving process, in R.W. Bremmer, M. Jungermann, P. Lourens & G. Sevon (eds.) *New Direction in Research on Decision Making,* Amsterdam: North-Holland.

Johnson E.J. & Payne J.W. (1985), Effort and accuracy in choice, *Management Science* 31, 395-314.

Klayman J. (1982), *Simulations of six decision strategies: Comparison of search patterns, processing characteristics, and response to task complexity,* Chicago: Center for Dicision Research.

Klein N. (1983), Utility and decision strategies: A second look on the rational decision-maker, *O.B.M.P* 31, 1-25.
Kleinmuntz D.N (1986), Human decision processes: Heuristics and task structures, in P.A. Hancok (ed.) *Human Factor Psychology*, Amsterdam: North-Holland.
Lee W. (1971), *Decision theory and human behavior*, NewYork: Wiley.
Lopes L. (1982), *Toward a procedural theory of judgment*, Madison: Human Information Processing Program, Technical Report 17.
May K.O. (1954), Intransitivity, utility and the aggregation of preference patterns, *Econometrica* 22, 1-13.
McAllister D.W., Mitchell T.R. & Beach L.R. (1979), The contingency model for the selection of decision strategies: the empirical test of the effects of significance, accountability and reductibility, *O.B.H.P* 24, 228-244.
Montgomery H. (1977), A study of intransitivities preferences using a think-aloud procedure, in H. Jungermann, G. de ZEEUW (eds.) *Decision Making and Change in Human Affairs*, Dordrecht: Reidel.
Montgomery H. (1983), Decision Rules and the search for a dominance structure: Toward a process model of decision-making, in P.C. Humphrey, O. Svenson & A. Vari (eds.): *Analyzing and Aiding Decision Process*, Amsterdam: North-Holland.
Montgomery H. & Svenson O. (1976), On decision rules and information processing strategies for choices among multiattribute alternatives, *Scandinavian Journal of Psychology* 17, 283-291.
Mullet E. (1984), *The heuristics of a flexible choice basis*, Paris: Service de Recherches de l'INETOP/CNAM.
Payne J.W. (1982), Contingent Decision Behavior, *Psychological Bulletin* 92, 382-402.
Raynard R. & Crozier R. (1983), Reasons given for risky judgment and choice: A comparison of three tasks, in P.C. Humphrey, O. Svenson & A. Vari (eds.): *Analyzing and Aiding Decision Process*, Amsterdam: North-Holland.
Russo J.E. & Dosher B.A. (1976), Strategies for multiattributes binary choice, *Journal of Experimental Psychology: Learning, Memory and Cognition,*
Schmalhofer F. & Gertzen H. (1986), Judgment as a component decision process for choosing between sequentially available alternatives, in R.W. Bremmer, M. Jungermann, P. Lourens & G. Sevon (eds.) *New Direction in Research on Decision Making*, Amsterdam: North-Holland.
Schmalhofer F. & Saffrich W. (1984), Effort-quality trade-off characteristics of selection information processing in binary choices, Paper presented at the 13th European Mathematical Psychology Meeting, Utrecht.
Shugan S.M. (1980), The cost of thinking, *Journal of Consumer Research* 7, 99-111.
Simon H.A. (1979), *Models of Thought*, New-Haven: Yale University Press.
Slovic P. (1967), *Structural determinants of one utilization in judgment: A polarisation and adjustment model for the computation of weighted averages*, unpublished manuscript.
Stillwell W.G., Seaver D.A. & Edwards W. (1981), *A* comparison of weight approximation techniques in multiattribute utility decision making, *O.B.H.P.* 28, 62-77.
Svenson O. (1979), Process description of decision making, *O.B.H.P* 23, 86-112.
Svenson O. (1983), Decision rules and information processing in decision making, in L.S. Sjöberg, T. Tyszka and J.A. WISZ (eds.): *Human Decision Making*, Bodafors: Bodaforlaget Doxa.
Tversky A. (1969), Intransitivity of preferences, *Psychological Review* 76, 31-48.

An Elementary Formal Categorization of a Corpus of Spelling Errors

Anton J. Smolenaars *
Psychological Laboratory University of Amsterdam

Abstract
If we take the complete mastery of orthography to be the productive knowledge of all spelling rules that exist within a language, then the orthography of an individual word can be identified with some subset of those rules. Accordingly, relations between words' orthographies can be framed in terms of formal relations between those subsets and partitioned into four categories:

identity: two words' subsets contain the same elements, i.e. the two orthographies contain the same spelling rules

exclusion: two words do not have any rule in common

inclusion: word **a**'s orthography contains all the rules of that of word **b**, plus some more

overlap: two words have some - but not all - rules in common. This category naturally is accompanied by some measure for the *amount* of overlap

The paper describes an algorithm to infer this partition from (co)variations of misspellings of words. The need for such an inference arises from (i) the want of a basis for a taxonomy of spelling errors which is less superficial or *ad hoc* than the common ones, and from (ii) the requirement to have an independent test for the psychological validity of recently developed software that converts 'sounds' to orthography for Dutch words. Eventually the inference is the first phase of a broad heuristic to detect the underlying cognitive processes that govern the behavior of persons who are in the process of building up the orthography of their mother's tongue, say children of about ten. These processes are not necessarily homomorph to the 'institutional' ones, i.e. the rules from textbooks or teachers.

The kernel of the algorithm consists of 3 independent criteria. The first criterion effects a relation between the scope of the deficit as to the orthography of some word and the likelihood of it distribution of spellings. The second one connects the relative *commonality* ('covariance') of two spelling distributions to *inclusion* and *overlap*. The third criterion, *heterogeneity*, focuses on the *amount* of difference between spellings.

* **Dr A.J. Smolenaars Psychological Laboratory University of Amsterdam Weesperplein 8, 1018 XA Amsterdam Netherlands phone 020-5253636 or 5253118.**

Each triple of words effects three pairs; allocation to one of the four categories of two of them puts constraints on the allocation of the third one. For instance: if **a** includes **b** and **b** and **c** have overlap, then **c** cannot include **a**, nor can **c** and **a** exclude each other. These 'triple constraints' are utilized to handle the stochastic aspect of the inference, which in itself is rather opaque: the algorithm has one free 'bias'-parameter which is assumed to be optimal when the number of violations of the 'triple constraints' is minimal.

The results of the application of the algorithm to real data are given.

It is indicated how this elementary categorization could be a precursor to a *taxonomy* of spelling errors, how it could reveal differences between 'normals' and 'dyslectics', and how it leads towards the notion of 'effective extent of errors': a way of counting the number of independent sources of error.

As the algorithm is purely formal, in the sense that no assumptions are involved that are specific to spelling processes, it can be generalized to all domains where incorrect cognitive performances can be discretely and finitely differentiated.

1. Background

Mastering the spelling of one's mother's tongue is difficult for most people, even up to a degree that full mastery is never attained. What exactly makes it that difficult is not clear at all to cognitive psychologists, who are stunned by the abundant variation of spelling errors that is produced, notably by extreme cases of spelling trouble, i.e. so-called 'dyslectics'. The natural tendency to use this affluence as a starting point for further inquiry, together with the need to restrain it, leads to a taxonomy of spelling errors. Such a taxonomy can have a linguistic basis, as well as a perceptual or cognitive one: spelling error taxonomies are ubiquitous, nevertheless they have been notoriously unsuccessful in revealing deeper insights into the spelling process and its aberrations.

One source of difficulties with these taxonomies is that they generally are developed from scratch: they focus onto the phenotypical aspects of the errors, which, together with some a priori about their etiology, tends to make them *ad hoc*, as well as equivocal. For instance, writing [poordost] for 'doorpost' can be attributed to (1) an acoustic deficit as to the differentiation of phonemes, in this case /p/ vs./d/, which brings it into one category with writing [doorfost], (2) a visual incapability in dealing with the spatial orientation of letter symbols, 'p' vs. 'd','q' or 'b', which brings the error on a par with writing [qoorpost], (3) a central inability to deal with sequential position: first /d/, then /p/, which makes it analogous to [toorposd] and (4) a deficit in the general linguistic ability to split up composed words - 'doorpost' = 'door' and 'post' - which relates the error to [dorpos].

This enumeration is by no means exhaustive, nor is it fully artificial: trying to fit a substantial corpus of spelling errors into some taxonomy in an unprejudiced way, inevitably ends up with only a minority of 'clear cases'.

This paper is the result of a confrontation of two demands. There was a need to give structure to a rich data base consisting of spelling errors from 'dyslectics' as well as a matched group of 'non-dyslectics'. Apart from that there was a requirement to evaluate in an independent way the 'psychological validity' of some recently developed software that converts 'sounds', i.e. phonological descriptions, of Dutch words into orthography , and that, by deliberate mutilation, can simulate quite a lot of common spelling errors (Verheyden, 1984, 1985). Both conditions together incited to give the treatment of spelling errors a fundamental twist, and to regard existing spelling error taxonomies as being either too specific, or prejudiced, or both, as a starting point for handling them. Does there exist a level of analysis that, by being more elementary, could evade the shortcomings of common taxonomies? Or, to put it differently, can we unveil characteristics of a corpus of spelling errors that are *preliminary* to a categorization of them?

Both questions are answered in the affirmative below, or, there is at least a clear promise that they could be. Given elementary empirical data, simple, virtually uncommitting assumptions together with some formal apparatus can reveal some abstract features of the orthographies of words.

These features, ideally, together embody a constraint that any software claiming to be 'psychologically real' should comply to. On the other hand the features potentially form some basis for an unbiased, unambiguous taxonomy.

2. The algorithm in general

2.1. Aim

We need a general and basic assumption to set things in motion: *the orthography of each word consists of a unique set of rules* i.e. from 'phonological input' to correct spelling there is a unique set of transformations.

This is a working hypothesis, whose plausibility should show up in the consistency of the results (section 4). Apart from this empirical claim, however, we would like to defend a general one: there is a level of description at which the hypothesis is uniformly true.

Orthography comes 'on top' of linguistic competence in general, and, unlike the latter, it has to be taught explicitly; whatever has been taught tends, however, to become fully implicit after its mastery so that even fluent spellers cannot enumerate the rules that guide their behavior, which brings the orthography eventually on a par with linguistic knowledge. As a result of this phenomenon it is sometimes held that adult spellers do not use any spelling rules at all, but simply *know how* to spell a word. But the native speaker does not consciously use any linguistic rule either but simply *knows how* to speak or understand a sentence. So there is no much body to this argument, except for the variant that, in some teaching systems, children learn to spell individual words by repetitious confrontation *only*. This variant, however, leads towards an empirical prediction as to the result of our analysis: each individual word has its own *exclusive* set of spelling rules.

Parallel to general linguistic competence, specification of spelling rules is not synonymous to a description of spelling behavior; subjects can use different *strategies* in applying them: besides to just using explicit rules that they happen to know, they can derive them by analogy to some other word, to put down a first approximation and evaluate whether it "looks good" etc. (v.d.Bosch, Elshout and Langereis, 1986). We claim, consequently, that there is a level of description somewhat more abstract than that of the strategies, and that - borrowing a distinction from linguistics - as a *competence* has more uniformity than the *performance* would suggest: violating or eliminating a specific rule leads to a specific error, whatever the strategy.[1)]

The orthography of a word is a *set* of rules, that is, it can be parsed, in principle, into parts that it has in common with other words; or, to put it differently, the orthography of a natural language is a finite set of spelling rules, whose cardinality is far less than the number of words. Of course, acknowledging this does not lead to the specification of the content of those rules, let alone to a (complete) enumeration of them. These endeavors should, to a high degree, be guided and constrained by empirical matters, and there is no a priori reason why the 'institutionalized' form of the spelling rules, i.e. the content of textbooks, should be optimal or realistic.

The reasoning so far gives rise to an analysis that is elementary indeed. For each pair of words we can ask which formal relation holds between the two orthographies, that is, the two sets of spelling rules.

Suppose we have five words whose orthographies consist of different rules *x*, *y*, or *z* in

1) Note that we do not claim that phenotypical identical errors point to one and the same rule, or, conversely, that different rules should necessarily lead to phenotypical different errors.

the following way **a** = $\{x\}$, **b** = $\{x\}$, **c** = $\{y\}$, **d** = $\{x,y\}$, **e** = $\{x,z\}$, then we can specify four formal relations:

identity: (**a**,**b**)

exclusion: (**a**,**c**); (**b**,**c**); (**c**,**e**)

inclusion: (**a**,**d**); (**a**,**e**); (**b**,**d**); (**b**,**e**); (**c**,**d**)

overlap: (**d**,**e**)

We have a partition here: the four relations exhaust all possibilities and each pair of words belongs to one and not more than one category. The assignment of a pair of words to one out of these four categories, together with some additional specifications, such as which word is included by which, and the *amount* of *overlap*, constitutes the level of analysis that was announced in section 1.

The notion of 'set of rules' used so far, suggests that the elements of those sets are independent and unordered. While this is unrealistic at the molecular level, the fact that the extent of those elements is left completely open, makes this assumption harmless. When two words' orthographies both contain the independent rules x and y but the sequence or frequency in which they should apply is different, we take it that each has in addition a specific 'super' rule that monitors the sequence or frequency of x and y; the two words' orthographies consequently have *overlap*. It will be clear that considerations like these do not move *in vacuo*: trivializations will show up empirically. For example, when each word consists of just one (super-)rule, so that complete 'independency' is achieved, all word-pairs will turn out to be either *exclusion* or *identity*. We do not know, of course, in advance the cardinality of each word's orthography, but, as we said we leave the extent of the 'rules' completely open, this notion does not make much sense either. For the subsequent reasoning we can do with the formulation that at each pair of words we recognize mutually exclusive *packages* of spelling rules, x, y, z. Accordingly, **a** = $\{x, y\}$ means: 'in order to spell word **a** correctly full mastery of the packages x and y is needed'.

2.2. *Nomenclature*

The algorithm that tries to assign some word-pair to one out of the four formal relations specified above, does so by the spellings of those both words by one and the same group of subjects. Each word-pair is analyzed separately, under the following standard nomenclature.

Word **a** is spelled correctly at least as often as word **b**. Subjects are divided into four groups according to the following scheme.

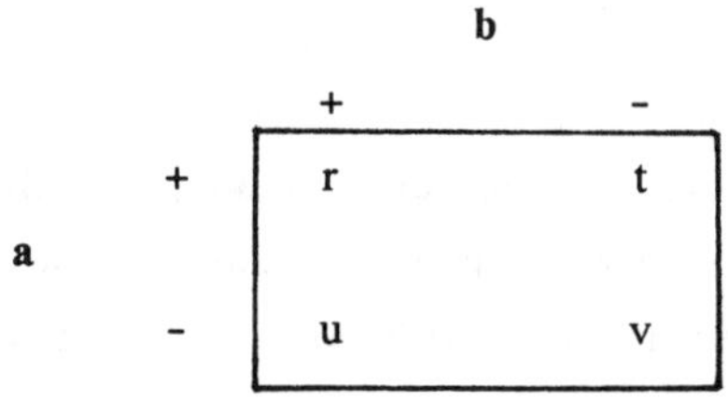

Figure 1 Initial division of subjects

Subjects from group 'r' spell both words correctly, subjects 't' spell **a** correctly but **b** wrongly, etc.

The number of subjects that belong to 'r' is called n_r and so on; n_a is the number of subjects that spell word **a** *correctly*, and so, by definition $n_a \geqslant n_b$. Obviously, $n_a = n_r + n_t$ and $n_b = n_r + n_u$. We take ${}^bE^t$ for the enumeration of all (incorrect) spellings of word **b**, by subjects 't' (as the correct spellings generally are uninteresting, we will often use E^t instead of ${}^bE^t$); $nd({}^aE^t)$ = the number of different spellings within ${}^aE^t$.

2.3. *Initial formalization*

At first sight it appears that the arrangement of fig.1 would suffice for our diagnostics: it is necessary for *identity* that $n_t = n_u = 0$, while for *inclusion* (**b** includes **a**) n_u must be = 0, analogously to the notion of 'error cell' at cumulative scaling *à la* Guttman, and so on. This impression of diagnostic value is deceptive, however, in that the conditions mentioned above surely are necessary but not sufficient, as will be shown below.

Let **a** = $\{x\}$ and **b** = $\{y\}$, so that there is *exclusion* between **a** and **b**. Supposing that subjects are in the midst of learning the spelling of their mothers tongue, (as our subjects happen to be), it is perfectly possible that within the spelling curriculum *y* comes *after x*, so that some subjects have mastered *x* but not *y yet*, while the reverse is impossible. In such a situation n_u will be = 0 under *exclusion*, so $n_u = 0$ (and $n_t = 0$) is not a sufficient condition for *inclusion*, as might be supposed naively.[2] Analogously, if **a** = {*x*} and **b** = {*x*,*y*}, *inclusion*, that is, then, if *y* comes before *x* in the curriculum then we could get $n_t = n_u = 0$, making the latter an insufficient condition to *identity*.

In order to be complete, then, one should specify all three 'curriculum conditions' among *x* and *y*: (i) simultaneous, (ii) *x* comes before *y*, iii) *y* comes before *x*, and check their consequences as to the frequencies n_r, n_t, n_u and n_v.

Taking *overlap*, **a** = {*x*, *z*}, **b** = {*y*, *z*}, into these considerations, working out all curriculum conditions and their consequences becomes rather complicated; so we omit details here, and only report that, in total, one gets 19 possible curriculum by formal relations combinations which we will call *cases* from now on. From these *cases* we will have to find our way towards the formal relations. It will be clear that the relation between the latter and the 'syndromes' (i.e. $n_t = 0$, $n_v = 0$ etc.) will be too fuzzy to be of any use. The cases constitute an intermedium and in connection to them we will have to rely on criteria of a complicated kind to do the work; we found three of those 'kernel criteria', to be described in the next paragraph.

Consequently this 'initial formalization' stage is only preliminary to the real algorithm. It generates the possible cases from the 'syndromes', or, possibly, diagnoses the task unfeasible i.e. at least one of the words is spelled correctly by all subjects: in such a case the algorithm, relying on spelling errors, can do nothing but conclude that the relation between **a** and **b** is 'undecidable'.

For the sake of completeness we mention the implicit assumption that the likelihood of the data is reasonable. That is to say, under *any* case, *each* cell frequency in fig. 1 *can* be = 0, provided some stochastic utmost has taken place (in the sampling of subjects), but, taking into consideration the weakness of assumptions all over the algorithm, the likelihoods that are excluded must be extreme indeed.

---

2) This possibility, which we overlooked at first, was brought to our attention by H. Verheyden in personal communication.

3. Kernel criteria

3.1. Scope of the deficit

What happens if the deficit as to the relevant knowledge to spell a word is complete (as if the average English speaker suddenly had to spell a word in Chinese, having at its disposal only a list of Chinese characters)? All spellings would be equally likely and over a group of English spellers the likelihood of the distribution of spellings could be derived from the multinomial distribution with some uniform p. If the English spellers happened to know that the correct spelling had to consist of 7 characters, their distribution of spellings would become less likely under the multinomial distribution with uniform p; if, in addition, they recognized one vowel and could choose the correct grapheme, the distribution would become still less likely, and so on. Together with the likelihood maxim from the end of the former section, we generalize this into an assumption: the larger the scope of the deficit as to the orthography of some word within a group of spellers the larger the likelihood of the distribution of spellings under the multinomial distribution with uniform p.

Now suppose **a** = $\{x\}$ and **b** = $\{x, y\}$, i.e there is *inclusion*. If there is no specific curriculum constraint upon x and y, that is, if they are taught simultaneously, there are four types of subjects according to the following scheme

	x	y
I	+	+
II	-	-
III	+	-
IV	-	+

Figure 2; scheme of subjects; x, y simultaneous.
'+' means 'mastery of the package'
'-' means 'some deficit in the package'

Subjects of type II have a deficit that has more impact at word **b** (x *and* y) than at word **a** (the deficit in y is irrelevant as to **a**); according to the assumption, then, their distribution of spellings of word **b** has a larger likelihood than that of word **a** under the multinomial distribution with uniform p.[3)] There is, on the other hand, no reason to expect a systematic difference in the impact at the two words of the deficit of subjects of type IV, and consequently there is no ground for differentiation of the two likelihoods.

Of course, having only the spellings there is no way to tell apart subject types II and IV, but there is no need to: both are in subgroup 'v' (cf. fig. 1), and, moreover, exclusively so. Consequently, the reasoning so far leads to the prediction, that for this case

$$\text{likelihood}({}^{a}E^{v}) < \text{likelihood}({}^{b}E^{v}) \qquad [1]$$

under the multinomial distribution with uniform p.[4)]

We can set up analogous reasonings for other cases, comparing, as before, the spellings of two words by one subgroup of subjects, or, alternatively, the spellings of one word by two subgroups of subjects. Some cases lead to a parallel prediction, some to the equality of two likelihoods. A lot of cases, however, lead to no prediction at all, either because some cells of fig.1 are empty, or because comparisons of the deficits make no sense: for instance, supposing **a** = $\{x\}$ and **c** = $\{y\}$, the scheme of fig.2 leads to no prediction as to likelihoods for these two words.

The 'scope (of the) deficit' algorithm compares two sets of spellings as to their likelihood under the multinomial distribution with uniform p. Let $f_1,...f_k$ be frequencies of spellings within ${}^{a}E^{v}$, then

$$\text{likelihood}({}^{a}E^{v}) = n_v!/(f_1!).,....,.(f_k!).p^{n_v} \qquad [2]$$

We need an estimation of p, which is the inverse of the number of different spellings under a complete deficit. As we can take this number to be a fixed positive monotonic function of the number of letters of the (correctly spelled) word, the assumption that p is a negative monotonic function of that number seems reasonable. Consequently, when we compare, say, likelihood(${}^{a}E^{v}$) with likelihood(${}^{b}E^{v}$), if both multinomial factors ($n_v!/f_1!,..f_k!$) are equal, and the number of letters of **a** equals that of **b**, we can take the two likelihoods to be equal (but cf. fn.4) without actually estimating p; also, if the multinomial factor of ${}^{b}E^{t}$ is larger than that of ${}^{b}E^{v}$, and $n_t < n_v$, we can infer that likelihood(${}^{b}E^{t}$) >likelihood(${}^{b}E^{v}$), again without estimating p, and so on. In most cases,

3) Note that it is not assumed that both p's are equal.
4) We leave the stochastics of sampling variation aside until section 4.

however, we have to estimate *p* explicitly. As it is the inverse of the number of different spellings of a word under a complete deficit, in fact we have to estimate that number. We estimate a *lowerbound* for it, which is the number of different spellings we actually have (concrete subjects seldom are completely deficient), i.e. at $^aE^v$ we take nd($^aE^v$). From separate materials, consisting of more than 550 spellings of 92 words each, we were able to fit a positively monotonic curve between word length and maximum number of different spellings. We used that curve to estimate an *upper bound* for the number of different spellings.

Upper and lower bound each lead to a *p*, and thus to a multinomial likelihood under that uniform *p*. The likelihoods of two sets of spellings are compared twice: under the lower bound and the upper bound *p*'s respectively. When both comparisons agree, the 'scopedeficit' algorithm has come to its final conclusion, when they do not the algorithm does not come to a conclusion at all.

3.2. Commonality

Each word's orthography consists of a package of spelling rules, but the individual rules are not all alike as to an attribute that we could call 'complexity', 'difficulty to learn', or something like that. Clearly, a word's 'complexity' is some function of the 'complexities' of its constituent rules; we name it the 'cognitive scope' (cs) of the word.

Now, let us express this cognitive scope as an amount of hypothetical atomic, equivalent cognitive abilities, c_1,.......c_n. Each spelling rule can be thought of as relying on a specific combination of c_i. We take a spelling - heterogeneous group of subjects and picture these as a matrix in which the rows are the subjects and the columns are the c_i. A matrix cell consists of either a '0' (the row subject does not have the column cognitive ability) or a '1'. If we want to fit in different words, it will be clear that each word's orthography relies on some c_i but not on others; we can, accordingly, depict the word's orthography as a *window* over the columns. In figure 3 we picture the situation for three words.

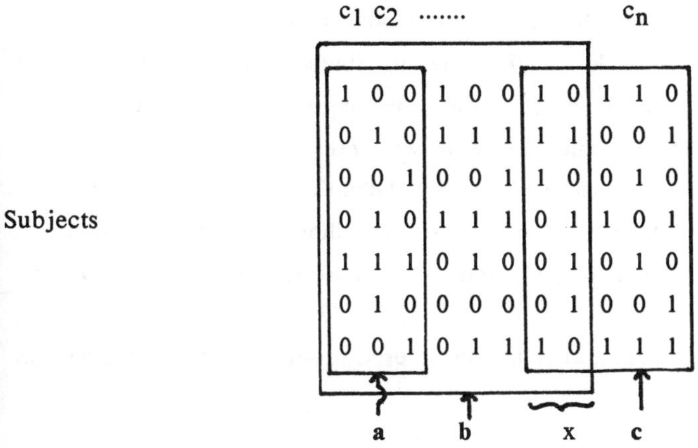

Fig. 3 A window for three words

Provided that we stick to one specific matrix, that is, to one and the same set of subjects, the following reasoning makes sense.

1. The cognitive scope of a word is proportional to the 'breadth' of its window, which, in its turn must parallel the number of different spellings within the group. The cognitive scope is implicitly calibrated to a hypothetical 'atom' word that spans one column (and consequently has two different spellings) and, likewise, a hypothetical 'super' word that spans the whole matrix, and, in the limit has a number of different spellings that equals the number of subjects. So, in fig.3 cs(**a**) < cs(**b**).

2. The *overlap* between two words is proportional to the relative overlap of their windows, which, in turn, must parallel the proportion of those pairs of subjects that spell *simultaneously* **a** and **b** either identical or different; we will call the latter proportion the *commonality* of **a** and **b**, comm(**a**,**b**). One can see clearly that for two identical windows, i.e. full overlap, the commonality must be = 1 (as is the commonality of a word with itself); when one of the two windows starts to 'grow', the commonality decreases proportionally. Again, there is the implicit calibration as to a 'superword', **s**, that spans all columns, in that comm(**a**,**s**) = cs(**a**) in the limit; moreover, any two words that approximate **s** must of necessity show a substantial commonality. It thus makes sense to put that in fig.3

$$\text{comm}(\mathbf{a},\mathbf{b})=\text{cs}(\mathbf{a})/\text{cs}(\mathbf{b}) \text{ and} \qquad [3]$$

$$\text{comm}(\mathbf{b},\mathbf{c}) = \text{cs}(x)/\{\text{cs}(\mathbf{b}) + \text{cs}(\mathbf{c}) - \text{cs}(x)\} \qquad [4]$$

Altogether, even if we weaken substantially the already modest assumptions, we retain
(i) leaving stochastics aside again, *within a fixed set of subjects*, we can differentiate between **a** vs. **b** on the one hand and **b** vs. **c** on the other as in the former -(*inclusion*)- comm(**a**,**b**) tends towards cs(**a**)/cs(**b**), while in the latter -(*overlap*)- comm(**b**,**c**) must be substantially smaller than cs(**b**)/cs(**c**) as cs(x) < cs(**b**) by definition and this fact affects both numerator and denominator. There will be also a clear indication for the other two formal relations, as in *identity* cs(**a**) = cs(**b**) and comm(**a**,**b**)=1, while in *exclusion* comm(**a**,**b**)=0;
(ii) if there is overlap comm(**a**,**b**), cs(**a**) and cs(**b**) can be used to set up a senseful index for the *amount* of overlap.

The 'commonality' algorithm works exclusively on the group 'v' of subjects (fig.1). It computes cs(**a**) from nd($^{a}E^{v}$), likewise cs(**b**),comm(**a**,**b**), and, with the help of these, can come to a conclusion, following the reasoning given above.

3.3. Heterogeneity

Until now we have differentiated between spellings that were either identical or different, without, in the latter case, considering the *amount* of difference. Let us return to fig.2, at which **a** = {x} and **b** = {x,y}. Among the subjects that spell both incorrectly the misspellings of **a** are, without exception, effected by some deficit in x, the misspellings of **b**, however, are effected either by some deficit in x, or by a deficit in x as well as y. As to the spelling of **a** those subjects are consequently more homogeneous as to their deficits, than to the spelling of **b** and this effect consists of two components. On the one hand, among the misspellers of **b** the *range* of potential deficits is larger than among the misspellers of **a**. On the other hand the misspellers of **b** tend to constitute two separate *clusters*, those of group II and IV respectively (fig.2), while the misspellers of **a** do not show such a tendency. Seen from the spellings of **a**, two subjects within group II can be arbitrarily close as to their deficits, the same holds for subjects within IV and a member of II can be very close, even identical to a member of IV as well. However, seen from the spellings of **b** the first two relations do hold, but it is *impossible* for a subject from II to be arbitrarily close to a subject from IV: there is always the deficit in y that holds for the one, but not for the other. Consequently, there must be some 'schism' among the misspellers of **b**, but not so among the misspellers of **a**. Altogether, if we had a sufficiently sophisticated measure for differences among spellings we would predict a smaller mean measure among $^{a}E^{v}$ than among $^{b}E^{v}$.

Now suppose we have an *un*sophisticated measure for differences among spellings, i.e. one that makes havoc with all kind of subtilities, sometimes transforming small differences in spelling into a large measure and vice versa. Surely, the range component, mentioned above, would not be mirrored within this measure, but it would not be too far fetched to assume that this coarse measure would still be somewhat sensitive in one way or another to the clustering component. With such a measure, meeting a condition that is minimal indeed, the prediction about mean differences would not hold, but it would be logical to predict a larger *variety* among measures within $^{b}E^{v}$ than within $^{a}E^{v}$.

The 'heterogeneity' algorithm uses a primitive measure for differences between spellings: it counts the number of times the characters on parallel positions of the spellings differ; (assuming a 'blank' to be a character, the measure never exceeds the number of characters of the largest spelling). It computes the standard deviation of this distribution of differences and calibrates it to a maximum=1 by dividing it by the maximum possible standard deviation for that distribution.[5] Reasoning and predicting like we did above, it compares these calibrated coefficients.

4. Additional features of the algorithm

4.1. Stochastics

We left the stochastics out explicitly in the foregoing; the reason to do so may be clear: they are complicated and opaque. Yet, we can not do without them: all three kernel criteria center on judgments like 'equal' and 'larger than' for ordered pairs of coefficients. Were we to take these in their literal, discrete sense, the first judgment would virtually never appear, effecting, in general, an enormous bias of the algorithm towards the judgment of *overlap*, at the expense of the other three formal relations. On the other hand, if we were too lenient in considering coefficients 'equal' the bias would become reversed.

---

5) The proof that this maximal standard deviation = 1/2(maximal spelling length) is straightforward. It makes sense, furthermore, to substitute 'length of correctly spelled word' for 'maximal spelling length'. We omit details here.

As the coefficients of interest for all 3 kernel criteria are such that they vary between 0 and 1, we introduce one free bias parameter ($0<bp<1$) for the whole algorithm. For any two coefficients c_1 and c_2 we put

$$c_1 > c_2 + bp \Rightarrow c_1 \text{ larger than } c_2 \text{ and } c_2 \text{ smaller than } c_1 \qquad [5]$$
$$\text{otherwise} \Rightarrow c_1 \text{ equal to } c_2$$

Bp could be optimized, taking the following reasoning. For any set of word pairs there exists one real, true partition into the four formal relations; it is characterized by being *consistent*, that is, it conforms to constraints of the type

if **b** includes **a**, and there is overlap between **b** and **c**
then **a** can not include **c**.

It turns out that there exist 13 meaningful 'triple constraints' like the one just mentioned. Clearly, a satisfactory empirical result should approximate the true partition in this respect as close as possible, i.e. in having a minimal number of violated triple constraints, without degeneration. (A 'degenerate approximation' would consist of only *exclusions*, for instance). So we have here a necessary condition for an optimal *bp*, that we expect to be sufficient too: the values of *bp* that meet the condition could be of a very restricted range.

4.2. Interconnecting the three criteria

After the possible *cases* have been specified in the initial formalization (2.3), the role of each of the 3 kernel criteria is to eliminate some, viz. those that are explicitly contradicted by the result, if any, of the crucial comparison. After each application of a criterium, an 'ambiguity' algorithm evaluates the *cases* that are left: if all can be allocated to the same formal relation, the situation is unambiguous, and the algorithm has come to its final decision. If not, the algorithm has to proceed, unless there is nothing left to proceed with, and consequently the formal relation remains undecided.

While the 'commonality' criterium (3.2) fits only to one comparison of spellings (${}^aE^v$ *versus* ${}^bE^v$), the other two, 'scope of deficit' (3.1) and 'heterogeneity' (3.3) can handle any of the pairs out of E^t,E^u,${}^aE^v$ and ${}^bE^v$. Of the 6 possible pairs only (${}^aE^v$, ${}^bE^v$), (E^t, ${}^bE^v$) and (E^u, ${}^aE^v$) turn out to make sense, however, in that clear differential predictions as to *cases* are possible. From these, the algorithm starts for both criteria with $({}^{a}E^{v}, {}^{b}E^{v})$: this is preferable while the number of subjects in the comparison is constant. In order to cancel some potential effect stemming from the sheer numbers of subjects, 'scope' takes $(E^{t}, {}^{b}E^{v})$ at first and then $(E^{u}, {}^{a}E^{v})$, while 'heterogeneity' does the reverse ($n_t > n_u$,cf. 2.2). All three subalgorithms require some minimal cardinality of the relevant sets of spellings. As each subalgorithm potentially eliminates some cases, it makes sense to check whether those cases are 'alive' at the moment before starting the - sometimes elaborate - computations.

Although we meant the reasonings for the three kernel criteria to be conceptually equivalent, in fact they are not. To this touchstone, the 'scope of the deficit' algorithm is superior to the other two by its explicitly stochastic argumentation. The 'heterogeneity' algorithm comes last, in our opinion, because of the arbitrariness and consequent coarseness of the measure of spelling differences. It is for this reason that the main algorithm applies the three sub algorithms in the order in which they are given in section 3: the situation in which the 'heterogeneity' algorithm need not be applied because the 'scope' algorithm has come to a conclusion, is preferable to the opposite one.

5. Application

A data base of 109 different words, spelled by 26 'normal' subjects, about 10 years of age, was subjected to the algorithm over a range of *bp*'s. From the 5886 word pairs, about 96 per cent turned out to be 'undecidable' (mostly because of n_v not being large enough). In order to optimize *bp* we computed for each *bp* the *incohesiveness*, i.e. the proportion of testable 'triple constraints'(4.1) that were violated (not all 'triple constraints' are testable, because what is needed is a formal relation for *each* of the pairs out of the triplet **a**,**b**,**c**). It turns out that there is a clear convergence of the optimal *bp* towards about .019. At the optimal *bp* - which has the satisfactory 'fit' of about 7 per cent violated triple constraints - we have no *identitie*s, 51 *exclusion*s, 22 *inclusion*s and 142 *overlap*s.

We made a list of those results, ranking the *overlap*s as to the amount of overlap. Next, we made a 'fake' list, consisting of the same word-pairs and categorizations, but with the word-pairs scrambled. Computing 'inclusion', 'amount of overlap' etc. downright from the factual rules in independently developed spelling software (cf. section 1) enabled to differentiate unequivocally between 'real' and 'fake' results. So the algorithm has at least a minimum of 'external validity'.

6. Conclusion and prospects

The foregoing served the purpose of demonstrating that manipulations with spelling errors that are preliminary to a taxonomy of them are possible, conceptually as well as empirically. It obviously is far too early to put any claims as to their use within a wider context; we plan the following analyses

- explorations into the formal structure of sets of orthographies departing from he partition that our algorithm has generated. It must be possible to fit all four formal relations into one coherent structure, although it is not clear at the moment how to proceed this way. A fair guess would be that a 'features of similarity' approach (Tversky 1977) is a good starting point. Such a formal structure could function as a plausible basis for a taxonomy of spelling *errors*. A relevant parameter would be the minimal number of rules that could generate such a structure of orthographies.

-comparison of the results so far to the ones on spelling errors of 'dyslectics' (cf. section 1). We expect a dramatic difference, but we are not sure which direction it will take: either there will be a trend towards a monopoly for *exclusion*, because dyslectic children in fact have no systematic rules, but spell each word *ad hoc*, or all pairs will tend to *overlap*, because dyslectic children use just a few rules for all words undiscriminatingly. In any case we expect the distribution over the formal relations to be far more uneven than at the normals.

- we could explore the concept of *effective error mass (eem)*, viz. two spelling errors, one in each of two words, that, as a pair, show large *overlap*, 'weigh' less than two errors at a pair that shows *exclusion*: the number of errors of a subject should be transformed into one *eem* score.

As a final remark, we note that the algorithm as such has nothing in it that is specific to spelling. In all (cognitive) domains where a response can be unequivocally characterized as either 'correct' or 'wrong', and where pairs of errors can become unambiguously differentiated into 'same' or 'different', those errors can be made input to the 'scope of the deficit' and 'commonality' sub algorithm. If the errors can, moreover, be submitted to some coarse notion of 'amount of difference', the complete algorithm can work on them. One could think, among other things, of arithmetic errors and recognition tasks. Whether the reasoning that brought about the algorithm will apply, should, of course, be the subject of a separate investigation.

ACKNOWLEDGEMENTS

This research was carried out under the"VF-project" 'Knowledge Acquisition in Formal Domains' at the University of Amsterdam.
Periodic discussions on spelling issues with Prof. Dr J.J. Elshout, Drs M.P. Langereis, Drs N. van Ruyven and Drs H. Verheyden advanced the construction of the algorithm.

REFERENCES

Bosch, K. van den, Elshout, J.J. and Langereis, M.P. (1986) *Spellingstrategieen bij tweede en vijfde klas basisschoolleerlingen'* [*Spelling strategies of 4th and 7th grade elementary school pupils,*]. Unpublished manuscript, Psychological Laboratory, University of Amsterdam.

Tversky, A (1977) Features of similarity. *Psychological Review*, *84*, 327 - 352.

Verheyden, H. (1984). Een programma ter sturing van het spellingsproces [A program for coaching the spelling process] In H.J.Breimer and E.J.W.M. van Hees (Eds.) *Technologie in het onderwijs Onderwijs Research Dagen 1984* (pp. 63 - 68), Lisse, The Netherlands: Swets and Zeitlinger.

Verheyden,H.(1985). De diagnose van spellingfouten' [The diagnosis of spelling errors]. In P.W.Verhagen and B.J.Wielinga (Eds.). *Media in het onderwijs Onderwijs Research Dagen 1985* (pp 43 - 50) Lisse, The Netherlands: Swets and Zeitlinger.

Rules for parallelprocessing networks with adaptive structure

Matthias Müller[*)]
Academy of Science, ZKI

1. Introduction

When using self-adjusting networksystems for modelling cognitive processes one has to remember that network systems have several limitations according to their respective design. For example, there are limits to the capacity which, if exceeded, make the system suddenly 'forget' everything in the sense of a 'total confusion' because of the superposition of the memory traces. Recently, attempts have been made to solve this problem, for example by implementing the ability to gradually 'forget' former memory traces.

An other problem arises from certain limitations to both the learning rules and the elementary network modules. Within these limitations only those sets of patterns can be correctly learned by the system that possess certain properties, such as single linear separability. One way of solving this problem is to assume additional units in the system, the so-called 'hidden' or 'internal' units, which are covered by the input and output units and which usually do not have a direct connection to the input of the external world. These units, through their ability to discriminate, make the insertion of additional hyperplanes into the feature-space possible. This is how the 'XOR'-problem ('exclusive-or'-problem) could be solved, as described in Rumelhart, Hinton & Williams (1986), pp. 330-34.

Both the problems mentioned lead to the question of how many units a network system needs to solve a learning task. In general one either assumes a system with a multiple of the presumably needed number of units or the needed number of units is calculated in advance according to the specific task.

Both ways, however, require to determine or at least to estimate the degree of difficulty of the task in advance. This leads to a paradoxical situation, because this also requires to put a certain knowledge about the task to be solved into the system structure before the actual learning process of the system starts. Moreover, a network with such a fixed structure will still be statically limited in its capacity which in turn will limit its adaptive property.

Such limitations might not play an important role in many fields of network application. However, in modelling certain psychological processes (in our case the learning of

---

*) Department of Psychology, Academy of Science, ZKI, 1086 Berlin, GRD.

stimulus-response assignments or of sequences of actions) we proceed on the assumption that in the system there is no internal representational structure of the patterns yet to be learned. Therefore we have chosen a different approach in order to achieve a network structure suitable for the task.

We proceed on the assumption that the number of hidden units needed for solving a certain learning task can be adaptively produced by the system itself during the training. Speaking in modeltheoretical terms, this means that we have a self-adjusting network system with the property of selforganization of its processing structure.

We have only just started to explore this approach. Therefore this paper will focus on the principle idea of this approach and on some preliminary results.

2. The pattern associator module and learning tasks

I would like to explain our basic-idea using a simple pattern associator module. In such a module there is at first one input level and one output level, consisting of several input and output units respectively. This module is given the task to associate pattern pairs in a learning task in such a way that the module responds to a certain input pattern with the respective output pattern. To illustrate this, let us consider the example of a module with four input units and one output unit, as shown in figure 1.

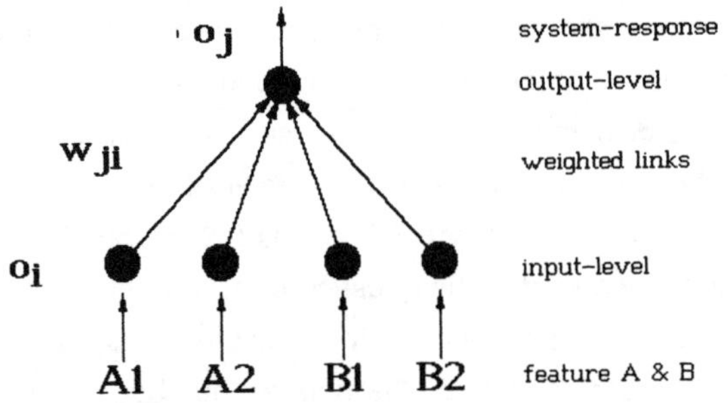

FIGURE 1. A Pattern-Associator-Module.

The activations in the input units which have been built up according to the input pattern are transferred to the output unit via weighted links. There they are used to calculate the system response, i.e. the output value. The units' output function is a logistic function with the net input (i.e. the sum of the transferred activation weighted by the links) as the argument. According to this nonlinear function, the units are threshold units with a moveable threshold, called Theta, as used by Rumelhart, Hinton & Williams (1986), p. 329, equation 15:

$$o_j = \frac{1}{1+e^{-(\sum_i w_{ji} \cdot o_i + \upsilon)}} \qquad (1)$$

where

o_j is the output of unit j

o_i is the output of unit i

w_{ji} is the weight of the link ji

υ is the threshold of unit j

How are the input units activated according to the features of an object presented to the system? Let us imagine that each object has two different features (A; B), and each of these feature dimensions has in turn two different valences (A1, A2 resp. B1, B2). With these features you can describe altogether four different objects (A1, B1; A1, B2; A2, B1; A2, B2).

Two input units at the time are to be interpreted as two valences of one and the same feature dimension of an object presented to the system. An activation of the value 1 in an input unit corresponds with the occurrence of the respective feature valence. An activation of the value 0 means the absence of this feature valence. Since in an input pattern only one valence of a feature dimension can be activated at a time, the two units of one dimension behave alternatively in the state of activation.

With the state of the activation of the input units we can now describe the feature-space as follows:

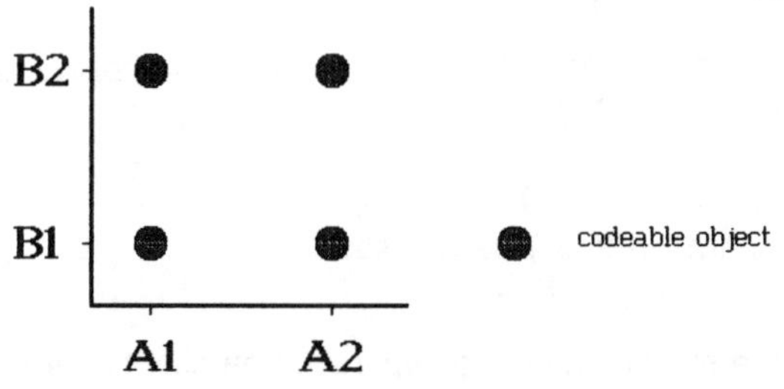

FIGURE 2. The Feature Space.

In this feature-space we have exactly four discrete points, each of them representing one codeable object within the set of possible objects.

Since the output level consists of only one unit which can assume a value of activation of 1 or 0, we can consider the module as a classificator which is to separate the four codeable objects into two classes. Let us now consider what possibilities there are to separate the set of objects into two classes. Leaving out the two trivial separations with all object being in one class, we are left with fourteen possibilities. Generalizing, we get three principle ways of dividing this set of objects into two classes through linear separation, as shown in figure 3.

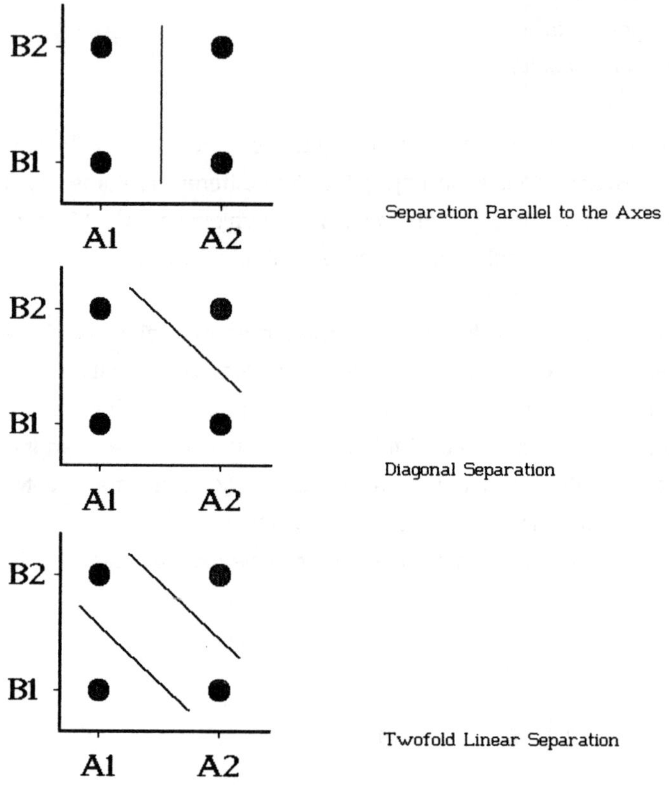

FIGURE 3. Linear Separation Into Two Classes.

First of all, there is the simple case of a separation parallel to the axes, where one and only one dimension is relevant for distinguishing the two classes (a respective Boolean expression would be for example [0 = A1]). In the case of diagonal separation both feature dimensions are relevant. This separation can be achieved through an 'and'- or an 'or'-function in the Boolean sense (for instance [0 = A1 or B1]). The third possibility for separation is the above-mentioned 'XOR'-function (for example [0 = R1 XOR B1]), which can only be achieved with at least two linear separations.

3. Learning and the consolidation of links

How does the system get the weights enabling it to respond correctly to an input pattern? Several learning rules for such networks have been developed and used. We have chosen a learning rule similar to the so-called Delta-rule which causes an error-driven search in the weight-space of the system:

In general:

$$\Delta w_{ji} = f(\eta\ ,\ \pi_{ji}\ (t)\ ,\ o_j\ ,\ t_j\ ,\ o_i\ \ldots) \tag{2}$$

For the purpose of simulation, we specified (2) as:

$$\Delta w_{ji} = \eta \cdot \pi_{ji}\ (t) \cdot \mathrm{sgn}\ (t_j - o_j) \cdot o_i \cdot o_j \cdot (1 - o_j) \tag{3}$$

where

η is the learning rate

t_j is the target signal of unit j

π_{ji} is the plasticity of the link ji

The sterm $o_j\ (1 - o_j)$ is the first derivative of the output function (see eq. 1) and is used for reasons shown and deduced in Rumelhart, Hinton & Williams (1986), pp. 329. The Signum-function with the error $(t_i - o_i)$ as the argument allows for considering the direction of the error without taking into account its absolute value. We have introduced this Signum-function in order to eliminate the influence of high error values which appear when isolating subsets of the set of object (as described below).

In addition to this general idea of the variation of the weights, we are suggesting a principle, that we have called 'consolidation of links'. We assume, that each link has the property of what we called 'plasticity'. When a link is generated, plasticity P_i has the value 1. Afterwards this value can change towards 0. This plasticity P_i expresses the possible span of a links' change of weight. Towards one link a plasticity has the same function as the learning rate Eta, which influences the span of change of all links in the system. The change of plasticity works as follows:

In general:

$$\Delta \pi_{ji} = f(\lambda\ ,\ \pi_{ji}\ (t)\ ,\ o_j\ ,\ t_j\ ,\ o_i\ \ldots) \tag{4}$$

For the purpose of simulation, we specified (4) as:

$$\pi_{ji} = \begin{cases} -\lambda \cdot (1 - | t_j - o_j|) \cdot (1 - | t_j - o_{ji} |) \cdot \pi_{ji} & \text{if} \quad | t_j - o_{ji} | < 0.5 \\ 0 & \text{else} \end{cases} \quad (5)$$

where

λ is the consolidation rate

t_j is the target signal of unit j

π_{ji} is the plasticity of the link ji

o_j is the output of unit j

$$o_{ji} = \frac{1}{1 + \exp(-w_{ji} \cdot o_i)}$$

Proportionally to its contribution to generating a correct system response, each link loses the ability to change its weight. In other words, if the function of the link to lead the system to a right response is correct, the link is consolidated according to this rule.

How is the correctness of one single link's function defined? The transferred activation $w_{ji}\, o_i$ needs to have a positive value in order to contribute to the desired output value 1. If the output value is to be 0, the transferred activation needs to have a negative value. This follows directly from the definition of o_{ji} (see eq. 5) as j unit's response to the transferred activation $w_j\, o_i$ and the comparison of the response with the desired target.

As the criterion of the correct response, caused by activation transfer via link ij, we consider the 0.5-mark of the target/response-comparison ($| t_j - o_{ji} | < 0.5$). Is the result of this comparison below the 0.5-mark, the link is consolidated in proportion to the correctness of the system's response ($1 - | t_j - o_j |$) and the correctness of the system's partial response ($1 - | t_j - o_{ji}|$) produced by the contribution of the activation transferred via the link ij. If the result of the comparison is above the 0.5-mark, the link is not consolidated.

The selective reinforcement of the links enables the system to isolate the learnable subset out of the entire patternset, which otherwise cannot be learned by the system, as in the case of the 'XOR'-problem. In addition, the system drives towards a state where it cannot change its weights considerably because the links' plasticity is exhausted, or in other words, all links are consolidated. Speaking in system theoretical terms, correct system responses gradually reduce the searching space in the weight space of the system.

4. The implementation of hidden units and the generation of their target signals

In our rule, the properties of the above-described learning rules are used for adaptively forming the structure of hidden units within the system according to the following algorithm:

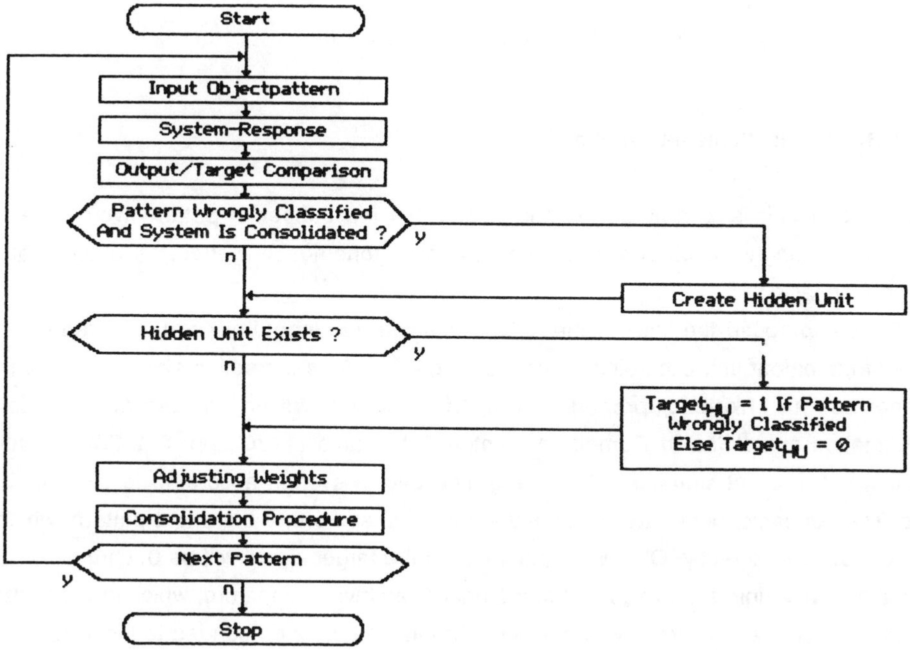

FIGURE 4. The Algorithm.

This figure is mainly to show the basic principle. The most adequate expression in formulas, parameters etc. can vary and is still being worked on.

At first, the system learns according to learning rules that cause a change of weights and plasticity. However, when the consolidated system is confronted with patterns that are not classified correctly, a new hidden unit comes into operation. The algorithm checks whether the system is consolidated and whether the system gives a wrong response to a pattern. If that is the case, a hidden unit is implemented, as shown in figure 5.

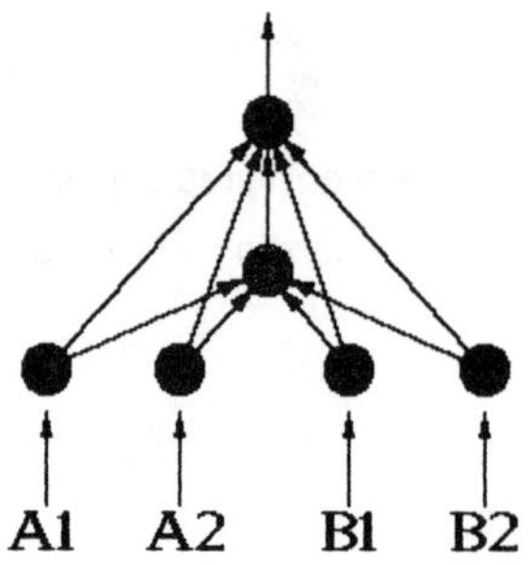

FIGURE 5. Implementation of an Hidden Unit.

This hidden unit is to abstract invariances within the subset of pattern which are still classified wrongly. In other words, the system autonomously generates a subgoal for solving the task.

For this purpose the links of the hidden unit with the input units are adjusted like the links of the output unit according to the learning rules. As a correction signal, however, we do not use an error-back-propagation signal, however, we do not use an error-back-propagation signal (as in Rumelhart, Hinton & Williams (1986), pp. 322-28) or similar signals but a target signal which is generated by the system according to the following rule: The target signal needed is given the value 1 if and only if there is a pattern, which is responded to incorrectly. Otherwise the value of the target signal will be 0. One could also say, the hidden unit is to extract out of the pattern an invariant feature, which may consist of several features and which appears whenever this pattern is responded to incorrectly.

5. Results of the computer simulation of such a module

At present we do not yet have proof of convergence towards a minimum of the error function of such a system for all possible pattern pair sets. However, such a module has been tested by using computer simulation of several learning tasks.

In this test all three possible principle variations of pattern pair sets (as shown in section 2) were used. Each training consisted of 200 trials with objects being presented in a random order and each of the two classes being represented with 100 trials respectively. The results of the test are summarized in figure 6:

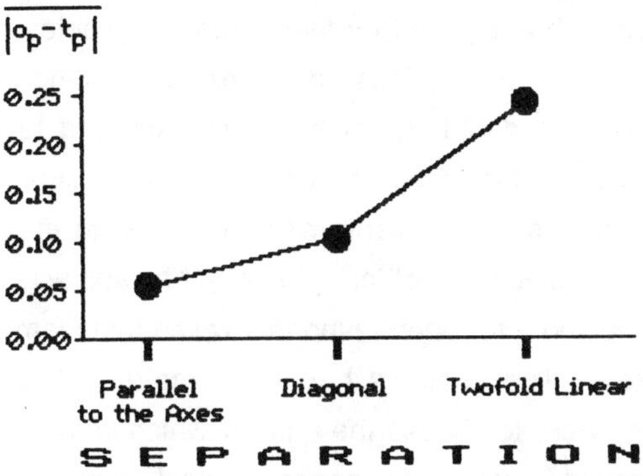

a) Mean error of system responses in 200 trials for the three separations

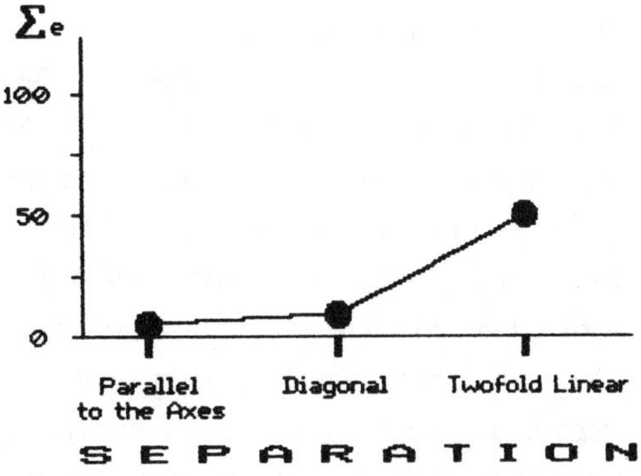

b) Number of wrong classifications in 200 trials made by the network

FIGURE 6. Simulation.

Figure 6a shows the mean error of the system response (i.e. the absolute value of the difference between the system response and the target) during the 200 trials for each one of the three possibilities of separation. Figure 6b shows the number of absolute errors made by the system during one training with 200 trials (as an 'absolute error', i.e. wrong classification of objects, we consider here error-values above 0.5 in the target/response-comparison).

In the case of separation parallel to the axes and diagonal separation no hidden unit was created within the system. In both these cases only a small number of objects were classified wrongly at the beginning (in the 200 trials only 5 resp. 9 errors occurred, i.e. each object needed to be shown only once resp. twice in order to be classified correctly).

In the case of the twofold linear separation a hidden unit was produced and the system needed considerably more presentations (after about 140 trials no more wrong classifications occurred, up to then about 50 errors had been made by the system) to solve the problem than in the two previous cases.

6. Testing the approach for psychological relevance using experimental data

In order to test whether the results of the method we have developed for our purposes are relevant for modelling cognitive phenomena we have carried out learning experiments with human subjects according to the learning tasks described in the previous section. As objects to be learned we have chosen combinations of two meaningless syllables. Each of these syllables consisted of three letters. They were presented to the subjects in the middle of a computer display in a vertical order. For one learning task each of the two possible positions (the upper or the lower one) could be engaged by two different syllables. This allowed for coding four different objects, as in our previous examples (for instance BEG/FID; BEG/FOS; BUN/FID; BUN/FOS). Having decided which object belonged to which of the two classes, the subject had to press a key on either the right or left hand side.

Starting the training the subjects did not know how the objects were assigned to the classes (i.e. whether to respond to the object by pressing the left or right key). The subjects were to learn this through the feedback they received after each response, which told them whether the response had been right or wrong. The subjects had been instructed to respond as quickly as possible. If uncertain they were to choose the answer which to them seemed most likely to be correct. Our reasons for asking to respond quickly were to minimize reflective responses and to make the responses as spontaneous as possible.

Twelve subjects took part in the experiment. After instruction and brief training each subject had to solve six different learning tasks. The experiment could thus include two variants of the three principle ways of separations as described in section 2. The order of the variants of separation varied from subject of subject. Each learning task consisted of 200 trials, in which the four possible objects were presented to the subject in a random order with the two classes occurring equally often (as in the simulation described in the previous section). We measured the reaction time and counted the errors (i.e. wrong classification) in each learning task (200 trials)

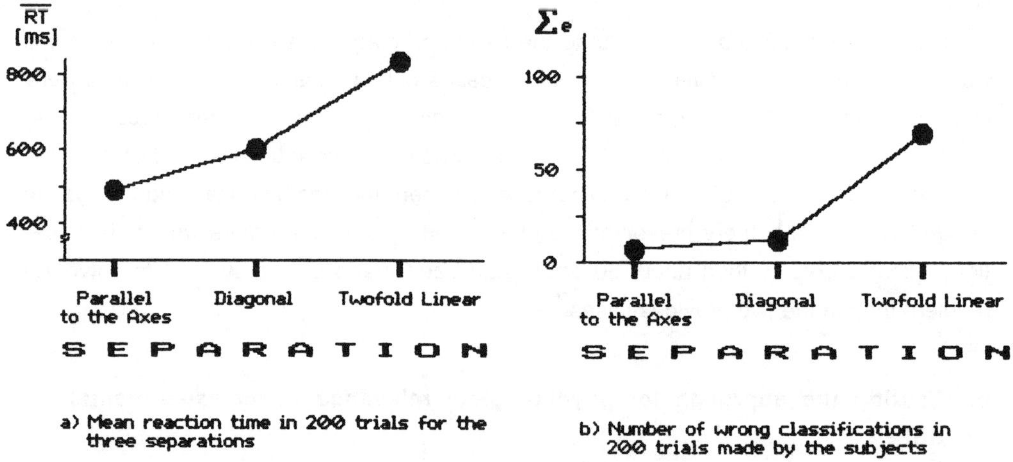

FIGURE 7. Experiment.

Figure 7 shows the summarized results of the experiments. The upper diagram shows (7a) the mean reaction time for each of the three possible ways of separation. In order to compare the mean reaction time with the simulation data we make an additional assumption as follows: The smaller the value of the response error of the network (i.e. the absolute value of the difference between system response and target), the faster is the activation of the respective response. A simple addition to the model could be an integrator with threshold output (it is easy to imagine that the output unit itself could take over this function, if the process of activation runs over a period of time which is divided into several small time steps).

Comparing the upper diagram curves of figure 6 and 7 we can see that the relations of the mean values of the three separation tasks are very similar.

An equal correspondence of simulation and experiment can be seen in the lower diagrams (figure 6b and 7b) which describe the number of absolute errors in a learning task (i.e. wrong classifications in 200 trials). Here we do not even need our above-mentioned additional assumption.

Apart from our model there are other approaches for explaining these experimental data; a simple one is for instance a sequential comparison. However, we intended to test the relevance of our method for modelling processes of the development of conceptual representation in general.

7. Summary

Summary of the properties of our model method: The learning algorithm is relatively fast and autonomous (for instance, the XOR-problem is responded to correctly after about about 130-140 trials, which is similar to the speed human subjects would need).

In addition to being a self-adjusting system, its property of selforganization produces the internal structure of processing.

This is how the system adapts itself to the learning task during the training. The degree of difficulty of the task does not have to be determined by the system in advance.

The rule is feature-selective in terms of correctness of the system response.

It fixes memory traces through consolidation, existing and confirmed memory traces remain in the system and cannot be wiped out.

This makes the system dependent on the order of patterns presented to the system.

The method abandones the principle of strictly distributed storage through implementing processing units for certain subsets of the entire pattern pair set.

There are still a number of problems remaining: To what extent are the hidden units involved in the process before they are actually needed? How does the system behave when many of the above-mentioned, elementary modules come together? (as shown in figure 8)

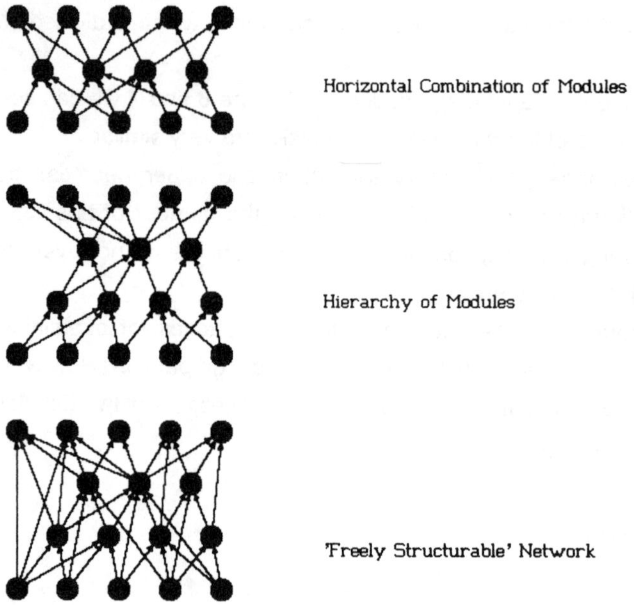

FIGURE 8. Adaptive Development of More Complex Structures.

Is there a finite number of hidden units that can be created by the system? How could a hierarchy of such hidden units be developed?

There are still a lot of further questions. In order to further develop our idea and to improve the method, we intend to use more complex network systems and more difficult learning tasks, for example standard tasks as the parity problem, the symmetry problem, addition of binary numbers and so on. In addition we are exploring effective variants of the formulas and parameters in the framework of the basic principle introduced in this paper.

References

Rumelhart, D.E., Hinton, G.E., Williams, R.J. (1986). Learning Internal Representation by Error Propagation. In D.E. Rumelhart, & J.L. McClelland (1986). *Parallel Distributed Processing. Explorations in the Microstructure of Cognition. (vol. 1)* Foundations. Part II: Basic Mechanisms, Chapter 8, MIT Press. Cambridge.

PART III

PSYCHOMETRICS AND THEORY OF DATA

New Results in Test Theory Without an Answer Key

William H. Batchelder and A. Kimball Romney

University of California, Irvine †

This paper discusses some recent developments in a new methodology for the social sciences being developed jointly by the authors. The methodology is called cultural consensus analysis, and it is designed to aggregate informant responses to test items about their common culture. The object is to determine correct knowledge about the nature of that culture. Our methods estimate informant competency parameters and "correct" answers to each item from the informant response data. The methodology is designed for anthropological field studies and related research designs. This paper studies the consequences of relaxing the axioms of our model for dichotomous items, and it presents new models for other testing formats.

1. INTRODUCTION

In a series of recent papers (Batchelder & Romney, 1986, 1988; Romney, Batchelder & Weller, 1987; Romney, Weller & Batchelder, 1986), we have been developing a new methodology for questionnaire research in the social sciences. We call this methodology *cultural consensus analysis*. It is designed to discover "culturally shared beliefs" from responses to questions obtained from informants on their culture. Anthropology is the prototypical social science in need of such a methodology; however, research in other social sciences such as psycholinguistics, sociology, and social psychology may benefit from its use.

The methodology fits into the category of information pooling methods (see Grofman & Owen, 1986). In an information pooling problem, one has answers from several "experts" to a fixed body of "objective" questions. The object is to aggregate rationally the responses to select the most likely "correct answers" to the questions, and perhaps also assess one's degree of confidence in these selections. Most information pooling schemes incorporate parameters that calibrate the relative competencies of the experts (hereafter informants), and these parameters are typically determined exogenously, that is, from a source other than the questionnaire data itself. Further, the prior beliefs of the aggregator are often reflected mathematically in the aggregation process.

In anthropological research, one usually lacks reliable, *a priori* assessment of the competence of the informants used. Further, it is a long standing tradition in anthropological research, as well as most scientific research in the social sciences, that one tries to avoid the

---

† School of Social Sciences, Irvine, CA 92717, USA. Work on this paper was supported by NSF Grant No. SES-8808358 to the authors.

influence of one's prior beliefs on the conclusions from one's research. What we set out to develop was an information pooling methodology that does not incorporate a researcher's prior beliefs, and both calibrates the informants' competencies and pools their responses from the same set of questionnaire data.

In the social sciences, there are two classes of methodology that we have used to develop our new methodology. They are test theory (for example, Lord & Novick, 1968) and latent class analysis (for example, Lazarsfeld & Henry, 1968). Test theory models assume that the "correct" answers to each item are known to the researcher. Consequently, it is possible to "score" a respondent's data and analyze the performance data consisting of corrects and errors. Our models are technically test theory models; however, we do not have the "correct answers" *a priori*. Hence the phrase "test theory without an answer key" that appears in the title of this paper.

Latent class analysis does not assume that there are correct answers to the items. Instead, it is assumed that there are two or more classes of respondents, where the classes represent common viewpoints (cultures in our terms); however, they are not known to the researcher *a priori*. Within a class, all respondents are assumed to be homogeneous in that they are postulated to have the same response probabilities to each item. Because there are no "correct" answers, it is necessary to analyze a respondent's data directly rather than scoring it as test theorists do. In our models, as with the latent class analysis, it is necessary to analyze respondent data directly; however, there is only one latent class of informants (however, see Section 3.1), and more important, the response probabilities can differ within that class owing to competence and perhaps response bias differences.

Much of our efforts have been devoted to formulating, statistically analyzing, and applying a model for a dichotomous (true-false) testing format. This model is reviewed next in Section 2 along with the estimation theory that we have developed for it. In Section 3, we describe how to generalize the model by weakening several of its axioms. In Section 4, we show how to extend our approach to several other testing formats.

2.1 A MODEL FOR DICHOTOMOUS ITEMS

Before describing our model for aggregating true-false questionnaire data, we need to establish a little notation. In any study, N informants each answer M questions. Whenever possible i and j will index informants and k and l will index items. For dichotomous items, we will arbitrarily code the items by 1 for "yes ("true," etc.) and by 0 for "no ("false," etc.). With these conventions and the fact that the "correct" answer to a question is not known *a priori*, there are three important classes of random variables as follows:

1. *Response Profile Data.* $\mathbf{X} = (X_{ik})_{N\times M}$, where

$$X_{ik} = \begin{cases} 1 & \text{if informant } i \text{ answers "yes" to item } k \\ 0 & \text{if informant } i \text{ answers "no" to item } k. \end{cases} \tag{1}$$

2. *Answer Key.* $\mathbf{Z} = (Z_k)_{1\times M}$, where

$$Z_k = \begin{cases} 1 & \text{if correct answer to item } k \text{ is "yes"} \\ 0 & \text{if correct answer to item } k \text{ is "no".} \end{cases} \tag{2}$$

3. *Performance Profile Data.* $\mathbf{Y} = (Y_{ik})_{N\times M}$, where

$$Y_{ik} = \begin{cases} 1 & \text{if informant } i \text{ correct on item } k \\ 0 & \text{if informant } i \text{ wrong on item } k. \end{cases} \tag{3}$$

The answer key random variables require some comment. If the Z_k are known, as they are to a test theorist, then performance profile data can be obtained from response profile data by the scoring rule

$$Y_{ik} = X_{ik}Z_k + (1 - X_{ik})(1 - Z_k)\,, \tag{4}$$

for $i = 1,\ldots,N$ and $k = 1,\ldots,M$. When the Z_k are not known, we regard them as random variables much as a Bayesian might. We also refer to them as parameters, and in this case we also regard them as having a prior distribution.

The usual distribution we assume is that the Z_k are independent and identically distributed Bernoulli random variables with $\Pr(Z_k = 1) = \pi$, $0 < \pi < 1$, $k = 1,\ldots,M$. To be consistent with our later derivations, it is helpful to think of the M items as testing M topics in a fixed order. Then the actual k^{th} item can be put in the positive or negative mode by the researcher. In any event, the reader can ignore these details about the technical interpretation of the Z_k without much loss of comprehension.

The model for dichotomous questions that we proposed and analyzed extensively in Batchelder & Romney (1986, 1988) is called the *general Condorcet model* (GCM). It is closely related to a model by Gelfand & Solomon (1973). It is expressed by the following three axioms:

Axiom 1. *Common Truth.* There is a fixed answer key "applicable" to all informants, that is, each item k has a correct answer, $z_k = 1$ or $z_k = 0$, $k = 1, 2, \ldots, M$.

Axiom 2. *Local Independence.* The informant-item response random variables satisfy conditional independence given by

$$\Pr\big[(X_{ik})_{N\times M} = (x_{ik})\,|(Z_k)_{1\times M} = (z_k)\big] = \prod_{k=1}^{M}\prod_{i=1}^{N} \Pr(X_{ik} = x_{ik}|Z_k = z_k)\,, \tag{5}$$

for all possible response profiles (x_{ik}) and the fixed answer key (z_k).

Axiom 3. *Homogeneity of Items.* Each informant i has a fixed "hit rate" P_{1i} and a fixed "false alarm rate" P_{0i} such that

$$\Pr(X_{ik} = 1 | Z_k = z_k) = \begin{cases} P_{1i} & \text{if } z_k = 1 \\ P_{0i} & \text{if } z_k = 0. \end{cases} \tag{6}$$

Most of our results are obtained for a special case of the GCM called the ***high threshold model*** (HTM) defined by

$$P_{1i} = D_i + (1 - D_i)\, g_i \tag{7a}$$

and

$$P_{0i} = (1 - D_i)\, g_i, \tag{7b}$$

where $0 < D_i,\ g_i < 1,\ i = 1, \ldots, N$. The model assumes the informant knows the correct answer with probability D_i and otherwise guesses with probability g_i of a "yes" response. The advantage of the HTM for our purposes is that the D_i serve directly as competence parameters, whereas the g_i are just nuisance parameters representing guessing bias and can often be set to 1/2. Further, the HTM is equivalent to the GCM with the restriction $P_{1i} \geq P_{0i}$ (which should characterize an earnest informant).

Both the GCM and the HTM are restricted in several ways. First, the assumption of item homogeneity seems unrealistic. Second, the assumption of a single underlying culture is too strong for some purposes. Third, it would be desirable to have methods for dealing with response modes other than dichotomous. These three restrictions are successively relaxed in Sections 3 and 4; however, first we need to briefly review the essential properties and results of the HTM that appear in Batchelder & Romney (1988).

2.2 ESTIMATION THEORY FOR THE HTM

If we assume the HTM, then there are $2N$ competence and response bias parameters and M answer key parameters to estimate from the MN observations in the response profile data in (1). In Batchelder & Romney (1988), we develop the estimation theory for the HTM (and GCM).

First, the likelihood function is easily derived; however, the nonpolynomial explosion of possible answer keys, namely 2^M, prohibits a direct approach to obtaining maximum likelihood estimates (MLEs) from it except for small M. Second, technically the model is equivalent to the two-class latent class model described in Lazarsfeld & Henry (1968), however, with the roles of items and respondents reversed. The two classes of items are the items with $z_k = 1$ and the items with $z_k = 0$. This means that various computer programs that obtain iterative MLEs—for example, Clogg's (1981) MLLSA—can be used in some cases. Unfortunately, these programs only work for a small number of informants (actually items in their intended application) for reasons analogous to the 2^M explosion of possible answer keys.

Third, given values of the D_i and g_i, the answer key parameters can be conditionally estimated. For example, if $\pi = 1/2$, then the value of $\hat{\mathbf{z}} = (\hat{z}_k)_{1\times M}$ that maximizes the likelihood function is given by the rule $\hat{z}_k = 1$ iff

$$G_k = \sum_{i=1}^{N} \left\{ X_{ik} \ln\left[\frac{[D_i + (1-D_i)\,g_i]\,[1-(1-D_i)\,g_i]}{(1-D_i)^2 g_i\,(1-g_i)}\right] - \ln\left[\frac{1-(1-D_i)\,g_i}{(1-D_i)\,(1-g_i)}\right]\right\} \geq 0. \tag{8}$$

In particular, if $g_i = 1/2$ for all respondents, $\hat{z}_k = 1$ iff

$$G_k = \sum_{i=1}^{N} (2X_{ik} - 1) \ln\left[\frac{1+D_i}{1-D_i}\right] \geq 0. \tag{9}$$

Results like (8) and (9) are well known in the information pooling literature (Nitzan & Paroush, 1982).

These and related results necessitated that we devise new estimation methods for the HTM to handle cases of large N and M. This was accomplished by utilizing the fact that a great deal of information about the D_i is contained in informant by informant association measures (computed over items).

To see this, let

$$\mathbf{X}_i = (X_{i1}, X_{i2}, \ldots, X_{iM}) \tag{10}$$

be the random vector of response random variables for the ith informant. Next define the following random variables characterizing the mean and variance of $\mathbf{X}_i$:

$$\overline{X}_i = \sum_{k=1}^{M} \frac{X_{ik}}{M} \tag{11}$$

and

$$S_i^2 = \sum_{k=1}^{M} \frac{(X_{ik} - \overline{X}_i)^2}{M-1}. \tag{12}$$

Finally, define the following random variable characterizing the association between two informants:

$$C_{ij} = \sum_{k=1}^{M} \frac{(X_{ik} - \overline{X}_i)\,(X_{jk} - \overline{X}_j)}{M-1}, \tag{13}$$

namely the covariance between i and j, and

$$M_{ij} = \sum_{k=1}^{M} \frac{X_{ik}X_{jk} + (1-X_{ik})(1-X_{jk})}{M}, \tag{14}$$

namely the proportion of response matches between i and j, for all $1 \leq i \neq j \leq N$.

The key to our estimation methods is presented in Observation 6 of Batchelder & Romney (1988, p.76). In essence, it says that if $\mathbf{Z}$ is governed by a Bernoulli process with $\Pr(Z_k = 1) = \pi, 0 < \pi < 1$, then if $C^*_{ij} = C_{ij}/\pi(1-\pi)$,

$$\mathrm{E}(C^*_{ij}) = D_i D_j, \tag{15}$$

and if $g_i = g_j = 1/2$ and $M^*_{ij} = 2M_{ij} - 1$,

$$\mathrm{E}(M^*_{ij}) = D_i D_j. \tag{16}$$

Both (15) and (16) have empirical counterparts by putting actual informant responses into (13) and (14), so one way to estimate the D_i is to pick one of these measures, say $M^*_{ij} = 2M_{ij} - 1$, where M_{ij} in (14) is computed with actual responses, and seek the $\hat{D}_i$ that minimizes the squared error function given by

$$\mathrm{SS}(\mathbf{D}) = \sum_{\substack{i=1 \\ i \neq j}}^{N} \sum_{j=1}^{N} \left(M^*_{ij} - D_i D_j\right)^2. \tag{17}$$

Fortunately, there is a method for minimizing (17) invented by Comrey (1962) called the "minimum residual method of factor analysis" (hereafter MINRES) that is available in most standard statistical packages. The method is designed to perform a factor analysis on a correlation matrix by ignoring the main diagonal of the matrix; however, when the off diagonal terms of an $N \times N$ matrix are filled with the M^*_{ij}, the program produces a vector $\hat{\mathbf{D}} = (\hat{D}_1, \hat{D}_2, \ldots, \hat{D}_N)$, which we take as least squares estimates of the D_i. This method is called the *matching method*, and its counterpart with C^*_{ij} is called the *covariance method.* Once $\hat{\mathbf{D}}$ is obtained, we estimate the answer key by using the $\hat{D}_i$ in (8) or (9). Thus the matching method is a two-phase procedure.

Batchelder & Romney (1988) and especially Maher (1987) report a number of Monte Carlo studies that show that the matching method appears to have little or no bias and a surprisingly high efficiency relative to MLEs with a known answer key. Further, in cases where both the matching method and latent class methods (MLLSA) can be used, the results are quite close when the model assumptions are true.

We have used the matching method on empirical data in Romney *et al.* (1986) and Batchelder & Romney (1988) with interesting results. Finally, the matching method provides a mild goodness-of-fit measure for the model, namely, within sampling variability, the N by N matrix of M^*_{ij} should yield a "one factor structure" with all positive entries when MINRES is applied (see discussion around (23)), that is, only "noise" should exist in the matrix of M^*_{ij} after the first factor, $\hat{\mathbf{D}}$, is extracted by MINRES.

3. WEAKENING THE AXIOMS

Axioms 1 and 3 of the GCM and HTM defined by (7*a*) and (7*b*) appear to be undesirably strong. This section, describes some new results we have obtained in weakening them.

3.1 THE ASSUMPTION OF ONE CULTURE

One of the strong assumptions of the GCM and HTM is Axiom 1, namely, that each item has a "correct answer" applicable to all informants. Latent class models weaken this assumption by allowing several classes of respondents; however, within a class there is no provision for differential competence, or cultural knowledge, among informants. It is easy to formulate a unification of the HTM and latent class models by retaining local independence in Axiom 2 and substituting appropriate changes to reflect multiple cultural groups. The model described next is dubbed the multiple culture high threshold model (MHTM).

Axiom 1. *Multiple Cultures.* There are C cultural groups, for some $C \geq 1$. For each cultural group, G_α, and each item k, there is a correct answer, $z_{\alpha k} = 1$ or $z_{\alpha k} = 0$, applicable to all informants in that group, $\alpha = 1, \ldots, C$, $k = 1, \ldots, M$.

Axiom 2. *Unique Membership.* Each informant i belongs to exactly one cultural group G_{α_i}, $i = 1, \ldots, N$.

Axiom 3. *Local Independence.* The informant-item response random variables satisfy conditional independence given by

$$\Pr[(X_{ik})_{N\times M} = (x_{ik}) \,|(Z_{\alpha k})_{C\times M} = (z_{\alpha k}), (\alpha_i)_{1\times N}] = \prod_{k=1}^{M}\prod_{i=1}^{N} \Pr(X_{ik} = x_{ik}|Z_{\alpha_i k} = z_{\alpha_i k}). \quad (18)$$

Axiom 4. *Homogeneity of Items.* Each informant i has a fixed competence D_i and response bias g_i such that

$$\Pr(X_{ik} = 1|Z_{\alpha_i k} = z_{\alpha_i k}) = \begin{cases} D_i + (1 - D_i)\, g_i & \text{if } z_{\alpha_i k} = 1 \\ (1 - D_i)\, g_i & \text{if } z_{\alpha_i k} = 0, \end{cases} \quad (19)$$

$0 < D_i$, $g_i < 1$, $i = 1, \ldots, N$.

The MHTM has a total of $3N + MC$ parameters ($2N$ bias and competence parameters, N group membership parameters, α_i, and MC answer key parameters), so as long as $3N + MC \leq MN$, the model is potentially estimable. However, unless N and C are quite small, the sorts of methods employed for latent class models described earlier are not applicable for reasons that were discussed in Section 2.2.

If there are only two groups ($C = 2$) and if there is no bias ($g_i = 1/2$), some progress can be made by modifying the matching method described earlier in (16) and (17). First, let a denote the proportion of the M items that both cultural groups agree on, namely,

$$a = \sum_{k=1}^{M} \frac{Z_{1k}Z_{2k} + (1 - Z_{1k})(1 - Z_{2k})}{M}. \tag{20}$$

Let M_{ij} and M_{ij}^* be defined as in (14) and (16). Then it is straightfoward to extend the result in (16) as follows:

$$\mathrm{E}(M_{ij}^*) = \begin{cases} D_i D_j & \text{if } \alpha_i = \alpha_j \\ (2a - 1)\, D_i D_j & \text{if } \alpha_i \neq \alpha_j. \end{cases} \tag{21}$$

Further,

$$\mathrm{Var}(M_{ij}^*) = \frac{1 - D_i^2 D_j^2}{M}. \tag{22}$$

for all pairs of informants i and j regardless of class membership.

Equation (21) is especially interesting, for example, in the extreme case where $a = 0$ (no overlap in the answer keys), the $N \times N$ matrix of observed M_{ij}^* should yield a "one factor" MINRES solution except, unlike (17), the best fitting column vector, $\hat{\mathbf{D}}$, should contain both positive and negative values. The absolute value of each entry is an estimate of each informant's competence, D_i, and membership in the two cultural groups can be estimated by separating the positive and negative entries into two groups—these are the estimates of class membership parameters. Then, separate MINRES analysis by the matching method of these two groups should yield one factor structures, along with revised competence estimates and answer keys for each group. We have found that this approach works on some Monte Carlo data (with $D_i > 1/2$), and equally important, that "randomally distorted" response profile data are unlikely to produce a solution where separate MINRES analysis of the positive and negative groups will yield one factor structures.

If $0 < a < 1$ in (20), MINRES applied to the M_{ij}^* matrix should not yield a "single factor" solution. In other words, there will be information about the parameters in the off diagonal terms of the $N \times N$ residual matrix

$$\left(M_{ij}^* - \hat{D}_i \hat{D}_j\right)_{N \times N}, \tag{23}$$

where $\hat{D}_i$ is the quantity in $\hat{\mathbf{D}}$ that minimizes (17), (of course, in this case, $\hat{D}_i$ is not a good estimator of D_i). We have been working on reasonable and practical estimation methods to work with (17) and (23) for the MHTM; however, this problem is still under investigation.

The overall conclusion is that it is easy to extend the one culture HTM in a natural way to allow for multiple cultures. The problem, as with the one culture model, is to develop both principled and practical estimation theory for the models. While we think we have a satisfactory, robust solution to this problem for the one culture HTM (in Batchelder & Romney, 1988; Maher, 1987), more work will be required to handle the MHTM extension. Nevertheless, based on our work so far, if there are only two cultural groups, sometimes disaggregating the informants into two groups based on the sign of their first factor in the MINRES solution to (17), followed by separated MINRES analyses of the two groups, may yield satisfactory estimates of the parameters.

3.2 HOMOGENEITY OF ITEMS

Perhaps the most troublesome assumption of the GCM and HTM is Axiom 3, item homogeneity. For example, within any culture, we would expect some cultural items to be less well known than others. In this section, we pose and analyze several possible substitutions for the item homogeneity assumption.

If we drop Axiom 3 altogether, then (6) for the GCM becomes

$$\Pr(X_{ik} = 1 | Z_k = z_k) = \begin{cases} P_{1ik} & \text{if } z_k = 1 \\ P_{0ik} & \text{if } z_k = 0, \end{cases} \tag{24}$$

where $0 < P_{1ik}, P_{0ik} < 1$, $i = 1, \ldots, N$, $k = 1, \ldots, M$.

Also the counterpart to (7*a*) and (7*b*) for the HTM becomes

$$P_{1ik} = D_{ik} + (1 - D_{ik})g_i \tag{25a}$$

and

$$P_{0ik} = (1 - D_{ik})g_i, \tag{25b}$$

where $0 < g_i, D_{ik} < 1$. Note that g_i is not subscripted by items because in the HTM an informant guesses only when he or she does not know the answer to an item.

The extensions of the GCM in (24) and the HTM in (25*a*) and (25*b*) are not interesting as models because they have more parameters ($M(2N+1)$ and $M(N+1)+N$, respectively) than data observations (MN). Nevertheless, it is possible to obtain counterparts to (15) and (16) so we can see the impact of arbitrary item inhomogeneity on the covariance and matching methods.

In order to proceed, we need to define

$$\text{Cov}(P_{1i}, P_{1j}) = \sum_{k=1}^{M} \frac{(P_{1ik} - \bar{P}_{1i})(P_{1jk} - \bar{P}_{1j})}{M - 1}, \tag{26}$$

where $\bar{P}_{1i}$ is the mean over items of informant i's hit rates and $1 < i \neq j < N$. Also $\text{Cov}(P_{0i}, P_{0j})$ and $\text{Cov}(D_i, D_j)$ can be defined similarily. Then the following relationships are easily obtained:

$$\text{Cov}(P_{1i}, P_{1j}) = (1 - g_i)(1 - g_j)\,\text{Cov}(D_i, D_j) \tag{27a}$$

and

$$\mathrm{Cov}(P_{0i}, P_{0j}) = g_i g_j \mathrm{Cov}(D_i, D_j)\,. \tag{27b}$$

Now we can generalize (15) and (16) for the HTM. Suppose $\mathbf{Z}$ is governed by a Bernoulli process with parameter $0 < \pi < 1$, then

$$\mathrm{E}(C^*_{ij}) = \left[1 + \frac{M\,(\pi - g_i)\,(\pi - g_j)}{(M-1)\,\pi\,(1-\pi)}\right] \mathrm{Cov}(D_i, D_j) + \bar{D}_i\bar{D}_j; \tag{28}$$

and if $g_i = g_j = 1/2$,

$$\mathrm{E}\big(M^*_{ij}\big) = \mathrm{Cov}(D_i, D_j) + \bar{D}_i\bar{D}_j. \tag{29}$$

The derivations of (28) and (29) are tedious but straightforward. The only difficult step is to obtain

$$\mathrm{E}\left(\sum_{k=1}^{M} X_{ik}X_{jk}\right) = \sum_{k=1}^{M} \Pr(X_{ik} = 1, X_{jk} = 1)\,. \tag{30}$$

Equation (30) can be solved by conditionalizing on z_k, using (25a) and (25b), then summing, and using the identity

$$\sum_{k=1}^{M} \frac{D_{ik}D_{jk}}{M-1} = \mathrm{Cov}(D_i, D_j) + \bar{D}_i\bar{D}_j. \tag{31}$$

Equation (28) and (29) are interesting because they show that the departure from the results in (15) and (16) are proportional to $\mathrm{Cov}(D_i, D_j)$. A reasonable restriction on the D_{ik} is *item monotonicity*, namely, if $D_{ik} > D_{jk}$ for any item k, then $D_{il} > D_{jl}$ for all items $l = 1, \ldots, M$. With item monotonicity, we see that $\mathrm{Cov}(D_i, D_j)$ will be positive, so the effects of item inhomogeneity are to inflate the quantities in (15) and (16). This consequence would introduce a positive bias in estimating the D_i for both the covariance and matching methods.

Batchelder & Romney (1988) introduced a substitute for Axiom 3 based on the Rasch (1960) model of item response theory. The idea was to model the D_{ik} in (25a) and (25b) by the equation

$$D_{ik} = \frac{D_i\,(1 - e_k)}{D_i\,(1-e_k) + e_k\,(1 - D_i)}, \tag{32}$$

where $0 < D_i,\ e_k < 1$. The D_i in (32) function as informant ability parameters and the e_k as item difficulty parameters. One version of the Rasch model in Lord (1974) for dichotomous items gives performance probabilities by

$$\Pr(Y_{ik} = 1) = \frac{1 + [1 + \exp -\,(\Theta_i - \beta_k)]^{-1}}{2}, \tag{33}$$

where the Θ_i represent respondent ability and the β_k represent item difficulty, and $-\infty < \Theta_i, \beta_k < \infty$. We adopted this idea by scaling the Θ_i and β_k to the unit interval and modeling the D_{ik} rather than performance data. The scaling change $\Theta_i^* = \Theta_i + A$ and $\beta_k^* = \beta_k + A$, for $-\infty < A < \infty$, leaves the Rasch model probablities invariant. In our version, D_{ik} is left invariant by the transformation $D_i^* = D_i / [1 + A(1 - D_i)]$ and $e_i^* = e_k / [1 + A(1 - e_k)]$, where $0 < A < \infty$. To get a "fixed" competence, D_i^*, one could try and pick A so that the mean of the e_k^* is 1/2. In fact, if $e_k = 1/2$ for all items, then the HTM with homogeneous items in (7a) and (7b) results.

Maher (1987) conducted a number of Monte Carlo studies with the HTM augumented by the Rasch model in (32). She found that the matching method of (17) produces good answer key recovery and acceptable competence estimates even if the variance of the e_k is pretty large. There is not space here to describe her results in detail; however, the conclusion we accept now is that the matching method of parameter estimation for the HTM is pretty robust under violations of the item homogeneity assumption. We are currently developing a practical way to estimate the e_k in (32) from response profile data.

4. OTHER RESPONSE FORMATS

One important aim in developing our methodology is to extend it to other testing formats. Such extensions are not routine because, in each case, response profile data must be analyzed since there is no answer key. While it is easy to formulate models in the spirit of the GCM and HTM for each new format, it is a much more difficult matter to develop principled and practical estimation methods to recover informant competence parameters as well as an estimate of the correct answer key.

So far we have obtained solid results for multiple choice and fill-in-the-blank formats. These extensions first appear in Romney *et al.* (1986), while Maher (1987) provides a very detailed empirical and Monte Carlo study of our estimation methods for the multiple choice format. In addition, we have improvised a method of dealing with a ranking format in Romney *et al.* (1988), and we have applied it successfully to several empirical examples.

In the remaining two subsections, we present new models and results for a matching exam format and a format requiring responses on a continuum.

4.1 A MATCHING EXAM FORMAT

In a matching format, each informant has M test items and M possible responses, $R_1, \ldots,$ R_M (we can think of them as on a nominal scale), and the task is to pair the responses to the items in a one to one fashion. To simplify, let the first M positive integers denote the responses. Unlike the testing formats considered so far, a matching exam entails dependencies among the items because a response used for one item can not be applied to another item. Thus the local independence axiom must be replaced by something that reflects these dependencies. This is accomplished by Axiom 3 and 4 of the matching model, which is expressed by the following four axioms.

Axiom 1. *Common Truth.* There is a correct answer z_k to each item k. So the correct answer key is $\mathbf{Z} = (z_k)_{1\times M}$, where $\mathbf{Z}$ is some permutation of the first M natural numbers.

Axiom 2. *Homogeneneous Items.* Each informant i has a competence D_i, $0 < D_i < 1$, of "knowing" the correct answer to any item k. If i knows the correct answer to an item, then a correct response is made.

Axiom 3. *Knowledge Independence.* Let

$$S_{ik} = \begin{cases} 1 & \text{if informant } i \text{ knows item } k \\ 0 & \text{otherwise,} \end{cases}$$

and $\mathbf{S} = (S_{ik})_{N\times M}$. Then

$$\Pr[\mathbf{S} = (s_{ik})] = \prod_{i=1}^{N}\prod_{k=1}^{M} \Pr(S_{ik} = s_{ik}) = \prod_{i=1}^{N}\prod_{k=1}^{M} D_i^{s_{ik}}(1-D_i)^{1-s_{ik}}, \tag{34}$$

for all possible $(s_{ik})_{N\times M}$.

Axiom 4. *Random Guessing.* If informant i knows K_i items, then random guesses without replacement are made to the remaining $M - K_i$ items from the $M - K_i$ unused response alternatives, $K_i = 0, 1, \ldots, M$.

One way to think about the matching model is that it assumes a type of independence among items at a hypothetical knowledge level. Then the violation in our usual "local independence" axiom is entirely through the without replacement guessing process.

It is possible to derive quantities like the informant hit and false alarm rates of the GCM. The results are

$$\Pr(X_{ik} = r \mid Z_k = r) = D_i + \frac{1 - D_i^M}{M} \tag{35}$$

and

$$\Pr(X_{ik} = r \mid Z_k \neq r) = \frac{M(1-D_i) - (1 - D_i^M)}{M(M-1)}. \tag{36}$$

Equations (35) and (36) are a bit tedious to derive. They follow by conditionalizing on the number of items other than item k that are known and then using (34) to show that this number is binomially distributed. Combinatorial work with binomial sums finishes the derivation.

The matching model has N competence parameters, D_i, and $M - 1$ answer key parameter, and the response profile data provide $N(M-1)$ unknowns; so for most values of N and M, one could, in principle, find estimates for the parameters. Standard approaches are unlikely to work because the parameter space for the answer key is unusual, namely, the $M!$ permutations of the first M integers, which grows in a non-polynonial way with M. We have devised an approximate method to estimate the D_i based on informant by informant matching indices as follows.

Suppose two informants i and j have competencies D_i and D_j, respectively. Let M_{ij} be the observed proportion of response agreements between i and j. Then

$$\mathrm{E}(M_{ij}) = \left[D_i + \frac{1-D_i^M}{M}\right]\left[D_j + \frac{1-D_j^M}{M}\right] + \left[M(1-D_i) - (1-D_i^M)\right]\frac{M(1-D_j)-(1-D_j^M)}{M^2(M-1)}. \quad (37)$$

Equation (37) can be obtained by noting that M_{ij} can be expressed linearly by

$$M_{ij} = \sum_{k=1}^{M} \frac{M_{ij,k}}{M},$$

where

$$M_{ij,k} = \begin{cases} 1 & \text{if } i \text{ and } j \text{ match on item } k \\ 0 & \text{otherwise.} \end{cases}$$

Since expectation is a linear operator and items are homogeneous,

$$\mathrm{E}(M_{ij}) = E(M_{ij,k}), \quad (38)$$

for any item k. Next from Axiom 3, informants i and j independently obtain hits or false alarms on item k with probabilities given by (35) and (36), repectively. All that remains to see (37) is to consider the possibilities that produce a match.

An approximate estimation method in the spirit of the matching method for the HTM discussed earlier is possible. For M not small ($M \geq 5$) and D_i fairly large ($1/2 \leq D_i$), an excellent approximation to $\mathrm{E}(M_{ij})$ is

$$\mathrm{E}(M_{ij}) \approx \left[D_i + \frac{1-D_i^M}{M}\right]\left[D_j + \frac{1-D_j^M}{M}\right]. \quad (39)$$

If an $N \times N$ matrix of observed M_{ij} is factored with MINRES (ignoring the main diagonal), the ith entry, f_i, should be approximately given by

$$f_i = D_i + \frac{1-D_i^M}{M},$$

and these N equations can be solved separately for the $\hat{D}_i$.

Even if we accept the estimates, $\hat{D}_i$, as true values of the D_i, it is not an easy task to determine the "most likely" answer key (among the $M!$ possibilities) from the response profile data. If we pick any item k, it is easy to determine the most likely response for it, however, the entire key can not be estimated in this way because of the fact that a given response can only be used for one item.

Let us pick, say, item k. Then by Bayes rule

$$\Pr(Z_k = r|\mathbf{X}_{\cdot k}) = \frac{\Pr(\mathbf{X}_{\cdot k}|Z_k = r)\Pr(Z_k = r)}{\Pr(\mathbf{X}_{\cdot k})},$$

where $\mathbf{X}_{\cdot k} = (X_{1k}, \ldots, X_{Nk})$. From (35) and (36),

$$\Pr(\mathbf{X}_{\cdot k}|Z_k = r) = \prod_{i=1}^{N} \left[\frac{D_i + (1 - D_i^M)}{M}\right]^{b_r(i,k)} \left[\frac{M(1 - D_i) - (1 - D_i^M)}{M}\right]^{1-b_r(i,k)}, \quad (40)$$

where

$$b_r(i,k) = \begin{cases} 1 & \text{if } X_{ik} = r \\ 0 & \text{otherwise.} \end{cases} \quad (41)$$

If all possible answer keys are equally likely *a priori*, then it is easy to see that the most likely response to item k is the r that maximizes (40), $r = 1, \ldots, M$.

One easily implemented method to obtain the entire answer key is to determine the answer for the item with the most clear-cut marginal decision from (40). Then that response is dropped from the possible response set, and the most clear-cut second decision is made, etc. Unfortunately this approach is rather *ad hoc*. It is an open problem to see if a computationally feasible method can be worked out to obtain the most likely answer key given the response profile data and estimates of the D_i.

4.2 CONTINUOUS RESPONSE FORMAT

In this section, we first describe a very simple model for items calling for responses on a ratio scale, and then several directions in which we are generalizing the model will be discussed. To simplify our discussion, suppose the informants all have a common ratio scale of a quality like height of people or yearly rainfall in a region. Each informant i is asked to give a guess X_{ik} as to the amount of the quality possessed by each item k. The goal is to develop plausible models along with satisfactory estimation schemes that permit the calibration of each informant's competency and, more importantly, the rational aggregation of their responses to obtain consensus point estimates of the "correct" answer for each item.

The model that follows is adapted from classical test theory (Lord & Novick, 1968) by reversing the roles of subjects and items—a frequently exploited device in our work. The model is unrealistic on psychophysical grounds; however, as we will see, it provides the bases for productive generalizations. To permit easy comparison with our other models, the model is presented in the following format:

Task. Each of N informants answers with a positive real number to each of M items.

Data. Let X_{ik} be a random variable representing the response of the ith informant to the kth item, and $\mathbf{X} = (X_{ik})_{N\times M}$ be the response profile matrix.

Axiom 1. *Common Truth.* There is a fixed answer key applicable to all informants, that is, each item k has a correct answer z_k in $(0,\infty)$. Let $\mathbf{Z} = (z_k)_{1\times M}$ be the correct answer key.

Axiom 2. *Random Error.* The ith informant's response to the kth item is a random variable given by

$$X_{ik} = z_k + E_{ik}, \tag{42}$$

where the E_{ik} are zero mean gaussian random variables, that is, each E_{ik} is normally distributed with mean zero.

Axiom 3. *Local Independence.* The E_{ik} are all mutually stochastically independent.

Axiom 4. *Inhomogeneous Variances.* Each informant i has a competence parameter D_i in $(0,\infty)$ such that E_{ik} has variance D_i^{-1}, for all $k = 1, 2, \ldots, M$.

It is possible to analyze the preceding model in ways analogous to how Lord & Novick (1968) analyze structurally related models for estimating subject (informant) aptitude. Define, for each informant, a random variable X_i, which represents the response of informant i to a randomly drawn item k. That is

$$\Pr(X_i = x_i) = \begin{cases} 1/M & \text{if } x_i = x_{ik} \\ 0 & \text{otherwise,} \end{cases} \tag{43}$$

for $k = 1, \ldots, M$. Also, let the variance of the unknown correct answers be given by

$$\sigma_Z^2 = \sum_{k=1}^{M} \frac{(z_k - \bar{z})^2}{M}, \tag{44}$$

and the variance of X_i be σ_i^2. Then it is easy to derive that the covariance between all pairs of informants i, j is a constant given by

$$\text{Cov}(X_i, X_j) = \sigma_Z^2, \tag{45}$$

and the correlation is given by

$$\rho_{ij} = \frac{\sigma_Z^2}{\sqrt{\sigma_i^2 + \sigma_Z^2}\sqrt{\sigma_j^2 + \sigma_Z^2}} = \rho_{iZ}\rho_{jZ}, \tag{46}$$

where ρ_{iZ} is the correlation of X_i with **Z**and σ_i^2 is the variance of X_i. One can think of ρ_{iZ} as the correlation of informant i's responses with the "truth." Equation (46) is a version of Spearman's famous item tetrad law (see, Lord & Novick, 1968) that applies here to informants rather than items, and it frequently holds in some form for process models that we formulate including the GCM and HTM (with homogeneous items).

One approach to estimating the parameters of the model (the z_k and the D_i) is to use the method of maximum likelihood estimation. It is easy to obtain the likelihood function for the model, namely,

$$\mathrm{L}(\mathbf{D},\mathbf{Z}) = \prod_{k=1}^{M}\prod_{i=1}^{N}\sqrt{\frac{D_i}{2\pi}}\exp\left(\frac{-D_i\left(X_{ik}-Z_k\right)^2}{2}\right). \tag{47}$$

By differentiating log L with respect to each parameter and setting the resulting equations to zero, it is easy to obtain the following equations that must be satisfied if MLEs exist:

$$\hat{z}_k = \frac{\sum\limits_{i=1}^{N}\hat{D}_i X_{ik}}{\sum\limits_{i=1}^{N}\hat{D}_i} \tag{48}$$

and

$$\hat{D}_i = \frac{M}{\sum\limits_{k=1}^{N}(X_{ik}-\hat{z}_k)^2}. \tag{49}$$

Equations (48) and (49) have the nice feature that $\hat{z}_k$ is defined entirely in terms of the $\hat{D}_i$; and $\hat{D}_i$, in turn, is defined entirely in terms of the $\hat{z}_k$. These facts suggest a two-phase estimation scheme. First one starts with some initial values of, say, the z_k, and then they are passed through (49) to obtain initial values of the D_i. These later quantities are passed through (48) to obtain revised values for z_k, etc. Such a scheme is easy to implement, and in many structurally related problems, it will converge to a solution (a fixed point) that maximizes the target function (in this case (46)), if certain technical conditions obtain that support a type of "fixed point" theorem (see, for example, Kuhn 1986).

In our Monte Carlo runs, the two-phase proceedure sometimes recovered the underlying parameters well; however, in many instances, especially with small N, it produced estimates that resulted in exactly one $\hat{D}_i$ diverging to positive infinity for some i. From (48), such an informant becomes a "dictator" in the aggregation process in the sense that $\hat{z}_k = X_{ik}$, for all items k. These empirical results led us to take a closer look at the likelihood function in (47).

Actually, without constraints, (47) does not have a maximum in the positive reals. The technical reason for this is that the likelihood function in (47) diverges to positive infinity if a particular competence D_i diverges to positive infinity as the z_k converge, at an appropriate rate, to the corresponding X_{ik}. We could think of such an informant as an "error free dictator" in the aggregation rule. However, the corresponding estimators based on a dictator do not have any particular properties that recommend them. Moreover, we cannot expect the usual asymptotic properties of the maximum likelihood approach to hold even if (48) and (49) can be solved, since the number of unknown parameters, $N+M$, goes up whenever the dimensionality of the response profile matrix, NM, increases. Nevertheless, since there are fewer parameters than observables, one can expect to find suitable parameter estimators by some rational means.

Fortunately, we have found a reasonable way to estimate parameters that has worked well in Monte Carlo runs. The idea is to use (45) and (46) to get point estimates of the σ_i^2 and from these and (48), estimates of the D_i and z_k follow. More specifically, this two-phased procedure first computes the mean of the observed covariances in (45) to obtain a point estimate of σ_Z^2. Second, the observed ρ_{ij} correlation matrix is analyzed by MINRES described earlier (see (17)). This provides least squares estimates of the ρ_{iZ} in (46). Finally, the estimate of σ_Z^2 coupled with the estimates of ρ_{iZ} can be inserted into (46) to obtain a point estimate $\tilde{\sigma}_i^2$ of σ_i^2 for each informant. The final step involves noting that $1/\tilde{\sigma}_i^2$ is reasonable point estimate of D_i. Once the D_i are estimated, these can be put into (48) to obtain a sort of conditional maximum likelihood estimate of each z_k. This two-phased proceedure is analogous to the matching method for the HTM in that estimates of the D_i are first obtained from informant by informant association measures, using MINRES, and then the answer key is reconstructed by a conditional maximum likelihood method. Monte Carlo work with this two-phased procedure has been promising so far; however more work is needed.

There are several reasonable ways to generalize the model presented here. All of these generalizations follow from psychophysical considerations. First, it is unrealistic to assume that a particular informant has the same error variance over a range of physical magnitudes. This follows both from empirical results and theoretical work in psychophysics (for example, McKenna, 1985; Pradhan & Hoffman, 1963). One practical way to handle this problem would be to attempt some sort of a variance equating transformation of the response profile data before applying the model.

Next, lets assume for the moment that the error variance within an informant on the analyzed data is constant. It is consistent with psychophysical theory that the ith informant's responses are given by some psychophysical function, Ψ_i, of the true magnitude plus a random error of some sort, that is,

$$X_{ik} = \Psi_i(z_k) + E_{ik}. \tag{50}$$

The simple model corresponds to $\Psi_i(z_k) = z_k$ and is psychophysically unrealistic. An obvious candidate for the psychophysical function in (50) is Steven's power law given by

$$\Psi_i(z_k) = a_i z_k^{b_i}, \tag{51}$$

where $a_i > 0$ and b_i are real valued parameters associated with each informant. Another version related to (51) might apply if a log transform of the X_{ik} produced the desired variance equating transformation discussed earlier. It is given by

$$\Psi_i(z_k) = a_i + b_i z_k, \tag{52}$$

which of course is the parametric form of the log of (51).

The likelihood function in (47) can be augmented to include (52) in place of z_k and then its log can be differentiated on the parameters (the D_i, a_i, b_i, and z_k). When these results are equated to zero to yield the extremum conditions, the results are

$$\hat{D}_i = \frac{M}{\sum_{k=1}^{M}(X_{ik} - \hat{a}_i - \hat{b}_i\hat{z}_k)^2}, \tag{53}$$

$$\hat{a}_i = \frac{\sum_{k=1}^{M}(X_{ik} - \hat{b}_i\hat{z}_k)}{M}, \tag{54}$$

$$\hat{b}_i = \frac{\sum_{k=1}^{M}(X_{ik} - \hat{a}_i)}{\sum_{k=1}^{M}\hat{z}_k} \tag{55}$$

and

$$\hat{z}_k = \frac{\sum_{i=1}^{N}\hat{D}_i\hat{b}_i(X_{ik} - \hat{a}_i)}{\sum_{i=1}^{N}\hat{D}_i\hat{b}_i^2}. \tag{56}$$

As with the simple model, the likelihood function does not have a maximum in the parameter space when all of the parameters are free to vary. However, if some way can be found to estimate one class of parameters, then a subset of (53), (54), (55), and (56) provides simple equations that provide conditional MLEs of the other parameters.

We have begun to look at the model in (52) and some other natural variations from an estimation theoretic standpoint. We have made some progress, but more work is needed. If we can successfully model psychophysical situations, then in a group psychophysical experiment we should be able to recover estimates of the underlying physical magnitudes by aggregating suitably transformed responses. In a theoretical sense, we would be doing psychophysics without the need of physical measurement. Of course, this would require some sort of usable way of estimating all the parameters in (50) from response profile data alone. We are currently working out estimation theory for several such models.

Hopefully, our methods can then be applied with confidence to scaling situations that do not naturally possess an underlying physical scale, for example, utility measurement.

In fact, one graduate student, Alan Brothers, is working with us to try and adapt our methodology to better understand the elusive concept of personal risk in decision making experiments. Another potentially valuable application would be to aggregate information from a set of witnesses to a physically quantifiable event. The goal would be to model both perceiver bias and informant competence in the same model.

Models like the ones analyzed in this section have an advantage over most traditional ways of pooling continuous measures over "experts" (see, for example, Grofman & Owen, 1986; and Hogarth, 1975). This advantage is that they determine expert weights as well as aggregated responses simultaneously. Most schemes in use require exogenous assessment of experts at some level (for example, Winkler & Cummings, 1972). Also, models like ours permit a quantitative answer to questions about how to use group judgments to obtain the best performances. For example, Einhorn, Hogarth, and Klempner (1977) compare models that attempt group judgments based either on equal weighting schemes or variously chosen "dictators." Our model not only differentially weights all informants, but it obtains estimates of these weights from the same data source that provides the to-be-aggregated responses.

5. REFERENCES

Batchelder, W.H. & Romney, A.K. (1986). The statistical analysis of a general Condorcet model for dichotomous choice situations. In B. Grofman & G. Owen (Eds.) *Information Pooling and Group Decision Making.* Greenwich, CN: JAI Press.

Batchelder, W.H. & Romney, A.K. (1988). Test theory without an answer key. *Psychometrika,* 53, 193–224.

Clogg, C.C. (1981). New developments in latent structure analysis. In D.M. Jackson & E.F. Borgatta (Eds.) *Factor Analysis and Measurement in Sociological Research.* Beverly Hills, CA: Sage.

Comrey, A.L. (1962). The minimum residual method of factor analysis. *Psychological Reports,* 11, 15–18.

Einhorn, H.J., Hogarth, R.M., & Klempner, E. (1977). Quality of group judgements. *Psychological Bulletin,* 84, 158–172.

Gelfand, A. & Solomon, H. (1973). A study of Poisson's models for jury verdicts in Criminal and Civil trials. *Journal of American Statistical Association,* 68, 271–278.

Grofman, B. & Owen, G. (Eds.). (1986). *Information Pooling and Group Decision Making.* Greenwich, CN: JAI Press.

Hogarth, R.M. (1975). Cognitive processes and the assessment of subjective probability distributions. *Journal of the American Statistical Association,* 70, 271–294.

Kuhn, H.W. (1986). How to compute economic equilibria by pivotol methods. In S. Reiter (Ed.) *Studies in Mathematical Economics.* The Mathematical Association of America.

Lazarsfeld, P.F. & Henry, N.W. (1968). *Latent Structure Analysis.* New York: Houghton Mifflin.

Lord, F.M. (1974). Individualized testing and item characteristic curve theory. In D.H. Krantz, R.C. Atkinson, R.D. Luce, & P. Suppes (Eds.) *Contemporary Developments in Mathematical Psychology (Vol.2).* San Francisco: Freeman.

Lord, F.M. & Novick, M.R.. (1968). *Statistical Theories of Mental Test Scores.* Reading, MA: Addison-Wesley.

McKenna, F.P. (1985). Another look at the "new psychophysics." *British Journal of Psychology,* 76, 97–109.

Maher, K.M. (1987). *A multiple choice model for aggregating group knowledge and estimating individual competencies.* Ph.D. Dissertation, Universtiy of California, Irvine.

Nitzan, S. & Paroush, J. (1982). Optimal decision rules in uncertain dichotomous choice situations. *International Economics Review,* 23, 289–297.

Pradhan, P.L. & Hoffman, P.J. (1963). Effect of spacing the range of stimuli on magnitude estimation judgements. *Journal of Experimental Psychology,* 66, 533–541.

Rasch, G. (1960). *Probabilistic Models for Some Intelligence and Attainment Tests.* Copenhagen: Denmarks Paedagogiske Institute.

Romney, A.K., Batchelder, W.H., & Weller, S.C. (1987). Recent applications of cultural consensus theory. *American Behavioral Scientist,* 31, 163–177.

Romney, A.K., Weller, S.C., & Batchelder, W.H. (1986). Culture as consensus: a theory of culture and informant accuracy. *American Anthropologist,* 88, 313–338.

Winkler, R.L. & Cummings, L.L. (1972). On the choice of a consensus distribution in Bayesian analysis. *Organization Behavior and Human Performance,* 7, 63–76.

Item Sampling, Guessing, Partial Information and Decision-Making in Achievement Testing

*Miguel A. García-Pérez**
Universidad Complutense de Madrid

Abstract
This paper addresses the problem of determining the number of items in a test and the cutting score to make a binary decision on mastery with prescribed precision. Previous attempts to solve this problem have been based on simplistic models assuming all-or-none knowledge. The same approach as in those papers is adopted here, but from the standpoint of a finite state model of test behaviour. The required number of items is shown to be smaller than previous results suggested. In contrast with previous attempts, this method is applied to true-false and multiple-choice tests responded to in the conventional mode, and to multiple-choice tests responded to in answer-until-correct and Coombs' modes. The effects of varying guessing behaviour on the part of the examinees are also studied. It is shown that the smallest number of items needed to make a mastery decision with a predetermined error rate occurs when the testees respond without guessing. This behaviour is unlikely to be followed by examinees, but it is also shown that this lower limit can be reached at by administering multiple-choice tests under Coombs' response mode.

1. Introduction

When an objective test is administered, the examiner's goal is to infer something about the testee. The most basic thing that an examiner is usually interested in knowing is whether the testee's ability or knowledge is above or below a certain critical point which is thought of as defining the boundary between masters and non-masters. This type of mastery decisions is frequent in educational settings and personnel selection: the use of mastery criteria is commonplace in assigning passing course grades to students or moving them to a higher level of instruction, in issuing drivers' licenses, or in job promotion, termination and hiring (Weiss & Davison, 1981; Guion & Gibson, 1988). In practice, a cutting score is preset that serves as a threshold with which the testee's observed score is compared. If the observed score is above the cutting score then the testee 'passes the test' and is regarded as master; otherwise he/she 'fails the test' and is regarded as non-master.

These decisions are not free of error, however. It is possible that a testee whose true ability/knowledge is clearly not that of a master gets an observed score that is above the cutting score, and viceversa. Some modifications of the multiple-choice test have been proposed in an attempt to segregate or, at least, compensate for irrelevant influences on test scores that are attributable to the format of administration of the test. However, the extent to

* Departamento de Metodología, Facultad de Psicología, Universidad Complutense, Campus de Somosaguas, 28023 Madrid, Spain.

which these proposed modifications attain their goal does not seem to have been thoroughly investigated (but see Frary, 1980a, 1982).

If errors in mastery decisions can not be completely eliminated, examiners can try to minimize them or, at least, to assess their magnitude. The mastery decision can be viewed as the testing of the null hypothesis that the testee's ability/knowledge is at or below the critical point against the alternative hypothesis that it is above. A sample of n items is used to gather the data to test this hypothesis. Then, fixing the probability of a Type I error, the probability of a Type II error can be determined and controlled by varying n, since this probability is known to decrease with increasing sample size (Hogg & Tanis, 1977, Sec. 8.4). An interesting byproduct of this approach is that the cutting score can also be immediately obtained. Fhanér (1974) and Wilcox (1976) made such analysis assuming that testees either know the correct response to an item and mark it out or do not know it and leave the item unanswered. This assumption has been criticized by van den Brink & Koele (1980), who assumed that, instead of omitting, testees guess at random on all items whose correct answer they do not know with certainty. They further assumed that testees have a probability $1/a$ of getting the right answer when guessing at an a-alternative item. With these amendments, they concluded that the number of items required is much larger than that calculated by Fhanér (1974), and that this number decreases with increasing number of choices per item. Also, the analyses in these papers were made assuming tacitly that all of the items in the test have the same difficulty.

A closer look at the papers just mentioned reveals some flaws in their method. Firstly, the models assumed by Fhanér (1974) and Wilcox (1976) do not take into account guessing nor partial information, which are known to play a role in multiple-choice testing. And it is unlikely that testees do not guess since the expected number-right score of guessing is positive. On the other hand, the model assumed by van den Brink & Koele (1980) is the simple knowledge or random guessing model which has been disproven repeatedly. Their assumption that guessing is among all choices is not valid since partial information makes testees eliminate some distractors at certain items (Coombs, Milholland & Womer, 1956; Cross & Frary, 1977; Bliss, 1980). Finally, these models apply only to the conventional response mode, where testees mark out the alternative believed to be correct in each item.

In this paper, the same general approach as in those papers is followed to determine the required number of items in the test and the cutting score to make a mastery decision with a predetermined error rate. A finite state model of objective test behaviour is adopted instead. The model is briefly reviewed in section 2 to show how it provides equations for the probability of each possible response outcome in each particular situation. A complete listing of all the equations corresponding to the situations selected for study is given in section 3. The general approach to determining the test size and cutting score is described in section 4. This approach is applied in section 5 to true-false tests and multiple-choice tests (with a ranging from 2 to 4) responded to in conventional mode with examinees following three different answering strategies. Section 6 presents similar results for multiple-choice tests (with a ranging from 3 to 4) responded to under Coombs' (1953) and answer-until-correct modes. The paper concludes with a discussion of the results with an eye towards choosing a test format for use in criterion-referenced testing.

2. Finite State Model

A full description of the finite state model, including its assumptions, can be found in García-Pérez (1987). It will be merely said here that it takes item sampling, guessing, and knowledge at the alternative level (partial information) into account to determine the probability of each possible response outcome to an item as a function of the testee's ability/knowledge λ ($0 \leq \lambda \leq 1$, representing the proportion of statements in the item pool whose truth value the subject knows) and willingness to guess γ ($0 \leq \gamma \leq 1$, representing the probability that a subject guesses at an item whose correct answer is not known with certainty). In the sequel, the test is regarded as a random sample of *n* items each of the same, average difficulty. It has been shown (García-Pérez & Frary, in press) that the model is rather insensitive to variations in item difficulties, since the probability of a subject's correctly responding to an item of average difficulty is valid to characterize performance on a test with items of varying difficulties.

The model is illustrated using the tree diagram shown in figure 1. This diagram depicts all

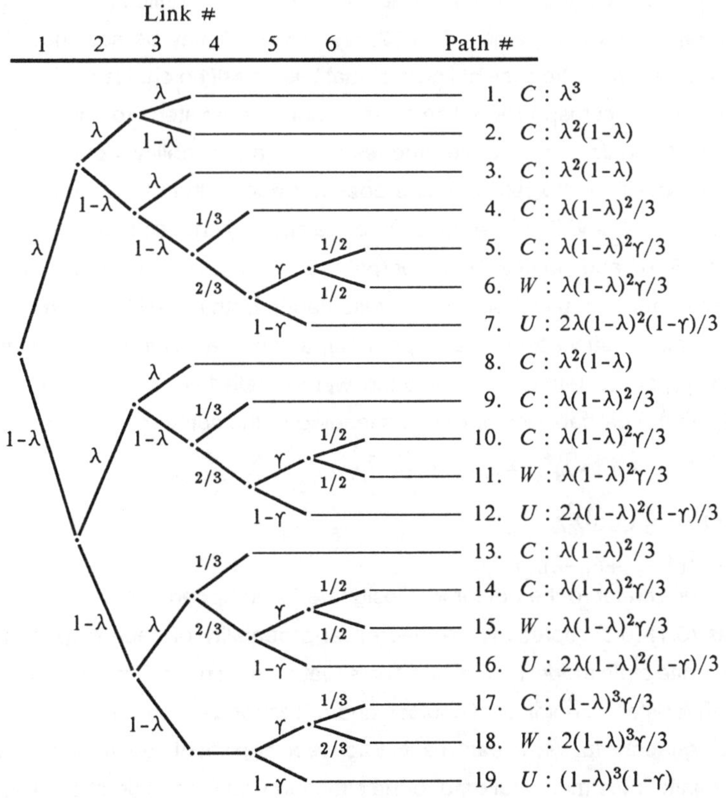

FIGURE 1. Tree diagram describing the possible sequences of events when responding to a 3-choice item.

the possible sequences of events that may take place before a subject responds to a 3-choice item in conventional mode. There are 19 paths corresponding to 19 possible situations which ultimately result in only three possible response outcomes: correct (*C*), wrong (*W*), or unanswered (*U*). There are at most 6 links in each path, depending on how many steps are needed to arrive at a response outcome. All three elements (number of paths, number of links, and possible response outcomes) depend on the number of alternatives in the item and the response mode.

In the case of figure 1, the first link within each path refers to the attempt at classifying the first choice in the item as true or false as applied to the item stem: a correct classification occurs with probability λ while the choice remains unclassified with probability $1-\lambda$. García-Pérez & Frary (1989) show that items of average difficulty are implied when the probability of correctly classifying a choice is taken to be λ. The second and third links are similar to the first, but applied to the second and third alternatives in the item, respectively. Whenever all choices are classified (total knowledge, represented in path 1) or a-1 choices are classified (highest degree of partial knowledge, represented in paths 2, 3, and 8), the testee may give the correct answer without further steps. That is why these paths have only 3 links, and the probability of each of these situations is shown to the right of the corresponding path, as is done for the rest of the paths too. If only one choice can be classified (lowest degree of partial knowledge, represented in paths 4-7, 9-12, and 13-16) it may be assumed that there is a probability $1/a$ (i.e. 1/3 in the case of figure 1) that this classified choice be the correct answer, in which case a correct response will be given without further steps (paths 4, 9, and 13). If this single classified choice is a distractor, the testee has a probability γ of guessing at random among the unclassified choices. If he/she does not guess, then the item is left unanswered (paths 7, 12, and 16), and if he/she does there is a fifty-fifty chance of marking out the correct answer (paths 5, 10, and 14) or a distractor (paths 6, 11, and 15). Finally, if the testee is unable to classify any choice (total ignorance, represented in paths 17-19) then the correct answer may be given after a successful guess (path 17), a wrong answer may be given by a wrong guess (path 18), or the item may be left unanswered (path 19).

Summing up the probabilities of all paths leading to the same response outcome,

$$c=\lambda^3+3\lambda^2(1-\lambda)+\lambda(1-\lambda)^2(1+\gamma)+\tfrac{1}{3}(1-\lambda)^3\gamma, \tag{0.1}$$

$$w=\lambda(1-\lambda)^2\gamma+\tfrac{2}{3}(1-\lambda)^3\gamma, \tag{0.2}$$

$$u=2\lambda(1-\lambda)^2(1-\gamma)+(1-\lambda)^3(1-\gamma), \tag{0.3}$$

where c, w, and u refer to the outcomes designated with uppercase characters.

Equations (0.1)-(0.3) represent the theoretical probability of each response outcome as given by the finite state model for the item and situation described. Tree diagrams constructed for items with a different number of choices and/or responded to in different modes yield the appropriate equations for use in each case. Each resulting set of equations can be considered in itself as a finite state model tailored to the situation under consideration. The next section presents the equations (models) that apply to the situations which will be studied in this paper.

3. Probabilities of Response Outcomes for Selected Cases

The equations just presented assume that testees guess inspired solely by their particular willingness to do so. This may be the case in some situations if the examinees are not aware of the consequences of guessing, but this event should be avoided for two reasons. Firstly, it adds an irrelevant source of score variation whose effects depend on both the scoring model to be used and the degree of partial information that the testee had on the particular item (Frary, 1980a). Secondly, the differential adoption of consistent guessing strategies on the part of examinees can be a source of test bias (Frary, 1980b). For these reasons, a more plausible and desirable assumption about guessing will be used. In fact, three different answering strategies will be considered for adoption with tests administered in conventional mode.

The first of these strategies will be referred to as *No Guessing* (NG) and it results in $\gamma=0$. Hence, subjects do not guess at all. The tree diagram and equations for this response strategy can be obtained from the diagram in figure 1 and equations (0.1)-(0.3) by replacing γ with 0. It follows that the probability of a wrong response is 0 under the NG strategy. This strategy is unlikely to be followed by examinees unless a severe penalty is applied to disuade them from guessing. Regardless, it is included in the study because the results obtained for this strategy represent a lower bound with which the results for other strategies can be compared.

The next two strategies have been described in García-Pérez & Frary (in press). In the *Number Right* (NR) strategy, examinees answer all items regardless of knowledge and, hence, act as if $\gamma=1$. The corresponding tree diagram and equations can be obtained in a manner completely similar to that mentioned above for the NG strategy. It is evident that the probability of omitting is 0 when the NR strategy is followed.

Under the Formula Scoring (FS) strategy, γ is no longer constant within items. This strategy represents perfect adherence to the directions that are supplied when formula scoring will be used. This means that $\gamma=1$ in all cases of partial knowledge while $\gamma=0$ in case of total ignorance. Replacement of these values in figure 1 and equations (0.1)-(0.3) leads to the tree diagram and equations that apply to this case.

Table 1 presents the probability of each possible response outcome to true-false (T-F) and multiple-choice (a-C) items with $2 \leq a \leq 4$ for each response strategy. Equations for true-false and 2-choice items under the FS strategy are not presented since they are the same as for the NG strategy. This is because the only situation in which subjects can not mark out the correct answer with assurance is total ignorance, and the FS strategy advocates not to guess in these cases. Note also that there are only two response outcomes except for the FS strategy when $a \geq 3$.

When the test is responded to in non-conventional modes, there is not always room for variations in answering behaviour. This is particularly true for the answer-until-correct (AUC) response mode, in which subjects are immediately informed as to the correctness of their first attempt and continue making attempts until they find the correct answer. Hence, the NR strategy is implied, since subjects have to answer every item. There are a possible outcomes

TABLE 1. Probabilities of outcomes under the conventional response mode

Item	Strategy	Equations	
T-F	NG	$c=\lambda$	(1.1)
		$u=1-\lambda$	(1.2)
	NR	$c=\lambda+\frac{1}{2}(1-\lambda)$	(2.1)
		$w=\frac{1}{2}(1-\lambda)$	(2.2)
2-C	NG	$c=\lambda^2+2\lambda(1-\lambda)$	(3.1)
		$u=(1-\lambda)^2$	(3.2)
	NR	$c=\lambda^2+2\lambda(1-\lambda)+\frac{1}{2}(1-\lambda)^2$	(4.1)
		$w=\frac{1}{2}(1-\lambda)^2$	(4.2)
3-C	NG	$c=\lambda^3+3\lambda^2(1-\lambda)+\lambda(1-\lambda)^2$	(5.1)
		$u=2\lambda(1-\lambda)^2+(1-\lambda)^3$	(5.2)
	NR	$c=\lambda^3+3\lambda^2(1-\lambda)+2\lambda(1-\lambda)^2+\frac{1}{3}(1-\lambda)^3$	(6.1)
		$w=\lambda(1-\lambda)^2+\frac{2}{3}(1-\lambda)^3$	(6.2)
	FS	$c=\lambda^3+3\lambda^2(1-\lambda)+2\lambda(1-\lambda)^2$	(7.1)
		$w=\lambda(1-\lambda)^2$	(7.2)
		$u=(1-\lambda)^3$	(7.3)
4-C	NG	$c=\lambda^4+4\lambda^3(1-\lambda)+3\lambda^2(1-\lambda)^2+\lambda(1-\lambda)^3$	(8.1)
		$u=3\lambda^2(1-\lambda)^2+3\lambda(1-\lambda)^3+(1-\lambda)^4$	(8.2)
	NR	$c=\lambda^4+4\lambda^3(1-\lambda)+\frac{9}{2}\lambda^2(1-\lambda)^2+2\lambda(1-\lambda)^3+\frac{1}{4}(1-\lambda)^4$	(9.1)
		$w=\frac{3}{2}\lambda^2(1-\lambda)^2+2\lambda(1-\lambda)^3+\frac{3}{4}(1-\lambda)^4$	(9.2)
	FS	$c=\lambda^4+4\lambda^3(1-\lambda)+\frac{9}{2}\lambda^2(1-\lambda)^2+2\lambda(1-\lambda)^3$	(10.1)
		$w=\frac{3}{2}\lambda^2(1-\lambda)^2+2\lambda(1-\lambda)^3$	(10.2)
		$u=(1-\lambda)^4$	(10.3)

TABLE 2. Probabilities of outcomes under AUC response mode

Item	Equations	
3-C	$c_1=\lambda^3+3\lambda^2(1-\lambda)+2\lambda(1-\lambda)^2+\frac{1}{3}(1-\lambda)^3$	(11.1)
	$c_2=\lambda(1-\lambda)^2+\frac{1}{3}(1-\lambda)^3$	(11.2)
	$c_3=\frac{1}{3}(1-\lambda)^3$	(11.3)
4-C	$c_1=\lambda^4+4\lambda^3(1-\lambda)+\frac{9}{2}\lambda^2(1-\lambda)^2+2\lambda(1-\lambda)^3+\frac{1}{4}(1-\lambda)^4$	(12.1)
	$c_2=\frac{3}{2}\lambda^2(1-\lambda)^2+\lambda(1-\lambda)^3+\frac{1}{4}(1-\lambda)^4$	(12.2)
	$c_3=\lambda(1-\lambda)^3+\frac{1}{4}(1-\lambda)^4$	(12.3)
	$c_4=\frac{1}{4}(1-\lambda)^4$	(12.4)

to an a-alternative item since a number of attempts from 1 to a may be needed to find the correct answer. Tree diagrams for this response mode are easily constructed and some examples can be found in García-Pérez (in press). Denoting the probability of a correct response at the ith attempt by c_i, Table 2 shows the probability of each possible response outcome to multiple-choice items (with $3 \leq a \leq 4$) responded to in AUC mode. Note that, obviously, the equation for c_1 for each value of a is the same as the equation for c following NR strategy when the same item is responded to in conventional mode.

The last response mode to be considered here is that proposed by Coombs (1953), in which testees are asked to mark out as many distractors as they can recognize. This gives rise to $2a$-1 possible outcomes: any number of marked choices from 0 to a–1, with the correct answer having been marked or not in each case save, obviously, when no marks are made. One point is awarded for each correctly recognized distractor and a penalty of a–1 points is applied if the correct answer is marked. Given this scoring scheme, the only neutral guessing strategy directs subjects to behave in exactly the opposite way as formula scoring directions suggest: guessing at random only in case of total ignorance, making from 1 to a–1 marks at will. It will be assumed here that subjects are equally inclined to make any allowable number of marks

TABLE 3. Probabilities of outcomes under Coombs' response mode

Item	Strategy	Equations	
3-C	IFS	$r_{20}=\lambda^3+3\lambda^2(1-\lambda)+\lambda(1-\lambda)^2+\frac{1}{6}(1-\lambda)^3$	(13.1)
		$r_{11}=\frac{1}{3}(1-\lambda)^3$	(13.2)
		$r_{10}=2\lambda(1-\lambda)^2+\frac{1}{3}(1-\lambda)^3$	(13.3)
		$r_{01}=\frac{1}{6}(1-\lambda)^3$	(13.4)
	NG	$r_{20}=\lambda^3+3\lambda^2(1-\lambda)+\lambda(1-\lambda)^2$	(14.1)
		$r_{10}=2\lambda(1-\lambda)^2$	(14.2)
		$r_{00}=(1-\lambda)^3$	(14.3)
4-C	IFS	$r_{30}=\lambda^4+4\lambda^3(1-\lambda)+3\lambda^2(1-\lambda)^2+\lambda(1-\lambda)^3+\frac{1}{12}(1-\lambda)^4$	(15.1)
		$r_{21}=\frac{1}{4}(1-\lambda)^4$	(15.2)
		$r_{20}=3\lambda^2(1-\lambda)^2+\frac{1}{6}(1-\lambda)^4$	(15.3)
		$r_{11}=\frac{1}{6}(1-\lambda)^4$	(15.4)
		$r_{10}=3\lambda(1-\lambda)^3+\frac{1}{4}(1-\lambda)^4$	(15.5)
		$r_{01}=\frac{1}{12}(1-\lambda)^4$	(15.6)
	NG	$r_{30}=\lambda^4+4\lambda^3(1-\lambda)+3\lambda^2(1-\lambda)^2+\lambda(1-\lambda)^3$	(16.1)
		$r_{20}=3\lambda^2(1-\lambda)^2$	(16.2)
		$r_{10}=3\lambda(1-\lambda)^3$	(16.3)
		$r_{00}=(1-\lambda)^4$	(16.4)

in these cases, and this strategy will be referred to as *Inverse Formula Scoring* (IFS). However, the expected score of guessing in these cases is 0 and, therefore, examinees might well leave these items unanswered as they actually do under formula scoring directions in the conventional response mode. In this event, then, subjects behave under the NG strategy, which is also of interest to us here. García-Pérez (1985) shows the tree diagram for a 3-choice item responded to with Coombs' mode in the general case. Letting r_{ij} be the probability (associated with the response outcome R_{ij}) of making $i+j$ marks, i of which are correct and j of which are wrong, Table 3 shows the probability of each possible outcome to multiple-choice items (with $3 \leq a \leq 4$) responded to in Coombs' mode with the IFS and NG strategies. Note that the right-hand sides of equations (14.1) and (16.1) are the same as those of equations (5.1) and (8.1), respectively. Note also that response outcomes involving classification of the answer as a distractor have a probability 0 under the NG strategy.

4. Determination of the Test Length and Cutting Score

Attention will be first drawn to cases which give rise to only two possible response outcomes one of which is, obviously, to give the correct answer. In these situations, the number-right score, x, follows a binomial distribution $b(n,p)$ where n is the number of items in the test and p is the probability of a correct answer as given by the expression for c in Table 1 that applies to the case under consideration. Formulated in the hypothesis testing framework, the null hypothesis $H_0{:}\lambda \leq \lambda_c$ is to be tested against the alternative $H_1{:}\lambda > \lambda_c$, where λ_c is the critical point defining the mastery boundary. For reasons that are discussed in detail in van den Brink & Koele (1980), an indifference zone (see Wilcox, 1987, Ch. 12) is set, and the hypothesis $H_0{:}\lambda \leq \lambda_c - \varepsilon$ is tested instead against $H_1{:}\lambda > \lambda_c + \varepsilon$, where ε is a predetermined error tolerance. Then, the Type I error probability α is associated with $\lambda_0 = \lambda_c - \varepsilon$ and the Type II error probability β is associated with $\lambda_1 = \lambda_c + \varepsilon$. Hence,

$$\text{Prob}(x \geq x_c \mid n, p_0) = \alpha, \text{ and} \tag{17.1}$$

$$\text{Prob}(x < x_c \mid n, p_1) = \beta, \tag{17.2}$$

where x_c is the cutting score of the test and p_0 and p_1 are the values for c when $\lambda = \lambda_0$ and $\lambda = \lambda_1$, respectively.

Using the normal approximation with a correction for continuity and letting z_0 and z_1 be standard scores such that $\text{Prob}(Z \geq z_0) = \alpha$ and $\text{Prob}(Z < z_1) = \beta$, equations (17.1) and (17.2) give rise to

$$z_0 = \frac{(x_c - \frac{1}{2} - np_0)}{\sqrt{np_0(1-p_0)}}, \text{ and} \tag{18.1}$$

$$z_1 = \frac{(x_c - \frac{1}{2} - np_1)}{\sqrt{np_1(1-p_1)}}. \tag{18.2}$$

Solving these two equations for n and x_c yields

$$n = \left[\frac{z_0\sqrt{p_0(1-p_0)} - z_1\sqrt{p_1(1-p_1)}}{p_1 - p_0}\right]^2, \text{ and} \tag{19}$$

$$x_c = z_0\sqrt{np_0(1-p_0)} + \frac{1}{2} + np_0. \qquad (20)$$

Then, obtaining n and x_c for situations in which only two outcomes are involved requires solving equations (19) and (20) after fixing λ_c, α, β, and ε, and determining p_0 and p_1 by means of the expression for c that applies to the case under consideration.

When the guessing behaviour and/or response mode give rise to more than two possible outcomes, scoring schemes other than number-right are usually applied. Formula scoring and the usual scoring under AUC or Coombs' response modes are well-known examples. The distribution of the random variable denoting the score awarded by these scoring schemes can not be determined analytically (but see the Discussion section). We shall, nonetheless, adapt the above procedure to cope with these cases too. Situations in which k response outcomes exist will be reduced to k binomial cases, taking in turn one of the possible outcomes as defining one category and all the remaining outcomes as defining the other. Then, the same analysis as above will be made for each binomial case, and several minimum number of items and cutting scores will be presumably obtained for a single situation. In these cases, the best result (i.e. that requiring the smaller number of items) will be chosen with the prescription to base the mastery decision on a comparison of the observed frequency of that outcome, x, with the proper x_c.

Two observations must be made with regard to this approach. Firstly, some of the equations pertaining to these events describe monotonically increasing functions (the probability of answering correctly is an increasing function of λ), while some others are monotonically decreasing (the probability of omitting is a decreasing function of λ). In the latter case, the obtained x_c must be regarded as an upper (instead of lower) limit for the observed frequency of such outcome: the testee fails the exam if $x \geq x_c$. This leads to straightforward modifications of the above procedure since the sign of the parenthetical inequalities in equations (17.1) and (17.2) is reversed.

Secondly, response outcomes whose probability is not a monotonic function of λ must be disregarded. This is because, in these cases, there is not a biunivocal relationship between λ and the probability of the response outcome under consideration. Hence, there will be always ambiguity as to the ability of a subject regardless of how accurately his/her probability of arriving at the outcome of interest is estimated.

As an example, c in equation (7.1) is an increasing function of λ while u in equation (7.3) is a decreasing function of λ. Then, the number of items required to make a decision based on correct answers or omissions will be separately considered and the result requiring the fewer items will be chosen. Also, x_c will represent the minimum passing number of correct responses or the maximum passing number of omissions. On the other hand, w in equation (7.2) is non-monotonic in λ and it will be left out from consideration. It can be easily seen that, in the case of equation (7.2), $w=0$ both when $\lambda=0$ and when $\lambda=1$. Hence, the number of wrong responses is useless as a decision aid to distinguish among examinees of high versus low ability.

The results of these calculations are presented in the next two sections.

5. Response Modes Involving a Single Mark

Table 4 presents the solution to equations (19) and (20) for the NG strategy and probabilities of correct response as given by equations (1.1), (3.1), (5.1), and (8.1). In this table, and those which follow, an arbitrary value λ_c=0.5 is chosen. This choice will be commented on in the Discussion section. Also, α is made the same as β and results are presented for several values for them and for ε. The results of Fhanér (1974) are exactly reproduced here for true-false tests. Perhaps surprisingly, n does not vary motonically with the number of choices per item. The minimum seems to occur at a=3. The value calculated for n in the case of 5-choice items (not shown in any table) came out greater than that reported in Table 4 for 4-choice items. Further comments on this issue will be deferred to the Discussion section. Note that n rapidly decreases with only slightly increasing ε and/or α and β.

Table 5 shows the results for the NR strategy. As compared with Table 4, these values seem disproportionately large. All the comments made with regard to Table 4 apply here too, except that now n seems to decrease monotonically with increasing a. As compared with the results of van den Brink & Koele (1980), only the values they got for 2-choice items are reproduced

TABLE 4. Results for NG strategy in the conventional response mode

		ε=0.050		ε=0.075		ε=0.100		ε=0.125		ε=0.150	
Item	$\alpha=\beta$	n	x_c	n	x_c	n	x_c	n	x_c	n	x_c
T-F	0.05	270	136	119	60	66	34	41	21	28	15
	0.10	163	82	72	37	40	21	25	13	17	9
	0.15	108	55	47	24	26	14	17	9	11	6
2-C	0.05	202	153	89	68	49	38	31	24	21	16
	0.10	122	92	54	41	30	23	19	15	13	10
	0.15	81	61	36	27	20	16	13	10	9	7
3-C	0.05	162	102	71	45	39	25	25	16	17	11
	0.10	98	62	43	28	24	16	15	10	10	7
	0.15	65	41	29	19	16	11	10	7	7	5
4-C	0.05	170	96	75	43	41	24	26	15	17	11
	0.10	102	58	45	26	25	15	16	10	11	7
	0.15	68	39	30	18	17	10	11	7	7	5

TABLE 5. Results for NR strategy in the conventional response mode

		ε=0.050		ε=0.075		ε=0.100		ε=0.125		ε=0.150	
Item	$\alpha=\beta$	n	x_c	n	x_c	n	x_c	n	x_c	n	x_c
T-F	0.05	814	612	360	271	201	152	128	97	88	67
	0.10	490	368	217	164	121	92	77	59	53	41
	0.15	324	244	143	108	80	61	51	39	35	27
2-C	0.05	475	416	210	185	117	104	75	66	51	46
	0.10	286	251	127	112	71	63	45	40	31	28
	0.15	189	166	84	74	47	42	30	27	21	19
3-C	0.05	318	253	140	112	78	63	50	40	34	28
	0.10	191	152	85	68	47	38	30	25	21	17
	0.15	127	101	56	45	31	26	20	17	14	12
4-C	0.05	276	204	122	90	68	51	43	32	29	22
	0.10	166	123	73	55	41	31	26	20	18	14
	0.15	110	81	49	37	27	21	17	13	12	10

here, but for true-false items. Nonetheless, in some cases there is a one-item difference between these results and theirs, probably due to the fact that they seem to have rounded to the nearest integer instead of the nearest greater integer. Consideration of partial information results in smaller number of items than van den Brink & Koele (1980) calculated for multiple-choice tests.

The results for the FS strategy are presented in Table 6 for $3 \leq a \leq 4$. (Recall that the same equations as for strategy NG apply when $a \leq 2$.) As compared with those for the NR strategy, these results are much closer to the lower limit. Also, the best choice seems to be to base the decision on the number of correct answers, regardless of the particular formula score assigned to the testees. Note that the results for *C* with 3-choice items in Table 6 reproduce those for 2-choice items in Table 4. This is not surprising since equations (3.1) and (7.1) can be shown to be identical.

TABLE 6. Results for FS strategy in the conventional response mode

			$\varepsilon=0.050$		$\varepsilon=0.075$		$\varepsilon=0.100$		$\varepsilon=0.125$		$\varepsilon=0.150$	
Item	Outcome	$\alpha=\beta$	n	x_c	n	x_c	n	x_c	n	x_c	n	x_c
3-C	*C*	0.05	202	153	89	68	49	38	31	24	21	16
		0.10	122	92	54	41	30	23	19	15	13	10
		0.15	81	61	36	27	20	16	13	10	9	7
	**U*	0.05	210	26	92	11	51	6	32	4	22	2
		0.10	127	16	56	7	31	4	20	2	13	1
		0.15	84	10	37	4	21	2	13	1	9	1
4-C	*C*	0.05	218	158	96	70	53	39	33	25	22	17
		0.10	131	95	58	42	32	24	20	15	14	11
		0.15	87	63	38	28	21	16	14	10	9	7
	**U*	0.05	253	16	112	7	62	4	39	2	26	1
		0.10	153	9	67	4	37	2	24	1	16	1
		0.15	101	6	45	3	25	1	16	1	11	1

(Asterisks indicate response outcomes for which x_c designates a maximum)

6. Response Modes Involving Multiple Marks

6.1. AUC response mode

Results for the AUC response mode are presented in Table 7. As expected by the identity of the right-hand sides of equations (6.1) and (11.1) on the one hand, and (9.1) and (12.1) on the other, basing the decision on the number of correct responses at the first attempt under AUC response mode is the same as basing the decision on the number-right score under the conventional mode and the NR behaviour on the same items. And, in the case of AUC, no other response category seems to provide the basis for a better decision.

6.2. Coombs' response mode

Table 8 shows the results for Coombs' response mode under the IFS strategy. Note that the response outcome indicating assured knowledge of the answer and all distractors ($R_{(a-1)0}$, i.e. R_{20} when $a=3$ and R_{30} when $a=4$) represents an appropriate basis for taking a decision on mastery, involving a number of items that is only slightly above the lower limit represented by

TABLE 7. Results for AUC directions

Item	Outcome	$\alpha=\beta$	$\varepsilon=0.050$		$\varepsilon=0.075$		$\varepsilon=0.100$		$\varepsilon=0.125$		$\varepsilon=0.150$	
			n	x_c	n	x_c	n	x_c	n	x_c	n	x_c
3-C	C_1	0.05	318	253	140	112	78	63	50	40	34	28
		0.10	191	152	85	68	47	38	30	25	21	17
		0.15	127	101	56	45	31	26	20	17	14	12
	*C_2	0.05	605	100	269	44	151	24	96	15	67	10
		0.10	364	60	162	26	91	15	58	9	40	6
		0.15	241	40	107	17	60	10	39	6	27	4
	*C_3	0.05	695	29	308	12	173	7	110	4	76	3
		0.10	418	17	186	7	104	4	66	3	46	2
		0.15	276	11	123	5	69	3	44	2	31	1
4-C	C_1	0.05	276	204	122	90	68	51	43	32	29	22
		0.10	166	123	73	55	41	31	26	20	18	14
		0.15	110	81	49	37	27	21	17	13	12	10
	*C_2	0.05	1101	187	488	82	274	45	175	28	121	19
		0.10	662	113	294	49	165	27	105	17	73	11
		0.15	438	74	194	33	109	18	70	11	48	7
	*C_3	0.05	559	43	249	19	140	10	90	6	63	4
		0.10	336	26	150	11	85	6	54	4	38	3
		0.15	222	17	99	7	56	4	36	3	25	2
	*C_4	0.05	1070	16	475	7	266	4	170	2	117	2
		0.10	644	10	286	4	160	2	102	1	71	1
		0.15	425	7	189	3	106	2	68	1	47	1

(Asterisks indicate response outcomes for which x_c designates a maximum)

TABLE 8. Results for IFS strategy under Coombs' response mode

Item	Outcome	$\alpha=\beta$	$\varepsilon=0.050$		$\varepsilon=0.075$		$\varepsilon=0.100$		$\varepsilon=0.125$		$\varepsilon=0.150$	
			n	x_c	n	x_c	n	x_c	n	x_c	n	x_c
3-C	R_{20}	0.05	196	127	86	57	48	32	30	20	21	14
		0.10	118	77	52	34	29	20	18	13	13	9
		0.15	78	51	35	23	19	13	12	9	8	6
	*R_{11}	0.05	695	29	308	12	173	7	110	4	76	3
		0.10	418	17	186	7	104	4	66	3	46	2
		0.15	276	11	123	5	69	3	44	2	31	1
	*R_{01}	0.05	1421	29	631	13	355	7	227	4	157	3
		0.10	855	18	380	8	214	4	137	3	95	2
		0.15	565	12	251	5	141	3	90	2	63	1
4-C	R_{30}	0.05	182	104	80	46	44	26	28	17	19	12
		0.10	110	63	48	28	27	16	17	10	12	7
		0.15	72	42	32	19	18	11	11	7	8	5
	*R_{21}	0.05	1070	16	475	7	266	4	170	2	117	2
		0.10	644	10	286	4	160	2	102	1	71	1
		0.15	425	7	189	3	106	2	68	1	47	1
	*R_{11}	0.05	1615	16	717	7	402	4	257	2	178	2
		0.10	972	10	431	4	242	2	155	1	107	1
		0.15	642	7	285	3	160	2	102	1	71	1
	*R_{01}	0.05	3248	17	1443	7	811	4	518	2	359	2
		0.10	1955	10	868	4	488	2	312	1	216	1
		0.15	1291	7	573	3	322	2	206	1	143	1

(Asterisks indicate response outcomes for which x_c designates a maximum)

the results for the NG strategy with the conventional response mode. The remaining outcomes under Coombs' response mode and the IFS strategy would require a disproportionately large number of items to make the mastery decision under similar circumstances.

Table 9 shows that compliance with the NG strategy under Coombs' response mode reduces the required number of items to exactly the lower limit for the number of choices involved when the response outcome indicating assured knowledge of the answer is considered. This is an expected result since the right-hand sides in equations (14.1) and (16.1) equal, respectively, those in equations (5.1) and (8.1). On the other hand, use of the response outcome indicating total ignorance (R_{00}) requires a larger number of items, although this number is not as high as when response outcomes other than $R_{(a-1)0}$ were considered in the case of the IFS strategy.

7. Discussion

It is clear from inspection of Tables 4-9 that the smallest number of items is required when the NG strategy is followed, that is, when only knowledge is involved in responding to the test. In this case, true-false items should be preferred because they are easier to write as compared with multiple-choice items. Put another way, the error values α, β, and ε associated with an a-choice test with n items can be reduced to some extent by splitting each of its items to form a true-false version of the same test which will then consist of a times n items. However, the NG strategy is unlikely to be followed by examinees if the final decision on mastery is known to be made according to the number-right score: subjects will probably adopt the NR strategy since they can increase their number right score by guessing at items whose correct answer they do not know with assurance. If this strategy were followed, then the criteria shown in Table 5 should be applied instead. This requires a rather larger number of items. Since there are a times as many statements as there are items in an a-choice test, true-false items seem to be best again in the sense that fewer statements are required to make a decision with

TABLE 9. Results for NG strategy under Coombs' response mode

			$\varepsilon=0.050$		$\varepsilon=0.075$		$\varepsilon=0.100$		$\varepsilon=0.125$		$\varepsilon=0.150$	
Item	Outcome	$\alpha=\beta$	n	x_c	n	x_c	n	x_c	n	x_c	n	x_c
3-C	R_{20}	0.05	162	102	71	45	39	25	25	16	17	11
		0.10	98	62	43	28	24	16	15	10	10	7
		0.15	65	41	29	19	16	11	10	7	7	5
	*R_{00}	0.05	210	26	92	11	51	6	32	4	22	2
		0.10	127	16	56	7	31	4	20	2	13	1
		0.15	84	10	37	4	21	2	13	1	9	1
4-C	R_{30}	0.05	170	96	75	43	41	24	26	15	17	11
		0.10	102	58	45	26	25	15	16	10	11	7
		0.15	68	39	30	18	17	10	11	7	7	5
	*R_{00}	0.05	253	16	112	7	62	4	39	2	26	1
		0.10	153	9	67	4	37	2	24	1	16	1
		0.15	101	6	45	3	25	1	16	1	11	1

(Asterisks indicate response outcomes for which x_c designates a maximum)

selected α, β and ε.

Substantial reductions (about 33%) in the required number of items can be accomplished by administering multiple-choice tests with formula scoring directions and basing the decision on the number-right score. If subjects are aware of this, they can adopt the NR strategy which is to their benefit. However, subjects violate the model for the FS strategy only in case of total ignorance, which can be relatively rare when there are several alternatives per item. Regardless, it seems that the criteria shown in Table 6 should not be adopted without an additional constraint to guarantee that testees do not follow the NR strategy. This can be done by checking whether the goodness of fit of each testee's data to the FS strategy is better than the fit to the model for the NR strategy. This procedure is thoroughly described in García-Pérez (in press).

On the other hand, there seems to be no benefit in administering a multiple-choice test in AUC mode. Table 7 makes the point that AUC mode is no better than the administration of the same test in conventional mode asking testees to answer every item, at least as far as a controlled mastery decision is concerned.

An interesting result shown in Tables 8 and 9 is that Coombs' response mode is the best choice as regards the required number of items, which reaches the lower limit when the NG strategy is followed and the decision is based on $R_{(a-1)0}$. This criterion should be applied with the same caveat as mentioned above for the FS behaviour in the conventional response mode: an additional constraint should be imposed to make testees refrain from adopting the NR strategy. Reference to the usual scoring method for this response mode is particularly useful in this case since it heavily (but fairly) penalizes guessing. An additional means to check the testees' compliance with the assumed behaviour would be to perform goodness-of-fit tests as mentioned above.

From a comparison of score characteristics, Frary (1982) concluded that there is little justification for the use of scoring modes other than number-right and response modes other than the conventional mode. It is now clear from our results that there is justification for the use of Coombs' response mode in criterion-referenced testing, since it requires the theoretically minimum number of items to make a mastery decision with prescribed precision.

Gibbons, Olkin & Sobel (1979) made a related analysis which also resulted in recommendations for the use of subset selection techniques (of which Coombs' response mode is a special case) instead of the conventional response mode. Several assumptions allowed them to derive the distribution of the score awarded by suitable scoring schemes. Specifically, they assumed values for the (linear) correlations between classification of any two distractors and between classification of any distractor and the correct answer to each item. Yet, it is unlikely that these relationships can be regarded as linear. In fact, the model adopted here specifies a non-linear relationship between the probabilities of classifying distractors and answers. On the other hand, the model implied in the paper by Gibbons *et al.* (1979) assumes that, regarding the correct answer, testees may either correctly classify it or leave it unclassified whereas, concerning distractors, testees either classify them as such or misclassify them as correct answers. Also, the model assumes that testees do not guess. These flaws prevent their results from being comparable with those presented in this paper.

The results presented in this paper are specific to a situation in which several parameters have been kept constant. Their values were chosen so as to allow a direct comparison between these results and those in available papers dealing with this topic, specially that by van den Brink & Koele (1980). However, a word is worth about how varying these parameters may affect the results of the study. Firstly, some insight as to the effect of varying α, β, and ε has been provided by presenting results for several values for them. Their effect on required sample size is well known to those acquainted with statistical power analysis, and will not be further discussed here. The reader is referred to van den Brink & Koele (1980) for some thoughts about this.

Secondly, the choice λ_c=0.5 merely served for illustrative purposes. The setting of mastery criteria is not a trivial issue and the critical point should probably have to be placed in a different position in different contexts depending on several factors (Shepard, 1980; Weiss & Davison, 1981; Guion & Gibson, 1988). It is important to note that the results presented in Tables 4-9 depend heavily on this choice. Different n and x_c would be found for every possible λ_c. This is largely because the probabilities of response outcomes are non-linear functions of λ (save for a couple of exceptions). In equation (19), n depends on the sum of transformations of p_0 and p_1 in the numerator (since $z_1=-z_0$ when $\alpha=\beta$) and on their difference in the denominator. Since p_0 and p_1 are the probabilities for $\lambda=\lambda_c-\varepsilon$ and $\lambda=\lambda_c+\varepsilon$, the non-linear dependence of these probabilities on λ makes n in equation (19) depend on the location of λ_c. If λ_c is placed at a point in the ability scale where the function relating probability of the response outcome to λ is steep, then p_0 and p_1 will be quite different and equation (19) will give rise to a small n; if λ_c is placed at a point where the function is almost flat, then p_0 and p_1 will be very similar, and a larger n will be obtained.

This influence of the steepness of the curves at $\lambda=\lambda_c$ is also responsible for the seemingly paradoxical variations in the number of items required when different outcomes are considered and λ_c is left unchanged (see, for example, the results for 4-choice items in Tables 7 and 8). A large number of items is needed whenever a response outcome is considered whose probability varies only slightly around the selected λ_c; and fewer items are needed if another outcome is considered that gives rise to larger differences in probability in the neighbourhood of λ_c. To illustrate this, figure 2a shows plots of equations (12.1)-(12.4) and figure 2b shows plots of equations (15.1), (15.2), (15.4), and (15.6). These are the equations for 4-choice items for which results were presented in Tables 7 and 8. Given the steepness of each curve at λ_c=0.5, the results in those Tables can be readily understood. It is important to realize that response outcomes that would require a large number of items to serve as a decision aid for a given λ_c may nonetheless require many fewer items if λ_c is placed at a different location. Therefore, knowledge of the shape of the curve that applies to each outcome may be informative as to which one is best to make a decision on mastery.

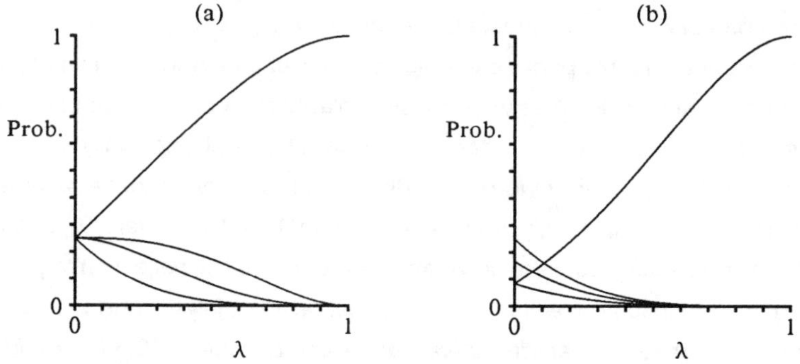

FIGURE 2. Plot of the probabilities of outcomes to 4-choice items responded to in AUC and Coombs' modes as a function of λ. (a) From top to bottom, curves for c_1, c_2, c_3, and c_4. (b) From top to bottom, curves for r_{30}, r_{21}, r_{11}, and r_{01}.

The results presented here are based on a model that has proven to be empirically supported (e.g. García-Pérez, 1987, in press) to a larger extent than the models used thus far in similar analyses. At present, this model does not give account of misinformation although it can be extended to incorporate it. A step forward in this direction would be to regard that testees may also wrongly classify each alternative, and not only correctly classify it or leave it unclassified as has been assumed here. Nonetheless, the extent to which examinees may be misinformed is surely small, and consideration of this should not lead to results very different from those presented here. The flexibility of the model allows a number of variations to be made in the assumptions that lead to expressions for the probability of each possible response outcome, some of which have been presented elsewhere (García-Pérez, in press; García-Pérez & Frary, in press). The same analysis as above could, therefore, be made for specific tests meeting some particular set of conditions.

Acknowledgements

I am indebted to Klaas Sijtsma for his suggestions to improve the readability of the paper, and to Bob Frary for his always insightful comments. I am most grateful to Juan Souza for the many hours of expert typesetting and for his willingness to comply with the publisher's and my own requests.

References

Bliss, L.B. (1980). A test of Lord's assumptions regarding examinee guessing behavior on multiple-choice tests using elementary school children. *Journal of Educational Measurement*, *17*, 147-153.

van den Brink, W.P., & Koele, P. (1980). Item sampling, guessing and decision-making in achievement testing. British *Journal of Mathematical and Statistical Psychology*, *33*, 104-108.

Coombs, C.H. (1953). On the use of objective examinations. *Educational and Psychological Measurement*, *13*, 308-310.

Coombs, C.H., Milholland, J.E., & Womer, F.B. (1956). The assessment of partial information. *Educational and Psychological Measurement*, *16*, 13-37.

Cross, L.H., & Frary, R.B. (1977). An empirical test of Lord's theoretical results regarding formula scoring of multiple-choice tests. *Journal of Educational Measurement*, *14*, 313-321.
Fhanér, S. (1974). Item sampling and decision-making in achievement testing. *British Journal of Mathematical and Statistical Psychology*, *27*, 172-175.
Frary, R.B. (1980a). The effect of misinformation, partial information, and guessing on expected multiple-choice test item scores. *Applied Psychological Measurement*, *4*, 79-90.
Frary, R.B. (1980b). Multiple-choice test bias due to answering strategy variation. Paper given at the Annual Meeting of the National Council on Measurement in Education, Boston, MA.
Frary, R.B. (1982). A simulation study of reliability and validity of multiple-choice test scores under six response-scoring modes. *Journal of Educational Statistics*, *7*, 333-351.
García-Pérez, M.A. (1985). A finite state theory of performance in multiple-choice tests. *Proceedings of the 16th European Mathematical Psychology Group Meeting*, Montpellier, France, 8-11 September. Pp 55-67.
García-Pérez, M.A. (1987). A finite state theory of performance in multiple-choice tests. In: E.E. Roskam & R. Suck (Eds.), *Progress in Mathematical Psychology-I*, 455-464. Amsterdam: Elsevier.
García-Pérez, M.A. (in press). A comparison of two models of performance in objective tests: Finite states versus continuous distributions. *British Journal of Mathematical and Statistical Psychology*.
García-Pérez, M.A., & Frary, R.B. (in press). Psychometric properties of finite state scores versus number-right and formula scores: A simulation study. *Applied Psychological Measurement*.
García-Pérez, M.A., & Frary, R.B. (1989). On the mathematical form (and psychological justification) of item characteristic curves. Manuscript submitted for publication.
Gibbons, J.D., Olkin, I., & Sobel, M. (1979). A subset selection technique for scoring items on a multiple choice test. *Psychometrika*, *44*, 259-270.
Guion, R.M., & Gibson, W.H. (1988). Personnel selection and placement. *Annual Review of Psychology*, *39*, 349-374.
Hogg, R.V., & Tanis, E.A. (1977). *Probability and Statistical Inference*. New York, NY: Macmillan.
Lord, F.M., & Novick, M.R. (1968). *Statistical Theories of Mental Test Scores*. Reading, MA: Addison-Wesley.
Shepard, L. (1980). Standard setting issues and methods. *Applied Psychological Measurement*, *4*, 447-467.
Weiss, D.J., & Davison, M.L. (1981). *Review of test theory and methods*. Research Report 81-1. Minneapolis, MN: University of Minnesota, Department of Psychology, Psychometric Methods Program.
Wilcox, R.R. (1976). A note on the length and passing score of a mastery test. *Journal of Educational Statistics*, *1*, 359-364.
Wilcox, R.R. (1987). *New Statistical Procedures for the Social Sciences*. Hillsdale, NJ: LEA.

The Linear Logistic Test Model and heterogeneity of cognitive strategies*

*Leo van Maanen*** *and Pieter Been*
University of Groningen
Klaas Sijtsma
Free University of Amsterdam

Abstract

Some properties of the Linear Logistic Test Model (LLTM) are discussed. Two prerequisites should be met in order to test a cognitive model by means of the LLTM. First, the items used in testing the cognitive model should make up a Rasch homogeneous scale. Second, the population under consideration should be homogeneous with regard to the cognitive strategy employed in solving items representing the task at hand. For a task consisting of solving balance problems it is demonstrated that the second prerequisite is not fulfilled. As a consequence the LLTM does not fit for the whole population. By dividing the population into four strategy homogeneous subpopulations a fitting LLTM could be found within one of these subpopulations. Consequently, it is recommended that in using the LLTM for testing cognitive models the population under consideration should be investigated with respect to different cognitive strategies.

Cognitive models may be tested by means of the Linear Logistic Test Model (LLTM) as has been shown by Schleiblechner (1972), Fischer (1974), Spada (1976) and Been, Jorna and Sijtsma (1984). The LLTM is an extension of the item response model of Rasch. In the Rasch model the difficulties of the items of a test are taken into account through a parameter for each item. Within the LLTM this parameter is considered as a weighted sum of a number of basic parameters. Each basic parameter represents the difficulty of an elementary cognitive process involved in solving a particular item. In this way the difficulty of an item is decomposed into difficulties of the basic cognitive processes that are called for.

---

*This is a modified version of a paper earlier published in Dutch: Het Lineair Logistisch Test Model en heterogeniteit van cognitieve strategieën bij balansproblemen. *Tijdschrift voor onderwijsresearch 13(1988)*, 301–310.

**Interdisciplinary Center for the development of Computer coaches and Expert systems, POBox 800, 9700 AV Groningen, the Netherlands, Bitnet/EARN: LVMAANEN @ HGRRUG5, UUCP: {... ! mcvax !} guvaxin ! guicce ! leo

The LLTM has been extensively treated by Fischer (1974; 1977; 1983), Fischer and Formann (1982) and Spada (1976). Only a short description of the model is therefore presented here. The basic feature of the model is the following equation:

$$\sigma_i = \sum_{j=1}^{m} q_{ij}\eta_j + c; \quad i = 1,\ldots,k; \quad j = 1,\ldots,m; \quad m < k. \tag{1}$$

In this equation σ_i represents the difficulty of item i as measured in the Rasch-model. Item i belongs to a set of k items, all measuring the same unidimensional trait or ability. The LLTM assumes that there are several subtasks underlying performance on items which the subject has to carry out. The difficulty of subtask j is represented in the model by η_j. Usually the weights q_{ij} reflect the number of times a subtask j is needed in the solution process of item i. However, formally any set of known weights can be used when estimating parameters and testing the model. The weights may equal zero, which implies that the subset of subtasks needed for solving item i is not necceserarily equal to the subset needed for item h. The symbol c is a normalization constant for the item parameters.

Substitution of the additive model (1) in the Rasch model for dichotomous item responses,

$$P(A_{vi} = a_{vi} \mid \xi_v, \sigma_i) = \frac{\exp(a_{vi}(\xi_v - \sigma_i))}{1 + \exp(\xi_v - \sigma_i)}; \quad v = 1,\ldots,n, \tag{2}$$

yields the LLTM,

$$P(A_{vi} = a_{vi} \mid \xi_v, \sigma_i) = \frac{\exp(a_{vi}(\xi_v - \sum q_{ij}\eta_j - c))}{1 + \exp(\xi_v - \sum q_{ij}\eta_j - c)}; \quad v = 1,\ldots,n. \tag{3}$$

In equation (2) and (3) the probability that subject v will give a correct ($a_{vi} = 1$) or an incorrect ($a_{vi} = 0$) response to item i is expressed as a function of subject ability, ξ_v, and item difficulty, σ_i in equation (2), or the difficulty of subtasks, η_j in equation (3).

A very important property of the Rasch model is that the item and subtask parameters can be estimated independently of the distribution of person parameters. This is a desirable property of a measurement model (see e.g. Fischer, 1974): general parameters describing items and subtasks should be estimated independently of individual person parameters. The sample-free estimation of item parameters implies that under the Rasch model estimates only differ because of sample fluctuations in randomly and even systematically differing subsamples. This property of sample independency is also valid for the person parameters in the Rasch model with respect to item subsampling.

The parameters in equations (2) and (3) can be estimated by means of the conditional maximum likelihood method. The reader is referred to Fischer (1974; 1983) for technical details about the estimation methods and conditions for the existence and uniqueness of the subtask parameters. In the same literature likelihood ratio tests for testing the validity of the LLTM are discussed.

The LLTM is a strong model indeed. As a consequence a fitting LLTM has not been reported until now. Tasks for which a LLTM has been proposed are: differential calculus problems (Fischer, 1973), balance problems (Spada, 1976), establishing functional relationships in science problems (Haeussler, 1977), statistical evaluation of psychological experiments (Kubinger, 1979, 1980), progressive matrices (Nährer, 1980), geometric analogies (Whitely & Schneider, 1981), fractions (Sijtsma, 1982), mental arithmetic tasks (Zwarts, 1983) and inductive reasoning (Van de Vijver, 1988). With the exception of the studies by Whitely & Schneider (1981) and Van de Vijver (1988), all authors report using items making up a Rasch homogeneous scale. Yet, none of them succeeded in composing a fitting LLTM for the task at hand.

Two conditions should be fulfilled before the LLTM can be applied. First, the items used for testing the cognitive model should comply with the requirements of the Rasch model. Second, a cognitive process model has to be specified that applies to every subject in the population. Thus it is presupposed that all subjects in the population will use the same cognitive strategy in solving a particular item. This seems to be a very strong assumption indeed in the light of growing evidence that different individuals will behave differently accomplishing the same cognitive task or that the same individual will behave differently accomplishing a similar task on different occasions, or even on different items on the same occasion. These variations can be attributed to changes in strategy (Underwood, 1978; Broadbent, 1984).

In work on human intelligence the weak relations often found between ability measures and basic information processing skills have led several authors to argue that global strategy differences may make a substantial contribution to individual differences in intelligence (Baron, 1978; Hunt, Frost & Lunneborg, 1973; Cooper, 1982). Individual differences in choice of strategy have for instance been demonstrated in solving items of Raven's Progressive Matrices test of General Intelligence (Hunt, 1974), in accomplishing Piagetian seriation tasks (Young, 1978), and in simple addition tasks (Groen & Parkman, 1972). Butterfield and Belmont (1971) found that individuals used a self-terminating or an exhaustive scanning strategy in detecting a presented item as belonging to a previous learned list, dependent on the instruction.

Correlations between abilities and choice of strategy also have been reported. Sternberg and Weil (1980) for instance found that the way linear syllogisms are solved is correlated with verbal and spatial ability. Similarly, choice of strategy in a sentence picture verification task is related to verbal and spatial ability (Macleod, Hunt & Mathews, 1978).

However, even within a fixed level of proficiency in solving algebra problems a flexible use of strategies occurs (Lewis, 1981). So one may suppose that choice of strategy may to a certain amount be influenced by individual differences in proficiency or by task characteristics (or both). Svenson and Hedenborg (1980) for instance found that reconstruction strategies in solving arithmetic tasks are used flexibly and unpredictably. One could argue that they neglected the possible influences of abilities and task characteristics. There is another explanation however. A strategy might be considered as an application of a set of rules. Practice in solving a class of problems enables individuals to acquire more sophisticated sets of rules gradually. In the process of acquiring a more sophisticated rule individuals use the sophisticated rule they are acquiring and the set of rules they previously mastered alternately in an unpredictable way. Among individuals solving fraction identification problems, Bergan, Towstopiat, Cancelli and Karp (1982) could identify such groups of transitioners between previously mastered rules and rules in the process of acquisition.

Now the existence of individual differences in choice of strategy — be it accomplishing relatively simple tasks or solving more complex problems — seems a well established fact, only illustrated here. Some authors choose to remove subjects not exhibiting consistency in strategy in advance from their investigations (Siegler, 1976; Siegler & Klahr, 1982), others to ignore the importance of strategies (Broadbent, 1984). If in solving an item different cognitive strategies are used then differences in cognitive strategies could explain why a fitting LLTM has not been reported until now.

The aim of this research is to demonstrate that a fitting LLTM can be obtained by taking strategy heterogeneity into account. This will be done within the domain of balance problems, because the cognitive processes involved in solving balance items are well known (Siegler, 1976; Siegler & Klahr, 1982). In a balance scale task, as used by Siegler, a subject is presented a two-arm balance with several pegs located at equal intervals along each arm. A number of (equal) weights are placed on any of these pegs but not on more than one peg at each side. It is the subject's task to determine which arm will go down or if equilibrium will result.

Models for balance problems

The Siegler and Klahr (1982) model for balance problems is well suited for our purpose. First, balance items are appropriate for a wide range of age-groups. Five year olds have some idea of weight while many grown-ups still have to master the formal rule that relates (im)balance to the product of weight and distance. Second, only two factors are of importance in solving balance problems: the distance of the weights from the tilting point and the number of the weights. This means that the problem domain is restricted. There is a limited number of conceivable item types and problem solving rules.

Spada (1976) has applied the LLTM to a slightly different version of balance problems but the model he proposed did not fit, although he used items making up a Rasch homogeneous scale. A possible explanation for this outcome is the heterogeneity in problem solving strategies used in the population that was examined, thus violating the assumption that the same LLTM applies to every member of the population.

Siegler and Klahr (1982) propose four possible strategies for solving balance items (Figure 1), ranging from an elementary strategy, which will only succeed for simple problems, to an expert strategy.

Subjects which use the elementary strategy (S1) only attend to the number of the weights on both sides of the balance, using the following rules:

Rule 1: If both sides have the same weights then respond balance.

Rule 2: If side X has more weight then respond X down.

The second strategy (S2) is the same as S1 extended with the following rule:

Rule 3: If both sides have the same weights and the weights on side X have the greater distance to the tilting point then respond X down.

The third strategy (S3) is the same as S2 extended with the following rules:

Rule 4: If side X has more weights and the weights on side X have the smaller distance to the tilting point then guess.

Rule 5: If side X has more weights and the weights on side X have the greater distance to the tilting point then respond X down.

As can be seen in Figure 1 the expert strategy (S5) includes the formal rule, using the product of weight and distance. It is S3 extended with the following rules:

Rule 6: If both sides have the same torque (product of distance and weight) respond balance.

Rule 7: If side X has more torque then respond X down.

In a pilot study we found that an additional strategy is required, which may be seen as a modification of S3. If items having the greater distance on one side and the greater weight on the other side (see conflict-items in Figure 1) are presented,

	Strategies				
Item types	S1	S2	S3	S4	S5
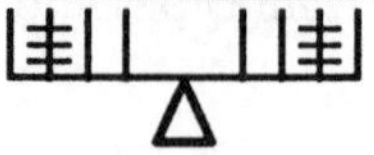 'Balance'	balance (100)	balance (100)	balance (100)	balance (100)	balance (100)
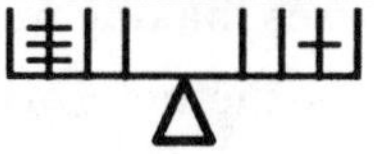 'Weight'	left down (100)	left down (100)	left down (100)	left down (100)	left down (100)
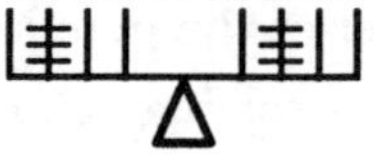 'Distance'	balance (0)	left down (100)	left down (100)	left down (100)	left down (100)
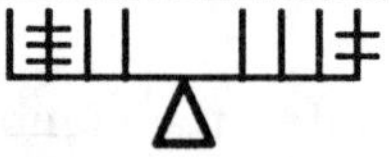 'Conflict weight'	left down (100)	left down (100)	guess (33)	balance (0)	left down (100)
 'Conflict distance'	right down (0)	right down (0)	guess (33)	balance (0)	left down (100)
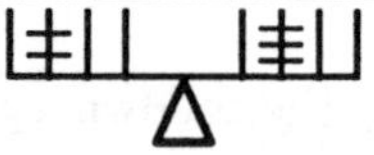 'Conflict balance'	right down (0)	right down (0)	guess (33)	balance (100)	balance (100)

Figure 1. Examples of predictions of answers and percentages of correct answers for 6 item types and 5 strategies. S1, S2, S3 and S5 are strategies from the balance model by Siegler and Klahr. S4 is the strategy found in the pilot study. The predictions hold for all item types and strategies. The only exception is in S4 for 'conflict weight' and 'conflict distance'. Depending on item characteristics the prediction will be left or right or balance; also see Table 3.

subjects using S3 guess (Rule 4) for the correct answer. In the additional strategy, instead of guessing a buggy rule (see Brown & VanLehn for a general discussion on buggy rules) is used:

Rule 4a: If side X has more weights and the weights on side X have the smaller distance to the tilting point then shift the weights on side X away from the tilting point until the distances on both sides are equal and remove for every shift on side X one weight on side X.

This rule (4a) replaces rule 4. After applying rule 4a the problem may be solved by applying rule 1 or rule 2. For subjects using this strategy (S4 in Figure 1), correct or incorrect responses to problems for which the buggy rule applies are predictable.

Whether subjects use the afore mentioned strategies indeed is detectable by asking them to solve six classes of problems (Figure 1):

Balance: weights and distances on both sides are equal.

Weight: distances are equal but weights differ.

Distance: weights are equal but distances differ.

The remaining three classes are prefixed conflict, because one side of the balance contains the greater distance and the other side the larger weight:

Conflict-Balance: the products of weight and distance on both sides are equal; equilibrium results.

Conflict-Weight: the side with the largest weight goes down.

Conflict-Distance: the side with the largest distance goes down.

Combining strategies and problem classes it is possible to predict response patterns of subjects using a particular strategy. Figure 1 shows the expected percentage of correct answers for each combination. In the case of balance problems only three answers are conceivable: equilibrium, right side down and left side down. Consequently guessing percentages are set to 33 percent. Of course the expert strategy (S5) — random mistakes left aside — will always lead to a correct answer.

The strategies used in solving balance problems can be used to specify the basic parameters of the LLTM. However, S5 must be left out of consideration because subjects using this strategy will solve all problems. The LLTM and the Rasch model do not allow for subjects with all answers wrong or right to be included in the analysis.

We already mentioned that in the pilot study all subjects turned out to solve all problems from the class of balance items correctly. So, items from this class do not discriminate subjects and as a consequence they can not be used in our analysis. The actual occurence of S1 up to S4 will be tested with the LLTM for the five remaining problem classes.

Specification of strategies in the LLTM

The actual occurence of the remaining four strategies can be tested with the LLTM. For every strategy a LLTM will be defined with item parameters consisting of a weighted linear combination of basic parameters. Within a strategy the basic parameters correspond to the difficulties of the cognitive subprocesses needed to solve a particular item. The weighted sum of the difficulties gives an estimate of the difficulty of the item. The weights of the difficulties correspond with the estimated frequency a cognitive subprocess is needed to solve a particular item. The relevant cognitive subprocesses and the basic parameters representing their difficulty are:

1. To solve item i the subject has to consider the weight (η_1). If this strategy (S1) is needed to solve item i the weight (q_{i1}) attached to η_1 equals one. If this strategy is not needed to solve a particular item this weight equals zero.

2. If the weights are equal, distance to the tilting point should be taken into account (η_2). This strategy (S2) is needed to solve distance items. Again a weight ($q_{i2} = 1$) is attached to η_2 if this strategy is needed, else $q_{i2} = 0$.

3. The subject has to attend to weight and distance (η_3). In the case of conflict items the subject guesses. Again a weight ($q_{i3} = 1$) is attached to η_3 if this strategy (S3) is needed, else $q_{i3} = 0$.

4. The subject has to compare weight and distance (η_4). Conflict items will be reduced — by use of a buggy rule — to an easier solvable balance item. Again a weight ($q_{i4} = 1$) is attached to η_4 if this strategy (S4) is needed, else $q_{i4} = 0$.

In the LLTM for every item the subtasks needed to produce the right answer are fixed. Within the LLTM the cognitive subprocesses required to solve the item are therefore represented by means of item characteristics and not by means of subject attributes. If there are differences between subjects in solving balance items this will have consequences for the fit of the LLTM. Differences in strategies can not be taken into account within the LLTM which allows only for a model based on item characteristics.

As we have learned balance items may be solved by means of different strategies. The purpose of this study is to test whether a fitting LLTM for balance problems — based on a Rasch homogeneous scale — can be obtained. We do not expect this to be the case, because subjects use different strategies. If a fitting LLTM can not be obtained for the whole population then we will examine subsequently whether a fitting LLTM within each strategy homogeneous subpopulation is obtainable.

Method

Sample

The research was conducted at twelve primary schools in the northern region of The Netherlands. The number of pupils joining in the research was 484 (235 in grade seven and 249 in grade eight). After collection of the data it turned out that data from six pupils were not useful, so that the item scores from 478 pupils were used in the analysis to be reported here.

Items and procedure

The balance model by Siegler and Klahr was used for the construction of the item set. Five item types from this model were used: weight, distance, conflict weight, conflict distance and conflict balance. Five different items were constructed for each item type. The resulting 25 items were presented to the pupils. For five items equilibrium is the right solution. For ten items the correct solution is right side down and for the remaining ten items the correct solution is left side down. These different solutions were distributed proportionally across the types of items, so that a specific item type is not connected with a specific type of solution.

At each school the purpose of the research was explained to the pupils and a standardized instruction was given, explaining how to fill in the answers. Next the pupils answered the 25 items in writing. To prevent learning and fatiguing from becoming systematic effects across pupils, the items were presented to each pupil in random order. It may be noted that this procedure does not prevent learning or fatiguing in individual cases, but it prevents systematic effects that are connected with specific items as might be the result of a fixed item order across pupils. Finally, item responses were dichotomously scored as either one (correct) or zero (incorrect).

Procedure of data analysis

Data analysis was performed as follows. First, it was investigated if the set of 25 items complied with the Rasch model in the complete group of pupils. Scalability according to the Rasch model is a necessary condition for the application of the LLTM.

Since the Rasch model did not fit within the complete group of pupils, its fit was next investigated within subgroups where each subgroup is characterized by the use of a specific strategy. These subgroups were constructed by means of cluster analysis on item response patterns for five items. Consecutive investigation of Rasch homogeneity within subgroups was based on the scores on the remaining twenty items. This partitioning of the data prevents that the construction of subgroups based on item response patterns leads to artifacts which would be obtained if Rasch homogeneity were examined on the same patterns.

Finally, after the establishment of Rasch homogeneity within separate strategy groups, the LLTM was applied to the scores on twenty items within each subgroup.

Results

Rasch homogeneity within the complete group of pupils

Andersen's (1973) likelihood ratio test was applied to a partitioning of the data (25 items, complete group of pupils) into two groups characterized by low and high total scores, respectively. This test procedure may be viewed as a global test for the Rasch model, indicating whether a set of items complies with the model. For our data, the Andersen test yielded a chi-square statistic equal to 983 given 24 degrees of freedom. This result clearly leads to a rejection of the Rasch model. As a result the LLTM can not be applied usefully within the complete group of pupils.

Rasch homogeneity within strategy homogeneous subpopulations

Two steps of data analysis are described in this subsection. The first is the construction of strategy groups. The second is the investigation of the fit of the Rasch model within separate strategy groups. In the first step, scores on five items, one of each item type, are used. In the second step, scores on the remaining twenty items are used.

Construction of strategy groups Hierarchical cluster analysis was used to construct strategy groups. The computer program CLUSTAN (Wishart, 1978) was used for this purpose. CLUSTAN was applied to response patterns produced by the pupils. These patterns were based on five items, one of each type (see Figure 1). Clusters of pupils were constructed, where each cluster consisted of response patterns that were more or less alike.

The application of CLUSTAN yielded four clusters of about equal size. The numbers of persons within each cluster can be found in Table 1. The answer patterns of persons in each cluster generally correspond fairly well to perfect to the answer patterns as predicted by the balance model. The identification of the group using S3 is more problematic than the identification of the other three groups. The answer patterns in the groups using S1, S2 and S4 are predictable with complete certainty. However, the expected proportion correct for conflict items in the group using S3 is one third. Therefore, pupils with answer patterns for conflict items which were different from the answer patterns of S1, S2 and S4 were placed in S3.

Results based on only five items may be rather unreliable. Therefore, cluster analysis was also performed on the response patterns concerning all 25 items. This analysis also lead to four clusters, each separate cluster corresponding to a strategy group as predicted by the balance model. Another important conclusion was that the formally correct Strategy 5 (S5) did not occur within this specific group of pupils. As was mentioned earlier, based on these results only four clusters were considered in the case of cluster analysis applied to five items.

Table 1
Results of investigating equal discriminating power property of the Rasch model for all items within each strategy group. The Andersen test is applied to a subdivision into subjects having low and high raw scores, respectively. Results concerning reliability estimates (KR20), limits of 95 percent confidence intervals, and range and standard deviation of raw scores are also given.

Strategy	n	Num. of items	χ^2	df	p	KR20	Lower limit	Upper limit	Range	Stand. dev.
1	118	12	25.1	11	0.01	0.54	0.40	0.66	7	1.3
2	135	17	32.0	16	0.01	0.49	0.36	0.60	12	2.0
3	111	17	28.2	16	0.03	0.35	0.15	0.52	10	2.4
4	114	17	29.8	16	0.02	-0.12	-0.46	0.17	5	1.1

Note. Since some items were answered either correctly or incorrectly by all persons within a specific group (characterized by either low or high raw scores), these items have been removed from the analysis. The numbers of items reported in the table are therefore smaller than twenty. The limits of the confidence intervals were obtained using a procedure proposed by Feldt (1965).

Fit of the Rasch model within strategy groups Scalability of the remaining twenty items according to the Rasch model was investigated within each separate strategy group.

First, the Andersen test was applied to a partitioning of the data into two groups of pupils having low and high total scores, respectively. According to Van den Wollenberg (1982), given this partitioning the Andersen test is especially sensitive to deviations from the Rasch property of equal discriminating power of all items. In Table 1 it can be seen that the Rasch model fits acceptably with respect to this property. This conclusion holds for all four strategy groups. The reliability estimates KR20 reported in Table 1 will be discussed in the final section of this paper. It may be noted at this place that based on the limits of the 95 percent confidence interval, the sample value of KR20 for S4 does not significantly differ from zero. Therefore, it does not contradict the fit of the Rasch model within S4.

Second, the Andersen test was applied to several partitionings of the data into groups of pupils based on their scores — either zero or one — on individual items. This procedure is known as the splitter-item technique (Van den Wollenberg, 1982).

Given this kind of partitioning of the data, the Andersen test is especially sensitive to violations of the Rasch assumption of unidimensionality of measurement. In Table 2, the results from a large number of applications of the splitter-item technique are given.

Table 2
Results of investigating unidimensionality within four strategy groups. The Andersen test is applied according the splitter-item technique.

Strategy	Item number	Proportion correct	χ^2	df	p
S1	2	0.06	10.3	8	0.24
	10	0.10	18.6	9	0.03
	19	0.18	35.3	10	<0.01
	21	0.92	21.6	10	0.02
S2	3	0.36	58.3	15	<0.01
	5	0.20	48.2	12	<0.01
	10	0.10	33.3	14	<0.01
	14	0.84	31.6	13	<0.01
	15	0.90	21.1	12	0.05
	16	0.83	36.4	13	<0.01
	17	0.80	47.3	15	<0.01
S3	1	0.32	29.3	15	0.02
	3	0.40	44.6	15	<0.01
	7	0.30	65.3	15	<0.01
	10	0.58	53.8	15	<0.01
	14	0.55	59.5	15	<0.01
	19	0.82	40.7	15	<0.01
S4	2	0.84	19.6	13	0.11
	10	0.75	8.8	13	0.78
	14	0.86	26.5	14	0.02
	15	0.88	22.1	12	0.04
	21	0.89	15.3	8	0.05

It appears that unidimensionality is not seriously violated in the groups using S1 and S4. This assumption is violated within the groups using S2 and S3, however.

It may be noted that the Andersen test should preferably be applied to subgroups of about equal size. The reason is that parameter estimation is by approximation equally accurate in subgroups of about equal size. For the splitter-item technique this would mean that the items used for the split of the total group into two subgroups should have p-values approximately equal to 0.50. In Table 2 it can be seen that p-values often deviate from 0.50. This deviation does not reflect a bad choice of p-values, but it is a necessary result from the specific strategy that was used by the pupils within a subgroup (see Figure 1 and Table 3).

Table 3
Proportions of correct answers (p-values) within strategy groups as well as the complete group. Items 4, 8, 12, 18, 22 have been used in the cluster analysis. In the table proportions correct for the remaining 20 items are given. An asterisk (*) means that an item is removed in the likelihood ratio test for the Rasch model as well as for testing the LLTM; also see the note below Table 1.

Item type	Item number	S1 (n=118)	S2 (n=135)	S3 (n=111)	S4 (n=114)	all (n=478)
Con. bal.	1	.05	.14	.32	.85	.33
Con. bal.	2	.06	.22	.30	.84	.35
Con. bal.	3	.04*	.36	.40	.90*	.42
Con. bal.	5	.07*	.20	.31	.75	.32
Con. dis.	6	.06	.17	.36	.06	.16
Con. dis.	7	.04	.13	.30	.03*	.13
Con. dis.	9	.03*	.18	.34	.06	.15
Con. dis.	10	.10	.32	.60	.75	.42
Con. wgt.	11	.92*	.60*	.29*	.16	.50
Con. wgt.	13	.87*	.55*	.26*	.06	.45
Con. wgt.	14	.92*	.84	.55	.86	.80
Con. wgt.	15	.98	.90	.56	.88	.84
Distance	16	.20	.83	.82	.97	.70
Distance	17	.14*	.80	.84	.97	.69
Distance	19	.18	.84	.81	.97	.70
Distance	20	.16	.84	.86	.97	.71
Weight	21	.92	.97	.91	.89	.93
Weight	23	.98*	.96	.94	.97	.96
Weight	24	.97	.96*	.94	.95*	.95
Weight	25	.98	.97	.97*	.97	.97

Note. The deviant p-values in S4 are explained in the caption of Figure 1.

Finally, we summarize the results from applying the Rasch model within strategy groups. From Tables 1 and 2 it can be concluded that the Rasch model adequately explains the data within the groups using S1 and S4. In S1 the splitter-item technique once yielded a relatively large chi-square value (item 19). We consider the general trend of the model test results for S1 to be satisfying, however. Within the groups using S2 and S3 unidimensionality is violated and as a result, the Rasch model does not apply. Strictly speaking, the LLTM can only be applied usefully in the groups using S1 and S4.

The LLTM and cognitive process models

Finally, the fit of the LLTM within strategy groups was investigated. Although the Rasch model did not fit to the data in the groups using S2 and S3, for exploratory purposes it was decided to investigate the fit of the LLTM within these groups as well. The results with respect to S2 and S3 should be interpreted tentatively, however.

The results of applying the LLTM to the group using S4 are discussed extensively. The results for the other groups are given briefly.

Table 4
A LLTM for S4.

Item type	Item number	q_{i1}	q_{i2}	q_{i4}	$\hat{\sigma}_i$	$\hat{\sigma}_i^+$	$\lvert\hat{\sigma}_i - \hat{\sigma}_i^+\rvert$
Con. bal.	1	1	0	1	-.38	-.22	.16
Con. bal.	2	1	0	1	-.31	-.22	.09
Con. bal.	5	1	0	1	.22	-.22	.44
Con. dis.	6	0	0	0	3.96	3.50	.46
Con. dis.	9	0	0	0	3.96	3.50	.46
Con. dis.	10	1	0	1	.25	-.22	.47
Con. wgt.	11	0	0	0	2.92	3.50	.58
Con. wgt.	13	0	0	0	3.96	3.50	.46
Con. wgt.	14	1	0	1	-.38	-.22	.16
Con. wgt.	15	1	0	1	-.60	-.22	.38
Distance	16	0	1	0	-1.99	-2.08	.09
Distance	17	0	1	0	-1.99	-2.08	.09
Distance	19	0	1	0	-2.45	-2.08	.37
Distance	20	0	1	0	-1.99	-2.08	.09
Weight	21	1	0	0	-.69	-1.46	.77
Weight	23	1	0	0	-2.45	-1.46	.99
Weight	25	1	0	0	-1.99	-1.46	.53
	$\hat{\eta}_j$	5.0	5.6	-1.2			

According to the balance model, in the group using S4 three strategies are used to solve the items:

1. Attention is only given to weight (parameter η_1).

2. In case the weights are equal subjects take distance into account (parameter η_2).

3. In case of conflict items the problem is reduced to a simpler balance problem (parameter η_4). As a result, the four conflict balance items and items 10, 14 and 15 can be solved correctly, other conflict items are solved incorrectly.

It should be noted that $q_{ij} = 1$ if and only if the strategy involved contributes to the solution of the item. Sometimes (items: 6, 9, 11, 13) S4 does apply but does not result in a transformation of the problem such that application of S1 to the transformed problem gives the right answer: $q_{i1} = 0$ and $q_{i4} = 0$. On the other hand, if S4 does apply and results in a transformation of the problem such that application of S1 to the transformed problem gives the right answer, both S1 and S4 contribute to the solution. As a consequence $q_{i1} = 1$ and $q_{i4} = 1$ in that case.

Items which were answered either correct or incorrect by all persons using S4, can not be used for analysis by means of the LLTM. Such items were removed from the analysis; see Table 3 where such items are indicated for each strategy group. In Table 4 the weights q_{i1}, q_{i2} and q_{i4} for the remaining items are presented.

The estimates of the basic parameters are given below the columns for q_{i1}, q_{i2} and q_{i4}. The estimated difficulty parameters ($\hat{\sigma}_i$) for the Rasch model are also given as well as the estimates ($\hat{\sigma}_i^+$) for the LLTM. The more the estimates $\hat{\sigma}_i$ and $\hat{\sigma}_i^+$ differ the more the LLTM fails to explain cognitive behavior within the group using S4. The absolute differences of the estimates $\hat{\sigma}_i$ and $\hat{\sigma}_i^+$ are also given in Table 4. They can be used to detect items contributing most to a possible misfit.

Table 5
Results from testing the LLTM within strategy groups.

Strategy	n	Number of basic parameters	Number of items	χ^2	df	p	R
1	118	1	12	52.4	10	<0.01	0.96
2	135	2	17	68.2	14	<0.01	0.96
3	111	3	17	60.0	13	<0.01	0.96
4	114	3	17	30.2	13	<0.01	0.98

Note. The correlation between item parameters estimated given the LLTM and item parameters estimated given the Rasch model is denoted by R.

In Table 5 it can be seen that based on a chi-square distributed test statistic (Fischer, 1974) the LLTM must be rejected at the one percent significance level. This means that the model outlined in Table 4 does not fully describe the strategy used by the pupils. Nevertheless the LLTM explains 96 percent (R^2) of the variance of the item difficulties ($\hat{\sigma}_i$) of the Rasch model. Comparison of the chi-square test statistic with the number of degrees of freedom also reveals that the misfit is only mild. An examination of the residuals in the last column of Table 4 suggests that items 21 and 23 contribute most to the misfit of the LLTM. Since we have no substantive explanation for the misfit of these two items, no further modification of the item set or the LLTM was tried in order to find a fitting LLTM.

The results for the other strategy groups are given briefly. In Table 6 the weights of the S1, S2 and S3 models are displayed for the interested reader. The linear logistic test models that were defined for the groups using S2 and S3 have to be rejected at the one percent significance level (see Table 5).

Table 6
Weights (q_{ij}) defining the LLTM for S1, S2 and S3. For S1 the weights for the modified LLTM are given within parentheses. A minus sign means that an item is removed for testing the Rasch model as well as for testing the LLTM; also see the note below Table 1.

Item type	Item number	S1		S2		S3		
		q_{i1}	q_{i2}	q_{i1}	q_{i2}	q_{i1}	q_{i2}	q_{i3}
Con. bal.	1	0	(0)	0	0	0	0	1
Con. bal.	2	0	(0)	0	0	0	0	1
Con. bal.	3	-	-	0	0	0	0	1
Con. bal.	5	-	-	0	0	0	0	1
Con. dis.	6	0	(0)	0	0	0	0	1
Con. dis.	7	0	(0)	0	0	0	0	1
Con. dis.	9	-	-	0	0	0	0	1
Con. dis.	10	0	(0)	0	0	0	0	1
Con. wgt.	11	-	-	-	-	-	-	-
Con. wgt.	13	-	-	-	-	-	-	-
Con. wgt.	14	-	-	1	0	0	0	1
Con. wgt.	15	1	(0)	1	0	0	0	1
Distance	16	0	(1)	0	1	0	1	0
Distance	17	-	-	0	1	0	1	0
Distance	19	0	(1)	0	1	0	1	0
Distance	20	0	(1)	0	1	0	1	0
Weight	21	1	(0)	1	0	1	0	0
Weight	23	-	-	1	0	1	0	0
Weight	24	1	(0)	-	-	1	0	0
Weight	25	1	(0)	1	0	-	-	-

For the S1 group a fitting model was obtained by applying the S2 model. The S2 model was applied for the following reason. Inspection of the difference between the estimates $\hat{\sigma}_i$ and $\hat{\sigma}_i^+$ revealed that compared with the Rasch difficulty estimates, distance items (with an equal amount of weights on both sides but with a different distance to the tilting point) are estimated too difficult by the LLTM. Such items can be solved by strategy S2. As can be seen in Table 3 distance items are somewhat easier for the S1 group than conflict balance and conflict distance items but far more difficult than for the S2, S3 and S4 groups. However, it is legitimate to suppose that the S1 group is in the process of acquiring rule 3 (If both sides have the same weights and the weights on side X have the greater distance to the tilting point then respond X down) but has not mastered it yet. According to Bergan et al. (1982) mentioned earlier, they are in the stage of transition. Model S2 applied to the S1 group gives an acceptable fit ($\chi^2_{df=9} = 13.2, \quad p = .16$).

Within the group using S2 relatively large residuals were observed for several types of items. Because of this diversity of item types, no substantive reason for the misfit of the LLTM could be given. No further analysis were carried out within S2.

Within the group using S3 all residuals had approximately the same size. Therefore, no further clues for modification of the item set or the LLTM could be found.

Discussion

Though balance items seem to set up a homogeneous set of items at first sight, it was not possible to construct a Rasch homogeneous scale with the whole set for the whole population. By dividing subjects into four subgroups a Rasch homogeneous scale could be constructed for two out of four cases. In testing the LLTM versions a fitting model was found for S1. This result is rather striking because in the literature no descriptions of fitting LLTM models are mentioned.

It is clear that several strategies exist among subjects solving balance items. The results from cluster analysis point out that the three strategies as predicted by the balance model of Siegler and Klahr (1982) and the fourth strategy we discovered in our pilot study are used consistently to a high degree in the population examined. Evidence comes from the result that the four response patterns which are characteristic of the four strategies unequivocally dominate the data. This strategy heterogeneity affects the usefulness of the LLTM and the Rasch model.

Although strategy heterogeneity can be prohibitive for application of the LLTM, strategy homogeneity is not a sufficient condition for a successful application. The following line of reasoning will make this clear.

A strategy homogeneous group consists of subjects which generate in principle the same answer pattern. In practice differences will show up but these differences are not very large. The consequence is that the raw scores of the respondents will not show much variation; see Table 1. For the Rasch model this means that all subjects are allocated to a rather small interval of the scale on which they are measured. In the extreme case in which all subjects are allocated to exactly the same point, the Rasch model would fit by definition (Wood, 1978). In short, investigating the fit of the Rasch model is useless in this situation and a serious test of the LLTM can not take place.

In this research the standard deviation (Table 1) of the raw scores in the four strategy homogeneous groups is relatively small in every case. In Table 1 it can be seen that within the groups using S1, S2 and S3 the lower bound to the reliability, KR20, has medium values, which differ significantly from zero (Feldt, 1965). This means that the variance of the raw scores contains a relatively large systematic (true score) component. Within the group using S4, KR20 has a low value, not significantly differing from zero (Feldt, 1965), meaning that raw score variance is mostly due to error. The question arises what impact the afore mentioned artifact could have, especially in the group using S4. After all one can argue that an analysis of the data with a latent class model should be preferred. Nevertheless this was definitely not the purpose of this research, where we tried to empirically establish the conditions under which the LLTM applies. As a consequence new problems show up as is evident now, which were not mentioned in the literature about the LLTM until now.

A consequence of a relatively large systematic score component in the groups using S1, S2 and S3 is that deviations from ideal response patterns (see Figure 1) are also systematic to a certain extent. In Table 3 it can be seen that the p-values of the items deviate from the expected values of zero, unity and one third (Figure 1). Within S1, S2 and S3, these deviations are probably partly due to error, but certainly, they also reflect systematic differences among pupils in their ability to apply a specific strategy.

Apart from an eventual artifact in the results within S4 one can conclude that taking strategy heterogeneity into account makes sense. The statements from Newell (1973): "Know the method your subject is using to perform the experimental task" and "never average over methods" are applicable here.

Summing up, the conclusion for the time being with respect to the usefulness of the LLTM is as follows. In case one uses the LLTM to test cognitive process models empirically, homogeneity of cognitive solution strategy appears to be a prerequisite for empirical validity of the LLTM. Anyhow, an examination of strategy homogeneity must precede the application of the LLTM. Nevertheless, if one has constructed strategy homogeneous groups, it is possible that the respondents within one group do not vary anymore on the attribute measured. In that case, a serious test of the LLTM can not take place.

All in all it is clear that the application of the LLTM is rather complicated and results which are obtained with this model should be interpreted with great care.

References

Andersen, E.B. (1973). A goodness of fit test for the Rasch model. *Psychometrika, 38*, 123–140.

Baron, J. (1978). Intelligence and general strategies. In G. Underwood (Ed.), *Strategies in Information Processing.* London: Academic Press.

Been, P.H., Jorna, R.J. & Sijtsma, K. (1984). Over kijken, meten en modellen bij breukrekentaken. In P.G. Vos, K.B. Koster & J. Kingma (Eds.). *Rekenen. Balans van standpunten in theorievorming en empirisch onderzoek.* Lisse: Swets & Zeitlinger.

Bergan, J.R., Towstopiat, O., Cancelli, A.A. & Karp, C. (1982). Replacement and component rules in hierarchically ordered mathematics rule learning tasks. *Journal of Educational Psychology, 74*, 32–38.

Broadbent, D.E. (1984). The Maltese cross, a new simplistic model for memory. *The Behavioral and' Brain Sciences, 7*, 55–95.

Brown, J.S. & VanLehn, K. (1980). Repair theory: a generative theory of bugs in procedural skills. *Cognitive Science,2*, 379–426.

Butterfield, E.C. & Belmont, J.M. (1971). Relations of storage and retrieval strategies as short-term memory processes. *Journal of Experimental Psychology, 89*, 319–328.

Cooper, L.A. (1982). Strategies for Visual Comparison and Representation: Individual Differences. In R.J. Sternberg (Ed.). *Advances in the Psychology of Human Intelligence.* Hillsdale (N.J.): Lawrence Erlbaum.

Feldt, L.S. (1965). The approximate sampling distribution of Kuder-Richardson reliability coefficient twenty. *Psychometrika, 30*, 357–370.

Fischer, G.H. (1973). The linear logistic test model as an instrument in educational research. *Acta Psychologica, 37*, 359–374.

Fischer, G.H. (1974). *Einführung in die Theorie psychologischer Tests.* Bern: Huber.

Fischer, G.H. (1983). Logistic latent trait models with linear constraints. *Psychometrika, 48*, 3–26.

Fischer, G.H. & Formann, A.K. (1982). Some applications of logistic latent trait models with linear constraints on the parameters. *Applied Psychological Measurement, 6*, 397–416.

Groen, G.J. & Parkman, J.M. (1972). A chronometric analysis of simple addition, *Psychological Review, 72*, 329–343.

Haeussler, P. (1977). Investigation of mathematical reasoning in science problems. In H. Spada & W.F. Kempf (Eds.). *Structural Models of Thinking and Learning.* Bern: Huber.

Hunt, E.B., Frost, N. & Lunneborg, C.L. (1973). Individual differences in cognition: A new approach to intelligence. In G. Bower (Ed.). *The Psychology of Learning and Motivation.* New York: Academic Press.

Hunt, E.B., (1974). Quote the Raven? Nevermore! In L. Gregg (Ed.). *Knowledge and Cognition.* Hillsdale (N.J.): Lawrence Erlbaum.

Kubinger, K.D. (1979). Das Problemlöseverhalten bei der statistischen Auswertung psychologischer Experimente. Ein Beispiel hochschuldidaktischer Forschung. *Zeitschrift für experimentelle und angewandte Psychologie, 26*, 467–495.

Kubinger, K.D. (1980). Die Anwendung von Fischers linear logistischen Test Modell zur Leistungssteigerung in Lehrveranstaltungen — Einige neuere Ergebnisse. *Archiv für Psychologie, 133*, 69–79.

Lewis, C. (1981). Skill in Algebra. In J.R. Anderson (Ed.). *Cognitive skills and their acquisition.* Hillsdale (N.J.): Lawrence Erlbaum.

MacLeod, C.M., Hunt, E.B. & Mathews, N.N. (1978). Individual differences in the verification of sentence-picture relationships. *Journal of Verbal Learning and Behavior, 17*, 493–507.

Nährer, W. (1980). Zur Analyse von Matrizenaufgaben mit dem linearen logistischen Testmodell. *Zeitschrift für experimentelle und angewandte Psychologie, 27*, 553–564.

Newell, A. (1973). You can't play 20 questions with nature and win. In W.G. Chase (Ed.). *Visual Information Processing.* New York: Academic Press.

Scheiblechner, H. (1972). Das Lernen und Lösen komplexer Denkaufgaben. *Zeitschrift für experimentelle und angewandte Psychologie, 19*, 476–506.

Siegler, R.S. (1976). Three aspects of cognitive development. *Cognitive Psychology, 8*, 481–520.

Siegler, R.S. & Klahr, D. (1982). When do children learn? In R. Glaser (Ed.). *Advances in Instructional Psychology*, vol 2. Hillsdale (N.J.): Lawrence Erlbaum.

Sijtsma, K. (1982). Een lineair logistisch model ter verklaring van de moeilijkheidsparameters van breukrekenitems. In J.G.L.C. Lodewijks & P.R.J. Simons (Eds.). *Strategieën in leren en ontwikkeling.* Lisse: Swets & Zeitlinger.

Spada, H. (1976). *Modelle des Denkens und Lernens.* Bern: Huber.

Sternberg, R.J. & Weil, E.M. (1980). An Aptitude x Strategy Interaction in Linear Syllogistic Reasoning. *Journal of Educational Psychology, 72*, 226–239.

Svenson, O. & Hedenborg, M.L. (1980). Strategies used by children when solving simple subtractions. *Acta Psychologica, 4,* 1–13.

Underwood, G. (1978). *Strategies of Information Processing.* New York: Academic Press.

van de Vijver, F.J.R. (1988). Systematizing the item content in test design. In R. Langeheine & J. Rost (Eds.). *Latent Trait and Latent Class Models.* New York: Plenum Press.

Whitely, S.E. & Schneider, L.M. (1981). Information structure for geometric analogies: A test theory approach. *Applied Psychological Measurement, 5*, 383–397.

Wishart, D. (1978). *CLUSTAN 1C.* Utrecht: Centrum voor Data-Analyse, Rijksuniversiteit Utrecht.

Wollenberg, A.L. van den (1982). A simple and effective method to test the dimensionality axiom of the Rasch model. *Applied Psychological Measurement, 6*, 83–91.

Wood, R. (1978). Fitting the Rasch model — A heady tale. *British Journal of Mathematical and Statistical Psychology, 31*, 27–32

Young, R.M. (1978). Strategies and the structure of cognitive skill. In G. Underwood (Ed.). *Strategies of Information Processing.* New York: Academic Press.

Zwarts, M.A. (1983). *Criteriumtoetsen bij aansluiting van primair en secundair onderwijs.* (unpublished dissertation). Rijksuniversiteit Utrecht.

Testable conditions for the existence of a qualitative J scale in unfolding*)

*Bernhard Orth***)
Universität Hamburg

Abstract
A new approach toward a measurement theoretical characterization of the method of (unidimensional) unfolding is outlined. It is shown that this approach yields sufficient conditions for the existence of a qualitative J scale. These axioms are empirically testable. They are illustrated by applications to three sets of hypothetical data.

1. Possible representations for unfolding

The method of unfolding (Coombs, 1950, 1952, 1953, 1964) may be considered as the most influential method for scaling preferential choice data. A measurement theoretical characterization of unfolding is still missing, however, and very little is known about the axiomatic foundations of this method. This paper suggests a new representation for unfolding and gives empirically testable conditions for the existence of what is called a qualitative J scale. In principle, the present approach can be extended to the existence of a so-called quantitative J scale. (This work is still in progress and will be presented elsewhere.)

Unfolding is concerned with a set A of stimuli or objects, which will be denoted by a,b,c,..., and a set P of persons or subjects denoted by p,q,r,... It is assumed that each person has ordered all objects according to his or her preference. We are thus faced with a family of preference orderings. These are called individual scales or I scales. According to a basic assumption of unfolding, a person p prefers object a over object b if and only if his or her "ideal point" (i.e., an assumed ideal object) is closer to a than to b, that is, if and only if the absolute difference between the ideal point and object a is smaller than that between the ideal point and object b. In terms of this ordering of absolute differences, the family of preference orderings can be written as a binary relation on the set $A \times P$ denoted as $\succsim$. It must be pointed out, however, that we cannot have $ap \succsim bq$ unless $p = q$. We are thus concerned with an empirical relational structure $\langle A \times P, \succsim \rangle$ where $ap \succsim bp$ is to be interpreted as "the absolute difference between a and p is at least as large as that between b and p" or, equivalently, "p (weakly) prefers b over a".

---

*) This paper is dedicated to Clyde H. Coombs (1912-1988).

**) Psychologisches Institut I, Universität Hamburg, Von-Melle-Park 6, D-2000 Hamburg 13, F.R. Germany.

The method of unfolding aims at "unfolding" the individual preference orderings (I scales) in order to obtain a joint scale (J scale) for the stimuli which is common to all subjects. An ordering of the stimuli in this sense is called a qualitative J scale. If also metric information (i.e., information about the ordering of differences between stimuli) is obtained from the data a so-called quantitative J scale can be constructed. Moreover, in either case the subjects (or rather, their assumed ideal points) can be ordered, too, along the J scale.

Any measurement theoretical characterization of unfolding has to look for a suitable representation to capture these ideas. For example, one might think of a scale ϕ with the following property:

$$ap \succsim bp \leftrightarrow |\phi(a) - \phi(p)| \geqq |\phi(b) - \phi(p)| \tag{1}$$

for all $a, b \in A$ and $p \in P$. This representation has been proposed by Suppes & Zinnes (1963) and by Krantz, Luce, Suppes & Tversky (1971).

Although this representation corresponds well to the unfolding model it does not fully take into account what is achieved by the actual unfolding technique. For a given set of data, the unfolding method does not yield a scale common to both stimuli and subjects (or their ideal points) because ideal points can only be located within certain regions of a J scale. They cannot be determined as points of such a scale. For example, if an ideal point is fairly close to a stimulus then there is no way, in general, to decide on which side of the stimulus this ideal point must be located. Therefore, a common scale for both stimuli and subjects cannot be constructed by the method of unfolding.

The following representation, due to Ducamp & Falmagne (1969), explicitly considers two distinct scales ϕ und ψ for stimuli and subjects (ideal points), respectively:

$$ap \succsim b| \leftrightarrow |\phi(a) - \psi(p)| \geqq |\phi(b) - \psi(p)| \tag{2}$$

for all $a, b \in A$ and $p \in P$. The problem with this representation is that it requires interval scale level for both scales (in order to become a meaningful statement) whereas the unfolding method only yields an ordering of ideal points (even in case of a quantitative J scale).

According to the actual unfolding method, the ordering of ideal points is directly given by the (qualitative or quantitative) J scale. The main task is thus the construction of the J scale. This notion leads to a representation (suggested by Orth, 1976, 1987) solely in terms of a stimulus scale ϕ:

$$ab \succsim^* cd \leftrightarrow |\phi(a) - \phi(b)| \geqq |\phi(c) - \phi(d)| \tag{3}$$

for all $a,b,c,d \in A$, where the binary relation $\succsim^*$ on $A \times A$ is "uniquely determined" by $\succsim$

(essentially, this means that $\succsim^*$ is appropriately defined in terms of $\succsim$). By constructing the function ϕ this approach closely corresponds to the actual unfolding technique. It is therefore possible to establish axioms which are sufficient for this representation. These axioms turn out to be fairly complex, however, since the representation is not stated in terms of the primitive notion $\succsim$.

While taking this approach the present paper is restricted to an axiomatization of unfolding in terms of a qualitative J scale. That is, we consider the following problem. Under which conditions does there exist a real-valued function on A, unique up to strictly increasing transformations, such that, for all $a, b \in A$,

$$a \succsim' b \leftrightarrow \phi(a) \geq \phi(b) \,? \tag{4}$$

Again, $\succsim'$ is a relation (on A) "uniquely determined" in terms of $\succsim$ (an exact definition will be given below).

2. An unfolding structure for a qualitative J scale

Let A and P be two nonempty sets and $\succsim$ a binary relation on $A \times P$. We first consider some very natural restrictions for $\succsim$. It has already been mentioned that, in the context of unfolding, we cannot have $ap \succsim bq$ unless $p = q$. This leads to the condition that $ap \succsim bq$ implies $p = q$. Furthermore, the individual preference orderings should be assumed to be weak orders. That is, they must be connected and transitive. These restrictions will be used as the following two axioms:

Axiom 1. Either $ap \succsim bp$ or $bp \succsim ap$;
and if $ap \succsim bq$, then $p = q$.
(For all $a,b, \in A$ and $p,q \in P$.)

Axiom 2. If $ap \succsim bp$ and $bp \succsim cp$, then $ap \succsim cp$.
(For all $a,b,c \in A$ and $p \in P$.)

Axiom 1 postulates that the relation $\succsim$ is conditionally connected. That is, $\succsim$ holds only for pairs of elements with a common element from P, and for those pairs, it is connected. Axiom 2 asserts transitivity of each individual preference ordering (that is, if p prefers c over b and b over a, then p must also prefer c over a).

It is well known that unfolding cannot be done when all subjects give the same preference ordering. In this case, a J scale cannot be constructed uniquely. A simple way for taking this fact into account is to incorporate an axiom as follows:

Axiom 3. There exists $r \in P$ such that $ar \gtrsim br$.
(For all $a,b \in A$.)

Essentially, this axiom asserts that the individual preferences are sufficiently distinct to allow for an unfolding analysis. It is satisfied when, for all pairs of distinct objects a and b, there is one subject who prefers a over b and another subject who prefers b over a. This does not imply the existence of mirrored I scales. Nevertheless, it is somewhat stronger than required as will be shown in the next section. Thus, this axiom can still be weakened. For the sake of simplicity, however, this version of the axiom will do.

Axioms 1,2, and 3 just characterize the (preferential choice) data unfolding is concerned with. Conditions which really impose constraints on a set of data still have to be incorporated. The basic idea of the present approach rests upon a betweenness relation on the set A which can be determined from the individual preference orderings. This betweenness relation can be defined as follows.

Definition 1. Let A and P be two nonempty sets and $\gtrsim$ a binary relation on $A \times P$. For all $a,b,c \in A$, b is said to be *between* a and c denoted $a \mid b \mid c$, if and only if, for some $p,q \in P$, $p \neq q$,

(1) $ap \gtrsim bp$ and $ap \gtrsim cp$;
(2) $cq \gtrsim bq$ and $cq \gtrsim aq$;
(3) either $a \neq c$ or $a=b=c$.

Thus, b is between a and c whenever there are two persons such that one of them prefers both b and c over a and the other one prefers both b and a over c. With respect to p, we have either $bp \gtrsim cp$ or $cp \gtrsim bp$ (by Axiom 1), and with respect to q, we have either $bq \gtrsim aq$ or $aq \gtrsim bq$. There are thus four possible cases leading to $a \mid b \mid c$: (1) $ap \gtrsim bp \gtrsim cp$ and $cq \gtrsim bq \gtrsim aq$; (2) $ap \gtrsim bp \gtrsim cp$ and $cq \gtrsim aq \gtrsim bq$; (3) $ap \gtrsim cp \gtrsim bp$ and $cq \gtrsim bq \gtrsim aq$; (4) $ap \gtrsim cp \gtrsim bp$ and $cq \gtrsim aq \gtrsim bq$

This betweenness relation quite naturally leads to an ordering of the objects and, hence, to the desired qualitative J scale. Moreover, a method for constructing this scale can be obtained from n-ary betweenness relations ($n > 3$) which are easily defined in terms of the ternary relation from Definition 1:

$a \mid b \mid c \mid d$ iff $a \mid b \mid c$, $a \mid b \mid d$, $a \mid c \mid d$, and $b \mid c \mid d$;
$a \mid b \mid c \mid d \mid e$ iff $a \mid b \mid c \mid d$, $a \mid b \mid c \mid e$, $a \mid b \mid d \mid e$, $a \mid c \mid d \mid e$, and $b \mid c \mid d \mid e$;
and so on (for all $a,b,c,d,e \in A$).

It should also be noted that the property of single-peakedness of the individual preference orderings (over the J scale) can easily be stated in terms of the betweenness relation:

If $a \mid b \mid c$, then either $ap \gtrsim bp$ or $cp \gtrsim bp$ (or both)

for all $a,b,c, \in A$ and $p \in P$. Hence, whenever $a \mid b \mid c$, single-peakedness is violated if there is a person preferring both a and c over b.

What is still needed is a condition which ensures that the elements of the betweenness relation are consistent among each other in the sense that they can be combined to yield n-ary betweenness relations. The essential condition serving this purpose is called transitivity of betweenness and is defined as follows.

Definition 2. A betweenness relation on a set A satisfies *transitivity of betweenness* if and only if, for all $a,b,c,d \in A$,

(1) If $a \mid b \mid c$ and $a \mid c \mid d$, then $b \mid c \mid d$ and $a \mid b \mid d$;
(2) If $a \mid b \mid c$, $b \mid c \mid d$, and $b \neq c$, then $a \mid b \mid d$ and $a \mid c \mid d$.

Transitivity of betweenness could be used as an axiom. It is then easy to show that the betweenness relation gives rise to a complete ordering of the set A. That is, a binary relation $\gtrsim'$ on A can be defined which is compatible with betweenness, in the sense that $a \gtrsim' b$ and $b \gtrsim' c$ imply $a \mid b \mid c$. Moreover, $\gtrsim'$ can be shown to be a simple order, hence, leading to the existence of a real-valued function ϕ on A which satisfies the desired representation. Within the present context of Axioms 1 to 3, however, transitivity of betweenness need not be stated as an axiom because it can be derived from the following condition.

Axiom 4. If $a \mid b \mid c$, $a \mid c \mid d$, and $b \neq d$, then either $bp \gtrsim cp$ or $dp \gtrsim cp$. (For all $a,b,c,d \in A$ and $p \in P$.)

Hence, this axiom is the most crucial and empirically interesting condition. Essentially, it is a type of single-peakedness condition. It would be violated if, whenever we have $a \mid b \mid c$ and $a \mid c \mid d$, there is a person preferring both b over c and d over c. In such a case, we cannot have $b \mid c \mid d$ because single-peakedness would be violated.

We are now in a position to summarize our discussion and to incorporate Axioms 1 to 4 into a definition of an unfolding structure.

Definition 3. Let A be a set with at least two elements, P a nonempty set, and $\gtrsim$ a binary relation on $A \times P$. The relational system $\langle A,P,\gtrsim \rangle$ is an *unfolding structure* if and only if, for all $a,b,c,d \in A$ and $p,q, \in P$, the following four axioms hold:

(1) Either $ap \gtrsim bp$ or $bp \gtrsim ap$; and if $ap \gtrsim bq$, then $p=q$.
(2) If $ap \gtrsim bp$ and $bp \gtrsim cp$, then $ap \gtrsim cp$.
(3) There exists $r \in P$ such that $ar \gtrsim br$.
(4) If $a \mid b \mid c$, $a \mid c \mid d$, and $b \neq d$, then either $bp \gtrsim cp$ or $dp \gtrsim cp$.

Because the sets A and P are not restricted to be finite we still need a typical "technical" condition in order to arrive at the desired representation theorem.

Axiom 5. A contains a finite or countable subset A' such that there is $b' \in A'$ with $a \mid b' \mid c$. (For all $a,c \in A$.)

Theorem. Let $\langle A,P,\gtrsim \rangle$ be an unfolding structure satisfying Axiom 5. Then there exists a real-valued function ϕ on A, unique up to strictly increasing transformations, such that, for all $a,b \in A$,

$$a \gtrsim' b \leftrightarrow \phi(a) \geqq \phi(b)$$

where $\gtrsim'$ is a binary relation on A uniquely determined by $\gtrsim$.

By "uniquely determined" it is meant that $\gtrsim'$ is the only simple order on A with the property: if $a \gtrsim' b$ and $b \gtrsim' c$, then $a \mid b \mid c$. The proof of the theorem is fairly simple. One can first show that transitivity of betweenness holds and then define the relation $\gtrsim'$ and show that it is a simple order. The details will be omitted.

3. Examples

We now analyze some sets of hypothetical data in order to illustrate empirical applications of an unfolding structure. The first example concerns the preference orderings given in Table 1.

Table 1: Hypothetical preference orderings of five objects (A = {a,b,c,d,e}) from eight persons (P = {p,q,r,s,t,u,v,w}). (For notation see text.)

dp	> bp	> cp	> ep	> ap
bq	> eq	> dq	> aq	> cq
br	> er	> ar	> dr	> cr
ds	> bs	> cs	> as	> es
bt	> dt	> et	> ct	> at
du	> cu	> au	> bu	> eu
bv	> ev	> av	> cv	> dv
dw	> cw	> aw	> ew	> bw

We first observe that the individual preference orderings are conditionally connected as well as transitive. Hence, Axioms 1 and 2 of an unfolding structure are satisfied. Moreover, it is easily checked that for every pair of objects, say a and b, there is at least one person, say r, weakly preferring b over a (i.e., ar ≳ br) and at least one person, say s, weakly preferring a over b (i.e., bs ≳ as). Thus, Axiom 3 holds, too.

In order to test Axiom 4, the betweenness relation has to be determined. For every triple (a,b,c) of objects, it must be checked whether a | b | c, b | a | c, or a | c | b holds. (Note that we have a | b | c if and only if c | b | a. Moreover, it can be shown that, for all a,b,c ∈ A, we have either a | b | c or b | a | c or a | c | b.) The betweenness relation obtained this way is given in Table 2. For a test of Axiom 4, we now consider all those

Table 2: The betweenness relation on A for the data from Table 1.

b | a | c	d | a | e
b | a | d	b | c | d
a | e | b	b | e | c
a | c | d	b | e | d
c | a | e	d | c | e

cases which satisfy a | b | c and a | c | d (with b ≠ d), for all a,b,c,d ∈ A, and check whether or not it is true that either bp ≳ cp or dp ≳ cp for all p ∈ P. These cases ("possible tests") are shown in Table 3. It turns out that every conclusion is satisfied. There is thus no

Table 3: Possible tests and conclusions of Axiom 4 of an unfolding structure for the data from Table 1.

b | a | c	and	b | c | d	→	either ap ≳ cp or dp ≳ cp
b | e | a	and	b | a | c	→	either ep ≳ ap or cp ≳ ap
b | e | a	and	b | a | d	→	either ep ≳ ap or dp ≳ ap
d | c | a	and	d | a | b	→	either cp ≳ ap or bp ≳ ap
d | c | a	and	d | a | e	→	either cp ≳ ap or ep ≳ ap
c | a | e	and	c | e | b	→	either ap ≳ ep or bp ≳ ep
e | a | c	and	e | c | d	→	either ap ≳ cp or dp ≳ cp
d | a | e	and	d | e | b	→	either ap ≳ ep or bp ≳ ep
b | e | c	and	b | c | d	→	either ep ≳ cp or dp ≳ cp
d | c | e	and	d | e | b	→	either cp ≳ ep or bp ≳ ep

violation of Axiom 4, too.

According to the representation theorem, there exists a qualitative J scale for the data in Table 1. This scale can now be constructed as follows. In Table 2, we find b | a | c, b | a | d, a | c | d, and b | c | d yielding b | a | c | d. Similarly, we obtain b | e | a | c, b | e | a | d, b | e | c | d, and e | a | c | d and hence b | e | a | c | d which gives the ordering of the objects on the qualitative J scale.

As a second example, we again take the data in Table 1 but now deleting the persons v and w, i.e., the preference orderings bv > ev > av > cv > dv and dw > cw > aw > ew > bw. (This example is taken from Orth, 1987.) Axioms 1 and 2 still hold. Now, however, Axiom 3 is violated because there is no person preferring d over c and no person preferring b over e. Nevertheless, we obtain the same betweenness relation as before (Table 2). Therefore, Axiom 4 is still satisfied. Moreover, the same qualitative J scale as before can be constructed. Hence, this example shows that Axiom 3 is somewhat stronger than required. In spite of its violation, the individual preference orderings are sufficiently distinct (as well as consistent among each other) to yield a uniquely determined qualitative J scale.

As a final example, we again consider the data in Table 1 but now with the addition of x ∈ P with bx > ax > dx > ex > cx. We already know that Axioms 1 to 3 hold. The betweenness relation turns out to be the same as those given in Table 2 but with the addition of a | d | e and a | e | d (because we now not only have, e.g., dp ≿ ap and dp ≿ ep as well as eq ≿ aq and eq ≿ dq, but also ax ≿ dx and ax ≿ ex). We thus have d | a | e, a | d | e, and a | e | d. This indicates a violation of Axiom 4. Indeed, Table 4

Table 4: Possible tests and conclusions (for all p ∈ P) of Axiom 4 of an unfolding structure for the data from Table 1 enlarged by an additional x ∈ P (see text).

b | a | c	and	b | c | d	→	either ap ≿ cp or dp ≿ cp (satisfied)
b | e | a	and	b | a | c	→	either ep ≿ ap or cp ≿ ap (violated with respect to x ∈ P)
b | e | a	and	b | a | d	→	either ep ≿ ap or dp ≿ ap (violated with respect to x ∈ P)
a | c | d	and	a | d | e	→	either cp ≿ dp or ep ≿ dp (violated with respect to p,s,t,u, w,x ∈ P)
d | c | a	and	d | a | b	→	either cp ≿ ap or bp ≿ ap (satisfied)
d | c | a	and	d | a | e	→	either cp ≿ ap or ep ≿ ap (violated with respect to x ∈ P)
c | a | e	and	c | e | b	→	either ap ≿ ep or bp ≿ ep (satisfied)
e | a | c	and	e | c | d	→	either ap ≿ cp or dp ≿ cp (satisfied)
d | a | e	and	d | e | b	→	either ap ≿ ep or bp ≿ ep (satisfied)
a | d | e	and	a | e | b	→	either dp ≿ ep or bp ≿ ep (satisfied)
e | d | a	and	e | a | c	→	either dp ≿ ap or cp ≿ ap (violated with respect to r,v, x ∈ P)
d | e | a	and	d | a | b	→	either ep ≿ ap or bp ≿ ap (violated with respect to u, w, ∈ P)
b | e | c	and	b | c | d	→	either ep ≿ cp or dp ≿ cp (satisfied)
d | c | e	and	d | e | b	→	either cp ≿ ep or bp ≿ ep (satisfied)
d | c | e	and	d | e | a	→	either cp ≿ ep or ap ≿ ep (violated with respect to q,r,t,v ∈ P)
e | c | d	and	e | d | a	→	either cp ≿ dp or ap ≿ dp (violated with respect to p,q,s,t,u,w ∈ P)

shows the possible tests and conclusions of Axiom 4 and indicates Its violations. Hence, there is no J scale compatible with the preferences of all persons. If it is noted, however, that x is the only person whose preferences are involved in the definition of both a | d | e and a | e | d (and, thereby, causing the violations of Axiom 4), then the previously obtained J scale, according to b | e | a | c | d, is a "dominant J scale" (Coombs, 1964) which is compatible with the individual preference orderings of eight out of nine subjects.

References

Coombs, C.H. (1950). Psychological scaling without a unit of measurement. *Psychological Review, 57,* 145-158.

Coombs, C.H. (1952). *A theory of psychological scaling.* Ann Arbor, MI: Engineering Research Institute, University of Michigan.

Coombs, C.H. (1953). Theory and methods of social measurement. In L. Festinger, & D. Katz (Eds.). *Research methods in the behavioral sciences* (pp. 471-535). New York: Dryden.

Coombs, C.H. (1964). *A theory of data.* New York: Wiley.

Ducamp, A. & Falmagne, J.C. (1969). Composite measurement. *Journal of Mathemtical Psychology, 6,* 359-390.

Krantz, D.H., Luce, R.D., Suppes, P. & Tversky, A. (1971). *Foundations of measurement, Vol. I.* New York: Academic Press.

Orth, B. (1976). *An axiomatization of unfolding.* Paper presented at the 7th European Mathematical Psychology Meeting, Stockholm.

Orth, B. (1987). Grundlagen des Entfaltungsverfahrens und eine axiomatische Analyse von Präferenzen für politische Parteien. *Zeitschrift für Sozialpsychologie, 18,* 236-249.

Suppes, P. & Zinnes, J.L. (1963). Basic measurement theory. In R.D. Luce, R.R. Bush, & E. Galanter, (Eds.). *Handbook of mathematical psychology, Vol. I* pp. 1-76. New York: Wiley.

Graph theoretical representations of proximities by monotonic network analysis (MONA)*)

*Bernhard Orth***)
Universität Hamburg

Abstract
Proximity data can be represented either geometrically or graph theoretically. Graph theoretical methods, however, are typically restricted to representations in terms of trees. As an new method, monotonic network analysis (MONA) allows for more general representations of proximity data. For a given set of data, MONA yields a connected graph, weighted by positive integers and possessing a distance function in such a way that (1) the vertices represent the empirical objects, (2) the number of edges is minimal, (3) the weights are minimal, and (4) the ordering of the distances coincides at least approximately (according to some prescribed error criterion) with the ordering of the dissimilarities. The rationale of MONA will be stated, and the method will be illustrated by applications to real data.

1. Mona representations

Proximity data can be represented either geometrically or graph theoretically. Graph theoretical methods, however, are typically restricted to representations in terms of trees. As a new method, monotonic network analysis (MONA) allows for more general representing graphs.

Representations by MONA are in terms of a connected and weighted graph possessing a path length metric. Consider a connected graph with its edges weighted by positive integers. Define the length of a path as the sum of the weights of its edges, and define the distance between two distinct vertices as the minimum of the lengths of all paths between those vertices. (Distances between identical vertices will be set equal to zero.) This yields a distance function which is usually called a "path length metric".

For a given set of (unconditional) proximity data, monotonic network analysis yields an order-preserving representation in terms of a connected graph weighted by positive integers and possessing a path length metric in such a way that (1) the vertices represent the empirical objects, (2) the number of edges is minimal, (3) the weights are as small as pos-

---

1*) The research for this paper was supported by a grant (Or 53/2) from the Deutsche Forschungsgemeinschaft.

**) Psychologisches Institut I, Universität Hamburg, Von-Melle-Park 6, D-2000 Hamburg 13, F.R. Germany.

sible, and (4) the ordering of the distances coincides either exactly or approximately with the ordering of the dissimilarities.

Approximate representations are allowed by means of incorporating an error criterion which is basically a count of those pairwise reversals of adjacent ranks that are necessary for complete agreement of both orderings. The criterion, called e_{max}, is the maximal number of such reversals (at any place in the dissimilarity ordering) the user is willing to accept. It is to be specified in advance.

For example, if $e_{max}=3$ is chosen then up to three pairwise reversals of adjacent ranks are allowed; thus the ranks, say, 13 and 16 may be interchanged but not the ranks 13 and 17. The value $e_{max}=0$ corresponds to an exact representation where no reversals at all are allowed. The e_{max} criterion is to be applied to rankings where the ranks are expressed as integers and where tied objects are given the same integers (i.e., rankings such as 1, 2, 2, 3, 4, 5, 5, 5, 6, 7).

Monotonic network analysis then determines a representing graph within this prescribed range of "error". This can be done for every value of e_{max} within the range of $0 \leq e_{max} < \binom{n}{2}$ where n is the number of objects. In general, increasing values of e_{max} lead to graphs with less edges until, ultimately, a tree is obtained.

Monotonic network analysis thus determines a connected graph with a path length metric such that, for all empirical objects a, b, c, d,

$$r(a,b) > r(c,d) + e_{max} \rightarrow d(A,B) > d(C,D)$$

where A, B, C, D, denote the vertices corresponding to the empirical objects, d is the path length metric, and r denotes the rank of a pair of objects in the dissimilarity ordering (where ranks are scored by integers only). Moreover, this graph is "minimal" in the sense that, first, the number of edges is minimized and, then, their weights are minimized according to some optional criterion (e.g., minimization of their sum).

2. Method

Monotonic network analysis is based on an analytic approach where the solutions are determined exactly. As a first step, MONA determines the edges of the representing graph. (Note that the vertices are given by the objects.) Their weights and, hence, the distances are calculated in a second step. The method can be outlined as follows.

From a given ordering of proximities, an ordinal betweenness relation will be derived according to the following definition:

$$a \mid b \mid c \text{ iff } r(a,c) + e_{max} \geq r(a,b) \text{ and } r(b,c),$$

for all pairwise distinct objects a, b, and c, where $a \mid b \mid c$ denotes "b is between a and c" and where the error criterion is already incorporated.

Next, a particular consistency condition on ordinal betweenness is imposed. It is essentially a monotonicity condition as used in some difference structures in measurement theory (cf. Krantz, Luce, Suppes & Tversky, 1971):

$$\text{If } a \mid b \mid c,\ d \mid e \mid f,\ r(a,b) \gtrsim r(d,e), \text{ and } r(b,c) \gtrsim r(e,f), \text{ then } r(a,c) \gtrsim r(d,f)$$

where e_{max} will be included in a manner similar as above. By the present representation, it can be shown that one cannot retain $a \mid b \mid c$ whenever this condition does not hold. Hence, some elements of the betweenness relation will typically be eliminated by testing this monotonicity condition.

In general, at least some edges can now be determined. For the remaining elements of the betweenness relation and for all pairs a and b, if there is no object between a and b, then the corresponding vertices A and B must be joined by an edge.

So far, the representing graph is not nessarily connected. In order to determined further edges, the simple paths between any two distinct vertices will be constructed. For the existence of a simple path between two vertices, two conditions must hold: (1) the edges belonging to this path must exist, and (2) the betweenness relation must hold for all objects corresponding to the vertices of this path. Hence, if there is no path between a certain pair of vertices then at least one additional edge is required. Furthermore, condition (2) can be used to determine all possible simple paths between those vertices (i.e., those paths being compatible with betweenness). The missing edges of possible paths thus become alternative candidates for additionally required edges. Considering every pair of vertices not joined by a simple path this way yields a set of alternatives for additional edges. A minimal set of edges satisfying these alternatives then gives a connected graph with a minimal number of edges for representing the given proximity data.

The calculation of weights can be done by means of an iterative method which determines positive integers as weights that are as small as possible. As a preliminary step, the pairs of vertices are ordered according to the empirical ordering, beginning with the smallest dissimilarities. Initially, positive integers being as small as possible, but preserving this ordering within the prescribed range of e_{max}, are assigned to those pairs of vertices that are connected by edges; furthermore, appropriate sums of these preliminary weights are assigned to those pairs of vertices that are joined by paths. (According to the path length metric, if there are two or more paths between a pair of vertices then the minimum of the respective sums of weights has to be taken as the (preliminary) distance.) In general, some of these sums will violate the order-preserving representation. In these cases, at least one of the weights of the respective sum must be raised. Typically, however, not every weight of a sum can be raised so as to remove such a violation. This is because raising a particular weight typically requires other weights and/or sums of weights to be raised, too, which in turn may force the particular sum under study to be raised again. In most cases, a particular weight which has to be raised by a certain amount can be determined uniquely. This gives rise to a set of new distances (i.e., weights and sums of weights) where violations of the order-preserving representation may occur again. Such violations will be removed again by raising particular weights, and this process continues until an order-preserving representation (within the range of e_{max}) has been established. Typically, most weights are determined uniquely by this procedure; sometimes, however, there remains a choice between raising either one of the two weights. In such a case, an auxiliary criterion will be adopted, such as minimizing the sum of weights, minimizing the sum of distances, or maximizing the rank correlation between both orderings.

3. Applications

Fig. 1 shows MONA representations of two sets of proximity data obtained by Schönemann, Dorcey & Kienapple (1985). They constructed nine rectangles varying in height and width according to a 3×3 factorial design, and they obtained dissimilarity judgements on these rectangles from 35 subjects. Because of large individual differences they classified these subjects into three groups. Most subjects (EQ group; N=20) apparently judged according to shape and area (or height and width) about equally. The MONA representation (with e_{max}=4) of the data from this group, as given in Fig. 1(a), mirrors exactly the physical stimulus design of the nine rectangles. Another group of subjects (UP group; N=9) apparently judged much more according to area than to shape. The representing graph in Fig. 1(b) obtained with e_{max}=5, now becomes a tree where the largest distance is those between the edges C and G representing the largest and the smallest rectangles with respect to area.

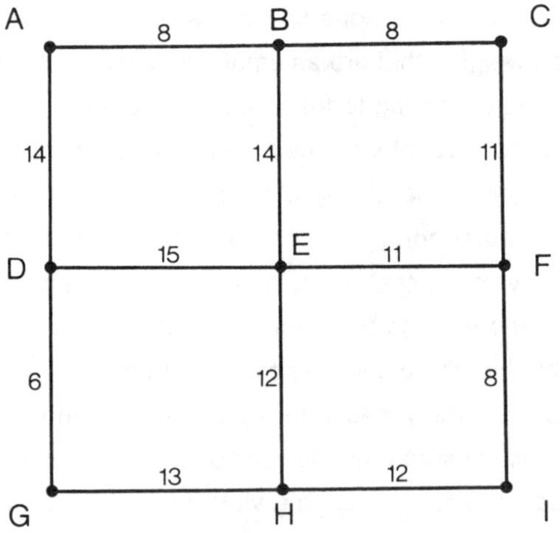

(a)

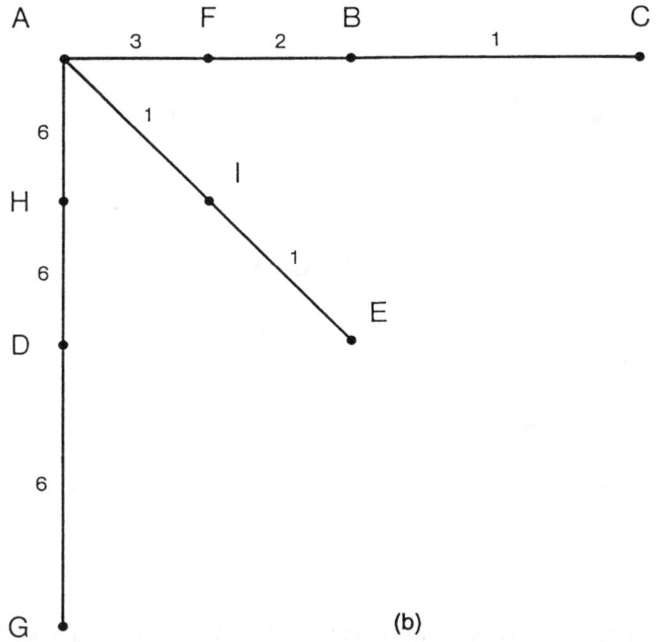

Fig. 1.: MONA representations of dissimilarities of rectangles:
(a) data of the EQ group; e_{max}=4 (from Orth, 1988);
(b) data of the UP group: e_{max}=5. Data from Schönemann, Dorcey & Kienapple (1985).

Trees are also shown in Fig. 2. These graphs are MONA representations (with e_{max}=0 or, in Fig. 2(d), with e_{max}=1) of communication frequencies in small social groups with 4, 5, 6, and 7 group members. The data are taken from Bales (1970). They were considered as conditional proximities, and distances between rows (i.e., persons as senders of information) were calculated according to Kemeny & Snell's (1962) distance measure between rank orders. For the four different sizes of groups, monotonic network analysis yields star-like trees to be interpreted as hierarchical communication structures having one and only one central position each.

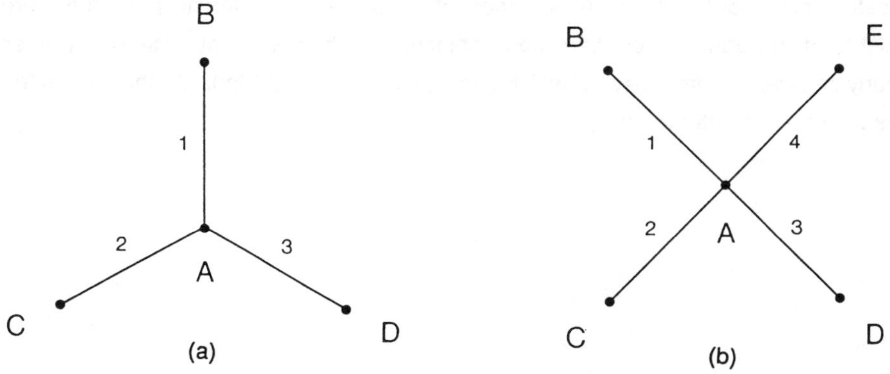

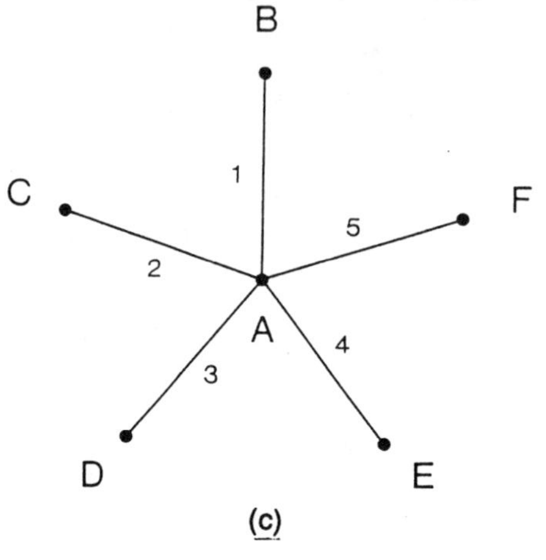

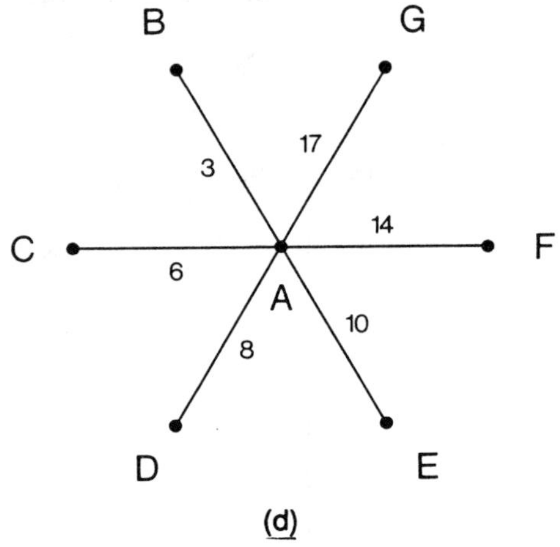

Fig. 2.: MONA representations of communication frequencies in small social groups:
(a) groups with 4 members; $e_{max}=0$;
(b) groups with 5 members; $e_{max}=0$;
(c) groups with 6 members; $e_{max}=0$;
(d) groups with 7 members; $e_{max}=1$.
Data from Bales (1970).

Feger (1985) obtained similarity judgements on fictitious vacation places defined by combinations of three characteristics (b, c, and d) where each of them was either present or absent. In a first study, the vacation place were described only by those characteristics that were present. This gives 7 objects, omitting the "empty" one. The MONA representation with $e_{max}=1$ of the corresponding data is given in Fig. 3(b). This graph represents the set theoretical structure of the objects very nicely. In a second study, all 8 vacation places were used; they were now described by both absence and presence of the three characteristics. Fig. 3(a) gives the MONA representation with $e_{max}=0$ of the proximity data. It shows the same subset structure as before but now enlarged by the "empty set", i.e., the vacation place defined by the absence of all three characteristics. Furthermore, the weights of the edges show that those objects for which characteristic d is present are clearly separated from those for which d is absent. This might indicate that characteristic d was the most important one.

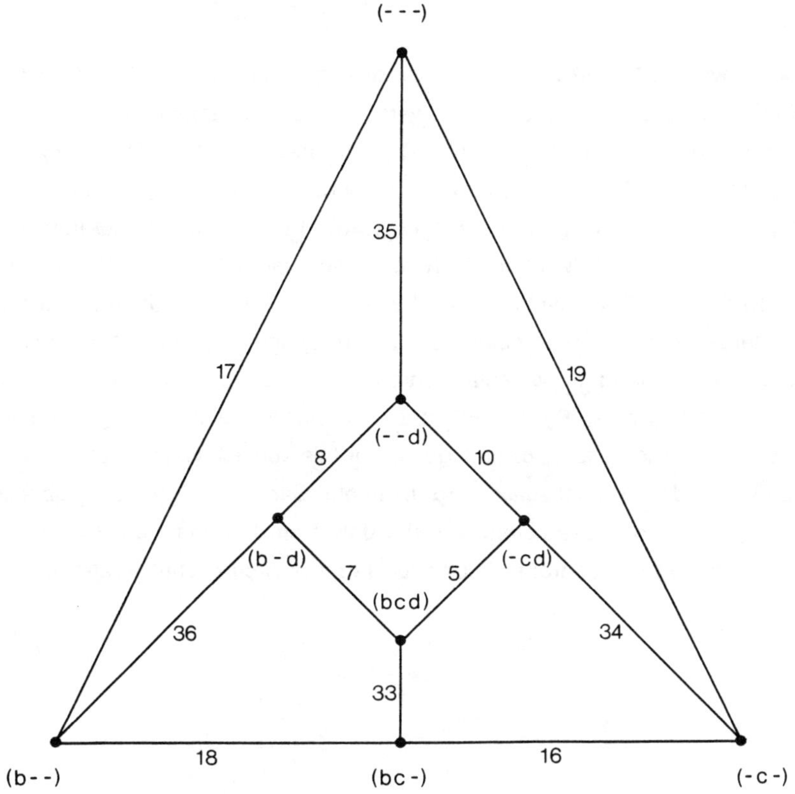

(a)

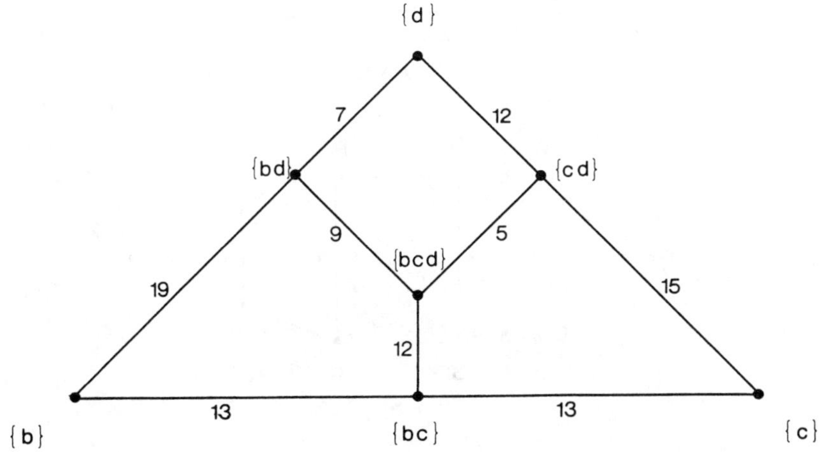

(b)

Fig. 3.: MONA representations of similarities of fictitious vacation places:
(a) 8 places described by absence and presence of three characteristics b, c, and d; $e_{max}=0$;
(b) 7 places described by the presence of these characteristics only; $e_{max}=1$.
Data from Feger (1985).

Fig. 4 shows two MONA representations of some well-known proximity data on color perception obtained by Helm (1959). The vertices of both graphs represent the colors red (R), yellow (Y), green-yellow (yellowish) (GY_1), green-yellow (greenish) (GY_2), green (G), blue (B), purple-blue (PB), purple (bluish) (P_1), purple (reddish) (P_2), and red-purple (RP). Fig. 4(a) gives a representing graph (with $e_{max}=3$) of the averaged data from 10 subjects with normal color vision. This graph nicely represents the color circle. The graph shown in Fig. 4(b) gives a MONA representation (with $e_{max}=4$) of the data from a single subject that was very deficient in red-green color vision. Correspondingly, the "color circle" now appears somewhat distorted. In particular, red and green as well as red-purple and blue (and also Y and GY_2 as well as P_2 and PB) are now joined directly by edges indicating that these colors appear to be fairly close together for this subject. Helm's data have also been analyzed by multidimensional scaling. For example, Carroll & Wish (1974) obtained an elliptical configuration of these colors with the data from the same color-deficient subject (whereas the averaged data from all subjects lead to a circular configuration).

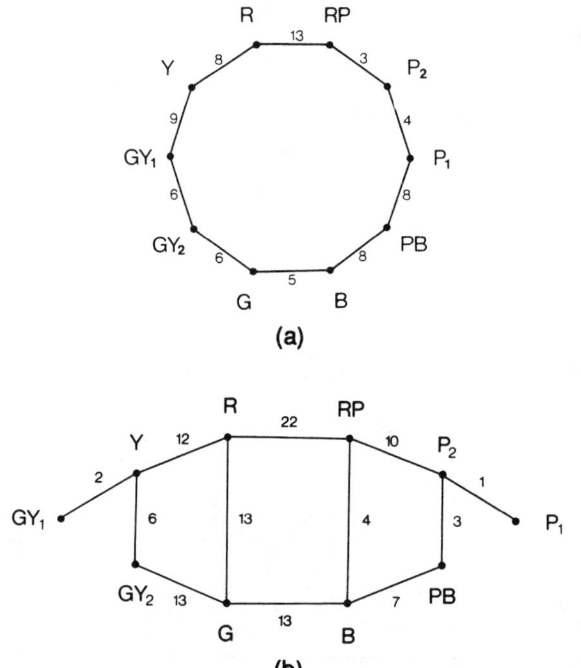

Fig. 4.: MONA representations of dissimilarities of colors:
(a) data from subjects with normal color vision; $e_{max}=3$ (after Orth, 1988);
(b) data from a subject with a red-green deficiency; $e_{max}=4$.
(See text for an explanation of colors.) Data from Helm (1959).

To illustrate "extended similarity trees", Corter & Tversky (1986) constructed 9 schematic faces differing in shape (top-heavy, even, bottom-heavy) and expression (smile, neutral, frown) according to a 3×3 design. These objects will be denoted here as follows:

a = (top, smile)	b = (top, neutral)	c = (top, frown)
d = (even, smile)	e = (even, neutral)	f = (even, frown)
g = (bottom, smile)	h = (bottom, neutral)	i = (bottom, frown)

Corter & Tversky obtained similarity judgements on these schematic faces as well as percentages of confusions between them from a study on paired associates learning. MONA representations (with e_{max}=3 and e_{max}=4, respectively) of both sets of data are shown in Fig. 5(a) and (b), respectively. Except for the weights and the labelling of the vertices, both graphs are identical. However, they differ sharply with respect to the labelled vertices. Whereas the graph for the similarity judgements shows three clusters corresponding to the three shapes, the representation of the confusion data shows three clusters corresponding to the three expressions. For the similarities, the three expressions are ordered (with "neutral" between "smile" and "frown") but not the three shapes (they are about equally far away from each other). For the confusions, however, the three shapes are ordered (with "bottom" between "top" and "even") but not the three expressions. These striking differences obtained by monotonic network analysis conform to results also observed and discussed by Corter & Tversky (1985).

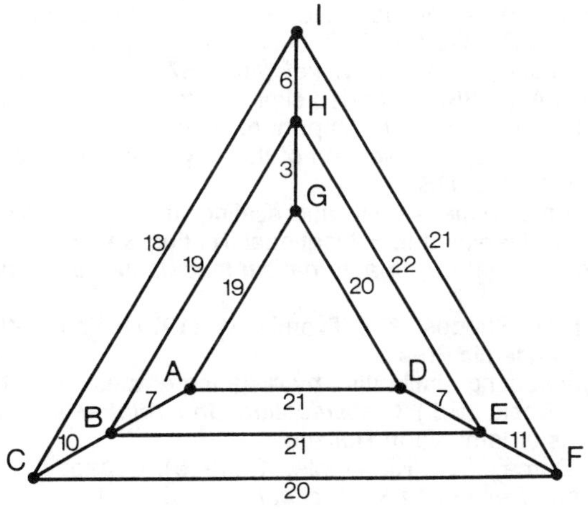

(a)

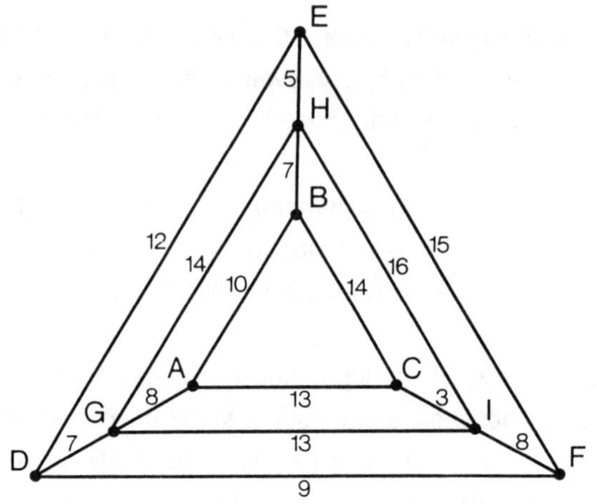

(b)

Fig. 5.: MONA representations of:
(a) similarity judgements (e_{max}=3), and
(b) perceptages of confusions (e_{max}=4) with schematic faces (from Orth, 1988).
Data from Corter & Tversky (1986).

References

Bales, R.F. (1970). *Personality and interpersonal behavior.* New York: Hot, Rinehart and Winston.

Carroll, J.D. & Wish, M. (1974). Models and methods for three-way multidimensional scaling. In D.H. Krantz, R.C. Atkinson, R.D. Luce, & P. Suppes (Eds.). *Contemporary developments in mathematical psychology, Vol. II* (pp. 57-105). San Francisco: Freeman.

Corter, J.E. & Tversky, A. (1986). Extended similarity trees. *Psychometrika, 51,* 429-451.

Feger, H. (1985). Ordinal testing of component models for attitude objects. Paper presented at the Fourth European Meeting of the Psychometric Society and the Classification Societies, Cambridge, GB.

Helm, C.E. (1959). A multidimensional ratio scaling analysis of color relations. Technical Report, Princeton University and Educational Testing Service.

Kemeny, J.G. & Snell, J.L. (1962). *Mathematical models in the social sciences.* New York: Blaisdell.

Krantz, D.H., Luce, R.D., Suppes, P. & Tversky, A. (1971). *Foundations of measurement, Vol. I.* New York: Academic Press.

Orth, B. (1988). Representing similarities by distance graphs: Monotonic network analysis (MONA). In H.H. Bock: (Ed.) *Classification and related methods of data analysis* (pp. 489-494). Amsterdam: North-Holland.

Schönemann, P.H., Dorcey, T. & Kienapple, K. (1985). Subadditive concatenation in dissimilarity judgement. *Perception & Psychophysics, 38,* 1-17.

MIDPOINT SEQUENCES, INTRANSITIVE J SCALES AND SCALE VALUES IN UNIDIMENSIONAL UNFOLDING

Rian A.W. van Blokland-Vogelesang
Free University, Amsterdam *)

ABSTRACT

Using combinatorial techniques, a number of procedures has been developed to find the best qualitative and quantitative J scales in unidimensional unfolding. On the basis of these procedures a computer program, UNFOLD, has been written. The criterion for a 'best' J scale is derived from nonparametric statistics: the minimization of the total number of inversions between the J scale and subjects' rankings. In defining a quantitative J scale as a 'midpoint sequence' some useful results are attained: 1) a transitivity check of a quantitative J scale can be done on the basis of the midpoint sequence; 2) scale values for individuals and stimuli can be found using the midpoint sequence and linear programming techniques. The procedures are illustrated on the Coombs' (1964) Grade Expectations data.

Keywords: unidimensional unfolding, combinatorics, backtracking, branch-and-bound-methods, linear programming.

1 INTRODUCTION

Coombs' (1964) unidimensional unfolding model was devised for the analysis of complete orderings of preference. Suppose there are n individuals ranking k stimuli from the most to least preferable. Each individual and each stimulus may be represented on a single dimension, called the J scale ('Joint'). The points representing the individuals are called 'ideal points', each representing the best possible object from the individual's point of view. Each individual's preference ranking of stimuli is given by the rank order of the distances of the object points from the ideal point, the nearest point representing the most preferable stimulus. In the unidimensional unfolding model possible orders of preference ('admissible patterns') correspond to intervals on the J scale. Other orders of preference do not correspond to intervals on the J scale and, hence, are called 'inadmissible patterns'. For four stimuli A, B, C and D, two different J scales ('4-scales') are possible, depending on the order of the midpoints *ad* and *bc*. The relative magnitude of the distances d(AB) and d(CD) depends on the order of the midpoints *ad* and *bc* (see Figure 1).

*) Department of Psychology, Provisorium I, H 120, De Boelelaan 1111, 1081 HV Amsterdam, The Netherlands

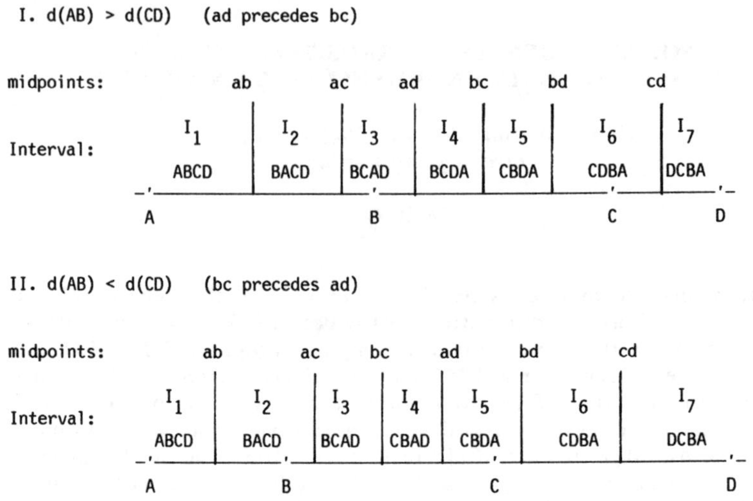

Figure 1: The two possible midpoint orders for 4-scale ABCD; ad precedes bc (top) and bc precedes ad (bottom)

Consequently, without restrictions on the order relations between the midpoints, there are eight admissible patterns on the 4-scale ABCD. This scale is called the **qualitative J scale.** With restrictions on the order relations of midpoints one of the fourth intervals I_4 is excluded (only one order of *ad* and *bc* is possible), this scale is called a **quantitative J scale.** A qualitative J scale contains 2^{k-1} patterns, a quantitative J scale $\binom{k}{2}+1$. The quantitative J scale can be represented by a unidimensional continuum, because of the fixed midpoint order; the qualitative J scale cannot.

Apart from the restrictions which follow from the ordering of the stimuli on the scale (see section 3), the midpoint order is not fixed on the qualitative J scale. With three stimuli only one midpoint order is possible, so the qualitative and quantitative J scales are identical. For four stimuli, two different quantitative J scales can be defined since there are two different midpoint orders given a particular order of stimuli on the J scale (see Figure 1). With increasing k there is an increasing number of midpoints the ordering of which is not implied by the mere ordering of the stimuli on the J scale. This means that there is an increasing number of possibilities to construct quantitative J scales from one qualitative J scale.

Thrall (1952) derived an upper bound, g_k, for the number of quantitative J scales for k stimuli:

$$g_k = \frac{\binom{k}{2}!\,(k-2)!(k-3)!\cdots 2!1!}{(2k-3)!\,(2k-5)!\cdots 5!3!} \tag{1}$$

This g_k equals the number of quantitative J scales that can be formed from one qualitative J scale; it is an upper limit because it includes scales with an intransitive metric, which may occur for $k \geq 6$.

If individuals' preference rankings are all consistent with one underlying J scale, this scale can be readily determined. For a variety of reasons mostly individuals do not all produce preference orderings which are consistent with one underlying J scale. In addition, much research is precisely aimed at finding a common reference frame for a group of individuals in some domain of research. So we have to decide on a criterion for the 'best' J scale. The best J scale will be defined aş that scale for which the total number of inversions from individuals' rankings is minimal. This is explained briefly in the following paragraph.

Each J scale has a certain number of admissible patterns, see Figure 1. Every individual is supposed to have a pattern of preference in mind, the 'latent pattern', which is identical to one of the admissible patterns of the J scale. In reporting his latent pattern of preference the subject may make errors. The 'manifest' pattern of preference may therefore be different from the latent pattern. For each admissible pattern of the J scale the number of inversions from an individual's manifest pattern of preference is assessed. That admissible pattern which has a minimum number of inversions from the individual's pattern is taken as the latent pattern for this individual. In this way, the number of inversions needed is minimized for each individual and, in general, for all individuals. The minimization of total numbers of inversions is a criterion often used in nonparametric statistics (cf. Lehmann, 1975). In the case of ranking data this criterion also follows from the Mallows (1957) and Feigin and Cohen (1978) models. Using this criterion, a computer program, UNFOLD (see Van Blokland, 1989a) has been written to find best J scales for rankings of preference.

In section 2 finding the best qualitative and quantitative J scales is treated. In section 3 it is shown that each quantitative J scale can be defined as a midpoint sequence. In using the midpoint sequence the (in)transitivity of a particular scale can be checked (section 4). Moreover, starting from the midpoint sequence and using linear programming techniques, scale values for stimuli and subjects can be assessed. This is dealt with in section 5. The procedures are illustrated on the Coombs' (1964) Grade Expectations. The test for goodness of fit of the unfolding model to the data is presented in section 6. In section 7 a discussion follows.

2 FINDING THE BEST J SCALE

Unidimensional unfolding is a technique for finding the latent dimension, called the 'J scale', on which the preference rankings are based. The data are complete orderings of preference of n individuals for a fixed set of k stimuli. The underlying J scale can be seen as a reference frame from which stimuli are judged. If a common frame of reference underlies people's preferences, rankings will unfold into a common J scale.

A 'best' J scale is that set of admissible patterns (2^{k-1} for a qualitative J scale and $\binom{k}{2}+1$ for a quantitative J scale) for which the total number of inversions from individuals' rankings is at a minimum (see section 1). To find best qualitative and quantitative J scales for rankings of preference, a number of procedures has been devised, see Van Blokland (1989a). The computer program UNFOLD, written by Piet van Blokland, is based on these procedures. It should be stressed that the minimization of the total number of inversions from subjects' rankings is the only criterion used to find the best J scale. No other criteria such as quasi independence (Davison, 1979), observed versus expected numbers of errors and uniqueness of the found scale (Van Schuur, 1984) are used. There is no user interaction and there are no parameters which have to be set by the user.

2.1 What does UNFOLD yield?

- best qualitative and quantitative scales for subsets of $4 \leq k \leq 9$ stimuli out of a maximum number of 15,
- a separate analysis for each number of stimuli. Results for any number or subset of stimuli are never dependent on previous steps in the analysis,
- a nested set of J scales if a stable continuum underlies the data: the stimuli of a smaller scale will be contained in the larger scale in the same order,
- scale values for stimuli, for midpoints between stimuli, for patterns of the J scale and for individuals,
- options to analyse specific qualitative or quantitative J scales,
- a test for goodness of fit based on a nonparametric error model for ranking data.

Best qualitative J scales can be determined for subsets of a maximum of 11 stimuli. Scale values and the test for goodness of fit are calculated for quantitative J scales only. All sets of data analysed to date yielded bipolar scales with a substantially meaningful interpretation.
The algorithms used in the program are based on:
- backtracking and branch-and-bound-methods,

- finding a good solution first,
- eliminating inferior scales as quickly as possible.

How best qualitative and quantitative J scales are found is discussed successively in 2.2 and 2.3. The test for goodness of fit of the unfolding model to the data using Feigin and Cohen's (1978) model is treated in section 6.

2.2 Finding the best qualitative J scale

The procedure to find the best qualitative J scale is based on an underestimate of the total number of inversions needed to fit all respondents' preference rankings into a J scale. An effective underestimate of the total number of inversions can be given with the help of 'inadmissible triples'. A **triple** (A,B,C) denotes a specific ordering of three objects A, B and C. For J scale ABCD... the triples ACB and CAB are **inadmissible triples,** as far as the objects A, B and C are concerned. In the same way, ADB and DAB are inadmissible triples for the objects A, B and D on J scale ABCD... It is not true that the total number of inadmissible triples is an underestimate of the total number of inversions. For example, pattern DCAB in J scale ABCD has one inversion from the J scale, (i.e., from admissible pattern DCBA). However, two inadmissible triples can be found in this pattern: DAB and CAB. Consequently, a selection of the possible inadmissible triples must be made, so as to insure that each ordered pair of objects occurs only once contiguously in the selected set of inadmissible triples. First, the frequency of occurrence is calculated for each triple. Next, the triples are ordered according to their frequency of occurrence. On investigating a certain scale, each successive inadmissible triple (p,q,r) is selected if this particular arrangement of the adjacent pairs (p,q) and (q,r) does not already occur in a previously selected inadmissible triple. For the 20 qualitative scales having the best underestimate of the total number of inversions the actual minimum number of inversions is assessed. Then all qualitative scales are investigated again and the ten best ones are retained and printed out.

2.3 Finding the best quantitative J scale

In the first part of the program the ten best qualitative J scales are found. These qualitative J scales will probably contain a very good quantitative J scale and are thus first investigated to assess the total number of inversions from subjects' preference patterns. Only at a later stage are all possible quantitative J scales investigated. In using the algorithm we want to find out whether an improvement, that is a drop in the number of inversions, on a hitherto best quantitative J scale can be made.

To describe the algorithm some notation is needed. Each pattern p of the qualitative scale has a distance, that is a certain number of inversions, from the first pattern (I_1) in the J scale. This distance is denoted as dist(p). Each quantitative J scale contains exactly one pattern with distance s ($0 \leq s \leq \binom{k}{2}$) and each pattern with distance s is contained in at least one quantitative J scale. If r is the number of patterns having a distance i from I_1, then for each j ϵ {1,...,r}, we define p_{ij} by dist(p_{ij})=i.

The set $P_{p_{ij}}$ is defined as the set of all quantitative J scales that contain pattern p_{ij}. If there are r patterns with distance m from I_1, then $P_{m1}, P_{m2} \cdots P_{mr}$ generates a partition on the set of all quantitative scales. A subpartition on the set of quantitative J scales can be attained by fixing another distance from I_1. Suppose that an admissible pattern with distance m from I_1 has been fixed. Only those quantitative J scales containing this pattern are examined in the next step. This means that the set of admissible patterns has been reduced. The algorithm does not work on the partitions themselves, but on the subdivision of admissible patterns they invoke.

The number of inversions needed to fit all subjects' rankings into a specific J scale or small collection of quantitative J scales is always larger than or equal to the number of inversions needed for a larger collection of quantitative J scales. If the number of inversions needed for a subset of quantitative J scales is larger than the minimum number of inversions for the best quantitative scale found so far, further investigation of this subset is not necessary. Subsequently, another pattern with distance m from I_1 is fixed. If the number of inversions is less than the minimum number of inversions found so far, an improvement is possible and a pattern with another distance from I_1 is fixed, and so on. In this way, all possible quantitative J scales belonging to this specific qualitative J scale are examined with respect to the total number of inversions from subjects' patterns.

Having determined a good quantitative J scale, most remaining scales can be eliminated as candidates for the best quantitative J scale. The ten best ones are retained and, on request, printed out.

3 MIDPOINT SEQUENCES AND QUANTITATIVE J SCALES

The number of midpoints on any J scale is equal to the number of pairs of objects. In passing a midpoint on the J scale, the corresponding pair of objects is interchanged in the preference order. The number of pairs of objects is $\binom{k}{2}$. Every pair of objects can be interchanged only once (there is one midpoint between two objects). So, given a fixed order of the midpoints on the J scale, the number of admissible patterns is equal to $\binom{k}{2}+1$.

The order of the midpoints between objects on the J scale is dependent on the ranks of the successive objects on the J scale. In general, there are two kinds of restrictions imposed upon the midpoint order for a qualitative k-scale ABCDE..., namely

1) ab → ac → ad → ...; bc → bd → be → ...; and so forth

2) ac → bc; ad → bd → cd; and so forth (2)

where "→" means "precedes".

The first restriction in (2) concerns the order of the midpoints with **following** objects, the second restriction the order of the midpoints with **preceding** objects. The only restrictions on the successive midpoints of the qualitative J scale are those which follow from the ordering of the objects along the J scale. Hence, the partial ordering of the midpoints between objects on a qualitative J scale is sufficiently characterized by the two kinds of restrictions in (2).

For 6-scale ABCDEF this means that object A's midpoints must be ordered as *ab*, *ac*, *ad*, *ae*, *af*. Similarly, object F's midpoints are ordered as *af*, *bf*, *cf*, *df*, *ef*. For 6-scale ABCDEF the $\binom{6}{2} = 15$ midpoints are represented in Figure 2. The first row shows the midpoints between each object and its immediate successor ('first' midpoints). In the second row the midpoints between each object and its second successor are given ('second' midpoints), and so on.

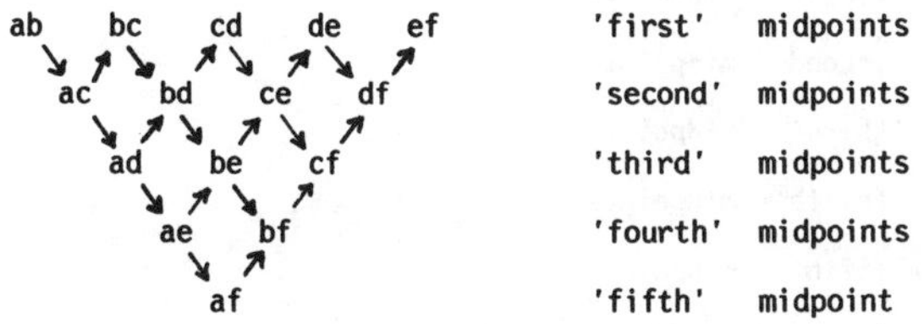

Figure 2. Midpoint order for six objects.

The last row shows the midpoint between the first and last object of the J scale. For k=6 this is the fifth midpoint *af*.

The arrows in the diagram show which order relations are imposed by (2). Diagonally, from 'north-west to south-east', the first type of restrictions can be found, and from 'southwest to north-east', the second type. If there is no path (sequence of arrows pointing in the same direction) from one midpoint to another, there is no order relation imposed upon these two midpoints. For example: the orders of *ad* and *bc*, of *be* and *cd*, of *ae* and *bd*, and of *af* and *be* are free. The number of possibilities to arrange 'higher' midpoints depends on the position of the 'lower' ones. For example, *ae* must be preceded by *ad* and followed by *be*. If *ad* → *bc* and *cd* → *be* there are four possible positions for *ae*: between *ad* and *bc*, between *bc* and *bd*, between *bd* and *cd*, or between *cd* and *be*. However, if *bc* → *ad* there are only three possible positions for *ae*. Hence, each third midpoint has two possible positions, the fourth midpoints have a maximum of four possible positions, the fifth midpoint has a maximum of seven possible positions. These possible positions are given in Figure 3 for the third midpoints, in Figure 4 for the fourth midpoints and in Figure 5 for the fifth midpoint. The lower order midpoints which can be passed are given within blocks.

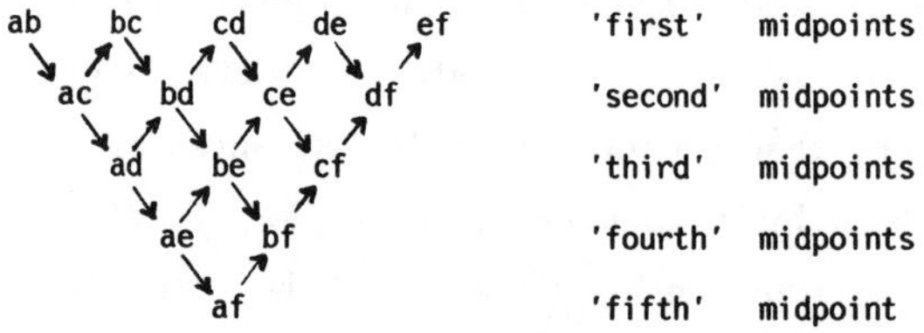

Figure 3. Two possible positions for every third midpoint. Every third midpoint can be placed before or after one lower midpoint.

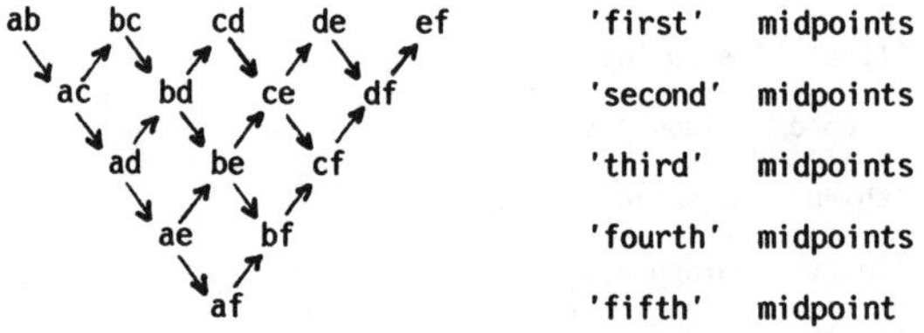

Figure 4. A maximum of four possible positions for every fourth midpoint. Every fourth midpoint can be placed before or after each of three lower midpoints.

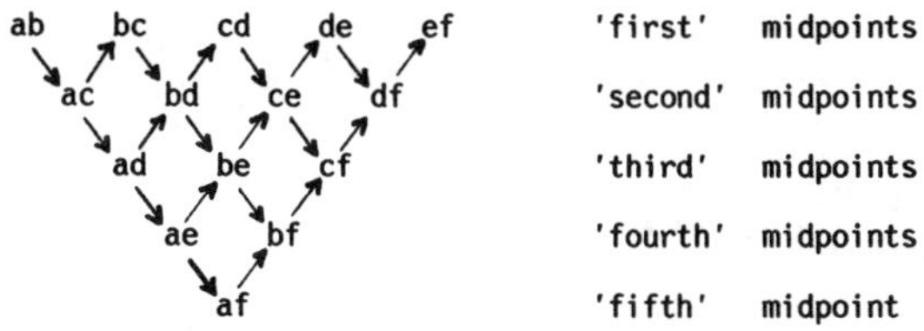

Figure 5. A maximum of seven possible positions for the fifth midpoint. Every fifth midpoint can be placed before or after each of six lower midpoints.

The number of combinations of possible arrangements of the higher order midpoints among the lower order ones determines the number of possible midpoint orders and hence constitutes an upper limit of possible quantitative k-scales. This upper limit can be shown to be equal to Thrall's g_k.

Using the midpoint sequence the transitivity of a found scale can be assessed. This is treated in the next section.

4 INTRANSITIVE J SCALES

Not all possible orders of midpoints between objects in the qualitative J scale form transitive quantitative J scales. An 'intransitive' J scale (Coombs, 1964) is a scale with inconsistent metric information. In order to find out whether a certain quantitative scale is intransitive, we have to know how to construct intransitive scales.

The order of the midpoints *ad* and *bc* on a 4-scale ABCD is not implied by the order of the objects on the qualitative J scale (see section 1). This midpoint order is thus 'indeterminate'. The first quantitative J scale in Figure 1 has d(AB)>d(CD). This is because of the midpoint order *ad*→*bc*. In the second scale these relations are reversed. From subjects' preference rankings it is inferred which of these order relations applies. So, from pure ordinal information (subjects' rankings) 'metric information' can be derived. Also, precisely these indeterminate midpoint orders yield the metric information. With increasing numbers of stimuli on the scale the number of indeterminate midpoint orders also increases and, hence, the number of metric relations. Sometimes the metric information is conflicting (intransitive).

There are two different methods to form (in)transitive relations, namely by way of **comparing** intervals and by way of **combining** intervals. The **comparing of intervals** ('COMP') is shown in Figure 6 (for k=6).

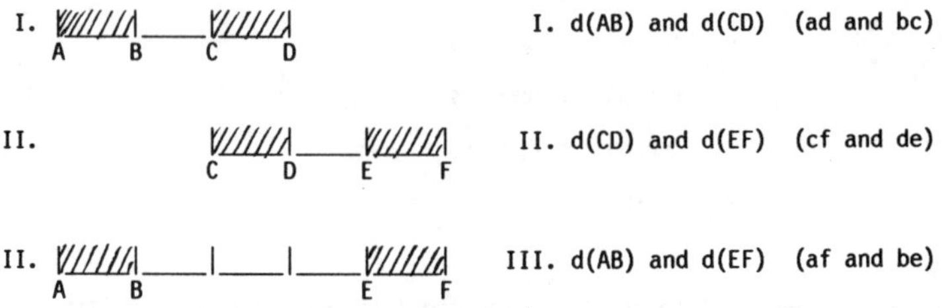

Figure 6. The comparing of intervals: a check of (in)transitivity of quantitative J scales.

Let d(XY) denote the distance between object X and object Y on the J scale. If d(AB)>d(CD) and d(CD)>d(EF), transitivity implies d(AB)>d(EF). An intransitive relation is obtained when d(AB)>d(CD) and d(CD)>d(EF), but d(AB)<d(EF). In terms of the corresponding midpoints this becomes: If *ad*→*bc* and *cf*→*de*, transitivity implies *af*→*be*. An analogous argument holds with all relations reversed.

There is another possibility to arrive at (in)transitive relations, namely by way of **combining intervals** ('COMB'). This is shown in Figure 7 for k=6.

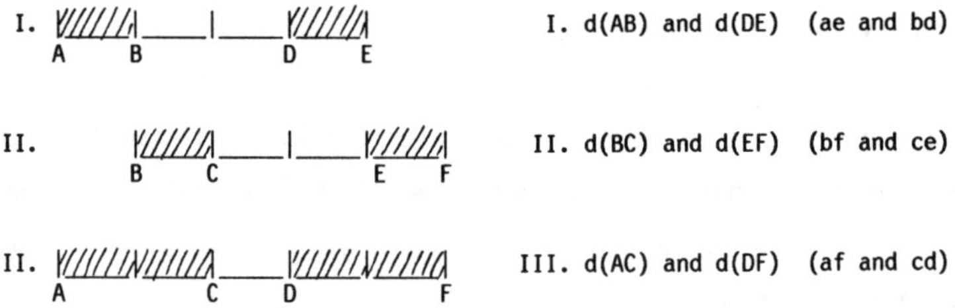

Figure 7. The combining of intervals: a check of (in)transitivity of quantitative J scales.

If d(AB)>d(DE) and d(BC)>d(EF), transitivity implies d(AC)>d(DF). In terms of the corresponding midpoints this becomes: if *ae*→*bd* and *bf*→*ce* transitivity implies *af*→*cd*. And again, an analogous argument holds with all relations reversed.

For the construction of an intransitive scale of type 'COMP' we need six objects, since three non-overlapping and non-adjacent intervals d(AB), d(CD) and d(EF) are being compared. The intervals d(AB) and d(CD) must be non-adjacent, because we need four objects to construct one midpoint order which is indeterminate (*ad* and *bc*). The same holds for the second 4-tuple: d(CD) and d(EF) must be non-adjacent to be able to construct the indeterminate midpoint order *cf* and *de*. It follows that d(AB) and d(EF) are non-adjacent so we have a third 4-tuple: A, B, E and F, with an indeterminate midpoint order for *af* and *be*. An analogous argument holds for the intransitivities of type 'COMB'.

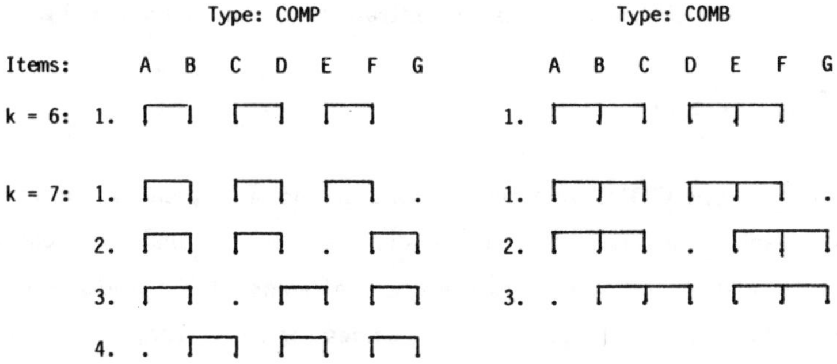

Figure 8. All possibilities to construct intransitive J scales of type COMP and type COMB with 6 and 7 objects.

With k=7 there are four possibilities to choose three pairs of objects, i.e. to compare three non-adjacent intervals of two neighboring objects. There are three possibilities to combine two triples of objects, i.e. to combine two non-adjacent intervals of three neighboring objects (see Figure 8). For k=6 and k=7 the intransitive relations in terms of the midpoints concerned are given below for the '→' relation.

Case k=6:

COMP: ad→bc, cf→de, and be→af   COMB: ae→bd, bf→ce and cd→af (3)

Case k=7:

COMP: 1) ad→bc, cf→de, and be→af   COMB: 1) ae→bd, bf→ce, and cd->af

2) ad→bc, cg→df, and bf→ag   2) af→be, bg→cf, and ag→ce

3) ae→bd, dg→ef, and bf→ag   3) bf→ce, cg→df, and de→bg

4) be→cd, dg→ef, and cf→bg (4)

In general, the number of ways to construct intransitive relations of type COMP for k objects is $2\binom{k-3}{k-6}$. The three 2-intervals are regarded as 'units', since choosing a left endpoint implies that the right endpoint is fixed. Also, there are (k-6) free points, not included in the three intervals. So, (k-3) points are distributed over (k-6) free points and three intervals. The number $\binom{k-3}{k-6}$ must be multiplied by two as for every triple pairs of midpoints two (in)transitive relations are defined (←,→).

In the same way, the number of ways to construct intransitive relations of type COMB is $2\binom{k-4}{k-6}$, as there are (k-4) points to distribute over (k-6) free points and two intervals, the two 3-intervals now being regarded as units.

In sum, the number of possibilities to construct intransitive relations is equal to

$$2\left\{\binom{k-3}{k-6}+\binom{k-4}{k-6}\right\} \qquad (k \geq 6)$$

The intransitive relations of type COMP and type COMB are not independent, however, but overlapping. In general, each intransitive relation gives rise to more intransitive J scales. This is because an intransitive relation only specifies the order of **some** of the midpoints. So, for each intransitive relation there is a set of quantitative J scales for which that relation holds. In constructing two intransitive relations, one of type COMP and one of type COMB, there may be more quantitative J scales for which both relations hold. For example, for k=6 there are at most 286 quantitative J scales (substitute k=6 in Equation 1). Also, for k=6 we can construct 2x30=60 intransitive scales of type COMP, 2x18=36 intransitive scales of type COMB, ten scales being member of both types. This is checked by constructing the lattice of admissible patterns for the qualititative J scale (see Van Blokland, 1988, 1989) and filling in the intransitive midpoint orders (one by one). The number of paths through this lattice having intransitive midpoint orders constitutes the number of intransitive quantitative J scales. So in all, 86 of the 286 6-scales are intransitive, 200 are not.

An example: The Coombs' grade expectations

As an example of the transitivity check of a found scale the Coombs' (1964) Grade Expectations data are used. The data are grade expectations of students in an introductory course in mathematical psychology at the university of Michigan (1959-1961) who were not planning to do any further work in mathematical psychology. Students were instructed to indicate by paired comparison which grade was nearest to the one they expected to get in the course. Seven grades were given: A+, A, A-, B+, B, B-, C+. If transitive, each student converted his own paired comparisons into a rank order. The total number of students was 62, 58 of whom gave transitive rankings.

The data are given in Coombs (1964, Table 5.4, p. 93). The intransitive patterns are indicated in the table with the intransitive stimuli in parentheses: $(F^{E}G)$DCBA indicates that the student 'preferred' F to E, E to G, and G to F. By ignoring these parentheses and reading the letters from left to right, these preference rankings were fed into UNFOLD. In doing so, Coombs' results could be perfectly reproduced, using a different method, however (see also sections 5 and 7).

The midpoint order for the resulting scale is given in Table 1.

Table 1. Midpoint order for the Coombs' (1964) Grade Expectations data. The midpoints within the brackets contain some metric indeterminacy.

ab ac bc ad ae bd af cd be bf ce [ag cf][bg de] cg [df ef dg] eg fg

The midpoint orders given in brackets contain some metric indeterminacy (cf. Coombs, 1964, Table 5.5, p. 94). These midpoint orders will be discussed successively. The first metric indeterminacy concerns the order of the midpoints [*ag*,*cf*]. Both orders are admissible, as can be verified from (4), the possible intransitivities listed for k=7. Arbitrarily, *ag*→*cf* is chosen for the final scale. The next metric indeterminacy concerns the midpoints [*de*,*bg*]. From (4), COMB(3), we see that *de*→*bg* yields an intransitive scale, so the order must be: *bg*→*de*. The last metric indeterminacy concerns [*df*,*ef*,*dg*]. The midpoints *df* and *ef*, and *df* and *dg* must be in this order, because the order of the objects on the J scale is ABCDEFG. So, we only have to check the order of *ef* and *dg*. From (4), COMP(3), we see that *dg*→*ef* yields an intransitive relation, so the order must be: *ef*→*dg*.

This yields the midpoint order given in Table 1, which is used in the next section to derive scale values for the stimuli.

5 SCALE VALUES BY LINEAR PROGRAMMING

For the assignment of scale values to **objects** in a quantitative unfolding scale a number of procedures are available. In the first place the 'equal delta' method by Goode (Coombs, 1964, pp. 96-102) and a comparable equal delta method by Van der Ven (1977, pp. 62-76) can be mentioned. A third procedure is the program ORDMET (McClelland and Coombs, 1975). The latter will not be discussed here, as a standard procedure for the solving of linear equations has been used. ORDMET has been used by Smolenaars (1984).

The equal delta procedure was devised by Goode (Coombs, 1964) to assign scale values to objects of the quantitative J scale, which satisfy a set of metric relations. This method departs from the partial order of the distances in the quantitative J scale. The smallest distance is set equal to some small positive quantity δ_1 and successively larger distances are obtained by introducing additional positive δ's. Assigning values to the δ's gives us interval scale values for the objects. Arbitrarily, a scale value of zero is assigned to stimulus A and a value of one to each δ. From this the scale values of the remaining stimuli follow.

The equal delta method as proposed by Van der Ven (1977) is comparable to the Goode-Coombs (1964) procedure. An advantage of Van der Ven's procedure is its simplicity: one need not construct the partial order of distances between stimuli. The procedure starts from the order of midpoints on the quantitative J scale. Since the midpoint sequence is in the output of UNFOLD, we used Van der Ven's equations. These equations can be solved by using linear programming techniques without using Van der Ven's "equal delta" assumption.

Let I, J, H and G denote arbitrary objects on the J scale, and let ij and ih denote the midpoints between stimuli I and J, and between I and H. Scale values of stimuli and midpoints will be denoted by s(I) for stimulus I, by s(ij) for the midpoint between stimuli I and J, etc. To represent these midpoints on an interval level scale, the distances between the midpoints must satisfy the restrictions:

$$d(ih,ig) = d(jh,jg). \tag{5}$$

(Van der Ven, 1977, p. 70). The distance between the midpoints ij and ih is defined as

$$d(ij,ih) = |s(ij) - s(ih)| \tag{6}$$

in which

$$s(ij) = \frac{s(I) + s(J)}{2} \quad \text{and} \quad s(ih) = \frac{s(I) + s(H)}{2} \tag{7}$$

To derive the scale values of the stimuli we use

$$s(I) = s(ij) + s(ih) - s(jh) \tag{8}$$

This can be verified, noting that 2s(ij) = s(I) + s(J), 2s(ih) = s(I) + s(H), etc. Let I, J and H be the first three stimuli on the scale, such that s(I) < s(J) < s(H). If stimulus I is assigned a scale value of zero, the scale value s(ij) of the first midpoint can be determined as follows:

$$s(ij) = d(ih,jh) \tag{9}$$

which can be expressed in terms of one or more δ's.

5.1 Solving the equations by linear programming

With larger numbers of stimuli the number of equations and unknowns becomes very large. These equations can be solved by using the techniques of linear programming. The equations are of the form (5) and constitute a system of linear equations with the δ's being the unknowns for which a solution has to be found. Since minimum values for the δ's are sought*) the

*) This is because with minimum values of δ a maximum difference in metric relations (distances between objects) is attained (see Coombs, 1964, p. 101).

problem is the minimization of

$$Z = \delta_1+\delta_2+....+\delta_r, \qquad r = \binom{k}{2}-1$$

as there are $\binom{k}{2}-1$ mutually independent distances between midpoints. The restrictions are the equations of the form (5). The solutions for the δ's are given by $\delta_i \geq 0$ (i=1,2,...,r). However, we need solutions $\delta_i \geq 1$, because distances between midpoints must be positive. So, the equations have to be adapted to this. The solutions obtained by minimizing Z then have to be corrected in the opposite direction. An example will clarify the procedure.

5.2 An example: The Coombs grade expectations

The Coombs (1964) Grade Expectations (see section 4) concerned seven grades. For k=7 the distances between the successive midpoints in the quantitative J scale should satisfy the following constraints:

$$\begin{array}{ll}
1)\ d(\underline{a}c,\underline{b}c) = d(ad,bd) = d(ae,be) = d(af,bf) = d(ag,bg) & \\
2)\ d(a\underline{b},a\underline{c}) = d(bd,cd) = d(be,ce) = d(bf,cf) = d(bg,cg) & \\
3)\ d(a\underline{c},a\underline{d}) = d(bc,bd) = d(ce,de) = d(cf,df) = d(cg,dg) & (10) \\
4)\ d(a\underline{d},a\underline{e}) = d(bd,be) = d(cd,ce) = d(df,ef) = d(dg,eg) & \\
5)\ d(a\underline{e},a\underline{f}) = d(be,bf) = d(ce,cf) = d(de,df) = d(eg,fg) & \\
6)\ d(a\underline{f},a\underline{g}) = d(bf,bg) = d(cf,cg) = d(df,dg) = d(ef,eg) &
\end{array}$$

where the underlined objects indicate the successive adjacent objects which are constant in each line. More constraints may be set up, but will be redundant (cf. Van der Ven, 1977, pp. 71-72). For k>7 these equations have to be extrapolated in an obvious way.

The transitive quantitative J scale according to Coombs' solution (Table 1) consisted of the following midpoint order:

ab ac bc ad ae bd af cd be bf ce ag cf bg de cg df ef dg eg fg

$\delta_1\ \delta_2\ \delta_3\ \delta_4\ \delta_5\ \delta_6\ \delta_7\ \delta_8\ \delta_9\ \delta_{10}\ \delta_{11}\ \delta_{12}\ \delta_{13}\ \delta_{14}\ \delta_{15}\ \delta_{16}\ \delta_{17}\ \delta_{18}\ \delta_{19}\ \delta_{20}$

The distances between the successive midpoints are denoted as $\delta_1 \cdots \delta_{20}$. The problem is to minimize

$$Z^* = \delta_1+\delta_2+\cdots+\delta_{20} \quad , \text{subject to } \delta_i \geq 1 \ (i=1,...,20), \qquad (11)$$

and to the constraints in (10). With linear programming techniques solutions ≥ 0 are attained. So, we have to transform the δ's to x's such that: $x_i = \delta_i - 1$ $(i=1,...,20)$. Now, in using linear programming, the following function is minimized:

$$Z = x_1+x_2+\cdots+x_{20} \quad \text{, subject to } x_i \geq 0 \ (i=1,2,...,20), \qquad (12)$$

and to the constraints (10). The first set of equations in (10) yields the following relations among the δ's:

$$\delta_2 = \delta_4+\delta_5 = \delta_5+\delta_6+\delta_7+\delta_8 = \delta_7+\delta_8+\delta_9 = \delta_{12}+\delta_{13} \qquad (13)$$

and analogous relations can be set up for the remaining set of equations. To minimize (12) we translate (13) into the following set of equations (using $x_i = \delta_i - 1$):

$$x_2 = x_4+x_5+1$$

$$x_2 = x_5+x_6+x_7+x_8+3$$

$$x_2 = x_7+x_8+x_9+2$$

$$x_2 = x_{12}+x_{13}+1$$

The remaining set of equations in (10) can be translated into restrictions on x's in a similar way. The minimizing of (12) was done by using SIMOPT (by E. Kalvelager, Free University, Amsterdam). The complete solution for the δ's is:

$$\delta_5 = \delta_6 = \delta_8 = \delta_{10} = \delta_{11} = \delta_{12} = \delta_{15} = \delta_{16} = 1$$

$$\delta_7 = \delta_9 = \delta_{14} = \delta_{20} = 2$$

$$\delta_1 = \delta_3 = \delta_{18} = 3$$

$$\delta_4 = \delta_{13} = \delta_{17} = \delta_{19} = 4$$

$$\delta_2 = 5$$

Using equations (8) and (9) scale values for the stimuli are obtained:

A=0 B=10 C=16 D=32 E=40 F=44 G=58,

which is equivalent to Coombs' solution (Coombs, 1964, Table 5.8, p. 100), apart from a scale factor of two. In fact, these scale values can be divided by two, to result in the set of smallest scale values for objects which are integer valued. The fact that our solution so closely resembles Coombs' is remarkable, the more because he left some metric relations undetermined and reported one intransitive relation (Coombs, 1964, Tables 5.4, 5.5). The final metric relations corresponded with our solution. By using Goode's equal delta method it was decided that AC>FG (*ag*→*cf*). According to our transitivity check of the midpoint order in section 4 however, the order of *ag* and *cf* was undetermined.

Again, SIMOPT was used to obtain a solution for the δ's corresponding to the midpoint sequence with *cf*→*ag*. A solution was found (see below) and from the consistency of this set of linear equations we can conclude that the corresponding metric relations are possible solutions. Hence, both orderings of the midpoints *ag* and *cf* are admissible. Since there are no observations for certain critical patterns in the J scale from which we can conclude that either

$ag \rightarrow cf$ or $cf \rightarrow ag$, these midpoints may coincide. This can be obtained by setting $\delta_{12}=0$, which corresponds to omitting x_{12} from the equations in (10). Again we found a solution, which appears to be a compromise between the previous ones. The scale values for the seven objects resulting from the three solutions are successively:

A=0 B=5 C=8 D=16 E=20 F=22 G=29 $ag \rightarrow cf$ and AC>FG (Coombs, 1964, our first solution)

A=0 B=5 C=8 D=17 E=21 F=23 G=31 $ag=cf$ and AC=FG

A=0 B=5 C=8 D=18 E=22 F=24 G=33 $cf \rightarrow ag$ and AC<FG

Hence, we obtained different solutions for the Coombs (1964) Grade Expectations. These solutions are all consistent with the data and are possible solutions for an indeterminacy of metric information. If such an indeterminacy occurs, due to lack of subjects in certain admissible patterns of the quantitative J scale, we are not forced to choose either one. A compromise solution is found by letting the concerned midpoints coincide. The result is that distances in the quantitative J scale are equalized instead of being stretched in one way or the other. This appears to be a sensible approach in the light of the lack of information from subjects' rankings.

Using equations (6) to (9) scale values for objects and midpoints between objects are derived. Most admissible patterns on the quantitative J scale are bounded by midpoints. So, each of these admissible patterns can be assigned the mean value of the bounding midpoints as a scale value. The assignment of scale values to the extreme patterns of the J scale is somewhat arbitrary, since these patterns are not bounded, they extend beyond the extreme objects. In UNFOLD to these extreme admissible paterns a scale value is assigned which is midway the scale values of the extreme object and the nearest midpoint.

The scale value of an individual can be set equal to the scale value of the admissible pattern which corresponds to his pattern of preference. This is done in UNFOLD. An inadmissible pattern is assigned the scale value of that admissible pattern which has a minimum number of inversions from it. It may happen that more admissible patterns exist which have the same number of inversions from that inadmissible pattern. In that case the inadmissible pattern gets the scale value of the admissible pattern which is closer to the median ranking (that is, the ranking that has less numbers of inversions from it). This seems reasonable since a unimodal and symmetric function of social preference is assumed to exist over the J scale (c.f. Coombs, 1964, p. 396; this is also implied by the Feigin and Cohen (1978) model). This rule corresponds to the principle of 'regression to the mean'.

In using the Van der Ven (1977) equations for the distances between midpoints in combination with a computer program for the optimization of linear equations, scale values are easily found for larger numbers of stimuli. The assignment of scale values to objects as well as to subjects on the basis of these procedures has been implemented in UNFOLD.

6 GOODNESS OF FIT OF THE UNFOLDING MODEL TO THE DATA

Coombs (1964) sought the 'dominant' J scale, that is, the number of perfect fitting rankings was maximized. With UNFOLD the total number of inversions from the J scale is minimized. In Coombs' solution (with $ag \rightarrow cf$) the number of rankings fitting the 7-scale perfectly was 47, the total number of inversions was 21. In our solution these numbers were 46 and 19, respectively. The goodness of fit of the unfolding model to the data will be tested using Feigin and Cohen's (1978) error model. If observed numbers of errors (inversions) fit the expected numbers of errors given by the Feigin and Cohen model, deviations from the perfect unfolding model can be explained by this error model. The adjustment of the Feigin and Cohen model to the unfolding situation has been treated in Van Blokland (1985, 1988, 1989b). Here, only its application is shown. The test for goodness of fit on the basis of Feigin and Cohen's model has been incorporated in UNFOLD.

Both Coombs' and our frequencies of observed numbers of inversions Y between the J scale (with $ag \rightarrow cf$) and subjects' rankings (n=62) are represented in Table 2. Expected numbers of inversions are derived from the Feigin and Cohen (1978) model. The parameter θ in this model is a measure for the dispersion of rankings among their latent rankings. Small values of θ indicate high levels of concordance (low spread) and vice versa. The θ parameter is estimated using $\bar{y}$, the mean number of inversions for subjects (see Van Blokland, 1989b). For the Coombs' solution $\bar{y}=21/62=.34$ and $\hat{\theta}=.08$, for the UNFOLD solution $\bar{y}=19/62=.31$ and $\hat{\theta}=.07$. The test for the goodness of fit is presented in Table 2. As a test statistic Pearson's χ^2 has been used.

The number of degrees of freedom for the test of goodness of fit is equal to the number of Y-categories minus two, since θ has been estimated. Categories for larger values of Y have to be combined because of small expected values. If we require all expected frequencies to be greater than 5, there are no degrees of freedom left for the test. So, only categories $Y \geq 2$ have been combined. With df=1, $.10<p<.25$ for the Coombs' solution and $.50<p<.75$ for the UNFOLD solution. Deviations from the UNFOLD solution fit Feigin and Cohen's model slightly better than those from Coombs' solution. This is not surprising, since both the error model and UNFOLD are based on a procedure that minimizes the number of inversions. We conclude that the unfolding model fits the data.

Table 2

Goodness of fit for the Coombs (1964) Grade Expectations (k=7), Coombs' solution and UNFOLD solution.

Coombs' solution γ=.34 $\hat{\theta}$=.08				UNFOLD solution γ=.31 $\hat{\theta}$=.07			
y	obs	exp	χ^2	y	obs	exp	χ^2
0	47	44.75	.11	0	46	46.11	.00
1	10	14.04	1.16	1	14	13.18	.05
2	4	2.75	.98	2	1	2.35	.19
3	1	.41		3	1	.32	
4	0	.05		4	0	.04	
≥5	0	.01		≥5	0	.00	
	62		χ^2=2.25		62		χ^2=.24

7 DISCUSSION

Using combinatorial techniques, a number of procedures has been developed to find a quantitative J scale from subjects' rankings. These procedures have been implemented in the computer program UNFOLD that seeks the best J scale in unfolding. The criterion for a 'best' J scale was derived from nonparametric theory. Using the concept of midpoint sequences, intransitive J scales can be traced and scale values can be determined quite easily. The procedures have been illustrated on the Coombs' (1964) Grade Expectations data. In general, Coombs' results have been confirmed. However, some differences emerged, partly because of the optimization criterion.

Coombs sought the 'dominant' J scale, that is the scale which fits a maximum number of subjects' rankings perfectly. Our criterion for the 'best' J scale is the minimization of the number of inversions from subjects' rankings. Despite this difference, the best qualitative J scales are the same in both Coombs' and our case, the quantitative J scales are slightly different.

The qualitative J scale contains 61 persons perfectly, not 62 as Coombs mentioned on p. 93, as pattern EDF(B^CG)A (I scale no. 16, Table 5.4, second column) is not admissible for J scale ABCDEFG. This can be verified by folding J scale ABCDEFG in the point of object E.

The quantitative J scale contains 47 persons perfectly in Coombs' solution (cf. Coombs, 1964, p. 95, who mentions 72%), 46 in our solution. In our solution the number of inversions was less: 19 versus 21 in Coombs' solution.

Also, the arrangement of the patterns in Coombs' Table 5.4 (p. 93, which gives the final scale) contains a number of flaws. We will not go into this.

ACKNOWLEDGEMENT

The author would like to express her appreciation to the anonymous reviewer for the many useful suggestions which have contributed to this paper.

REFERENCES

Blokland-Vogelesang, A.W. Van (1985). Unidimensional unfolding complemented by Feigin and Cohen's error model and by Davison's test for independence. *CSQ-Comp. Stat. Quart.*, *2*, 43-52.

Blokland-Vogelesang, A.W. Van (1988). Unidimensional unfolding complemented by Feigin and Cohen's error model. In W.E. Saris & I.N. Gallhofer (Eds.), *Sociometric Research*. London: MacMillan..

Blokland-Vogelesang, A.W. Van (1989a). *UNFOLD: a computer program for the unfolding of rankings of preference in one dimension. User's Manual.* Groningen: ProGAMMA.

Blokland-Vogelesang, A.W. Van (1989b). Unfolding and consensus rankings: a prestige ladder for technical occupations. In H. Feger & G. de Soete (Eds.), *Developments in psychological choice theory*. Amsterdam: North-Holland.

Coombs, C.H. (1964). *A theory of data.* New York: Wiley, 1964.

Davison, M.L. (1979). Testing a unidimensional, qualitative unfolding model for attitudinal or developmental data. *Psychometrika*, *44*, 179-194.

Feigin, P.D. & Cohen, A. (1978). On a model for concordance between judges. *JRSS (B)*, *40*, 203-213.

Lehmann, E.L. (1975). *Nonparametrics.* New York: Mc Graw-Hill.

Mallows, C.L. (1957). Non null ranking models I. *Biometrika*, *44*, 144-130.

McClelland, G.H. & Coombs, C.H. (1975). Ordmet: a general algorithm for constructing all numerical solutions to ordered metric structures. *Psychometrika*, *40*, 269-290.

Schuur, H. Van (1984). *Structure in political beliefs. Thesis.* Amsterdam: CT-Press.

Smolenaars, A.J. (1984). *Measuring sentences.* Thesis. Univ. of Amsterdam. Holland.

Thrall, R.M. (1952). A combinatorial problem. *Michigan Math. J.*, *1*, 81-88.

Ven, A.H.G S. Van der (1977). *Inleiding in de schaaltheorie.* Deventer: Van Loghum Slaterus.

Predicting an optimal threshold in Boolean analysis of questionnaires

Peter Theuns (*)

Vrije Universiteit Brussel

Abstract
In Boolean analysis of questionnaires, a main problem is the fact that the complexity of the *implication graphs* depends on the length of the *PCU's* (the terms in the minimal expression characterizing the *ignored response patterns*). A possible solution is the *dichotomization* of the consulted population, such that a (small) part of the population is ignored, resulting in intelligible *implication graphs* (valid for the remaining part). Some major problems with the determination of an *optimal threshold* for *dichotomization* are discussed. An approach to predict the lowest possible threshold, which may leave only *PCU's* of a given length or shorter, based on the study of a non-directed graph associated with the protocol, is presented.

1. Introduction

Binary questionnaires are frequently used in human sciences. Classical hierarchy-based methods for analysis, e.g. Guttman analysis, often force the researcher to ignore a significant part of the population. In order to generalize this classical method, Flament (1976) introduced the "Boolean analysis of questionnaires". This is a partial order generalization of the Guttman analysis, in which the assumption of "inclusion of classes" is abandoned. In doing so, one no longer states that the group of persons who passed one of 2 items always should contain (or be contained in) the group of persons who passed the other item. In essence Boolean analysis is based on the determination of an *ideal* of a Boolean algebra and of its quotient algebra.

(*) Center for Statistics and Operations Research, Vrije Universiteit Brussel, Pleinlaan 2, 1050 Brussels, Belgium.

The responses to the n questions of a questionnaire Q provided by an individual can be denoted as a series of 0's (for "false" or "not passed") and 1's (for "true" or "passed"), to which we will refer with the term "*response pattern*". The n questions make 2^n different response patterns possible. When submitted to N persons, each response pattern will be used a certain number of times f_j, named the *frequency*. Clearly $\sum_j f_j = N$.

Given the *protocol* R (the 2^n possible response patterns with their respective frequencies), one can partition R in a subset R^0 containing the *ignored patterns* (*frequencies* equal to 0) and a subset R^* containing the *actual patterns (non-zero frequencies)*. So we have $R = R^0 \cup R^*$ with:

R^0 = the set of patterns not obtained from any of the consultees,
R^* = the set of patterns that were actually obtained.

With "*subpattern of length k*" , we refer to a response pattern of a *subquestionnaire* of Q, consisting of k questions ($k \leq n$).

In Boolean analysis, R^0 is the ideal of a Boolean algebra. The *supremum* (the *Boolean sum*) of the patterns in R^0 is turned into its *minimal expression* by the use of Boolean laws. The resulting expression can completely be characterized by a number of equivalent *implication graphs*. These graphs represent the data and, in the end, will be subject of interpretation. In this procedure the terms in the minimal expression (of the Boolean sum of the ignored patterns) play a main role. Flament (1976, p.141) called these terms "*Projections Canoniques Ultimes*" (the French for *Ultimate Canonical Projections*), which he abbreviated to *PCU*'s. A *PCU* is denoted as a series of 1's, 0's and *'s, in which the latter stand for answers to questions in Q that are not considered in the subpattern.

1.1 Definition

S, a subpattern of length k, is a *PCU* of length k

iff

1) the set of all response patterns containing S is a subset of R^0, and
2) no subpattern, T, of S exists such that the set of all patterns in R containing T is a subset of R^0.

Thus defined, a *PCU* is a subpattern of length k, which characterizes the *maximal set* of patterns in *R* that contain the same subpattern (the *PCU)* and which are included in R^0. Every *PCU* of length k covers 2^{n-k} *patterns* and determines a number of (equivalent) *implications*.

1.2. Example

For a questionnaire *Q* consisting of 4 questions A,B,C,D, the patterns are denoted as a series of 0's and 1's, as indicated before. The pattern "1010" stands for: "*a positive answer to questions A and C together with a negative answer to B and D*". When we come to implications we will denote the answers as *characters* (for positive answers) and *primed characters* (for negative answers). For 1010 we thus would have A, B', C, D'. Suppose *Q* yields the following protocol (the patterns are ordered according to the frequencies):

pattern	f_i	pattern	f_i
0011	200	0010	0
0001	200	1101	0
0111	25	1110	0
0000	25	1100	0
1111	20	0110	0
0100	15	1011	0
0101	10	1010	0
1000	5	1001	0

Consequently:

$R^* = \{$ 0011,0001,0111,0000,1111,0100,0101,1000 $\}$

$R^0 = \{$ 0010,1101,1110,1100,0110,1011,1010,1001 $\}$

We find the following *PCU*'s:

**10 which covers 0010, 0110, 1010, 1110

110* which covers 1100, 1101

11*0 which covers 1100, 1110

101* which covers 1010, 1011

10*1 which covers 1001, 1011

1*01 which covers 1001, 1101

To find the covered patterns, in each *PCU*, the '*' are replaced with either '1' or '0', in all possible combinations. Every pattern in R^0 is covered by at least one *PCU*.

A number of (equivalent) implications correspond to every *PCU*:

PCU	**Implications for** R^*	
**10	$C \rightarrow D$	("YES" to C ***implies*** "YES" to D)
	$D' \rightarrow C'$	("NO" to D ***implies*** "NO" to C)
110*	$A \wedge B \rightarrow C$	("YES" to both A ***and*** B ***implies*** "YES" to C)
	$A \wedge C' \rightarrow B'$	
	$B \wedge C' \rightarrow A'$	
	$A \rightarrow B' \vee C$	("YES" to A ***implies*** "NO" to B ***or*** "YES" to C)
	$B \rightarrow A' \vee C$	
	$C' \rightarrow A' \vee B'$	
11*0	$A \wedge B \rightarrow D$	
	and ...	
101*	$C \rightarrow A' \vee B$	
	and ...	
10*1	$D \rightarrow A' \vee B$	
	and ...	
1*01	$D \rightarrow A' \vee C$	
	and ...	

One of the implication graphs that summarizes the above implications perfectly is:

$$\begin{array}{ccccccc} A \wedge B & \rightarrow & C & \rightarrow & D & \rightarrow & A' \vee B \\ & & \downarrow & & & & \\ & & A' \vee C & & & & \end{array}$$

Remark: Every *PCU* is represented by one implication, either explicitly or can be deduced using transitivity.

1.3. *PCU*-lengths and implications

As illustrated in the above example, a *PCU* determines different numbers of (equivalent) implications. For different values of *k* we have:

$k = 1$

A *PCU* of length 1, e.g. 1***, indicates that none of the patterns in the set R^* have a 1 in the first position. Consequently they all have a 0 in that position, meaning that all the persons considered answered A'.

$k = 2$

A *PCU* of length 2, e.g. *10*, indicates that nobody answered B together with C'. We thus have 2 implications: $B \rightarrow C$ and $C' \rightarrow B'$.

$k = 3$

A *PCU* of length 3 e.g. *001 yields six implications:

$B' \rightarrow C \vee D'$	$C' \wedge D \rightarrow B$
$C' \rightarrow B \vee D'$	$B' \wedge D \rightarrow C$
$D \rightarrow B \vee C$	$B' \wedge C' \rightarrow D'$

$k = 4$

A *PCU* of length 4 yields fourteen implications. For an example we refer to Van Buggenhaut (1987, p.12).

2. Preliminary results

As Van Buggenhaut and Degreef (1987, p.447) remark, the method presented above, often leads to graphs that are too complex to use for intelligible interpretation. As implication graphs become more and more complex with increasing k, Van Buggenhaut (1987, p.13) proposed to redefine R^0 and R^* in such a way that the resulting *PCU*'s have length $k \leq 3$ (or even ≤ 2). In this method an integer value β, referred to as "*dichotomization threshold*", is used as follows:

$$R^* = \{\text{response patterns with frequency} > \beta\}$$
$$R^0 = \{\text{response patterns with frequency} \leq \beta\}$$

Clearly, response patterns having a frequency $\leq \beta$ will be ignored.

Let $T_0, T_1, \ldots, T_m$ be the ordered set of (non-equal) *frequencies*:

$$0 \leq T_0 < T_1 < T_2 < \ldots < T_i < \ldots < T_m \leq N \quad (\text{with } m \leq 2^n)$$

Any of these T_i can be used as a threshold β resulting in, all together, m different sets R_i^* and R_i^0.

Let the *length of the longest PCU* for $\beta = T_i$ be denoted by $K(i)$. For $\mathbf{K}_i$ = { lengths of the *PCU*'s in R^0 if $\beta = T_i$ } we have:

$$K(i) = \max(\mathbf{K}_i)$$

Van Buggenhaut (1987, p.14) proposes to determine a minimal β-value (β_0), which he called *cohesion threshold*, in the following way:

$$\beta_0 = \underset{i}{\text{Min}}\ (T_i) \text{ for which } K(i) \leq \alpha \quad (\text{with } \alpha = 2 \text{ or } 3).$$

In his work, he made the conjecture (Van Buggenhaut, 1987, p.14) that increasing β would result in a decrease of $K(i)$. So, for all $T_i < T_j$ the following would hold:

$$K(i) \geq K(j) \qquad [1]$$

Unfortunately this inequality does **not** always hold. On the contrary, for $n > 2$, $K(i)$ may decrease as well as increase for some successive T_i.

2.1. Example

Ordering the frequencies in our example (1.2) gives

0 5 10 15 20 25 200

and thus: $T_0 = 0$, $T_1 = 5$, $T_2 = 10$, $T_3 = 15$, $T_4 = 20$ etc.

For $T_1 = 5$ we have:

$R_1^* =$ { 0011,0001,0111,0000,1111,0100,0101 }
$R_1^0 =$ { 1000,0010,1101,1110,1100,0110,1011,1010,1001 }

The corresponding *PCU*'s are 10**, 1*0*, 1**0 and **10. It follows that $K(1) = 2$. The *PCU*'s define the following implications:

10**	A → B	and	B'→ A'
1*0*	A → C	and	C'→ A'
1**0	A → D	and	D'→ A'
**10	C → D	and	D'→ C'

which can be put together in one (or more equivalent) comprehensive implication graph(s) as follows:

$$\begin{array}{ccc} B & & \\ \uparrow & & \\ A \rightarrow C \rightarrow D & & \end{array} \qquad \text{or} \qquad \begin{array}{c} B' \\ \downarrow \\ A' \leftarrow C' \leftarrow D' \end{array}$$

Clearly, T_1 is the lowest possible threshold for which all *PCU*'s have length ≤ 2, and thus for $\alpha = 2$ we would have: $\beta_0 = T_1$ (=5).

For T_2 = **10** we have:

$R_2^* = \{$ 0011,0001,0111,0000,1111,0100 $\}$
$R_2^0 = \{$ 0101 ,1000,0010,1101,1110,1100,0110,1011,1010,1001 $\}$

The emerging *PCU*'s are: 10**, 1*0*, 1**0, **10, *101. We have: $K(2) = 3$ (one *PCU* has length 3).

For T_3 = **15** we have:

$R_3^* = \{$ 0011,0001,0111,0000,1111 $\}$
$R_3^0 = \{$ 0100,0101,1000,0010,1101,1110,1100,0110,1011,1010, 1001 $\}$

The emerging *PCU*'s are: 10**, 1*0*, 1**0, **10, *10*, *1*0. Clearly $K(3) = 2$ (all *PCU*'s have length 2).
According to [1] we would expect $K(1) \geq K(2) \geq K(3)$ to hold. In our example, however, we have $T_1 < T_2 < T_3$, and clearly: $K(2) \geq K(3)$ but $K(1) < K(2)$. And so [1] indeed does not hold.

As a result, for the determination of β_0, one would have to compute the *PCU*'s for all successive β, starting from $\beta = T_0$ upwards, until one finds β_0 (the first β for which all *PCU*'s have lengths $\leq \alpha$).

The fact that $K(i-1)$ may be smaller than $K(i)$ is not only important from a theoretical point of view, but also from an algorithmical standpoint. Let us first have a closer look at the phenomenon. In a systematic approach to Boolean analysis, one will start with $\beta = T_0$, find the corresponding *PCU*'s and calculate $K(0)$. Then this procedure will be repeated for $\beta = T_1,\ldots,T_m$ systematically. Apparently $\#R^0$ grows as β increases. A *PCU of length* k emerges as soon as 2^{n-k} (i.e. all possible) patterns that contain the same subpattern (the *PCU*) are included in R^0. According to definition 1.1, however, there is a restriction to this: to be named *PCU* the common subpattern should not contain another *PCU*. We will call the 2^{n-k} patterns, that generate a *PCU* the "*generator patterns*". As the number of generator patterns increases for a decrease in k, we could hypothesize $K(i)$ to decrease when β raises. Necessarily this phenomenon exists as a trend, but this assumption does not always hold. Actually the reason to this is simple. In our example, all patterns in R_1^0 can be covered with *PCU*'s having a length 2. In R_2^0, two patterns, the entering pattern 0101 together with the already present pattern 1101, generate the *PCU* *101. Next, in R_3^0, the *PCU* *101 disappears: together with the already present patterns, the entering pattern 0100 generates two *PCU*'s (*10* and *1*0) having length 2. In R_3^0 the *PCU* *10* is contained in the subpattern *101, which thus meets the restriction put on *PCU*'s.

The restrictions on the difference $K(i)$ - $K(i-1)$ satisfy the following proposition.

2.2. Proposition 1

For $n > 2$ the following holds (*):

$$K(i) - K(i-1) \leq n-2 \qquad \text{(with } i \geq 1 \text{ and } T_0 = 0) \qquad [2]$$

Proof

It is clear that eq. [2] holds if $K(i) \leq K(i-1)$. Clearly, $0 < K(i) \leq n$ and so, eq. [2] will hold for all $K(i-1) \geq 2$. This leaves eq. [2] to be proven for the case $K(i-1) = 1$ (**). In this case all *PCU*'s, corresponding to $\beta = T_{i-1}$, have length 1. Such a *PCU* is generated by 2^{n-1} response patterns, each being build up by one field for the *PCU*, the other fields filled in with one of all 2^{n-1} possible combinations of 0's

(*) for $n \leq 2$ the following can easily be shown: if $K(i)$ and $K(i-1)$ exist, then $K(i) < K(i-1)$.

(**) the trivial case $\beta = T_m$ (with $R^0 \equiv R$) in which $K(i)$ doesn't exist (there are no *PCU*'s) is excluded, because [2] would not make any sense.

and 1's. When going further in the analysis with $\beta = T_i$ the new coming patterns to be covered all have two properties:

- they differ from all the patterns in R^0_{i-1} precisely in the field occupied by the *PCU*(s).
- for the non-*PCU*-fields all possible combinations were in R^0_{i-1}. So, for any pattern in R^0_i, that was not included in R^0_{i-1}, there is at least one pattern in R^0_i from which it differs in no more than 1 field. This causes a *PCU* of length $\leq n$-1 to emerge.

As result: $K(i) - K(i-1) \leq [(n-1)-1]$. ■

The resulting conclusion is that the eventual decrease in $K(i)$, when lowering β cannot be greater than n-2.

3. Main results

The fact that $K(i-1)$ may be less than $K(i)$ has an important implication for systematic optimal threshold seeking approaches. To our knowledge former approaches to this started from a high β-level and systematically lowered β until $K(i)$ exceeded a predetermined number α. Our findings suggest that β_0 might be lower than the β found this way. Still, the determination of β_0 would be more efficient if it could be done without computing all the *PCU*'s for all possible β-values.

In a first approach we can immediately state that **no** *PCU*-computation is needed if $\#R^0 < 2^{n-\alpha}$, as a *PCU* of length α covers $2^{n-\alpha}$ patterns. This simple expression already allows to reduce the range of β-values to process. However, the expression only provides a rather rough approximation of an optimal β, to which we will refer with β^*.

At its best one would be able to predict $K(i)$ for any $\beta = T_i$. Then β_0 would be equal to the lowest β for which $K(i)$ does not exceed α. To enable the introduction of an approach to predict $K(i)$, for a given β, without having to compute the *PCU*'s, we will first translate our problem in terms of graph theory. For this we need some definitions.

3.1. Definitions

In coding theory the *Hamming-distance* $d_H(x,y)$ between two patterns x and y is defined as the *number of places in which x and y differ* (e.g. van Lint, J.H., 1971, p.7). We define a *non-directed graph* on the patterns in R^0 in which 2 patterns are connected when their Hamming-distance is 1. For A_i, *incidence matrix of the graph* G_i, corresponding with β_i, we have:

$$\forall\ a_{xy} \in A_i : \quad a_{xy} = 1 \quad \text{iff} \quad d_H(x,y) = 1$$
$$a_{xy} = 0 \quad \text{else.}$$

remark: $a_{xy} = a_{yx} \quad (\forall\ x,y)$.

3.1.1. Example

For R_0^0 = {0010, 1101, 1110, 1100, 0110, 1011, 1010, 1001}, as above, we find the following Hamming-distances:

	0010	1101	1110	1100	0110	1011	1010	1001
0010	0	4	2	3	1	2	1	3
1101	4	0	2	1	3	2	3	1
1110	2	2	0	1	1	2	1	3
1100	3	1	1	0	2	3	2	2
0110	1	3	1	2	0	3	2	4
1011	2	2	2	3	3	0	1	1
1010	1	3	1	2	2	1	0	2
1001	3	1	3	2	4	1	2	0

It follows that:

$$A_0 = \begin{pmatrix} 0 & 0 & 0 & 0 & 1 & 0 & 1 & 0 \\ 0 & 0 & 0 & 1 & 0 & 0 & 0 & 1 \\ 0 & 0 & 0 & 1 & 1 & 0 & 1 & 0 \\ 0 & 1 & 1 & 0 & 0 & 0 & 0 & 0 \\ 1 & 0 & 1 & 0 & 0 & 0 & 0 & 0 \\ 0 & 0 & 0 & 0 & 0 & 0 & 1 & 1 \\ 1 & 0 & 1 & 0 & 0 & 1 & 0 & 0 \\ 0 & 1 & 0 & 0 & 0 & 1 & 0 & 0 \end{pmatrix}$$

is incidence matrix of graph G_0 (fig.1).

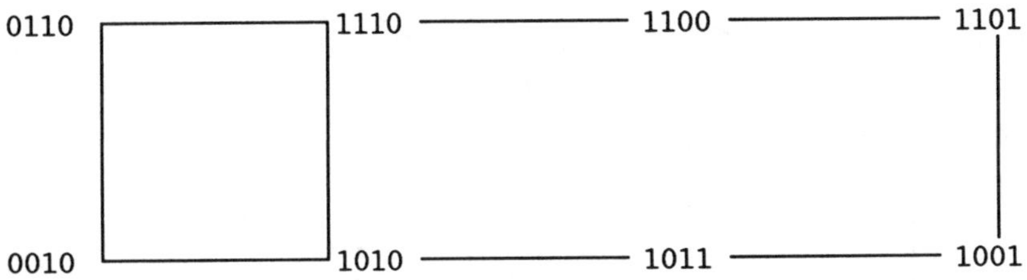

FIGURE 1: Graph G_0

The vertices of the graph can be grouped in subsets of R_0^0 according to the *PCU*'s generated:

the square 0110-1110-1010-0010 represents the *PCU* **10

1110-1100 represents the *PCU* 11*0

1010-1011 represents the *PCU* 101*

1100-1101 represents the *PCU* 110*

1011-1001 represents the *PCU* 10*1

1101-1001 represents the *PCU* 1*01

More generally a *PCU*, having a length k, can be represented by a *r-dimensional hypercube* (with $r = n-k$).

3.1.2. Examples

$r = 3$

For a *PCU* 0*** ($n = 4$, $k = 1$) we would get:

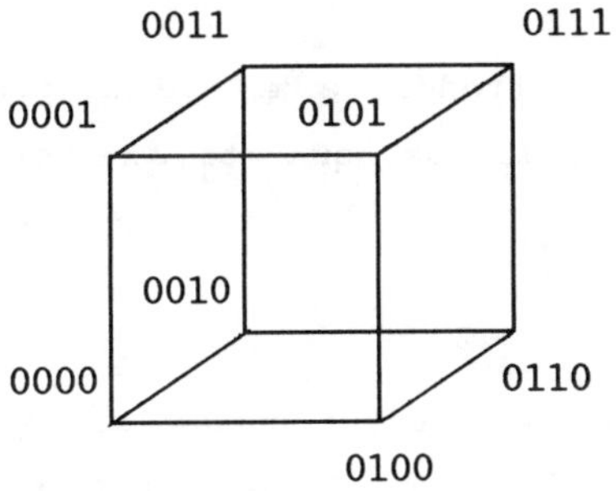

$r = 2$

A *PCU* *10* ($n = 4$, $k = 2$) results in:

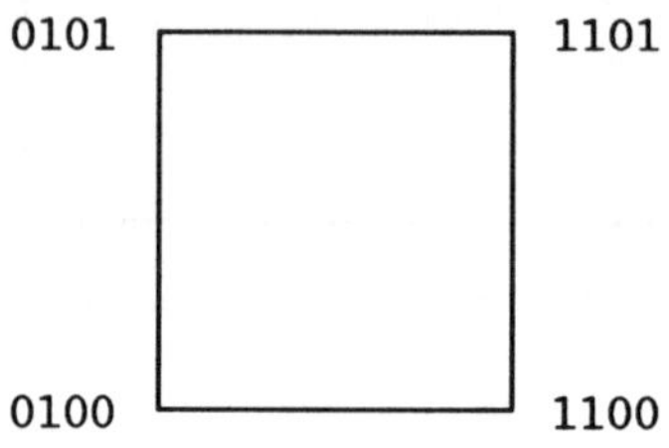

$r = 1$

A *PCU* *000 ($n = 4$, $k = 3$) would result in:

It follows that $K(i)$ will correspond to the dimension of a hypercube in the minimal hypercube covering of R^0. $K(i)$ will be equal to $n\text{-}r_0$ (with r_0 equal to the dimension of the hypercube with the lowest dimension in the covering). As a result, the determination of $K(i)$ becomes a *minimal covering* problem.

As far as we know (see e.g. Berge (1973), Lawler (1966) and Roy (1970)) this problem is not solved yet. Though some algorithms for (what we would call) *PCU*-computation are introduced, no methods are provided to predict $K(i)$. Adopting the prescribed methods would not result in a substantial gain in data processing speed because all *PCU*'s for all possible β would have to be computed.

In the following we will introduce a method to predict the lowest possible β-value for which $K(i)$ may be equal to α. For this we need an additional definition.

3.2. Definition

The *degree of a vertex* x is defined as the *number of edges incident with that vertex* (e.g. Chartrand, 1977, p.27). Starting from the matrix *A*:

$$deg_x = \sum_y a_{xy} \qquad \text{(row-sum)}.$$

Our prediction of $K(i)$ is based on the degree of the vertices in the graph G_i.

3.2.1. Property

For all vertices x in any r-dimensional hypercube the following holds:

$$deg_x = r \qquad [3]$$

In graphs related to response patterns, however, any vertex may be part of more than one hypercube (see i.e. vertex 1010 in our example), and thus eq. [3] has to be weakened to:

$$deg_x \geq r \qquad [4]$$

We are interested in the value of $K(i)$ corresponding to any β-value.

3.3. Proposition 2

$$K(i) \geq n - \min_x(deg_x) \quad \text{(with x = a vertex in } G_i\text{)}$$

Proof:

For any PCU, we have $k = n - r$ (in which r = dimension of the corresponding hypercube). Thus, according to eq. [4], in every hypercube in G_i: $k \geq n - deg_x$. As $K(i)$ is equal to the maximum of all k, we find:

$$K(i) \geq n - \min_x(deg_x).. \qquad \blacksquare$$

Using this expression, minor calculations will allow to find a β_0^* for which the corresponding $K(i)$ is $\geq \alpha$. This β_0^* is our prediction for β_0.

Starting from these results, the following approach is suggested for a Boolean analysis with a predetermined α:

- ordering of the frequencies (possible β-values).
- computation of β^*, the lowest β for which $\#R^0 \geq 2^{n-\alpha}$ holds.
- following to this step β_0^* is determined: the lowest $\beta \geq \beta^*$ for which $\min_x(deg_x) = n\text{-}\alpha$.
- from then on the computation of PCU's is started from the highest possible β-value down to and including β_0^*.

Theoretically it is possible that no β_0 exists: in our example this would have been the case if e.g. all frequencies ≥ 0 would have been equal. In practice, however, this will be very rare: mostly, the highest frequencies are unique, so, for high β-values, "short" *PCU*'s are likely to be found. The present approach has resulted in a significant gain in processing speed of as much as 75% with our recently developed computer software (Theuns, 1989).

4. Conclusion

The determination of "the optimal" threshold in Boolean analysis remains one of the central problems to the method. The choice of it depending on the goals of the researcher. However, practical work of ours confirms findings of Van Buggenhaut (1987) which suggest a maximal *PCU*-length of 2 or 3 to suit most when coming to an interpretation and a schematic representation (implication graph) of the results. For this reason a researcher will have to choose a maximal *PCU*-length (α) to be tolerated. Consequently he will have to dichotomize the response patterns in a part to be ignored and another to be retained. The goal of the researcher will be to minimize the number of persons ignored due to the dichotomization.

A possible method (for other methods see e.g. Van Buggenhaut and Degreef (1987, p.447)) to determine a dichotomization threshold which responds to this goal is based on the frequencies associated with the response patterns. So, a pattern will be considered "ignored" if its frequency does not exceed a certain threshold β. The goal of the researcher then becomes to find the **lowest possible** β, for which the corresponding *PCU*-lengths do not exceed α. Our findings suggest that former approaches to this will not necessarily lead to the lowest possible β.

A possible, but rather inefficient approach, would be to compute all *PCU*'s for all possible β-values and then choose the lowest β for which $K(i) \leq \alpha$.

Our findings supply a method which allows to reduce the number of β-values to process importantly. Firstly: β for which $\#R^0 \leq 2^{n-\alpha}$ are not to be processed, the reason for this being clear. Secondly: using the expression $K(i) \geq n - \min_{x}(deg_x)$ allows to predict, with minor calculations, the length of the longest *PCU* for any β. Consequently, β-values for which the $K(i)$ is predicted to exceed α are not to be processed either.

The decrease in the number of β to process allows an important gain in processing speed. For our recently developed computer software, the processing time can be reduced to a quarter of the time needed for an all-β-processing.

References

Berge, C. (1973). *Graphes et Hypergraphes*. Paris, Dunod.

Chartrand, G. (1977). *Graphs as Mathematical Models*. Boston, Prindle, Weber & Schmidt, Inc.

Flament, C. (1976). *L'analyse booléenne de questionnaire*. Paris, Mouton.

Lawler, E.L. (1966). Covering problems: duality relations and a new method of solution. *SIAM, Journal on Applied Mathematics*, Vol. 14, *5*, 1115 - 1132.

Roy, B. (1970). *Algèbre moderne et Théorie des graphes*, II. Paris, Dunod.

Theuns, P. (1989). *ISOBAN: Geïntegreerde Software voor Booleaanse analyse*. Center for Manpower Planning, Vrije Universiteit Brussel.

Van Buggenhaut, J. (1987). Questionnaires booléens: schémas d'implications et degrés de cohesion. *Mathématiques et Sciences Humaines*, *98*, 9 - 20.

Van Buggenhaut, J. and Degreef, E. (1987). On dichotomization methods in boolean analysis of questionnaires. In: Roskam, E.E. and Suck, R. (eds.), *Progress in Mathematical Psychology - 1*. North-Holland: Elsevier Science Publishers, 447 - 453.

van Lint, J. H. (1971). *Coding theory*, Springer-Verlag, Berlin.

An Impossibility Theorem for Fair Bidimensional Representation: Towards a Biproportional Solution[1].

Marjorie B. Gassner[2]

Université Libre de Bruxelles

Abstract

This paper concerns fair (proportional) representation of a population which is divided into categories according to **two** criteria as is the case, for example, when an electoral system takes into account the geographical as well as the political group of the elector. Our first model leads us to the conclusion that, on the one hand, there can be no fair representation - under our very weak conditions - as soon there are more than two constituencies or more than two parties, but on the other hand, a two by two situation can always be fairly represented. As these results are mainly negative, we go on to a second model and we give a necessary and sufficient condition for the existence of a **biproportional delegation**.

1. Introduction

It has now become classical, in mathematical voting and representation theory to seek normative or even ethical conditions for social and political processes. In this spirit, the concrete problem of a Dutch election led us to conceive equity conditions in the search for a two-dimensional fair representation.

When a population, classified according to a given criterion (such as belonging to a region, to a political party,....), is to elect delegates in order to form an assembly, the question of the fairness of the representation arises; the fundamental barrier is that the ideal apportionment, from the point of view of fairness, should be proportional (in the mathematical sense)

---

[1]Several conversations with G. De Meur, X. Hubaut and Ph. Vincke stimulated a revision of a first draft of this paper, including shortcuts in the proof of our possibility theorem.

[2]U.L.B., Faculté des Sciences Sociales, Politiques et Economiques, C.P.135, Av. F.D. Roosevelt, 50, B-1050 Brussels, Belgium.

to the respective populations of the classes, which is generally impossible to achieve in integers.

If many elections take into account a division of the population based upon one criterion only (geographical, for example), some others are based upon several criteria simultaneously (for example geographical and partisan). In the latter case, the same problem of fairness arises for each of the criteria taken separately; but an extra difficulty is created by the interference of the criteria with each other; a kind of "multi-dimensional" balance must be found.

Political scientists and mathematicians have broadly examined the one-dimensional problem (a complete survey of the subject can be found in Balinski and Young, 1982), but the only formalized study of a multi-criteria electoral system that we encountered, is one of a regional election in the Netherlands (Anthonisse, 1984). In this study, the electors of a region are ranked according to two criteria: the commune in which they vote and the political party of their choice. Among the communal councilors of a region, a delegation must be chosen which will form the regional council. This must be done while respecting as accurately as possible the political and geographical (parties, communes) distribution of the communal mandatories. The method described by Anthonisse, while respecting legal texts, cannot avoid certain impossibilities and, furthermore, is contrary to some aspects of fairness which seem fundamental to us (De Meur, Gassner, Hubaut, 1984 and 1985).

In § 2, we set ourselves in an institutional frame derived from real-life situations i.e. the total number of delegates will be predetermined, as will their distribution according to one of the two criteria; these numbers are not arbitrarily chosen, as they must obey some conditions. We chose, among the different fairness aspirations one could reasonably have, some conditions which we judged "minimal" in order to meet those demands. Even though these requirements were quite modest, we had to prove that it is impossible to satisfy the constraints when one of the two criteria offers more than two modalities. In § 3 however, we prove the existence of a fair representation, as we define it, when each of the dimensions offers two options only.

We judged that the latter results were not satisfactory, at least as far as democracy was concerned, on the one hand because of the unrealistic size of the only possible case (very few real-life election situations, for example, are limited to two constituencies and two political parties!); on the other hand, even when a "fair" delegation does exist, the total numbers of delegates per party can be forced very far away from those obtained by dealing out the total number of seats available to the parties proportionally to their scores by a one-dimensional rule of apportionment (Hamilton's or d'Hondt's method, for example); in § 4, following these remarks, we considered it most important that the total number of seats available should be allotted to constituencies and to parties proportionally to their respective strengths (i.e. by a classical one-dimensional rule of apportionment); we show that an integer delegation which sums up to these a priori determined fixed numbers and is "near" global proportionality does not necessarily exist and we give a necessary and sufficient condition for the existence of a biproportional delegation i.e. one which is "near" the classical econometric RAS biproportional solution.

2. An Impossibility Theorem

The distribution into classes of a population ranked by two criteria can be described by a matrix (c_{ij}) of non-negative integers where element c_{ij} is the number of individuals associated with option i of the first criterion and option j of the second. Examining real-life cases of two-dimensional settings (see Anthonisse, 1984, for example) convinced us of the interest to make a distinction between the two dimensions, and not to award them systematically identical properties.

In this manner, we retain the possibility of imposing "institutional" constraints on one of the criteria and purely logical ones on the other: for example, the size of the global representation of a constituency (first criterion) can be predetermined by an electoral law, while the size of the global representation of a party (second criterion) is a consequence of the considered political and geographical setting. In the same way, the ordinal structure induced by the initial sizes of the populations will be respected differently for the two dimensions. More precisely, we formalize the problem as follows:

from a given n by m matrix (c_{ij}) of non-negative integers, one must derive a matrix (r_{ij}) of non-negative integers of same dimensions, the row sums of which are predetermined (rows being associated with the first criterion, columns with the second). These given values and the unknown elements of (r_{ij}) must obey the following constraints of fairness:

Condition 1 (C_1)

$\forall$ i, $0 < r_{i.} < c_{i.}$ except if $c_{i.} = 1$ in which case $r_{i.} = 0$ or 1. (i)

$$\forall i,j: \begin{cases} c_{i.} < c_{j.} \Rightarrow r_{i.} \le r_{j.} \text{ and } r_{j.} - r_{i.} \le c_{j.} - c_{i.} \\ c_{i.} = c_{j.} \Rightarrow |r_{i.} - r_{j.}| \le 1 \end{cases} \quad \text{(ii)}$$

Condition 2 (C_2)

$\forall$ i,j : $0 \le r_{ij} \le c_{ij}$

$$\forall i,j,k: \begin{cases} c_{ij} < c_{ik} \Rightarrow r_{ij} \le r_{ik} \text{ and } r_{ik} - r_{ij} \le c_{ik} - c_{ij} \\ c_{ij} = c_{ik} \Rightarrow |r_{ij} - r_{ik}| \le 1 \end{cases} \quad \text{(iii)}$$

Condition 3 (C_3)

$$\forall i,j: \begin{cases} c_{.i} < c_{.j} \Rightarrow r_{.i} \le r_{.j} \text{ and } r_{.j} - r_{.i} \le c_{.j} - c_{.i} \\ c_{.i} = c_{.j} \Rightarrow |r_{.i} - r_{.j}| \le 1 \end{cases}$$

Commentary concerning the formalization

a) C_1, which restricts the number of allowed given values for the communes' delegations, increases the possibility of its existence as opposed to C_2 and C_3, which tend to reduce it.

b) Generally, one wishes a "true" delegation, meaning non zero and lower than the initial size for each option of the first criterion (i). The non zero condition justifies itself by avoiding immediate impossibilities, even in the simple case of 2 by 2 matrices:

$$\text{If } (c_{ij}) = \begin{pmatrix} 0 & 2 \\ 4 & 3 \end{pmatrix} \begin{matrix} 2 \\ 7 \end{matrix} \qquad \text{then } (r_{ij}) = \begin{pmatrix} a \le b \\ c \ge d \end{pmatrix} \begin{matrix} 0 \\ 1 \end{matrix}$$
$$\begin{matrix} 4 & 5 & 9 \end{matrix} \qquad\qquad\qquad \begin{matrix} a+c \le b+d & 1 \end{matrix}$$

which is clearly impossible to obtain.

On the other hand, the exception to this rule, in the elementary case where the initial size is 1, allows to prevent an immediate cul-de-sac.

c) One will see to it that the order induced by the marginal comparisons between $c_{i.}$ and $c_{j.}$ not be reversed in the delegation and that the increase of the initial difference between these two numbers is severely restricted: for a positive initial difference, no increase will be allowed; an initial zero difference will be allowed to reach one (ii).

d) The same kind of concern appears in the conditions involving elements r_{ij}; nevertheless, the little sense contained in comparing any two elements of the matrix, and the institutional character of the first criterion, made us limit internal comparisons to elements within a same *row* (iii).

We call **fair representation rule,** a rule which associates any matrix (c_{ij}) of $\mathbb{N}^{n\times m}$ and any n-uple $\bar{r} = (r_{1.}, r_{2.}, \dots, r_{n.})$ of $\mathbb{N}^n$ which obeys C1, with a matrix (r_{ij}) of $\mathbb{N}^{n\times m}$ such that, for each i, $r_{i.} = \sum_{j=1}^{m} r_{ij}$ and which obeys C2 and C3.

THEOREM 1: *if n or m is larger than 2, no such rule exists.*

Proof:

It is sufficient to exhibit two counter examples: one (a) of $\mathbb{N}^{3\times 2}$ and the other (b) of $\mathbb{N}^{2\times 3}$.

(a) Let $(c_{ij}) = \begin{pmatrix} 4 & 1 \\ 2 & 3 \\ 2 & 3 \end{pmatrix}$ and $\bar{r} = (1,1,1)$ which obeys C1.

To obey C2, (r_{ij}) must be $\begin{pmatrix} 1 & 0 \\ 0 & 1 \\ 0 & 1 \end{pmatrix}$, which does not respect C3.

(b) Let $(c_{ij}) = \begin{pmatrix} 3 & 4 & 1 \\ 3 & 1 & 4 \end{pmatrix}$ and $\bar{r} = (1,1)$ which obeys C1.

To obey C2, (r_{ij}) must be $\begin{pmatrix} 0 & 1 & 0 \\ 0 & 0 & 1 \end{pmatrix}$, which does not respect C3.

3. A Possibility Theorem for the Smallest Case

THEOREM 2: *If m=n=2, at least one fair representation rule exists*

Proof:

For any given matrix $(c_{ij}) = \begin{pmatrix} A & B \\ C & D \end{pmatrix}$ of $\mathbb{N}^{2x2}$ and any two non-negative integers k_1, k_2 obeying C1, we build a matrix (r_{ij}) of $\mathbb{N}^{2x2}$, the row sums of which equal respectively k_1 and k_2 and which respects C2 and C3.

(r_{ij}) can thus be written as $\begin{pmatrix} a & k_1 - a \\ k_2 - d & d \end{pmatrix}$

Without loss of generality, we suppose

$$A + C \geq B + D \quad \text{and} \quad A \geq B$$

We thus have to examine four cases:

1) $A > B$ and $C < D$
2) $A > B$ and $C > D$
3) $A > B$ and $C = D$ (identical to $A = B$ and $C > D$)
4) $A = B$ and $C = D$

CASE 1

$A > B$ and $C < D$ [1]

First step

$A + C > B + D$ [2]

Condition C2 imposes the following bounds for a and d:

$$\alpha = \max\left\{\frac{k_1}{2}, k_1 - B\right\} \leq a \leq \beta = \min\left\{k_1, \frac{(k_1 + A - B)}{2}\right\} \qquad [3]$$

$$\gamma = \max\left\{\frac{k_2}{2}, k_2 - C\right\} \leq d \leq \delta = \min\left\{k_2, \frac{(k_2 + D - C)}{2}\right\} \qquad [4]$$

Condition C3 implies

$$d - a \leq \frac{k_2 - k_1}{2} \qquad [5]$$

and

$$d - a \geq \frac{k_2 - k_1 - (A + C) + (B + D)}{2} \qquad [6]$$

In this case, we thus have to prove the existence of two non-negative integers a and d which obey [3], [4], [5] and [6].

Each of the intervals $[\alpha,\beta]$ and $[\gamma,\delta]$ obviously contains at least one non-negative integer. Let us use a geometrical representation in a real plane coordinated by axes a and d.

In this way, rectangle $\mathcal{R} = \{ (a,d) : \alpha \le a \le \beta \text{ and } \gamma \le d \le \delta \}$ contains at least one point with non-negative integer coordinates. [7]

[5] and [6] determine two half-planes:

$$\mathcal{Z}_1 \equiv d - a \le \frac{k_2 - k_1}{2}$$

and

$$\mathcal{Z}_2 \equiv d - a \ge \frac{k_2 - k_1 - (A + C) + (B + D)}{2}$$

Their intersection $\mathcal{S} = \mathcal{Z}_1 \cap \mathcal{Z}_2$ is a strip parallel to the bisectrix of axes a and d; the width of $\mathcal{S}$ is at least $\frac{1}{2}$. [8]

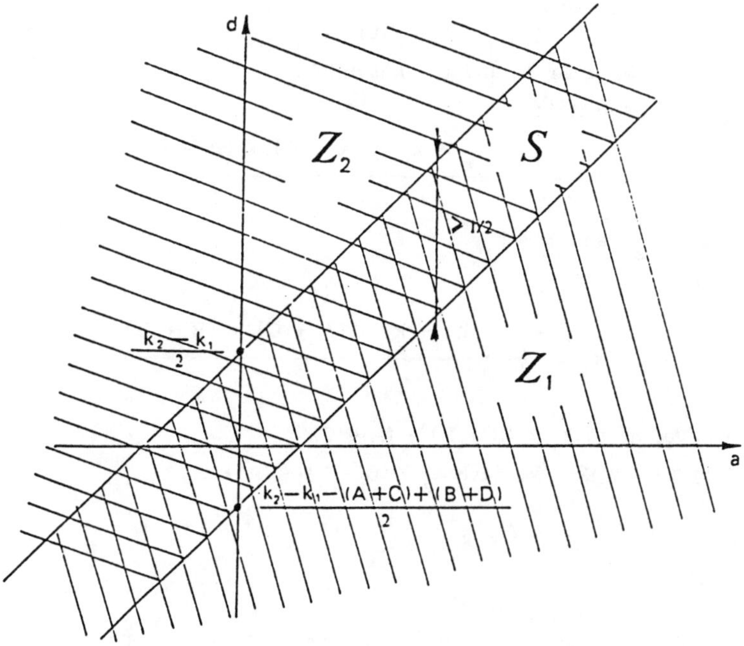

FIGURE 1

It is thus sufficient to prove the existence, in $\mathcal{R} \cap \mathcal{S}$, of at least one point with non-negative integer coordinates.

Lemma 1: *$\mathcal{R} \cap \mathcal{S}$ is non-empty.*

Proof:

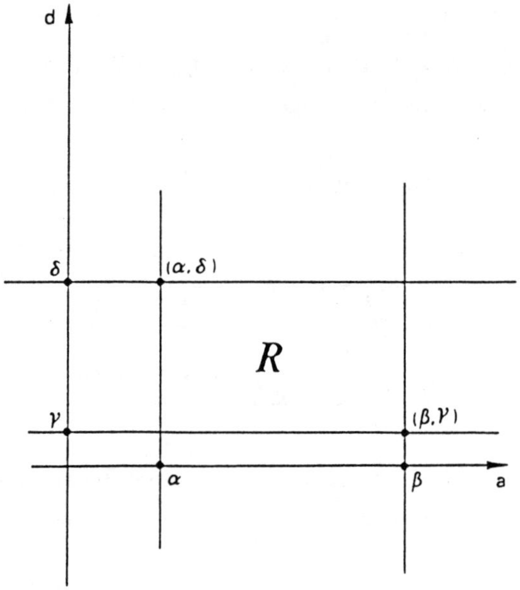

FIGURE 2

We prove that (α,δ) is in $\mathcal{Z}_2$ and (β,γ) is in $\mathcal{Z}_1$.
$(\alpha,\delta) \in \mathcal{Z}_2$ is equivalent to

$$\delta \geq \alpha + \frac{k_2 - k_1 - (A + C) + (B + D)}{2}$$

1) Suppose $\alpha = \frac{k_1}{2}$ and $\delta = k_2$
We must prove

$$k_2 \geq \frac{k_1}{2} + \frac{k_2 - k_1 - (A + C) + (B + D)}{2}$$

which is equivalent to $k_2 \geq (B + D) - (A + C)$.
As $k_2 \geq 0$ by C1, by [2], we have $k_2 > (B + D) - (A + C)$.

2) Suppose $\alpha = k_1 - B$ and $\delta = k_2$
We must prove

$$k_2 \geq k_1 - B + \frac{k_2 - k_1 - (A + C) + (B + D)}{2}$$

which is equivalent to $k_1 - k_2 \leq A + C + B - D$.

If $k_2 \geq k_1$, this is obviously true by [2].
If $k_2 < k_1$, two cases arise:

(i) $A + B > C + D$; then, by C1, we have:

$$k_1 - k_2 \leq (A + B) - (C + D) \leq A + C + B - D$$

(ii) $A + B = C + D$; then, by C1, we have $k_1 = k_2 + 1$ and we must prove $k_1 - k_2 \leq A + C + B - D$ which is equivalent to $1 \leq 2C$; this is true unless $C = 0$; however, in that case, $A + B = D$ and, by [2], $A > B + D$, a contradiction.

3) Suppose $\alpha = \frac{k_1}{2}$ and $\delta = \frac{(k_2 + D - C)}{2}$

We must prove

$$\frac{k_2 + D - C}{2} \geq \frac{k_1}{2} + \frac{k_2 - k_1 - (A + C) + (B + D)}{2}$$

which is equivalent to $0 \geq B - A$, obvious by [1].

4) Suppose $\alpha = k_1 - B$ and $\delta = \frac{(k_2 + D - C)}{2}$

We must prove

$$\frac{k_2 + D - C}{2} \geq k_1 - B + \frac{k_2 - k_1 - (A + C) + (B + D)}{2}$$

which is equivalent to $k_1 \leq A + B$; by C1, in this case, $k_1 < A + B$ as [1] and [2] do not allow $A + B = 1$.

Using the same arguments, (β,γ) is in $\mathcal{Z}_1$. □

In the four cases considered hereabove, it should be noted that (α,δ) is in fact in $\mathring{\mathcal{Z}}_2$ (interior of $\mathcal{Z}_2$) (resp. (β,γ) is in $\mathring{\mathcal{Z}}_1$) except eventually if $\alpha = k_1 - B$ and $\delta = k_2$ (resp. $\gamma = k_1$ and $\beta = k_2 - C$); however, in that case, (α,δ) (resp. (β,γ)) is in $\mathbb{N}^2$ and is thus a solution of the problem.

Let us note that all intersection points of the borders of $\mathcal{R}$ and $\mathcal{S}$ have integer or half-integer coordinates. [9]

If $\mathcal{R}$ is not degenerated (i.e. $\alpha \neq \beta$ and $\gamma \neq \delta$ or, equivalently, neither B nor C is zero), in general, by [8], [9] and lemma 1, $\mathcal{S} \cap \mathcal{R}$ contains one of the following configurations

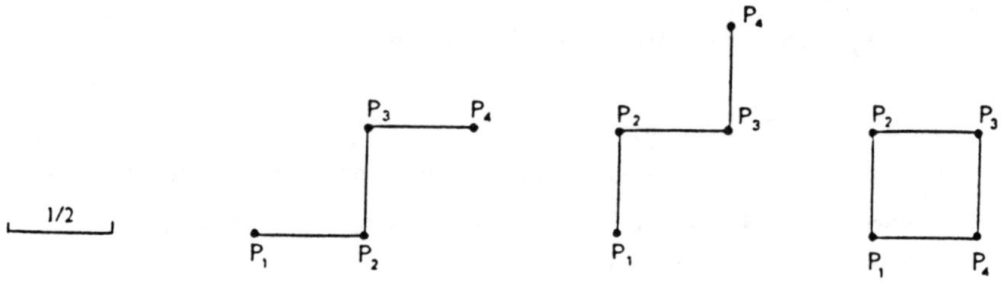

FIGURE 3

With P_1's (and thus all P_i's) coordinates being non-negative integers or half-integers.

Obviously, one of the P_i's has non-negative integer coordinates. The only exception is when $\mathcal{S} \cap \mathcal{R}$ is a right isosceles triangle, the edges of the right angle measuring $\frac{1}{2}$.

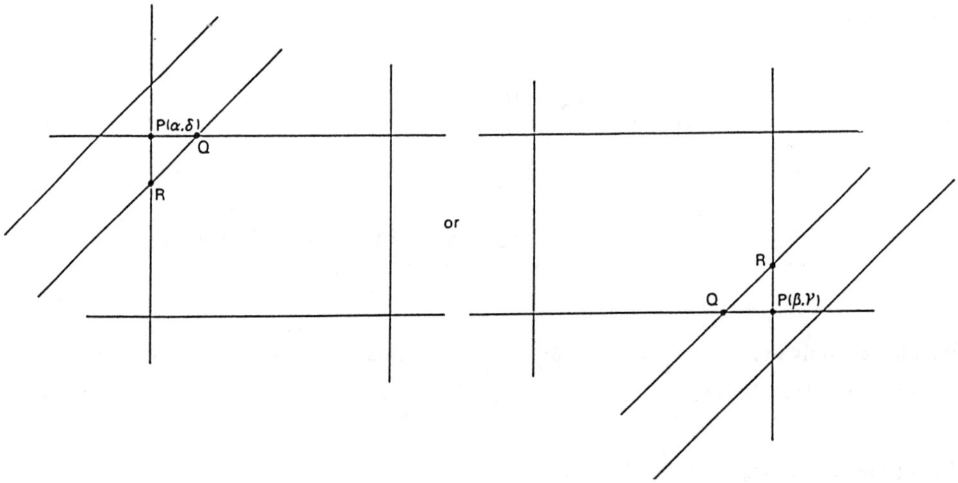

FIGURE 4

Euclidean distance $d(P,Q) = d(P,R) = \frac{1}{2}$

The only case to be examined is that where P's coordinates are both half-integer, as otherwise one of points P, Q, R is a solution. If α and δ (resp. β and γ) were both half-integer, then α would be $\frac{k_1}{2}$ and δ would be $\frac{(k_2 + D - C)}{2}$ (resp. β would be $\frac{(k_1 + A - B)}{2}$ and γ would be $\frac{k_2}{2}$).
Let us compute R's coordinates by two different ways:

on the one hand, as a point at distance $\frac{1}{2}$ from P, R's coordinates are $\left(\frac{k_1}{2}, \frac{(k_2 + D - C - 1)}{2}\right)$ (resp. $\left(\frac{(k_1 + A - B)}{2}, \frac{(k_2 + 1)}{2}\right)$);
on the other hand, as an intersection of the borders of $\mathcal{S}$ and $\mathcal{R}$, R's coordinates are

$$\left(\frac{k_1}{2}, \frac{(k_2 - (A + C) + (B + D))}{2}\right) \text{ (resp. } \left(\frac{(k_1 + A - B)}{2}, \frac{(k_2 + A - B)}{2}\right)\text{)}$$

This implies $\frac{(A - B)}{2} = \frac{1}{2}$ or $A = B + 1$, a contradiction by [1] and [2].

To end the proof of this first step, we must examine the cases in which $\mathcal{R}$ is degenerated:

1°) $B = C = 0$

In this case, $\mathcal{R}$ becomes $\{ (k_1,k_2) \}$ which is, by lemma 1, the unique solution.

2°) $B = 0 \neq C$

In this case, $\alpha = \beta = k_1$

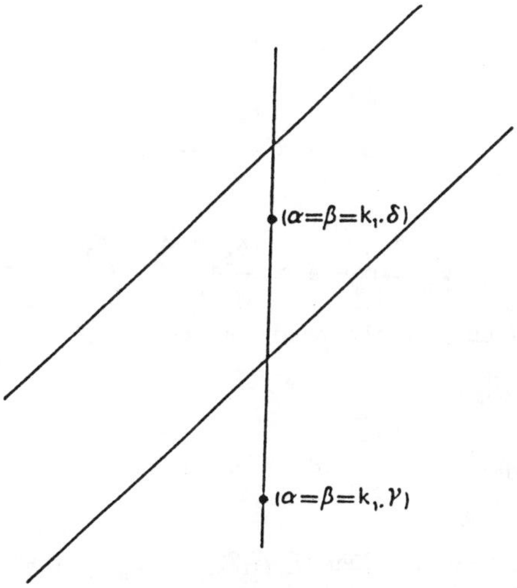

FIGURE 5

Lemma 1 shows that (k_1,γ) is in $\mathring{\mathcal{Z}}_1$ and (k_1,δ) is in $\mathring{\mathcal{Z}}_2$. It is thus obvious that $\mathcal{R} \cap \mathcal{S}$ contains a point with integer coordinates.

3°) $B \neq 0 = C$

Same argumentation as in 2°).

Second step

$$A + C = B + D \qquad [2']$$

[3] and [4] again give bounds for a and d.

C3 and [2'] imply that one of the following must hold:

$$d - a - \frac{k_2 - k_1}{2} = 0 \text{ or } \frac{1}{2} \text{ or } -\frac{1}{2}$$

$$\text{Let } D_1 \equiv d = a + \frac{(k_2 - k_1)}{2},\ D_2 \equiv d = a + \frac{(k_2 - k_1 + 1)}{2}$$
$$\text{and } D_3 \equiv d = a + \frac{(k_2 - k_1 - 1)}{2}$$

It is sufficient, in this case, to prove, rectangle $\mathcal{R}$ having been defined in the first step, the existence of at least one point with non-negative coordinates in $\mathcal{R} \cap (D_1 \cup D_2 \cup D_3)$.

Lemma 2: *$\mathcal{R} \cap D_1$ is non-empty*

Proof:

Let

$$\mathcal{Z}_4 \equiv d - a \leq \frac{(k_2 - k_1)}{2} + \frac{1}{2}$$

and

$$\mathcal{Z}_5 \equiv d - a \geq \frac{(k_2 - k_1)}{2} - \frac{1}{2}$$

By the same arguments used in the proof of lemma 1, we can prove that (α,δ) is in $\mathring{\mathcal{Z}}_5$ and (β,γ) is in $\mathring{\mathcal{Z}}_4$. □

If $\mathcal{R}$ is not degenerated:

(i) $D_1 \cap \mathcal{R}$ is not a singleton, then $D_2 \cap \mathcal{R}$ and $D_3 \cap \mathcal{R}$ are non-empty and

$\mathcal{R} \cap (D_1 \cup D_2 \cup D_3)$ thus obviously contains a solution.

(ii) $D_1 \cap \mathcal{R}$ is a singleton $\{ P(\alpha,\delta) \}$ (or $\{ P(\beta,\gamma) \}$), let us prove that it is impossible for both of P's coordinates to be half-integer.

Indeed, if this was the case, α would be $\frac{k_1}{2}$ and δ would be $\frac{(k_2 + D - C)}{2}$ (resp. β would be $\frac{(k_1 + A - B)}{2}$ and γ would be $\frac{k_2}{2}$) with $\frac{(k_2 + D - C)}{2} = \frac{k_1}{2} + \frac{(k_2 - k_1)}{2}$ which implies D = C (resp. with $\frac{k_2}{2} = \frac{(k_1 + A - B)}{2} + \frac{(k_2 - k_1)}{2}$ which implies A = B), a contradiction by [1].

If $\mathcal{R}$ is degenerated, the same arguments as in the first step hold.

CASE 2

A > B and C > D which implies A + C > B + D

Condition C2 implies, in this case:

$$\alpha = \max\left\{\frac{k_1}{2}, k_1 - B\right\} \le a \le \beta = \min\left\{k_1, \frac{(k_1 + A - B)}{2}\right\} \quad [3']$$

$$\gamma = \max\left\{\frac{(k_2 + D - C)}{2}, 0\right\} \le d \le \delta = \min\left\{\frac{k_2}{2}, D\right\} \quad [4']$$

Condition C3 is obviously, in this case, a consequence of [3'] and [4'], and it is thus sufficient to notice that there is at least one point with non-negative integer coordinates in $\mathcal{R}$ as defined in case 1.

CASE 3

A > B and C = D (and thus A + C > B + D)

Condition C2 implies, in this case:

$$\alpha = \max\left\{\frac{k_1}{2}, k_1 - B\right\} \le a \le \beta = \min\left\{k_1, \frac{(k_1 + A - B)}{2}\right\}$$

and

$$d = \frac{k_2}{2}\ (k_2\ \text{even})\ \text{or}\ d = \frac{(k_2 - 1)}{2}\ \text{or}\ \frac{(k_2 + 1)}{2}\ (k_2\ \text{odd})$$

Condition C3 is again a consequence of the latter and it is thus sufficient to notice that $[\alpha,\beta]$ contains at least one non-negative integer.

CASE 4

A = B and C = D (and thus A + C = B + D)

Condition C2 implies, in this case:

$$a = \frac{k_1}{2}\ (k_1\ \text{even})\ \text{or}\ a = \frac{(k_1 - 1)}{2}\ \text{or}\ \frac{(k_1 + 1)}{2}\ (k_1\ \text{odd})$$

and

$$d = \frac{k_2}{2}\ (k_2\ \text{even})\ \text{or}\ d = \frac{(k_2 - 1)}{2}\ \text{or}\ \frac{(k_2 + 1)}{2}\ (k_2\ \text{odd})$$

Condition C3 implies:

$$d - a - \frac{k_2 - k_1}{2} = 0\ \text{or}\ \frac{1}{2}\ \text{or}\ -\frac{1}{2}$$

Whether k_1 and k_2 are even or odd, it is obvious that a and d can be chosen in a way which satisfies C2 and C3 simultaneously. □

4. Towards a Biproportional Solution

The latter results are not satisfactory, at least as far as democracy is concerned, on the one hand, and mainly, because of the unrealistic size of the only possible case: indeed, very few real-life election situations are limited to two constituencies and two political parties; on the other hand, even when a "fair" delegation does exist, the total numbers of delegates per party can be forced very far away from those obtained by dealing out the total number of seats available proportionally to the parties' scores by a one-dimensional rule of apportionment[3].

The main feature in this type of representation problem is the necessity to take into account both dimensions simultaneously. Obviously, priorities must be set: on which parts of the delegation is it most important to set fairness constraints (knowing that it is impossible to demand too much), and what conditions should be chosen ? The answer is not, in our opinion, strait

---

[3]Hamilton's or d'Hondt's method, for example.

forward. Different problems trigger different priorities. However, most existing electoral systems of the type described[4] need the a priori determination of the numbers of delegates due to each constituency. This is achieved by dealing out a fixed number of seats to constituencies "proportionally" to their numbers of voters[5] using a classical rule of apportionment; secondly, "proportionality" should also hold globally between political parties with respect to the amount of votes they received (otherwise, why not simply consider each constituency separately, dividing the two-dimensional problem into several one-dimensional ones).

Following the latter remarks concerning existing systems, we found it was appropriate to award the seats to constituencies and to parties proportionally to their respective magnitudes by some one-dimensional rule of apportionment. The problem remaining is thus to find an integer delegation which sums up to these predetermined total margins. Recalling results of § 2 and § 3, one can obviously set up examples of situations for which no such delegation can respect condition C2; a natural question is then whether there always exists such a delegation, each element of which is an integer adjacent to the exact proportion of seats the corresponding number of votes is worth[6] (a sort of "global" proportionality). Unfortunately, the answer is "no". Indeed, consider the following matrix of vote results, each row representing a constituency, each column a political party. Suppose 16 seats are to be dealt out.

$$\begin{pmatrix} 3960 & 750 \\ 1960 & 800 \\ 1950 & 700 \\ 940 & 1700 \\ 1610 & 10 \\ 1610 & 10 \end{pmatrix} \begin{matrix} 4710 \\ 2760 \\ 2650 \\ 2640 \\ 1620 \\ 1620 \end{matrix}$$

$$\begin{matrix} 12030 & 3970 & 16000 \end{matrix}$$

Global exact proportionality yields:

---

[4]Such as those used for parliamentary elections in Belgium (Gassner, 1987) or for some regional elections in the Netherlands (Anthonisse, 1984).

[5]Or their populations.

[6]This means quantity $\frac{v_{ij} \cdot S}{\sum\sum v_{ij}}$ if v_{ij} is the number of votes for party j in constituency i and S is the total number of seats available.

$$\begin{pmatrix} 3.96 & 0.75 \\ 1.96 & 0.80 \\ 1.95 & 0.70 \\ 0.94 & 1.70 \\ 1.61 & 0.01 \\ 1.61 & 0.01 \end{pmatrix} \begin{matrix} 4.71 \\ 2.76 \\ 2.65 \\ 2.64 \\ 1.62 \\ 1.62 \end{matrix}$$

$$\begin{matrix} 2.03 & 3.97 & 16 \end{matrix}$$

Rounding row sums by either Hamilton's or d'Hondt's rule of apportionment yields (5, 3, 3, 3, 1, 1). As the rounded values of the first column must add up to a minimum of twelve, obviously at least one of the two last rows must be rounded up, making it impossible to obtain the imposed row marginal sums. This example thus shows that if one wishes to stay "near" exact proportions, it may be impossible for the rounded values to sum up marginally to predetermined numbers of delegates. As this is of major importance in many electoral systems we are concerned with here, we tried to find an alternative solution.
It can be easily shown that there exist integer matrices which add up to given integer row and column sums (as long as the sum of the row sums equals that of the column sums). If we impose, for example, that row sums be (5, 3, 3, 3, 1, 1) and the column sums be 12 and 4, we have, for example:

$$\begin{pmatrix} 5 & 0 \\ 3 & 0 \\ 2 & 1 \\ 0 & 3 \\ 1 & 0 \\ 1 & 0 \end{pmatrix} \begin{matrix} 5 \\ 3 \\ 3 \\ 3 \\ 1 \\ 1 \end{matrix}$$

$$\begin{matrix} 12 & 4 & 16 \end{matrix}$$

However, we must somehow include the notion of proportionality between the initial matrix of votes and an acceptable delegation matrix.

The latter sort of problem will undoubtedly remind economists of the well-known econometric "RAS" model designed to estimate the behavior of input-output relations through time: an initial matrix is known, and one must derive from it another matrix, the marginal sums of which are given.
Bacharach (1970) precised what he calls the **biproportional constrained matrix problem** as follows: given A, a non-negative m×n matrix and

$$\begin{cases} l = (l_1, l_2, \ldots, l_m) > 0 \\ c = (c_1, c_2, \ldots, c_n) > 0 \end{cases}$$

find $B = (b_{ij})$, a non-negative m×n matrix with

$$\sum_i b_{ij} = c_j \quad \forall\ j \in \{1,\ldots,n\}$$

$$\sum_j b_{ij} = l_i \quad \forall\ i \in \{1,\ldots,m\}$$

and $B = \lim \langle R^t\rangle\, A\, \langle S^t\rangle$ for some sequences $\{R^t\}$, $\{S^t\}$ of vectors, $R^t_1 = 1\ \forall\ t$ ($\langle M\rangle$ is a diagonal matrix).

He proved the problem has a unique solution if and only if:

$$a_{ij} = 0 \quad \forall\ i \in I',\ \forall\ j \in J \ \Rightarrow \begin{cases} \sum_{i\in I'} l_i \le \sum_{j\in J'} c_j \\ \sum_{j\in J} c_j \le \sum_{i\in I} l_i \end{cases}$$

where I and J are respectively subsets of $\{1,\ldots,m\}$ and $\{1,\ldots,n\}$, I' is $\{1,\ldots,m\} \setminus I$ and J' is $\{1,\ldots,n\} \setminus J$.

This **possibility condition** prevents the following immediate impossibility due to the eventual presence of zeros in the initial matrix. Indeed, obviously $a_{ij} = 0 \Rightarrow b_{ij} = 0$ so, if A is of the following form:

$$\begin{array}{c} \\ I' \\ I \end{array} \begin{pmatrix} J' & J \\ A_{I'J'} & 0 \\ \hline A_{IJ'} & A_{IJ} \end{pmatrix}$$

then B must be such that block $B_{I'J}$ contains only zeros; thus

$$B = \begin{array}{c} \\ I' \\ I \end{array} \begin{pmatrix} J' & J \\ B_{I'J'} & 0 \\ \hline B_{IJ'} & B_{IJ} \end{pmatrix} \begin{array}{l} \\ \} \sum_{i\in I'} l_i \\ \} \sum_{i\in I} l_i \end{array}$$

$$\qquad \underbrace{\qquad}_{\sum_{j\in J'} c_j} \qquad \underbrace{\qquad}_{\sum_{j\in J} c_j}$$

the possibility condition prevents the total sum of the elements of block

$B_{I'J'}$(resp. B_{IJ}) from exceeding that of those of block $B_{(I\cup I')J'}$ (resp.$B_{I(J\cup J')}$), an immediate impossibility.

Bacharach also describes a "natural" algorithm yielding the solution i.e.

$$A^{o} = A$$

$$A^{2t+1} = \langle R^{t+1}\rangle\, A^{2t}$$

$$A^{2t+2} = \langle R^{t+1}\rangle\, A^{2t}\, \langle S^{t+1}\rangle$$

$$\text{where } R_i^{t+1} = \frac{l_i}{\sum_j a_{ij}^{2t}} \quad \text{and} \quad S_j^{t+1} = \frac{c_j}{\sum_i a_{ij}^{2t+1}} \qquad t = 0,1,..$$

This process is simply the multiplication of each row by a scalar in order for it to add up to its prescribed sum, then the same for each column, and so forth.

It should be noted that the biproportional problem is closely akin to the search for a delegation matrix in a two-dimensional voting setting by the following points:

1)*Non-negativity*:

the initial and solution matrices are non-negative in both problems.

2)*Predetermined margins* :

the marginal row and column sums of the biproportional solution matrix are pre-imposed as are those of the delegation matrix[7]; their strict positivity is not in contradiction: rows or columns required to add up to zero can be discarded.

3)*Biproportionality*:

The type of solution matrix to be found ($B = \lim_{t\to\infty}\langle R^t\rangle A\langle S^t\rangle$),which can be seen as a "double-proportionality" to the initial matrix, is a compromize vis-à-vis strict proportionality. It should be noted, however, that if the imposed

---

[7]By dealing out the total number of seats by a one-dimensional rule of apportionment.

marginal sums **are** proportional (in the strict sense) to those of the initial matrix, then the solution matrix is strictly proportional to the initial one.

Unfortunately, the crucial point in the representation problem, the fact that the delegation matrix is required to be integral, is obviously generally not respected by the biproportional solution; so, once again, can the elements of the solution matrix be rounded to adjacent integers while preserving the imposed marginal sums?

This time, the answer is "yes"; let us call such a rounding a **biproportional delegation**.

THEOREM:

Let $A = (a_{ij})$ be a mxn matrix of votes and S, the total number of seats to be filled.

Let $l = (l_1,\dots,l_m) \in \mathbb{N}^m$ (resp. $c = (c_1,\dots,c_n) \in \mathbb{N}^n$) be the distribution of the S seats among the constituencies (resp. the parties) by a one-dimensional rule of apportionment.

If the possibility condition of the biproportional constrained matrix problem holds for initial matrix A and imposed marginal sums l and c, and if $B = (b_{ij})$ is the corresponding solution, then a **biproportional delegation** *exists for A i.e. a matrix $D = (d_{ij}) \in \mathbb{N}^{mxn}$ such that*

$$d_{ij} = b_{ij} \quad \text{if } b_{ij} \text{ is integer}$$
$$d_{ij} = [b_{ij}] \text{ or } [b_{ij}]+1 \text{ otherwise}$$
$$\text{and} \quad \forall i,\ d_{i.} = l_i,\ \forall j,\ d_{.j} = c_j$$

Proof:

Cox and Ernst (1982) proved the following result:

a **controlled rounding** of a given matrix of real numbers always exists i.e. each entry of the matrix (including marginal sums and grand total) can be rounded to an adjacent integer while preserving the additive structure of the array; furthermore, this existence result remains valid if **zero-restrictedness** is imposed i.e. if integers must be rounded to themselves. An example of the latter is the following:

$$\text{Let } \mathbf{A} = \begin{pmatrix} 2.17 & 3.75 \\ 1.33 & 2.43 \\ 0.75 & 3.01 \end{pmatrix} \begin{matrix} 5.92 \\ 3.76 \\ 3.76 \end{matrix}$$
$$\begin{matrix} 4.25 & 9.19 & \mathbf{13.44} \end{matrix}$$

A controlled rounding of A is, for example:

$$\mathbf{R(A)} = \begin{pmatrix} 2 & 4 \\ 2 & 2 \\ 0 & 4 \end{pmatrix} \begin{matrix} 6 \\ 4 \\ 4 \end{matrix}$$
$$\begin{matrix} 4 & 10 & \mathbf{14} \end{matrix}$$

Using this result, a zero-restricted controlled rounding of the biproportional solution matrix exists; since the marginal sums of the latter are integers, zero-restrictedness ensures that some controlled rounding sums up exactly to the pre-imposed margins. □

We have thus proven the existence of a biproportional delegation matching a priori determined total numbers of delegates per constituency and per political party. Of course, as unicity of a biproportional delegation is not guaranteed, the possibility of finding an eventual **best** solution among the existing controlled roundings of the biproportional solution must be discussed.

One must also examine in which circumstances the possibility condition of Bacharach's theorem is violated when dealing out seats to constituencies and to parties by a one-dimensional rule of apportionment; can this dead-end be avoided by some marginal apportionment rules, and why? If not, what should be done? (for example, should the problem be divided into two or more sub-problems?)

Finally, the priorities awarded to constraints to be set on different aspects of the delegation are not the same in every representation problem; a classification of such problems should thus be attempted in that direction.

References

Anthonisse, J.M. (1984). Evenredige Vertegenwoordiging in het Kader van Gemeenschappelijke Regelingen. Notitie OS-N8401, Centre for Mathematics and Computer Science, Amsterdam.

Bacharach, M. (1970). *Biproportional Matrices and Input-Output Change*. Cambridge University Press.

Balinski, M.L. and Young, H.P. (1982). *Fair Representation Meeting the Ideal of One Man, One Vote*. Yale University Press.

Cox, L.H. and Ernst, L.R. (1982). Controlled Rounding. *INFOR, 20*, 423-432.

De Meur, G., Gassner, M. and Hubaut, X. (1984). The Problem of Representation based upon Two Criteria. In: E. Degreef and J. Van Buggenhaut (Eds.), *Trends in Mathematical Psychology*. North-Holland.

De Meur, G., Gassner, M. and Hubaut, X. (1985), A Mathematical Model for Political Bipolarization. *European Journal of Political Research, 13*, 409-420.

Gassner, M. (1987). Elections Législatives Belges: Défauts connus et moins connus de la Méthode de Répartition des Sièges, to appear.

THRESHOLDS AND INDEPENDENCE IN PROPORTIONAL REPRESENTATION

Xavier HUBAUT[1]

Université Libre de Bruxelles

Abstract
Many papers have been devoted to the study of different methods of apportionment for proportional representation: Hamilton, Adams, Jefferson, Webster, Dean, Hill, Saint-Laguë... In particular Guilbaud (1985), Steinhaus (1964), Balinski and Young (1982), De Meur (1986), De Meur and Hubaut (1986), Petit and Térouanne (1987), and many others.
In this paper we prove that a very well-known property of Hamilton's method, i.e.the stability of the thresholds necessary to get a given number of seats may be extended to another class of methods. More precisely, in the frame of divisor methods, given a fixed number of parties and seats to be apportioned, the minimum and maximum percentages necessary for a party to get a given number of seats is independent of the results of the other parties if and only if the rounding used is a fixed decimal one. Among those methods let us mention Adams', Webster's and Jefferson's.

If there are p parties competing in a ballot, the results of the election may be represented by a point of $\mathbb{R}^p$ with coordinates $(x_1,x_2,\ldots,x_p)$ being the percentages of votes received by the p parties; the sum of the x_i must equal 1, and these points are located in a hyperplane. Moreover, all the x_i are positive and so all the possible results of an election are described by the points lying inside a simplex S of $\mathbb{R}^{p-1}$ (fig.1) Steinhaus (1964).

When n seats are to be distributed, among all the points of S somecorrespond to exact repartitions; let us call them exact points. Those points have coordinates x_i equal to n_i/n with $n_i \in \mathbb{N}$ and $\Sigma_i n_i = n$; in those (simple) cases, party i obviously receives n_i seats and the distribution is done strictly proportionally. In the other cases, one must associate the real

---

1 Département de Mathématique - Université Libre de Bruxelles - C.P.216 - Bd. du Triomphe - 1050 Bruxelles - Belgium.

distribution of percentages of votes (point of S) with an integer apportionment of the number of seats (exact points of S) (fig.2).

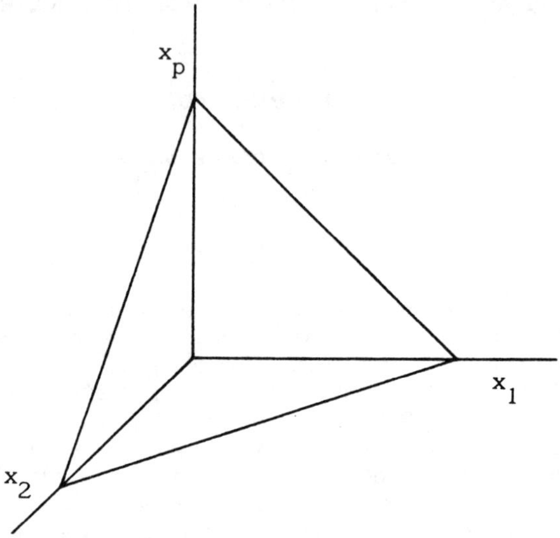

figure 1

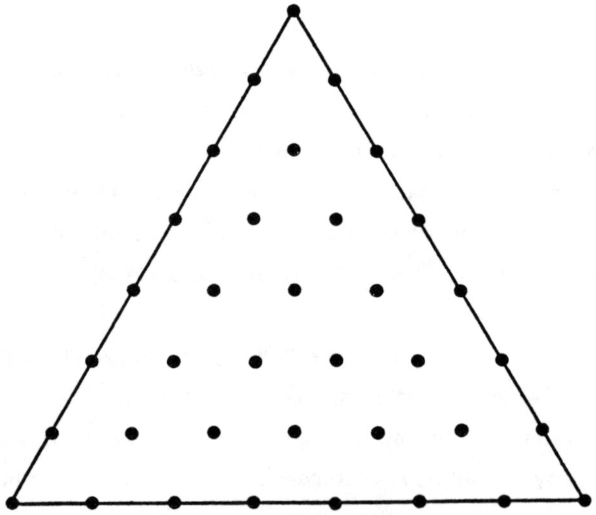

figure 2

Geometrically, to any point of S one must associate a unique exact point which is equivalent to a "reasonable" partition of S (strictly speaking it is not a partition because of the ties) De Meur & Hubaut (1986), De Meur (1986). To obtain this partition various methods are used; let us mention those of greatest remainders (Hamilton), of greatest quotients (Jefferson, D'Hondt), as well as many other methods named after their "discoverer": Webster or Saint-Laguë, Adams, Hill, Dean,...None of these methods is clearly "better" than the others: the choice of a method is very subjective. However people agree to admit some "obvious" conditions that must be fulfilled by a "reasonable" method; the most natural of them imply that the elements of the partition each contain an exact point, are connected and convex. It follows that the borders are portions of hyperplanes. Every domain of the partition is a convex polytope surrounding an exact point(fig.3).

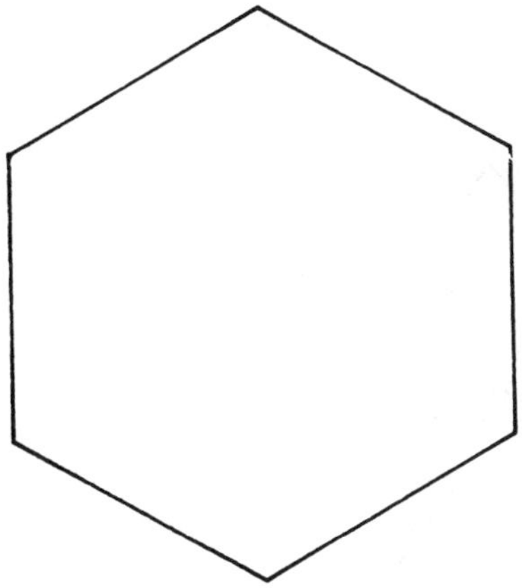

p = 3

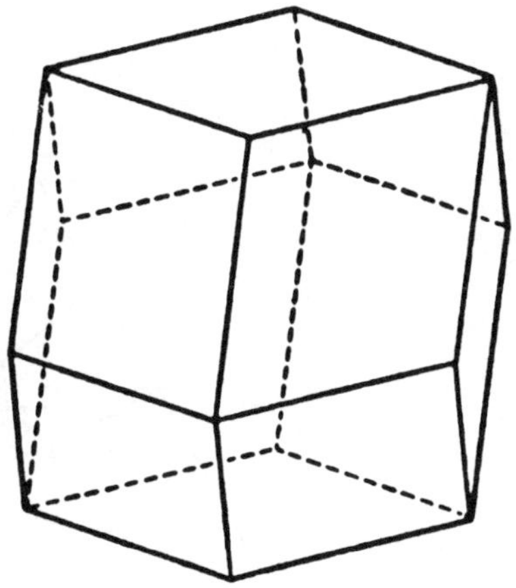

p = 4

figure 3

The hyperplanes bordering those polytopes (faces of codimension 1) correspond to results yielding a tie between two distributions of type $(n_1,n_2,\dots,n_i,\dots,n_j+1,\dots,n_p)$ and $(n_1,n_2,\dots,n_i+1,\dots,n_j,\dots,n_p)$; so the number of faces is equal to the number of pairs (i,j) and equal to p(p - 1)/2. The vertices (faces of codimension p - 1) correspond to ties between p distributions where n - k seats are distributed in a fixed way while the k remaining seats are distributed one by one between the p parties. There are then various types of vertices according to the different values of k lying between 1 and p - 1; so the total number of vertices is equal to $\Sigma_k\ p!/[(p-k)!k!] = 2^p - 2 = 2(2^{p-1} - 1)$.

Among the more commonly used methods, the greatest remainders'one (Hamilton) has many remarkable properties; in particular the following: for a party, the minimum and maximum percentages required to receive a given number of seats are obviously independent of the results of the other parties. Among the other methods, the so-called divisor methods (Jefferson, Dean, Hill Saint-Laguë, Webster, Adams, D'Hondt,...) have many interesting properties Balinski & Young (1982), but generally the lower and the upper thresholds leading to a given number of seats depend on the results of the other competing parties (fig.4). However, some divisor methods avoid this inconvenience and the purpose of this paper is to characterize them.

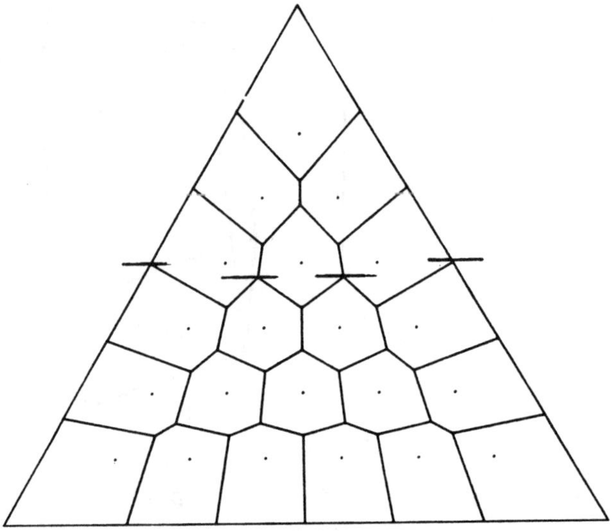

figure 4

Let us first recall the definition of divisor methods. Consider an election with p parties and n seats to be dealt out; let us suppose that from a total of N votes the party i gets N_i. Suppose the rounding law $\alpha:\mathbb{R}^* \to \mathbb{N}$ be given; α is a monotone and surjective application; this law may also be determined by a function d from $\mathbb{N} \to \mathbb{R}$ mapping any integer n onto the upper bound d(n) of the reals rounded to n. One usually supposes that every integer belongs to its rounding interval; in this case $d(n-1) < n < d(n)$; also $\alpha(d(n)) = n$. There is a one-to-one correspondence between a rounding law and a divisor method. The problem is to find a divisor D such that $\Sigma_i \alpha$ (Ni/D) = n; intuitively, one may think the divisor D is the "value" in voices of a seat.

The inconvenience of this definition is that the divisor is not uniquely determined; elementary properties of continuity do assure its existence in some interval. It is easier, from a practical point of view, to directly compute the distribution, and it may be done as soon as the critical cases (ties) are known, and in particular in the geometrical representation it is equivalent to locate the vertices of the polytope; they determine all the faces of every dimension.

Let us see how to compute the coordinates of a vertex of the polytope. Take a vertex corresponding to a tie of k seats between the p parties; it belongs to the domain corresponding to distributions $(n_1,n_2,\ldots,n_i,\ldots,n_j,\ldots,n_p)$ + V, where V is a vector with k components equal to 1 and p - k equal to 0; moreover one has also $\Sigma n_i + k = n$.

This tie will occur when the quotients by divisor D are equal to the limits of rounding. In that case the number of votes N_i are such that $N_i/D = d(n_i)$. Therefore we get $\Sigma_i \alpha(d(n_i)) = \Sigma_i n_i = n - k$ and there will be k seats (k < p) otherwise one should decrease divisor D to share between the p parties. There will be a tie of that kind when percentages $x_1,x_2, \ldots, x_p$ satisfy the relation: $x_j = (N_j/D)/(N/D) = d(n_j) / \Sigma \quad d(n_i)$ with sum $\Sigma_i n_i = n - k$.

In particular, let us estimate the minimum percentage needed by the jth party to receive $n_j + 1$ seats. In that case we are dealing with a tie such that n - 1 seats have been shared (each party k receiving n_k seats) and only one seat is left; one gets $\underline{x}(n_j) = d(n_j) / \Sigma d(n_i)$ with $\Sigma_i n_i = n - 1$. We may also determine the maximum percentage for which the jth party is not sure of receiving more than n_j seats; in this case the tie is of the following kind: n - p + 1 seats are shared, the jth party has received n_j of them, and p - 1 are to be shared. In that case one gets $\overline{x}(n_j) = d(n_j) / \Sigma_i d(n_i)$ with $\Sigma_i n_i = n - p + 1$ (fig.5) Petit & Térouanne (1987)

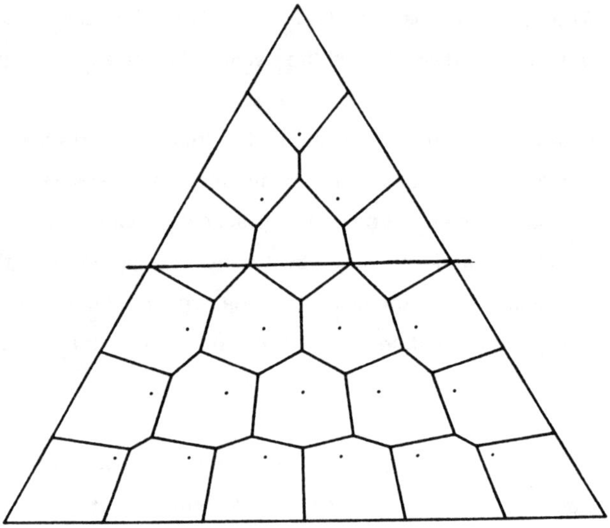

figure 5

It should be noticed that, in the most general case those percentages vary according to the distribution of the other seats n_i; indeed the expression $\Sigma_i d(n_i)$ with a given sum $\Sigma_i n_i$ is not a constant.

Let us show that this sum, and consequently the percentages $\underline{x}(n_j)$ and $\overline{x}(n_j)$, is independent of the distribution of the other seats if and only if the rounding determined by function d(n) is a fixed decimal rounding. First, if the rounding is a fixed decimal one, we get $d(n) = n + \delta$ with $0 < \delta < 1$ and the sum $\Sigma_i d(n_i) = \Sigma n_i + p\delta$. Conversely as the sum $\Sigma_i d(n_i)$ is a constant as soon as $\Sigma_i n_i$ is constant, we may fix all the n_i except n_j and n_k; for them, using a variation of one unit, it follows that:

$$d(n_j + 1) + d(n_k) = d(n_j) + d(n_k + 1)$$

equivalently:

$$d(n_j + 1) - d(n_j) = d(n_k + 1) - d(n_k).$$

It follows that taking into account the constraint $d(n - 1) < n < d(n)$, the constant value of this difference is 1 and the rounding is a fixed decimal one: $d(n) = n + \delta$.

Gathering those two results it follows that in the case of a divisor method with fixed decimal rounding, the interval in which party number k may receive n_k seats is given by:

$$\underline{x}(n_k)=(n_k - 1 + \delta)/(n - 1 + p) < x_k < (n_k + \delta)/(n - p + 1 + p)=\overline{x}(n_k)$$

Let us recall that among the most frequently used methods, δ is equal to 0 for Adams', 0.5 for Saint-Laguë - Webster's and 1 for the method of greatest quotients (Jefferson - D'Hondt). One may also notice that the amplitude of the interval is an increasing function of the number of parties.

References

Balinski,M.L. & Young,H.P. (1982) - Fair representation meeting the ideal, one man, one vote. Yale University Press: New Haven & London.

De Meur,G. & Hubaut,X. (1986) - Fair models of political fairness. European Journal of Political Research, **14**, 237-252

De Meur,G. (1986) - Simplexes and elections. Methods in Operation Research, **54** 486-496

Guilbaud,G,Th. (1985) - Leçons d'à peu près. C.Bourgeois: Paris

Petit,J.L. & Térouanne,E. (1987) - Proportional methods. Extremal values and Manipulability. submitted to SIAM Journal of applied mathematics.

Steinhaus,H. (1964) - Mathématiques en instantanés. Flammarion: Paris.

A
ab initio statistics 86 94 97
ability 249-251 257 263
achievement testing 249
adaptive automata 12
additive conjoint measurement 79ff 87ff
additive representation 53
additivity, interattributive 69-70
affine model of colour coding 173 176
ambiguity algorithm 210
answering strategy 250 253 255
anticipated utility 29-30 36-37 39-41 43
appearance space 176
attentional capacity, loss of 141
attitude models 69
attitudes towards risk 33
autocorrelation 115 117-118 120 123 127-130
axiomatization 77
axioms
  deterministic 99 107 109
  first-order 108 110
  probabilistic 99-101 106-109

B
Bayes rule 242
Bernoulli process 234
betweenness 292-296 300-301
bias parameter 198 210-211
bilineair models 69
binary principle 6
binary questionnaire 329
biproportional
  constrained matrix 360
  representation 347ff 363
Boolean
  algebra 342
    ideal of a 329-330
    minimal expression in 329-330
    quotient algebra of a 329
    supremum in 330
  analysis 329-330 335
  expression 159
  variable 159
boredom 140
bottom context 7
Bourdon test 115 118 123 125 128 131
brightness matching 175

C
capacity 39
cellular automata 10ff
change, measurement of 56-58
choice axiom 34
choice polynomial 184ff
Choquet-expected utility 39
Choquet-integral 29 39 43
CIE colour space 172-173
classical conditioning 13
closed (intersection,union) 160-161
cognitive models
  for balance problems 270
    buggy rules 272
    item types 273
    strategies 271-272
  individual differences 268-270
  strategies 267
cognitive scope of a word 206-207
cohesion threshold 334
colour cancellation method 175
colour circle 306
colour contrast 172
colour induction 172
colour matching 172-173 175
colour perception
  similarity judgements 306
colour vision 171
common truth 231 240 243
commonality algorithm 208 210 212
commonality of two words 197 206-207
communication frequencies 303
comonotonic(ity) 41
  (coordinate) independence 40-42
competence 239 241-242 247
computability 8
computable functions 16
computational reducibility 12-13
concatenation 53
concentration
  see also distraction
  tests 115 118 122-124 131
conditioning, finite automata 15ff
Condorcet model 231-232 235 237 239-240
confusion data 307
conjoint measurement 69-70
connectedness 70-71
consequence 163-166
consistent, minimal 165-166
constant utility model 101 106
context free grammars 5ff
contradictory 165-166
convex polytope 369
convexity space, structure 160
coordinate independence 40-41

covariance method 234 238
covering 334 340
criterion-referenced testing 251 262
cross context matching 172
cultural consensus analysis 229
cumulative distribution function 30 40

D
decision (making) 34 179ff 249
  choice polynomial 184ff
  moving basis heuristics 181ff
  rules 180ff
  under risk 29-30 39
  under uncertainty 39-41
  weights 33
decrement distinction 173
decrement in performance 133-134
decumulative distribution function 30-31 38-39
degree of a vertex 340-341
determinism and predictability 12
dichotomization 329
  threshold 333 342
dichotomous items 230
difference structure 87ff 91ff
differentiability of anticipated utility 41
dimensional invariance 63-64
distance function 299
distance measure 303
distraction(s) 115-121 124-125 130-131
  see also inhibition
  time 126 128-129
distribution
  binomial 256
  exponential 116 119 131
  function 30
  Poisson 116 119 126 130
distributivity 71
divisor method 370-371
double cancellation 71 73
dynamic behavior 77
dynamic structure 83
dyslectics 198-199 212

E
effective error mass 212
elections 345
equal delta method 321-322
equivalence 163-164 166
error (type 1,type 2) 250 256
error tolerance 256
essential component 81
estimation theory 230 232 239 246-247
expectations 30
expected utility 29-30 32 36 40-41 43
  with rank-dependent probabilities 30
expected value 30-31 38-39
expert judgement 157-158
expert system 157
extended similarity trees 307
extensive measurement 52
  alternative representations 54 63

F
failure space 160 162-164 168
failure state 160 168
fair representation 346ff
  biproportional solution 358ff
  rule 349ff
false alarm rate 232 240
fatigue 140
fill-in-the blank exam 239
filling in 175
finite automata 4
  stimulus-response models 15ff
finite state model 249-252
fixed point theorem 244
formal language 102 110
formal learning theory 8ff
foundations of measurement 50
Fréchet differentiability 41 43
freezing principle 6

G
gain control, multiplicative 173
Galois closure, connection 161ff
Gamma model 130-131
Ganzfeld conditions 175
gap 87ff
Gateaux-differentiable 43
generator patterns 336
Gliwenko's theorem 94
goodness of fit 262
grammars, context free 5
grammatical tree structure 6
graph 299-302 306-307 330 335 337 339 341-342
  incidence matrix of a 338
  non-directed 329 338
graph theoretical methods 299
Grassmann's linearity laws 172 176
guessing 249 251-252 257 261-262
  strategy 253 255
Guttman analysis 329

H
Hamilton's method 347 358 360
Hamming-distance 338
harmony theory 14-15
hazard rate 116-119

hedging 40
heterogeneity algorithm 197 208-211
hierarchical communication structure 303
high threshold model 232-233 235-239 241 245
higher-order stochastic dominance 41
hit rate 232 240
homogeneity of items 235 237 240
Hullian theory 3
hypercube 339 341
minimal covering and 340
hypothesis testing 256

I
I-component structure 81ff
I-scale 289 292
ideal of a Boolean algebra 329-330
ignorance 252-253 255 261
IMAX model 115-116 118 120 122-125 127 130-131 135 137-138
goodness of fit testing 121
parameter estimation 121 139
implication (graph) 329-335 342
implication relation 162-163 168
incidence matrix 338
increment distinction 173
independence 81
independence, quasi 312
independence condition 40
independence of equal coordinates 41
indifference zone 256
informant-learnable 5
information, partial 249
information pooling 229-230 247
information processing 148 154
inhibition 117-121
theory 136 141 153 155
Inhibition model 115-120 123 125 127-128 130-131 135 137
input function 78ff
internal programming 16ff
intransitive metric 311 317ff 323ff
intransitive triads 72
inversions, minimizations of 311-314 326-327
item difficulty 250-252
item homogeneity 232 239
item monotonicity 238
item pool 251
item response theory 238
item sampling 249 251

J
J-scale 309-316 319-327
dominant 298
qualitative 289-292 296-297
quanitative 289-290
Jensen inequality 128
joint independence 71 74
judgement
contradictory 167
expert 167-168

K
Kendall's
W 75
zeta 72
knowledge 249-251 253 259 261
all or none 249
assessment 157
partial 252-253
space 160 162
state 160
structure 157
total 252
knowledge or random guessing 250
Kolmogorov-Smirnov statistic 124

L
language learning 4ff
latent class analysis 230
latent class model 232 235
learnability 6 14
learning
language 4
register machines 16ff
stochastic models 4
theory, formal 8ff
learning effects 131
least squares
conditional 122 125
general 122
Lebesque-Stieltjes integral 90
lexical functional grammars 7
lexicographic rule 180ff
lexicographic semi-order 181
likelihood function 233 244 246
Lineair Logistic Test Model 267-268
cognitive models
balance problems 274 280-282
strategies 283-284
restriction of range 284
lineair operator 241
lineair programming 311 321-324
lineair system 78ff 83ff
linguistic analysis 6
local independence 231 235 243
loss of attentional capacity 141
lottery 30

M
magnitude estimation 56
majority rule 180
massed vs spaced work 120 131
Masstheorie 50
mastery decision 249-250 257 259 261-263
matching method, exam 234 238-239
mathematics 51
maximin decision making 41
maximum likelihood estimation 244-245
maximum likelihood ratio 232
meaningfulness 51 59ff
measurable sets 89
measurement
 conjoint 69-70 79ff 87ff
 deterministic 99-100
 difference structure 87ff 91ff 301
 of change 56-58
 of risk 54-55 59ff
 probabilistic 99-101 106 111
 structure 301
 theory 77 86ff 171-172 176 301
memory, register machines 19ff
memory (finite) 8
metamerism 171-172 175-176
metric, intransitive 317ff 323ff
metric, path length 299-300
midpoint sequence 311-325 327
minimal covering 340
minimal expression
 in a Boolean algebra 329-330
MINRES 234 236-237 241 245
misinformation 264
MLLSA 232 234
model theory 99 104 106 111
 probabilistic 100 110
monotonic network analysis (MONA)
 299-300 302 304 307
monotonicity condition 301
monotonous versus mixed tasks 140-141
 143-148 150
moving basis heuristics 181ff
multi-attribute models 69
multidimensional scaling 49 306
multinomial distribution 204-206
multiple choice test 239
multiplicativity, intraattributive 69-70

N
neural code 172
neural networks 13ff
 sensory processes 14
 traveling salesman 14
non-additive probabilities 33
non-determinate reinforcement 9
non-directed graph 329 338
non-polynomial growth 241
nonparametric 327
nonparametric error model 312
normal approximation 256
numbers 55

O
objective probability 40
octant model of colour coding 174-176
optimal threshold 329 337 342
optimism 40
order dense 90
order type η 87 90
ordered sets 87 90
orthography 197 199-201 204 206 212
 formal relations between 197 200-203
 208-212
outer measure 89

P
P-mixture 102-104 106-107 109
pair comparison 100-102 104-106
Parellel Distributed Processing 14
partial differential equations 11
partial order 161
partial recursive functions 16-18 20-22 24
path length metric 299 302
PCU (projections canoniques ultimes) 330
 338 340-341
 length of 331-337 339 342-343
 length of a 329-330
perceptron
 convergence theorem 10
 learning model 9ff
perceptual display 9-10
pessimism 40-41
photoreceptor output functions 172 174
phrase marker 5
phrase structure grammars 7
Poisson-Erlang model 115-118 120 124-125
 130-131
Poisson process 130
polytope 369
pooling assumption 109-111
possible world 102
power law 246
practice effects 131
premise 159 166
principle of transparancy 7
probabilistic choice theory 34
probabilistic condition 108-111
probabilistic order 106-108 110
probability, qualitative 86
probability space 90 94

processing time 115-120 124-129 131
product-summation models 69
production system 185
proportional representation 347ff 359 367ff
prospect theory 33 70
protocol of a questionnaire 329-331
proximity data 299 302 306
psychophysical function 56 245-246

Q
quantitation 50
quasi-order 162
questionnaire
  binary 329
  response pattern and 330 333 336 341-342
  subpattern and 330-331 336
  subquestionnaire of a 330
quotient algebra
  in Boolean algebra 329

R
Rabin-Scott definition of automata 16
raising principle 6
random guessing 255
random reals 101 111
random utility model 101 106-107
random variable 86 94 257
rank-dependent expected utility 30
rank-ordered expected utility 30
rank-ordering 41
ranking test 239
RAS model 360
Rasch homogeneity
  balance problems 276
    strategy groups 276-279
Rasch model 238-239 268
ratio principle in colour perception 176
ratio scale 242
rectangles 302
recursion 8
register machines 16-23
  axioms 20-21
  hierarchies 23ff
reinforcement 4
relation, implication 159
relational theory of colour perception 175-176
relativistic velocity 54
representation 99-101 105 111
  probabilistic 100-101 104-106 108
representation theorem 51
response continuum 239
response mode 257-259
  answer-until-correct 249-250 253-255 259-260 262 264
  conventional 249-250 252-256 258-259 261-262
  Coombs' 249-250 255-257 259-262 264
response pattern 330 333 336 341
response profile data 231 247
response time 116 119
  choice 124
  disjunctive 124
  series 115 118 120 123 125-126 129-131
  trend 115 117-118 120-121 123 125-127 129-131
risk
  attitude 41
  aversion 32-33
  perception 54-55
  Pollatsek & Tversky's theory of 59-65
  variance-expectation theory of 59-63
riskless choice 179ff
rule 157 166-167 169

S
satisficing model 185
scale, universal 87
scaling problem 51
schematic faces 307
scor(ing)
  answer-until-correct 257
  cutting 249-250 256-257
  expected 256
  formula 253 255-257 259 262
  number-right 250 256-257 259 261-262
  observed 249
self-organization 11
self-reproduction 11ff
sensory codes 13
sequential covering class 89ff 92
sigma-mixture, -structure 107 109-111
sign dependence 70 73
similarity judgements 304 307
single-peakedness 293
size
  sample 250 263
  test 250
social groups 303
solvability 81
spatial adaptation 172
Spearman's tetrad law 244
specific objectivity 57
spelling(s) (errors/deficit)
  categorization 199 211
  distribution 197 204-206
  rules 197 200-201 206 211-212
  taxonomy 197-199 212
St. Petersburg paradox 30

standard sequence 81ff
state-description 102
state space 40
states of nature 41
stationarity 82
statistical learning theory 4ff
Statistical power analysis 263
stimulus-response models
  and finite automata 15ff
stimulus-response theory 3ff
stochastic dominance 29 40
  first-order 36
structural assumption 100 103 109-110
structure 105
  deterministic 100-102 104 106-108
  probabilistic 100-103 106-108 110-111
    induced 104-105 108
subadditive representation 55
subjective probability 33
subpattern 330-331 336
subquestionnaire 330
superadditive representation 55
Suppes' theorem on finite automata 15ff
supremum, in Boolean algebra 330
sure-thing principle 40-41
surmise system 161
symbolic computation 15
system theory 77ff
  lineair 78

T

tautology 163-164
test
  behaviour 249-250
  bias 253
  length 256
  muliple-choice 253 255-256
  multiple-choice 249-250 259 261-262
  objective 249-250
  true-false 249-250 253 258-259 261
test theory 230 242
text-learnable 5
threshold for dlchotomization 329 333-335
  337 342
transformational grammars 6
transformed probabilities 29 33
transition function 78ff
transitivity 70-72 74 103 106-108
  of betweenness 293-294
tree 299 302
trend
  analysis 122-123 129
  exponential 115 117-118 120 127 130
  linear 120 126
triple, inadmissble 312
triple constraints 198 210-211
truth assignment, admissible 159
truth function, value 159
Turing machine 4 11 16ff

U

ultimate canonical projections 330
unfolding 289-292
  method 289-290
  quantitative vs qualitative 58-59
  structure 291 294-297
  unidimensional 309
uniqueness theorem 51
universal scale 87 90
universal sentence 110-111
utility function 32

V

vacation places 304
validity 197 199 212
voting 345ff 367ff

W

weak order 71
working memory 136
  register machines 19ff

Z

zero-restrictedness 363ff

A
Aczél, J. 34 43
Adelbratt, T. 183 195
Albert, D. 195
Allais, M. 44
Andersen, E.B. 276 285
Anger, B. 44
Anthonisse, J.M. 346-347 359 364
Arbib, M.A. 78ff 84
Arnold, W. 142 155
Arrow, K.J. 33 44
Asanuma, C. 14 25
Aschenbrenner, K.M. 180 183 195
Atkinson, R.C. 248

B
Bacherach, M. 360 362 365
Baddeley, A.D. 136 155
Baianu, I.C. 12 25
Bales, R.F. 303 308
Balinski, M.L. 346 365 367 370 373
Baratta, P. 33 45
Baron, J. 269 285
Barthélemy, J.P. 181 189 195
Baschera, P. 140 155
Batchelder, W.H. 229 231 234 237-238 247-248
Beach, L.R. 183 196
Beals, R. 49 66
Been, P.H. 267 285
Belmont, J.M. 269 285
Bergan, J.R. 270 283 285
Berge, C. 340 343
Bernoulli, D. 29 32-33 44
Bertelson, P. 133 155
Bettman, J.R. 184 195
Bezembinder, Th.G.G. 33 43-44
Billings, 185
Bills, A.G. 117 132
Birkhoff, G. 162 169
Bishof, W. 195
Bliss, L.B. 250 264
Boes, D.C. 119 132
Borgatta, E.F. 247
Bourdon, B. 134 155
Bowen, J. 59 66
Bresnan, J. 7 27
Broadbent, D.E. 269-270 285
Brothers, A. 247
Brown, J.S. 272 285
Buchanan, B.G. 157 169
Bunge, M. 50 66
Burigana, L. 162 169-170
Burks, C. 12 25
Burnham, R.W. 173 176
Bush, R.R. 4 25 45
Butterfield, E.C. 269 285

C
Cancelli, A.A. 270 285
Carnap, R. 110 112
Caroll, J.D. 306 308
Challands P.D.C. 175 177
Chartrand, G. 340 343
Chateauneuf, A. 44
Chew, S.H. 41 43-44
Choquet, G. 29 39 43-44
Clogg, C.C. 247
Codd, E.F. 12 25
Cohen, A. 311 313 325-326 328
Colonius, H. 99 112
Comrey, A.L. 234 247
Condorcet, C.M.J.A. de 195
Coombs, C.H. 33 44 55 58-59 66 180 195 250 255 264 289 298 309 311 317 320-328
Cooper, L.A. 269 285
Corbin, 185 195
Corter, J.E. 307-308
Cox, D.R. 119 132
Cox, L.H. 363 365
Crangle, C. 4 25
Crick, F 14 25
Crombag, H.F.M. 49
Cross, L.H. 250 265
Crozier, R. 183-184 196
Culicover, P.W. 5-7 28
Cummings, L.L. 247-248

D
Dahlstrand, V. 180 195
Davies, D.R. 140 156
Davis, Ph.J. 51 55 66
Davison, M.L. 249 263 265 312 328
Dawes, R.M. 180 195
De Groot, A.D. 50 66
De Hoog, R. 183 195
De Meur, G. 346 365 367 369 373
Debord, B. 180 195
Degreef, E. 159 170 333 342-343
Dellacherie, C. 44
Dennenberg, D. 44
Doignon, J.P. 157 159-160 162 169-170
Dorcey, T. 54 67 302 308

Dosher, B.A. 180 195
Droste, M. 87 90 97
Dubois, D. 44
Ducamp, A. 170 290 298

E
Ebert, U. 43-44
Edwards, W. 33 36 44 183 196
Ehrenfeucht, A. 9 26
Einhorn, M.J. 183 195 247
Eisler, H. 56 66
Ellis, B. 52 56 66
Elshout, J.J. 200 213
Ernst, L.R. 363 365
Estes, W.K. 4 26
Evans, R.W. 173 176
Eysenck, H.J. 131-133 156

F
Fahner, S. 250 258 265
Falmagne, J.C. 65-66 99 101 106 109 112
157 159-160 162 169-170 290 298
Farmer, D. 12 26
Feger, H. 304 308
Feigin, P.D. 311 313 325-326 328
Feldt, L.S. 277 284-285
Fellner, W. 45
Fischer, G.H. 56-58 66 267-269 281 285
Fishburn, P.C. 45 86 97 180 195
Fitch, F.B. 27
Flament, C. 185 195 329 343
Formann, A.K. 268 285
Forsyth, B.H. 46
Frankman, R.W. 4 28
Frary, R.B. 250-253 262 264-265
Friedman, A. 88-89 97
Frith, C.D. 131-133 156
Frost, N. 269 286

G
Gaifman, H. 110 112
Galanter, E. 45
García-Pérez, M.A. 251-253 255-256
264-265
Gassner, M.B. 346 359 365
Gelfand, A. 231 247
Gertzen, H. 185 196
Gibbons, J.D. 262 265
Gibson, W.H. 249 263 265
Gilboa, I. 40 44-45
Gilchrist, A. 176
Gold, E.M. 4-5 8 26
Goode, F.M. 33 44
Grandjean, E. 140 155
Grassmann, H. 171-172 176
Graybill, F.A. 119 132
Groen, G.J. 269 285
Grofman, B. 229 247-248
Groner, M. 195
Groner, R. 182 195
Grossberg, S. 13-14 26
Guilbaud, G.Th. 106 112 367 373
Guion, R.M. 249 263 265

H
Hölder, O. 50 66
Haeussler, P. 269 285
Hall, M. 27
Hamburger, H. 5 26
Harrison, M.A. 16 26
Hedenborg, M.L. 270 286
Heller, W.P. 46
Helm, C.E. 306 308
Helmholtz, H. 171
Henry, N.W. 230 248
Hersh, R. 51 55 66
Hess, C. 176
Heyer, D. 111-112
Hilton, R.W. 45
Hinton, G.E. 215-216 222 226
Hoffman, P.J. 245 248
Hogarth, R.M. 247-248
Hogg, R.V. 250 265
Holland, J.H. 12 26
Hoogenboom, W. 133 156
Hopfield, J.J. 14 26
Horn, A. 111-112
Hovland, C.I. 27
Huang, L. 55 66
Hubaut, X. 346 365 367 369 373
Huber, O. 180 182-183 185 195
Huber, P.J. 45
Hübner, R. 84
Hull, C.L. 3 26
Hunt, E.B. 269-270 286
Hurvich, L.M. 173 176

J
Jackson, D.M. 247
Jacobson, A. 176
Jacoby, J. 184 195
Jaffray, J.-Y. 44
Jameson, D. 173 176
Jansen, R.W.T.L. 115-116 118 121 132-135
137 156
Joffe, R. 133 155
Johnson, E.J. 183 195
Jorna, R.J. 267 285

K
Kahneman, D. 33-34 45 70 75
Kandel, E.R. 20 27
Kanerva, P. 9 27
Kaplan, R.M. 7 27
Karni, E. 41 44-45
Karp, C. 270 286
Kauffman, S.A. 12 27
Kay, D.C. 160 170
Kemeny, J.G. 303 308
Kempf, W.F. 285
Kendall, M. 75
Kienapple, K. 54 67 302 308
Kieras, D.E. 15ff 27
Klahr, D. 270-272 275 283 286
Klayman, J. 183 195
Klein, N. 179 196
Kleinmuntz, B. 183 195
Kleinmuntz, D.N. 183 185 195-196
Klempner, E. 247
Koele, P. 250 256 258-259 263-264
Koopmans, T.L. 82 84
Koppen, M. 162 169-170
Krantz, D.H. 45 49-50 54 56 62-63 66 71 75 77 81 84 86 88 92 94 97 99 105 112 171-173 176 248 290 298 301 308
Krauss, P. 104 110 112
Kubinger, K.D. 269 286
Kuhn, H.W. 244 248
Kuperstein, M 14 26

L
Land, E. 176
Langereis, M.P. 200 213
Langton, C.G. 12 27
Larimer J. 175-176
Lawler, E.L. 340 343
Lazarsfeld, P.F. 230 248
Lee, W. 180 196
Lehman, E.L. 311 328
Lehner, P.E. 59 66
Levine, M. 4 28
Lewis, C. 270 286
Lindman, 183
Loève, M. 89 97
Lopes, L. 185 196
Lord, F.M. 230 238 242-244 248 265
Los, J. 110 112
Luce, R.D. 33-34 45 49 59 65-66 75 77 85-86 97 99 105 112 248 290 298 301 308
Lunneborg, C.L. 269 286
Lyons, 183

M
Machina, M.J. 33 41 43 45
Mackworth, J. 133 156
MacLeod, C.M. 270 286
Maddy, P. 34 45
Mahler, K.M. 234 237 239 248
Mallows, C.L. 311 328
Marcus, 185
Mathai, A.M 97
Mathews, N.N. 270 286
Mausfeld, R. 111-112 176-177
May, K.O. 180 196
Mc Kenna, F.P. 245 248
McAllister, D.W. 183 196
McClelland, G.H. 321 328
McClelland, J.L. 14 28
McCulloch, W.S. 9 27
Medendorp, E.L. 50 66
Mehler, J. 14 27
Michel, J. 51 65-66
Micielsky, J. 9
Milholland, J.E. 250 264
Miller, H.D. 119 132
Minsky, M. 9 27
Mitchell, T.R. 183 196
Monjardet, B. 162 170
Montgomery, H. 180-181 183 185 192 195-196
Mood, A.M. 119 124 127-128 132
Morgenstern, O. 32 46
Mosteller, F.M. 4 25
Mullet, E. 181 189 191 195-196
Mychielski,J. 26
Myhill, J. 12 27

N
Nährer, W. 269 286
Nakamura, Y. 45
Narens, L. 65-66 85 90 97-99 104 112
Newell, A. 15 27 284 286
Newhall, S.M. 173 176
Newton, I. 171
Niederée, R. 55 66 111-112 176-177
Nitzan, S. 233 248
Novick, M.R. 230 242-244 248 265

O
Olkin, I. 262 265
Ore, O. 161 170
Orth, B. 290 296 298 306 308
Osherson, D.N. 8-9 27
Owen, G. 229 247-248

P
Padulo, L. 78ff 84

Papert, S. 9 27
Parasuraman, R. 133 140-141 155-156
Parkman, J.M. 269 285
Paroush, J. 233 248
Payne, J.W. 179 183 195-196
Pederzoli, G. 97
Perkins, D.T. 27
Peters, H.J.M. 46
Petit, J.L. 367 371 373
Pierce, C.S. 51
Pieters, J.P.M. 115-117 124 132
Pinker, S. 7 14 27
Pitts, W. 9 27
Pollatsek, A. 59 67
Posner, M.I. 142 156
Prade, H. 44
Pradhan, P.L. 245 248
Pratt, J.W. 33
Preston, M.G. 33 45
Pretori, H. 176

Q
Quiggin, J. 29 40 45

R
Röell, A. 45
Rasch, G. 238-239 248
Raynard, R. 183-184 196
Roberts, F.S. 52 67 88 98
Romney, A.K. 229 231 234 237-239 247-248
Rosenblatt, F. 9 27
Rosenstein, J.G. 87 98
Roskam, E.E. 67 115 132 135 137 156
Roskies, R.A. 71 75
Ross, R.T. 27
Rottmayer ,W. 19 28
Rouanet, H. 4 28
Roy, B. 340 343
Rumelhart, D.E. 14 28 215-216 222 226
Russo, J.E. 180 196

S
Saffrich, W. 183 185 196
Safra, Z. 41 43
Sanders, A.F. 133 156
Savage, L.J. 32-33 40 45
Schönemann, P.H. 54 67 302 308
Scheiblechner, H. 267 286
Schlee, E. 45
Schmalhofer, F. 183 185 195-196
Schmeidler, D. 29 40-41 46
Schneider, L.M. 269 287
Schrödinger, E. 177
Schrodinger, E. 171
Scott, D. 99 101 104 110 112
Seaver, D.A. 183 196
Segal, U. 46
Shackleton, V.J. 140 156
Shepard, L. 263 265
Shepherdson, J.C. 17 28
Shevell, S.K. 175 177
Shortliffe, E.H. 157 169
Shugan, S.M. 196
Siegler, R.S. 270-272 275 283 286
Sijtsma, K. 267 269 285-286
Simon, H.A. 179 196
Slovic, P. 185 196
Smit, J.C. 115 127 130 132-133 135 156
Smolenaars, A.J. 321 328
Smolenski, P. 14-15
Snell, J.L. 303 308
Sobel, M. 262 265
Solomon, H. 231 247
Spada, H. 267-269 271 285-286
Starr, R.M. 46
Starrett, D.A. 46
Steinhaus, H. 367 373
Sternberg, R.,J. 285
Sternberg, R.J. 269 286
Stevens, S.S. 51 67 246
Stiles, W.S. 172 174 177
Stillwell, W.G. 183 196
Stob, N. 8-9 27
Sturgis, H.E. 17 28
Suck, R. 67
Suppes, P. 3-4 6 15-16 19 25 28 33 45 75 77 84 86 97 99 105 112 248 290 298 301 308
Svenson, O. 180 183 185 196 270 286

T
Térouanne, E. 367 371 373
Tanis, E.A. 250 265
Tank, D.W. 14 26
Tarski, A. 8 111-112
Theuns, P. 342-343
Thorndike, L.L. 3 28
Thrall, R.M. 310 317 328
Towstopiat, O. 270 285
Turing, A.M. 11 28
Tversky, A. 33-34 45-46 49 59 66-67 70 75 77 84 86 97 99 105 112 180 185 192 196 212-213 290 298 301 307-308

U
Ulam, S. 11
Underwood, G. 269 286
Uttal, W.R. 172

V
Van Blokland, A.W. 311-312 320 326 328
Van Breukelen, G.J.P. 115-119 122 125 127-130 132-137 139 145 155-156
Van Buggenhaut, J. 333-334 342-343
Van de Vijver, F.J.R. 269 287
Van den Bosch, K. 200 213
Van den Brink, W.P. 250 256 258-259 263-264
Van den Wittenboer, G. 183 195
Van den Wollenberg, A.L. 145 156 277 287
Van der Kamp, C.A.J. 49
Van der Ven, A.H.G.S. 115 127 130 132-133 135 137 145 156 321-322 325 328
Van Lint, J.H. 338 343
Van Ruyven, N. 213
Van Schuur, H. 312 328
VanLehn, K. 272 285
Verheyden, H. 199 203 213
Vlek, C.A.J. 49
Von Kries, J. 171 173-174 176
Von Neumann, J. 11-12 28 32 46
Vrieze, O.J. 46

W
Wakker, P.P. 39-41 46
Wallach, H. 176-177
Wallsten, T. 33 46
Walraven, J. 171 173 175 177
Weber, E.U. 59 66
Weil, E.M. 269 286
Weinstein, S. 8-9 27
Weiss, D.J. 249 263 265
Welford, A.T. 140 155-156
Weller, S.C. 229 248
Wexler, K. 5-7 26 28
Whitely, S.E. 269 287
Whittle, P. 175 177
Wilcox, R.R. 250 256 265
Williams, R.J. 215-216 222 226
Winkler, R.L. 247-248
Wish, M. 306 308
Wishart, D. 276 287
Wolfram, S. 12 28
Womble, E.W. 160 170
Womer, F.B. 250 264
Wood, R. 284 287
Wyszecki, G. 172 174 177

Y
Yaari, M.E. 29 40 43 46-47
Yager, R.R. 47
Young, H.P. 346 367 370 373
Young, R.M. 269 287
Young, Th. 171 177

Z
Zinnes, J.L. 290 298
Zwarts, M.A. 269 287